THE UNITED NATIONS: *Peace and Progress*

Alf Ross

B̶P̶ The Bedminster Press 1966

The
United
Nations
Peace and Progress

PREFACE ❧

I T is possible to write about the United Nations in several ways. The subject may be treated historically, for example, and the main emphasis may be placed on the series of political situations and economic and social problems that the Organization has had to deal with in its time. It is also possible—as I myself have done in a previous work, *The Constitution of the United Nations* (1950)—to consider the United Nations from a juridical point of view and to describe, on the basis of the provisions of its Charter, the various organs that have been created, the manner in which these work, and the powers that have been given to them. Yet a third possibility is to describe the United Nations in the light of ideals—to proclaim the ideas the Organization is built on, and to preach the faith in its mission to save the world.

This book is written in none of these ways. Naturally, it contains historical, juridical, and ideological elements—not for their own sakes, however, and only to the extent that these can illustrate the object of this work: <u>to understand the United Nations as a *political* phenomenon.</u>

The new world organization, like its predecessor, has <u>not fulfilled the expectations</u> with which it was created. Is this due to external and relatively accidental circumstances that might perhaps be removed? Or does the faulty realization of the ideal plan mean that it was in fact incompatible with the conditions of international politics? Is the United Nations essentially just a piece of wishful thinking? Or dare we believe that this world organization is the little green shoot that, watered with good will, can grow into a world government? Or is the right and more modest answer that the significance of the United Nations lies in the fact that it offers new diplomatic machinery through which states can develop their power politics and which is particularly suitable for mobilizing world opinion as a factor in the struggle for power?

It is questions of this kind that this work deals with and tries to <u>answer realistically</u>, in order to create thereby a basis for a policy on the United Nations, the object of which must be something other and more than mere mirages.

The realism in political thinking that this book tries to live up to is in no way contrary to idealism, if this is understood, in the ordinary sense of the word, as directing one's efforts and strivings in accordance with disinterested views and aims. Political realism, in my sense, simply means unconditional objectivity in one's consideration of political reality, unhampered by dogmatic prejudice and moral postulates. This program sounds extremely simple but is difficult to carry out in practice. When it is a question of the study of man himself and human relations, it is difficult to approach the facts with the same dispassionate candor as in the study of nature.

Realism in determining political aims means, in accordance with this, refraining from setting ideal aims when one is unable to show any practicable way of achieving them. It is idle to propose schemes the realization of which clashes with fundamental traits in the nature of man and to suppose that conditions can be changed merely by an appeal to good will.

This realistic evaluation has especially crystallized, in this book, into the conviction that the widespread belief that peace among nations can be won, as people say, by setting law in the place of might and violence, is an illusion due to lack of understanding of the conditions under which law grows in the national community, and the fundamental differences between the national and the international communities. My analysis of these problems forms the natural conclusion, in political theory, of the study of constitutional law, international law, and the philosophy of law that has occupied me from the time of my youth.

✳ Since this book was written, Communist China has been added to the list of nations in possession of nuclear weapons. This fact makes the dim prospect of world peace still more unlikely and gives further weight to the main thesis of this book—that only an American–Russian *rapprochement* establishing a joint and exclusive nuclear control can save this world from the cataclysm of an atomic war. The apparent lack of understanding of this fact in American public opinion and the apparent carelessness with which American foreign policy follows traditional but outmoded patterns are deeply shocking. Experts tell us soothingly that it will be many years before China will be in possession of an effective atomic force and the necessary means of transportation. But what of 20 or, say, 50 years? The shortsightedness of this view reflects the same mentality as do the famous words with which Neville Chamberlain, on the eve of the Second World War, brought back to London his Munich agreement with Hitler: Peace for our time.

We in the small countries dependent on our great ally can do nothing but speak our mind in the hope that the United States will live up to its responsibilities for world peace.

A. R.

Copenhagen 1965

CONTENTS ❧

THE UNITED NATIONS: *Peace and Progress*

I ❧

ORIGINS
AND BACKGROUND

Rome was not built in a day. Nor was the United Nations. The Charter that was created when the representatives of 50 nations signed it on June 26, 1945, was not merely the result of months of discussion at the Conference at San Francisco. Beforehand, during the course of the Second World War, there had been extensive preliminary discussion between the Big Four—China, the Soviet Union, the United Kingdom, and the United States of America. The draft had been worked out and been the subject of lengthy discussions at Dumbarton Oaks, near Washington (Aug.-Oct., 1944) and at the Conference of Yalta in February 1945.

Moreover, the United Nations, like all human creations, has roots further back in history, both in the history of ideas and in the history of political institutions. It is obvious that in many respects the new world organization was inspired by the League of Nations, which was created by the peace treaties after the First World War. The Covenant of the League was used as a model, and, as a result of bitter experience in the years between the wars, efforts were made to correct and make good the errors and omissions revealed by the breakdown of the League. But the roots go even deeper, to the various projects for a universal organization for the maintenance of peace that, from the Middle Ages to the beginning of the 19th century, have been suggested by statesmen and philosophers.

In the Middle Ages it was the Turkish menace and the notion of the solidarity of Christendom that gave rise to various projects for the union of the Christian states, with the object of resisting the common enemy and maintaining peace among themselves. The oldest of these was set out by a Frenchman, Pierre Dubois, in his *De recuperatione Terre Sancte* (On the reconquest of the Holy Land) (c.1306). To maintain peace among the Christian princes, the indispensable condition for the reconquest of the Holy Land, he proposed that all disputes between these should be referred for decision to a court of arbitration of six members, three lay and three clerical, whose decision should be appellable to the Pope. After the fall of Constantinople (1453), George of Podebrad, King of Bohemia, put forward a similar proposal.

The best-known project of later times is the Great Design, which was ascribed to Henry IV of France, though its real author is now taken to be the Duke of Sully. According to this plan, Europe was to be divided into 15 states, united in an alliance and subject to a Grand Council of 66 members chosen by the princes in proportion to the size of the states.

In the 18th century, the Age of Rationalism, there appeared a multitude of plans proposed by authors who, untroubled by historical, social, or psychological considerations but guided by the light of reason and natural law, believed that it was possible to find eternally valid principles for the maintenance of peace. Particularly well known is a treatise written (1717) by the Abbé de St. Pierre, who had worked as a secretary during the negotiations for the Treaty of Utrecht in 1713. The title of his treatise is typical of his period: *Abrégé du Projet de Paix Perpetuelle inventé par le roi Henri IV . . . approprié à l'état présent des affaires générales de l'Europe, démontré infiniment avantageux pour tous les hommes nés et à naître* (Summary of King Henry IV's plan for perpetual peace . . . adapted to the present general state of affairs in Europe, and shown to be infinitely advantageous to all men born and to be born). The great philosophers, too, worked out peace projects, e.g. Rousseau, Bentham, and Kant. Kant's *Entwurf zum ewigen Frieden* (Plan for perpetual peace) marks the culmination and the end of the rationalistic plans for peace. Abstract speculation of this kind ceased in the 19th century, and the friends of peace concentrated on more realistic but less pretentious aims, such as efforts to promote disarmament and the peaceful settlement of international disputes by arbitration.

There is, however, nothing to indicate that these speculative products have made any particular mark on the Covenant of the League of Nations or on the Charter of the United Nations, though it may be that they have to some extent helped to keep alive the idea of a league for peace. More important have been the various arangements for international collaboration that developed in the course of the 19th century, i.e., the Concert of Europe for the maintenance of peace, a number of international organizations for dealing with matters of common interest, and the Hague Conventions development of international arbitration and other methods for the peaceful settlement of disputes between states.

It is of more than merely historical interest to see how these historical antecedents have prepared the way for and have influenced the Covenant of the League of Nations and thereby also the Charter of the United Nations. A deeper understanding and a critical evaluation of the charter will often be possible only when one knows its connection with the past.

1. The Concert of Europe

It seems to be almost a law of nature that great, constructive plans for an organization for peace should arise during long and extensive wars and be inspired by the collaboration imposed on the victorious powers by the necessities of war. Just as the United Nations is the child of the Second World War, and the League of Nations of the First, so the Concert of Europe was also born of a great war. In this connection the word "concert" means harmony, harmonious collaboration, and presumably originates from the Treaty of Chaumont, 1814, by which Austria, Russia, Prussia, and England entered into an alliance against Napoleon and promised to devote all their efforts to the war and to develop them *"dans un parfait concert"* (in perfect harmony).

Even before the threat of Napoleon had been definitively removed, all the princes of Europe or their representatives assembled for the Congress of Vienna (Sept. 1814 to June 1815) to re-establish order in Europe after the upheaval caused by Napoleon, to restore the legitimate monarchs to their thrones, and to protect absolutism against the revolutionary tendencies inspired by the libertarian ideas of the French Revolution. The four victorious Great Powers, three Continental—Russia, Austria, and Prussia—and England, naturally dominated the Congress. But France, too, brilliantly represented by that master-diplomat Talleyrand, played an important part, and a few years later she was accepted as the fifth in the circle of the Great Powers.

The results of the lengthy negotiations of the Congress were laid down in the Treaty of June 9, 1815. It was signed not only by the five Great Powers, but also by Sweden, Portugal, and (a little later) Spain. By gathering the whole of the new European arrangements into one document as a treaty between these eight states, it was thus emphasized that it was not a matter of a multiplicity of arrangements among the states of Europe, but of a common European arrangement, a European political system, a European code of public law, laid down by the signatories, with more or less voluntary accession of the other powers.

Hereby the eight signatories—and in practice this meant the five Great Powers—had set themselves up as a kind of European Directorate responsible for maintaining the political system they had themselves dictated. This implied that the Great Powers claimed the right to intervene in the internal or external affairs of the European states wherever attempts might be discerned to destroy or reform the system established in the final protocol of Vienna. Since this system was established by binding agreement among the eight states, none of them could act alone and acknowledge any change in the existing state of things but must consult with the others. This naturally led to the point that each of the principal powers, as soon as a political dispute or situation arose, had the right to demand that the signatory powers should be called to conference.

From 1815 to 1914 a long series of such conferences of the Great Powers was held. In general, it proved possible, throughout that century, to stave off crises and maintain the harmony of the Concert. Only occasionally was this harmony broken (Crimean War, 1853-56; Prussian-Austrian War 1866; and the Franco-Prussian War, 1870-71), but none of these wars was extensive or long, or such as to bring to an end the collaboration of the Great Powers.

Among the better known of the European political conferences which took place in the hundred years between the Napoleonic wars and the First World War are:

Vienna, 1814-15	New European system after Napoleon
Aachen, 1818	France received into the circle of the Great Powers
Verona, 1822	The Spanish colonies break free
London, 1830, 1831	Independence and neutrality of Belgium
London, 1832	Independence of Greece
Paris, 1856	Peace after the Crimean War
London, 1871	Russia's violation of the Peace of Paris
Berlin, 1878	Balkan problems
Madrid, 1880	Conditions in Morocco
Berlin, 1885	Interests in the Congo
Algeciras, 1906	Interests in Morocco
London, 1913	Balkan affairs

It is this that is usually called the Concert of Europe—the collaboration of the Great Powers, in the form of consultation and conference, for the maintenance of peace by preserving the existing state of affairs. This collaboration was not organized or elaborated institutionally, though various efforts were made to devise a more permanent framework.

It was especially the Russian Tsar, Alexander I, who, inspired by visionary religiosity and vague idealism, put forward lofty plans; in some of them there were ideas that were to be widely taken up. Immediately after the close of the Congress of Vienna, he took the initiative in establishing the Holy Alliance (Sept. 26, 1815). This appeared as a union of the three absolute monarchs, the Tsar of Russia, Francis I, Emperor of Austria, and Frederick William III, King of

Prussia. They described themselves as "delegated by Providence to rule over three branches of the same family" that form a part of the Christian nation, and as having no other lord than God Himself— and, of course, His deputies. They promised, in high-flown terms, that in all matters of government, both internal and external, they would be guided only by the precepts of the Sacred Scriptures, in justice, mercy, and peace. The Tsar, it has been said, wanted to make the world safe for Monarchy by Divine Right of Kings.

The ideas put forward by Alexander at the Congress of Aix-la-Chapelle in 1818 were more realistic. His main proposal was that all the states of Europe, large and small, should unite in guaranteeing the existing territorial and constitutional conditions, so that everyone was bound to march against the first state that violated the existing order. The Tsar had, in fact, launched the peace program that later became known as "collective security." But the time was not ripe for such a step. The English, in particular, firmly refused to undertake in advance to intervene in disputes on the Continent.

Alexander did succeed, however, in persuading England (Castlereagh) to agree to the holding of regular annual conferences, and such conferences were held from 1818 to 1822. But after the death of Castlereagh, England would not continue with this arrangement, and thereafter conferences were held as circumstances made them desirable.

The collaboration of the Great Powers, which began at the Congress of Vienna, was strengthened when the four victorious powers entered into an alliance at Paris in November 1815. When France, by the restoration of the Bourbons, had been brought back into the fold of legitimacy she became (in 1818) the fifth power in the alliance.

2. International organization and organizations

Contact between the organized centers of power, namely states, may assume two radically different forms: conflict and war, or community of interest and collaboration. Unfortunately, the most obvious aspects of international relations are the conflicts and the "cold" or "hot" wars pertaining to them, and, at certain stages of development, perhaps the only visible ones.

Progress in science and technology has made it evident that no state, however mighty, can stand alone. It has made every state dependent on all the others and sensitive to disturbances elsewhere. Just as a break in an electrical cable in Sweden can plunge a large area of Denmark into darkness and bring machines and traffic to a standstill, so economic or political events in one country produce effects and reactions in others. It is a common saying that science and technology have brought us to live in one world, and the truth in this saying is precisely that no one can live alone because we are all interdependent and our interests are so inextricably interwoven that they can be promoted only in collaboration with other states.

Take international communications. What would be the use of one state's building a splendid railway network if it were not possible to agree with the other states on a common gauge, through-traffic on international routes, exchange and mutual utilization of rolling stock, the use of through consignment notes, and so on? Or take the efforts of the public health administration to stamp out the most dangerous contagious diseases and to deal with epidemics. Of course, the individual state can make quarantine regulations and the like, but these measures would have little effect if elsewhere the diseases were allowed to spread unhindered.

One could go on in this manner. Many of the technological, economic, cultural, and social tasks that a state seeks to deal with are of such a nature that a satisfactory solution is possible only when they are tackled in co-operation with other states.

It is in itself a paradox that while the development of science and technology in the last hundred years has taken and is still taking us steadily toward union in a corporate community of interests, the world is at the same time being divided politically into more and more units, now considerably more than a hundred, each demanding the right to manage its own affairs in juridically sovereign independence of all the others. This discrepancy between actual dependence and legal independence is a challenge that requires an answer. And this answer hitherto has been primarily international organization.

Naturally, it is possible for states to collaborate by making simple agreements. But if collaboration is to be on a large scale, then a permanent institution is required to deal with it. It is this institutional character that is crucial for the concept of international organization.

An international organization may be defined as an institution established jointly by two or more states to deal with a certain collaboration between these states. It is not intended to exclude or supplant the states. It is still the states that perform the juridical and actual acts necessary to carry out the tasks in which they are collaborating. The role of the international institution is limited to the promotion and co-ordination of the national efforts in accordance with the agreed directives. The Universal Postal Union, for example, does not handle letters. That is exclusively the business of the national postal authorities. The purpose of the Union is limited to assisting the national authorities by preparing their negotiations on collaboration, making investigations, procuring material and disseminating information, and otherwise giving guidance to the national administrations in accordance with the Union agreement.

International organizations may be conceived as having any governmental function as their sphere of operation, but it is most natural that they should be concerned with some branch of administration (in contrast to the duties of the law-courts and the legislature). They are also called "administrative unions."

Administrative unions began to appear in the 1860's, and thereby began a new era in the history of international law and international relations. It was the telegraph that led to the establishment of the first administrative union, founded in Paris in 1865 (now replaced by ITU, the International Telecommunications Union). This was soon followed by the General Postal Union (Berne, 1874, now replaced by the Universal Postal Union, UPU). This development has continued, so that today there is a very large number of institutions of this type, for nearly all spheres of international administration: traffic (post, telegraph, radio, railways, road traffic, river traffic, and airways), trade (customs, import restrictions, currency, etc.) social and humanitarian matters (labor conditions, slavery, national minorities, refugees, human rights), health (communicable diseases, narcotics, etc.), trade conditions (literary and artistic industrial property rights, etc.), cultural matters (education, technology), and many others (Chap. V.3 and Chap. X.4).

An administrative union has, typically, three organs: (1) an ordinary conference of states, consisting of representatives of the contracting parties. This usually meets at regular intervals, e.g. every five years, with the object of revising the basic convention under which the organization was established in order to adjust the union to changed conditions; (2) an administrative council (executive committee or commission) consisting of a smaller committee of the participating states, acting as a kind of supervisory organ whose task it is to direct and watch over the work of the union; (3) a permanent office, often called the Bureau or the Secretariat, to deal with current business.

These unions brought into international relations new elements that were to be important for the development up to the League of Nations and its successor. These regular general conferences were of a very different type from those of the Concert of Europe. The union conferences knew nothing of Great Power privileges. All members were equal and had one vote each. As these unions typically aimed at universality, and were therefore open to any state that wished to take part, the conferences often took on the appearance of a general and equal representation of all the states in the world—a structure that thus pointed forward to the General Assemblies of the League of Nations and the United Nations. The invention of the secretariat was even more important. Even though the resemblance is incomplete in many respects, it may be said that the secretariat came to play a part similar to that of a civil service in relation to the successive governments it serves. The secretariat came to represent continuity, became professional and, gradually and to an increasing extent, independent of national interests. In the many international secretariats, a staff of technicians and administrators grew up who became accustomed to think in international terms and to feel the interests involved not as merely national but as common interests, not of the individual states but of the international community.

3. Institutions for settling international disputes

Besides the normal direct diplomatic negotiations between the two parties to a dispute, there are two ancient methods of settling disputes between states peacefully and preventing a dispute from turning into a war: mediation and arbitration. They have this in common, that both are what are called "third-party" methods—that is to say, that between the two parties at issue comes a third who is not involved in the dispute and whose function it is to secure a settlement of the dispute in one way or another. These methods have also this in common, that a state, unless it has previously entered into an obligation to do so, is not obliged to submit a dispute to mediation or arbitration. Otherwise, the two methods are very different.

Mediation is a decidedly political act. It occurs when a state steps in between the two parties to a dispute and, with good advice and the exercise of its influence, seeks to reconcile them. It is usually a Great Power with aspirations to a certain territorial hegemony that appears in the role of mediator. Mediation has greater authority, though it loses something of its voluntary character, when it is offered by a group of Great Powers acting in concert at a conference. The activity of the Concert of Europe was, in fact, largely mediatory.

Arbitration, on the other hand, is a judicial process. It is founded on the agreement of the parties to refer their dispute to binding decision on a legal basis given by an arbitration tribunal. This is composed of one or more arbitrators, chosen to deal with the dispute. Arbitration is very ancient, but the modern form of this settlement procedure originates from the famous Jay's Treaty of 1794 between the United States and England. Since then, the idea of arbitration has steadily grown. In the course of the 19th century, many arbitration treaties were concluded and hundreds of cases decided. But this by no means implies that the states were in general willing to allow their disputes to be settled in this way by recourse to law. In the first place, only purely legal disputes, not those of a political character, are suitable for settlement by arbitration. In the second place, most arbitration cases concern claims by private persons against a foreign state, and they acquire the character of disputes between states only because the claimant's own country can, under international law, make his claim its own, and so give it an international character.

The point of interest here is that at the turn of the 19th century, the idea arose of institutionalizing arbitration. This happened, in fact, when, at the first Peace Conference at the Hague in 1899, it was agreed to establish a Permanent Court of Arbitration. The name, in fact, is misleading, since this was not a real court. A court implies permanent judges, and this is incompatible with the concept of arbitration, which implies that a tribunal shall be set up to deal with individual cases, so that the parties can choose as arbitrators persons in whom they have especial confidence, or whom they consider to be expert in relation to the case in question. The "Court" is thus, in reality, merely a list of persons who are both suitable and willing to act as arbitrators.

At the same time, rules were laid down as to how the parties—in cases where nothing had previously been agreed upon to the contrary—were to proceed in choosing from among these persons those who were to constitute the tribunal for the individual case. Further, rules were also laid down defining the arbitration procedure in cases where the parties had not agreed on another method. Whether or not two states would submit a dispute to the Permanent Court of Arbitration remained a completely voluntary matter. What was achieved was the creation of an apparatus that stood ready for use, should two states desire it. This avoided the rock on which arbitration negotiations can easily founder, that is, the difficulties that can arise in an acute dispute, not merely on the matter of agreeing to go to arbitration, but also on the composition of the tribunal, the rules for its procedure, limitation of its competence, place of meeting, etc.

A further step toward fixing international administration of justice in permanent institutions would be the establishment of a real international court of justice, i.e. a judicial organ with permanent judges, seat, and secretariat. An attempt in this direction was made at the second Hague Conference in 1907, but it did not succeed. This was due to inability to agree on any method of appointing the judges. The Great Powers proposed the principle of rotation, used later in the League of Nations. According to this proposal, eight of the seventeen members would always be appointed by eight Great Powers, while the remaining nine would be appointed in rotation by the other participating states in accordance with certain rules that made allowance for the size of the states. But the smaller states, led by Brazil, firmly maintained the formal principle of absolute equality and equal rights of all states. In this case, adherence to this principle would have meant that every state should have its judge, and that the Court should thus consist of 44 members. This was obviously unwieldy, and so the plan fell through. The case is interesting in that it illustrates the zeal with which the small states, at conferences of this kind, upheld their position of equality with the Great Powers.

At the same conference an attempt was also made to set up a special world court to deal with prize cases. This also failed, but for other reasons. In the same year, however, the first international court of justice was successfully established, though only for a very limited group of states. This was the Central American Court, with obligatory competence in all disputes between Costa Rica, Guatemala, Honduras, Nicaragua, and San Salvador.

Realizing that not all disputes lend themselves to judicial decision by arbitration and that the states, even though a dispute may be suitable for such a decision, are often unwilling to submit to the obligation of a judicial decision, the two Hague Conferences recommended that, in that case, the parties in dispute should refer their dispute to a "commission of inquiry." Such a commission is very similar to an arbitration tribunal, and could be set up in the same way by application to the Permanent Court of Arbitration. The crucial difference is that the task of a commission of inquiry is limited to establishing, by an inquiry conducted under the forms of law, the actual facts of the case. It was considered that this method of proceeding would prove useful, especially in the case of disputes that had arisen in connection with some incident, e.g. a frontier incident, or skirmishes at sea related to fisheries inspection. In such cases, each of the parties will often, on the basis of one-sided and excited reports, entertain exaggerated ideas of apparent injustice. When the circumstances have been established by a court of inquiry and, at the same time, when the excitement has died down, it was considered that there would be a reasonable chance of settling the dispute.

Outside the Hague Conferences, other efforts were made to organize institutionally the peaceful settlement of disputes. On the initiative of William Jennings Bryan, the U. S. Secretary of State, even before the First World War a large number of treaties (about 30) were concluded between the United States and other states for the establishment of "permanent commissions of conciliation." These normally consisted of five persons, two chosen by each side, and an arbitrator. Their function lay between that of an arbitration tribunal and that of a commission of inquiry, for they were not only to seek to establish the facts but also to propose a solution. They were thus not bound by purely legal considerations, and their proposals were not legally binding on the parties.

4. The League of Nations

In 1914 Europe had been at peace for nearly half a century. A great deal of work had been done to create a number of international institutions for promoting collaboration between the states and the peaceful settlement of threatening conflicts, and several times it had proved possible to quench the sparks before they turned into a real conflagration. Many came to believe that a great war was now a thing of the past.

Then on June 28, 1914, came the shot at Sarajevo, which within a month led to the First World War. It will be clear from what has been said above that the failure to prevent the catastrophe was not due to lack of methods and institutions for preventing war. There had been ample opportunity to take up one or the other of the means recommended by the Hague Conferences, but apart from a few attempts at mediation, nothing was done. England, in accordance with the principles of the European Concert, tried in the opening phase to mediate between Austria and Serbia, but in vain, and at the last moment, the American President offered to mediate in accordance with the rules of the Hague Convention, also in vain. The fact is that if the parties, or only one of them, have determined on war, all the settlement machinery in the world is useless.

It was felt, however, that peace might perhaps have been maintained, all the same, had there been a more effective apparatus for dealing with threatening situations and removing the causes for war. Toward the end of the war, therefore, the idea occurred to the Allies of setting up a union of all peace-loving states for this purpose. A number of proposals were drafted, some on the initiative of various private peace movements, and some by commissions appointed by the English and French governments. Of great importance was the fact that the American President, Wilson, encouraged by his friend and adviser, Colonel House, took up the idea with almost religious faith and enthusiasm, and worked out a series of proposals for a founding covenant.

The crucial negotiations took place at the Peace Conference opened at Versailles on February 3, 1919. The Anglo-American draft (the Hurst-Miller draft) provided the basis for discussion. President

Wilson was received with enormous enthusiasm and, for a long time, himself took part in the discussions, until he had to go back to the United States to try to win the hesitating American public over to his cause. On June 28, 1919, the Versailles Treaty was signed, and the first 26 articles of this treaty form the Covenant for the League of Nations. The Covenant came into force on January 10, 1920—but without the participation of the United States. Although President Wilson, more than any other man, can be considered the father of the League, and although the efforts to allay American misgivings shackled the Covenant with various provisos—in favor of the Monroe Doctrine, domestic jurisdiction, and the right to withdraw— American ratification was prevented by the insurmountable opposition of the U. S. Senate. For the President, it was an unparalleled defeat.

When the structure of the League of Nations is examined, elements will be recognized, brick for brick, as having been taken over from the ideas and institutions of the 19th century, changed and adapted in the light of the experience gained during the war. What is new lies not so much in any detail as in the way in which the elements have been brought together under one roof, in one universal and general international organization.

Without describing the League of Nations in detail, I would remind the reader that in its organization it showed the same tripartite structure as the special administrative unions of the 19th century: (1) a General Assembly, where all the member states were equally represented, and which thus had the character of a general conference of states; (2) a Council, consisting of a chosen group of states, that met more frequently and worked as a kind of executive committee; and (3) a Permanent Secretariat, headed by a Secretary-General. To this was added an International Court of Justice, as prescribed in Article 14, and established under a special agreement in 1920.

The object of the League was described in all-embracing terms as being to promote international collaboration and to create international peace and security. There was no division of power between the General Assembly and the Council—either could at its meetings "deal with every question that comes within the competence of the League or touches world peace"—but there is no doubt that it was considered that major political questions concerning the maintenance of peace and the settlement of disputes belonged primarily to the Council. According to the original provisions of the Covenant, this was to be composed of the five Great Powers (the United Kingdom, the United States, France, Italy, and Japan) as permanent members, and four others elected periodically by the General Assembly. Since the United States did not accede to the League, the number of Great Powers was reduced to four, while later on the number of lesser states was raised to 11.

The League of Nations may be described as a universal, international organization, uniting in itself all the aims and activities that were previously distributed among many different bodies. Thus the Council exercised the same functions—maintenance of peace, mediation, settlement of disputes—that were formerly exercised by the Concert of Europe. The General Assembly, in which all states were equally represented, corresponded to the ordinary periodical intergovernmental conferences of the administrative unions, and, like these, functioned primarily to provide a forum for general discussion and to serve as a mouthpiece for world opinion. Through the General Assembly and its numerous subordinate commissions and affiliated special organizations, all the duties and functions involved in collaborating for the pursuance of common aims, which had previously been parcelled out among a number of scattered organizations, were now completed and co-ordinated. The Secretariat was clearly modeled on the bureaus of the various administrative unions, which had proved particularly effective in promoting continuity and objectivity in the work. Lastly, the Court dealt with the judicial functions previously distributed among a multitude of arbitration tribunals.

The League of Nations may therefore be described as the universal and general organization of its day. This must not be taken to mean that the League aimed to supersede and supplant the organizations and institutions that already existed. It was not intended, for instance, that the Court should preclude access to arbitration, or that the activities of the Council should abolish the traditional methods of dealing with disputes (inquiry, conciliation, mediation) as these had been elaborated by the Hague Conventions. Nor, finally, was it the intention to abolish or supersede the many and various administrative unions, but only to place them under the direction of The League, and thus co-ordinate them (Art. 24 of the Covenant).

The British draft proposals for the Covenant clearly show that the political function of the League was envisaged as an elaboration and improvement of the European Concert. As is clear from a draft in the archives of the Foreign Office, the Council was accordingly to have consisted exclusively of the Great Powers. Unfortunately, this realistic and traditional attitude did not prevail, and the proposals were watered down and partly displaced by a high-flown idea launched by Wilson: the idea of a mutual, automatic guarantee, or in short, collective security.

According to this idea, it was not the Great Powers as such that were to be made responsible for international peace and security. All, great and small, were to be responsible, in that each promised and guaranteed that it would automatically apply sanctions, at any rate, in the form of a complete economic blockade, and possibly also military action against any other member of the League that went to war contrary to the provisions of the Covenant.

Today, with our experience of the years between the wars, when we look back at the Covenant, belief in such an automatic system must seem extremely naïve. Wilson's belief in this system of security was linked with another, equally unrealistic belief—that wars arise because people are misled by absolute monarchs, who are not responsible to anyone for their acts, and because of secret diplomacy. He was convinced, therefore, that if a nation enjoys democratic government and all diplomatic questions are handled in public, an important impetus to war disappears. Accordingly, in Wilson's opinion, only states with free, democratic institutions should be admitted as members of the League.

The League of Nations thus united in itself various currents from the 19th century in its efforts for peace and progress. Seen against this background, the League appears as a systematic synthesis, completion, and co-ordination of given but isolated elements—now crowned by the idea of collective, automatic security. At the same time, the League bears all the marks of having been conceived during the world war and shaped by the victorious Allied and Associated Powers at the conference at which the terms of peace were dictated. The conquered Axis powers were, for the moment, excluded from the League. Nor could Russia, which from an ally had changed into a revolutionary power threatening her former allies with revolution from within, be considered eligible for membership. As stated above, the United States did not join the League. The idea of the concert of the Great Powers was thus incompletely realized from the very start. Of the remaining four Great Powers, the United Kingdom, France, Japan, and Italy, the last two soon showed tendencies to aggression that made them unsuitable for playing the part of guarantors of peace. The idea of the concert, a reality in the last century, was played out, and the League grew more and more to resemble an Anglo-French club. Nor did the subsequent acceptance as members of Germany, in 1926, and Russia, in 1934, do much to change this. Ideologically, both were far removed from the spirit of the League and neither would nor could bring any accession of strength.

The experiences of the war years and the problems of the peace marked the Covenant in various ways. During the war, the Allied and Associated Powers had been successful in jointly creating a series of common organs, from the Supreme War Council down. They had carried on such collaboration as had never been witnessed before, which reinforced the belief that it must be possible to organize a corresponding collaboration in peacetime, too. The blockade of Germany had shown that an economic boycott can be an extremely effective weapon, and the rules concerned economic sanctions in the Covenant are undoubtedly inspired by this experience.

The "mandate system" reflects one of the most difficult problems of the peace, i.e. how to reconcile Wilson's nonannexation principle with the Allies' demand to take over the German colonies and certain areas under Turkish suzerainty, which they had shared out among themselves in secret agreements during the war. The mandate system was a stroke of genius, a solution that satisfied the demands both of Wilson (in principle) and the Allies (in reality). The system held that it was the sacred duty of civilization to take care of the now masterless colonies and territories inhabited by peoples "not yet able to stand by themselves under the strenuous conditions of the modern world" (Art. 22 of the Covenant). The best method of giving practical effect to this principle, it was said, would be to entrust the tutelage of such peoples to advanced nations fit and willing to undertake this responsibility. In most cases, "mandate" differed but little from "annexation." But even though the mandate system was originally almost a pretext, its introduction was the first step toward the liberation of the colonial peoples. The idea that had thus found (more or less hypocritical) expression had a power in it that made its progress irresistible. The mandate system led to the trusteeship system of the United Nations, which has now almost made itself superfluous, since its objective, liberation, has been achieved in most cases.

The League of Nations lasted two decades. The first of these offered some encouragement. Various conflicts were dealt with successfully. In 1925 the Locarno treaties, which were to guarantee peace in Western Europe, were signed, and in 1928 came the Kellogg-Briand Pact, to which 62 states acceded, declaring formally, in the name of their respective peoples, that they condemned recourse to war for the solution of international controversies and renounced it as an instrument of national policy in their relations with one another. During those years, there was a certain optimism and a spirit of conciliation linked with names such as Briand, Stresemann, and Austen Chamberlain.

But it was soon to appear that fair words were not enough. In the 1930's the League was faced with a series of conflicts and flagrant breaches of the peace without being able to assert its authority for the maintenance of peace and justice. In that decade Japan, Italy, and Germany embarked on manifest aggressions, without causing any other reaction from the League than empty protests and half-measures. It began with Japan's attack on China, and conquest of Manchuria, camouflaged by the erection of Manchukuo as a Japanese puppet state (1932). The League was powerless, nor was the United States willing to do anything but protest. The episode gave rise to what is known as the Stimson Doctrine. In 1932, the American Secretary of State, Henry Stimson, in a note to Japan and China, declared that the United States had no intention of recognizing any situation, treaty, or agreement brought about by means contrary to the Kellogg-Briand Pact of 1928. This doctrine was approved shortly after by the League of Nations, when the Assembly passed a resolution declaring that it was the duty of members not to recognize any situation, treaty, or agreement brought about by means contrary to the Covenant of the League of Nations or the Kellogg-Briand Pact.

Faced with a fait accompli that one is not prepared to resist, however, it is doubtful whether there is anything to be gained by denying its existence. In any case, such an ostrichlike policy may involve its author in difficulties.

The Manchukuo affair was a serious blow to the prestige of the

League of Nations; nor did this improve when, some years later, Italy followed Japan's example, in open aggression against Ethiopia. In this case, and for the first and last time in history, sanctions were voted and set in motion by 50 states. The effect of these sanctions was also felt, and there is no doubt that Italy could have been brought to her knees by these means. But because they feared that an Italian defeat would throw Mussolini into the arms of Hitler, England, and France, outside the League, pursued a policy aiming at a solution that would satisfy Mussolini (the Hoare-Laval plan) while seeing to it that sanctions were not applied so thoroughly as to achieve their object. Thus sanctions never came to include the imports of oil without which the Italian war machine would have ground to a halt.

The weakness of the Western powers toward Mussolini must have given Hitler the all-clear for his aggressions. He had already, without meeting any resistance, unilaterally abolished the disarmament clauses of the Treaty of Versailles, and had soon after moved into the demilitarized zone in the Rhineland. The following year witnessed the occupation of Austria and Czechoslovakia. Italy had taken possession of Albania, and Japan had attacked China. Hitler's march into Poland was, finally, the beginning of the Second World War. In all these infringements of the Covenant, in the last years before the war, nobody mentioned the League of Nations. It was played out. The last sign of life was an empty demonstration: the Soviet Union, after its attack on Finland in the winter of 1939, was branded as an aggressor and ejected from the League.

The reason for the failure of the League of Nations has often been discussed. Perhaps the question is wrongly formulated, since it assumes that there was reason to expect a better result, and that the fiasco therefore needs to be explained by particular circumstances and causes. Here we have a profound and difficult problem, namely the question of what may reasonably be expected of international organizations, undertakings to maintain peace, and systems of guarantees, sanctions, and other juridical regulation, in a world where there is no monopoly of the power to use force, but where this is shared among a number of equally independent organs—the so-called sovereign states. Without going into the details of this problem here, I shall confine myself to emphasizing one obvious (and often pointed out) factor that must from the outset have made it unlikely that the League of Nations would be able to keep the peace. In the years between the wars there were seven Great Powers. Of these, only France and the United Kingdom were really able and willing to give their support to the League of Nations as the decisive factor in the maintenance of peace. The other Great Powers either stood outside the League or adopted a cool and reserved attitude to it, regarding it as an instrument of Anglo-French policy. It was thus never possible after the First World War to establish anything like a World Concert, which might perhaps have exercised in world politics an influence for the balancing of power and the preservation of peace similar to that exercised by the Concert of Europe in the politics of Europe. And here it is impossible to avoid the question of whether the political arrangements made under the Treaty of Versailles could measure up, in political wisdom and foresight, to those of the Congress of Vienna (Chap. VIII.2).

5. The origins of the United Nations

"From the moment when Hitler's invasion of Poland revealed the bankruptcy of all existing methods to preserve the peace, it became evident to us in the State Department that we must begin almost immediately to plan the creation of a new system." Thus writes Cordell Hull, then U. S. Secretary of State, in his *Memoirs*. A commission to study the question was soon appointed, and the same was done in the British Foreign Office.

These plans might have aimed at a reform of the League of Nations. There seems, however, never to have been any doubt that a new organization should be created, which, in the eyes of Russia or the United States, would not be tainted with unpleasant memories or inveterate prejudices.

The preparatory work, in general, was effected as follows. The fundamental investigations and deliberations were carried out by the American and the British commissions mentioned above. At a very late stage (the spring of 1944), the drafts were submitted to Russia and China for their comments. Then, in the autumn of 1944 (Aug. 21 to Oct. 7), at Dumbarton Oaks, there were long, confidential discussions between experts representing the four powers. Those questions on which agreement could not be reached were referred to the meeting at Yalta, in the Crimea, in February 1945, between Roosevelt, Churchill, and Stalin. The draft thus hammered out by the Big Four during long discussions and with hard-won compromises provided the basis for discussion at the final conference, which took place at San Francisco from April 25 to June 26, 1945, with the participation of 50 states.

It may be said, therefore, that the Charter of the United Nations is in all essentials the work of the four Great Powers, and, in particular, an Anglo-American product. The other states at the San Francisco Conference were unable to make any important changes in the original draft. There was certainly no lack of criticism or proposed amendments. Forty delegates tabled amendments, about 1,200 of them in all. And many of these, on points of lesser importance, were accepted. Indeed, the Great Powers seem even to have encouraged such amendments to avoid creating the impression that they were presenting the Charter as a quasi-ultimatum. But on crucial points, however, they held fast to what they had agreed among themselves. This was especially the case over the right of veto in Article 27, which is the political keystone of the Charter. This gave rise to a lengthy and lively debate. The lesser states were strongly in favor of certain modifications of the right of veto. At one moment it looked as though the Conference would be wrecked on this point. There is not the slightest doubt that if a free vote had been taken on this point, there would have been more than the necessary two-thirds majority for limiting the right of veto. But as Dr. Herbert Evatt, the leader of the Australian delegation and the leader of the opposition on this point, reports, the Great Powers let it be known that they would accept no amendment concerning the right of veto, and that the delegates must choose between a Charter on that basis and no Charter at all.

In my opinion, this procedure was both sensible and fortunate. Abstract democratic ideals of equality are not applicable to units, such as states, that in size, interest, power, and influence are incommensurables. If all the 50 states represented at the San Francisco Conference had participated on a footing of equality in the preparation and adoption of the Charter of the United Nations, it is probable that the discussion would have dragged on until the favorable moment had passed, and the result would have been reduced in value by national jealousies and intrigues. It is never quite wrong to let responsibility and influence march together.

That the states invited to the Conference were not allowed to meddle with the foundations does not mean that their contributions were without importance. They made improvements on a number of points. One of these, in fact, was to become of the first importance for future developments. It was due mainly to Dr. Evatt that, at the eleventh hour of the Conference, the competence of the General Assembly was extended so that it might discuss any question or any matters within the scope of the Charter, and also make recommendations unless the Security Council at that moment is exercising its functions in relation to the dispute or situation in question (Art. 10 and 12). This extension was made precisely because Evatt and others were skeptical about the optimism shown by the permanent members of the Security Council with regard to the continued harmony of their collaboration within that organ; and because they wanted to make it possible for the organization to work through the General Assembly should the Council be paralyzed by the exercise of the right of veto. It is not easy to see how the adjustment in favor of the General Assembly that has, in fact, been made, would have been possible if this reserve competence for the Assembly had not been created.

If one single person can, more than any other, be rightly described as the originator of the Charter, it must be the American Secretary of State, Cordell Hull. In his *Memoirs* he has given a detailed account of the preparatory work from the first days of the war right up to San Francisco. It is interesting to see that Churchill wanted security to be based on a series of regional councils under a world council, and he succeeded for a time in winning Roosevelt over to this view. After detailed studies and discussions, however, Hull won the President back to the idea of one universal organization for world peace. Without any protest from Churchill, this principle was laid down in the Moscow Declaration of October 30, 1943, in which the four leading powers declare that they recognize the necessity of establishing "a general, international organization" for the maintenance of international peace and security.

Cordell Hull also describes the confidential negotiations at Dumbarton Oaks. At the beginning, the main difference was on the field of action of the projected organization. The Russians were of the opinion that this should be confined to the maintenance of peace and security, and that economic and social collaboration should be left to special organizations. The American view, that the scope of the organization should also include economic and social matters, was very soon agreed to.

More serious, however, was the difference of opinion on the right of veto of the permanent members of the Security Council. On the main point, all four were agreed: the right of veto is the real political keystone of the Charter—the idea that it is a Russian invention is incorrect. But, while the Russians maintained this idea without limitation, Roosevelt urged very strongly that a permanent member might not apply the veto when the voting was on a dispute to which that member was a party. He said it was a fundamental principle of justice, imbedded in American law by the Founding Fathers, that no one may vote on his own case. He even wrote direct to Stalin, but without effect. The question was postponed till the Yalta Conference, and the compromise there agreed to is embodied in Article 27(3). No member may use the veto in his own case when it is simply a question of settling a dispute, as under Chapter VI, whereas it may be used, also in the member's own case, when it is a question of measures of enforcement under Chapter VII.

The Russian representative at Dumbarton Oaks, Ambassador Gromyko, had caused surprise by demanding that all of the 16 Soviet Socialist Republics should be recognized as original members of the United Nations. At Yalta, Roosevelt agreed to support the Russian request that two of these, White Russia and the Ukraine, should be acknowledged as original members alongside the Soviet Union itself.

Mindful of the unhappy fate of the League of Nations in the American Senate, Hull had taken care, from the beginning, to arrange that the American investigations and deliberations should be on a bipartisan basis, so that both Republicans and Democrats took part.

The San Francisco Conference itself was a gigantic undertaking. The invitations were issued by the four Great Powers to 42 states— all those who were co-signatories of or had acceded to the Common Declaration of January 1, 1942, and had declared war on either

Germany or Japan. At the Conference, it was agreed to invite also Argentina, White Russia, the Ukraine, and Denmark, so that 50 states in all were represented.

These came with delegations of varying size, from 4 up to the 175 members of the American delegation. There were 282 delegates, with 1,444 deputies, advisers, technical experts, and so on. The Secretariat included over 1,000 persons. To these must be added a number of representatives of public and private international organizations and, of course, countless representatives of the world press.

The results of the two months of negotiations were embodied in two treaties, both dated June 26, 1945. The first contained the Charter of the United Nations, comprising 111 Articles with an Appendix, the Statute of the International Court of Justice, of 70 Articles. The second covered the Preparatory Commission that was to make the necessary arrangements for the first session of the General Assembly, including the establishment of a secretariat.

In accordance with the customary rules, the Charter was not binding on the signatory states until the signature had been duly ratified by the authorities competent to do so, and it was not to come into effect until a sufficient number of states had ratified the Treaty (See Art. 110 of the Charter). The Charter thus came into effect October 24, 1945, the birthday of the United Nations. The organization took form and shape with the opening of the first session of the General Assembly in London on January 10, 1946.

The minutes of the negotiations at San Francisco have been published under the title *The United Nations Conference on International Organization* (UNCIO), in 15 volumes plus an Index, covering 12,000 pages in all. These minutes are naturally of great importance when it is a question of determining what the Fathers of the Charter meant and intended by the text they agreed on. Such historical and subjective interpretation, however, diminishes in importance and interest in proportion to the measure in which developments in practice cause the living organization to diverge from the organization in the text.

Even after the United Nations had come into being, the League of Nations still existed. Its liquidation required various measures:

(1) liquidation of the League's financial obligations, particularly those to its employees;

(2) transfer of various assets (buildings, libraries, equipment) to the new organization; and

(3) transfer to the United Nations of various functions and mandates exercised by the League of Nations by virtue of particular authority granted under special agreements between two or more states.

The first of these the League could itself carry out on its own authority. This was done by various resolutions passed at the 21st and last session of the Assembly, held at Geneva from April 8 to 18, 1946, whereby a pension fund was established and a Committee of Liquidation appointed.

The second question was dealt with in various agreements between the two organizations whereby the various assets were transferred to the successor organization on easy conditions.

As for the last point, it was clear that, in principle, there must be a new agreement between all the interested parties, if the United Nations was to take the place of the League. This principle was unconditionally applied to the political functions. As to nonpolitical functions, a simple solution was found, in that the United Nations declared itself willing to take over these functions, while it was determined, at the same time, that the members, by voting for this declaration, were to be taken as agreeing that the new organization should take over the role of the League of Nations.

The formal dissolution of the League of Nations was effected by a resolution passed by the Assembly on April 18, 1946, whereby the League, with effect from the next day, should cease to exist except for the single object of winding up its affairs.

References

1. THE CONCERT OF EUROPE
    Besides the textbooks in general political history, reference should be made to:
    Nussbaum, Arthur, *A Concise History of the Law of Nations* (rev. ed., 1954).
2. INTERNATIONAL ORGANIZATION AND ORGANIZATIONS
    Hill, Norman, *International Organization* (1952).
    Leonard, L. Larry, *International Organization* (1951).
    Mangrove, Gerard J., *A Short History of International Organization* (1954).
    Padelford, Norman J. and George A. Lincoln, *International Politics* (1954).

3. INSTITUTIONS FOR SETTLING INTERNATIONAL DISPUTES

Hull, William I., *The Two Hague Conferences* (1908).

Ross, Alf, *Lærebog i Folkeret* (Textbook of International Law) (4th ed., 1961), Chap. XIII. An earlier edition of his work is available in English, *Textbook on International Law* (London, 1947).

4. THE LEAGUE OF NATIONS

The literature is enormous. See, in particular:

Brierly, J. L., "The Covenant and the Charter," *British Yearbook of International Law* (1946).

Schücking, Walther and Hans Wehberg, *Die Satzung des Völkerbundes* (The Statute of the League of Nations) (1931).

Walters, F. P., *A History of the League of Nations* (1952).

Zimmern, Alfred, *The League of Nations and the Rule of Law, 1918-1935* (1936).

For the policy of nonrecognition, see Ross, *Lærebog i Folkeret*, pp. 134-5.

5. THE ORIGINS OF THE UNITED NATIONS

Besides the general accounts of the United Nations, see also:

Evatt, Herbert Vere, *The United Nations* (1948).

Goodrich, Leland M., From League of Nations to United Nations," *International Organization*, I (1947), 3-21.

Hull, Cordell, *Memoirs*, II (1948), 1625-1713.

Kopelmanas, Lazare, *L'organisation des Nations Unies* (The Organization of the United Nations), Vol. I (1947).

League of Nations: *The League Hands Over* (1946).

II ❧

THE UNITED NATIONS
ON PAPER
AND IN REALITY

WHEN the San Francisco Conference opened on April 25, 1945, Denmark was still occupied, and Hitler was still alive. When the Conference closed on June 26, the war was still raging in the Pacific, and the world was as yet ignorant of the atomic bomb. The Charter of the United Nations is a product of the world political situation as it appeared in the last phases of the Second World War. It was based on certain conditions—conditions that in a very short time no longer existed. No sooner had the Charter been signed than it was out of date, for, as certain presuppositions no longer held good, it was—to use an architectural metaphor—in reality impossible to erect the United Nations edifice in accordance with the architectural plan drawn at the Conference. When we now, twenty years after the creation of the Organization, consider the United Nations, we find a structure that in many respects differs radically from the original plan. Certain parts of the original project have never been built, and at other points additions have gradually been made, while some parts have been reconstructed in order to adjust the edifice to the changed conditions. Perhaps the architectural metaphor is not really appropriate, for a building lacks the capacity to adapt itself readily to changing conditions. Perhaps the United Nations may be better likened to something organic, a tree, for example, which can adjust its growth to changing climatic conditions: where conditions are unfavorable to growth, the branches die off, whereas new shoots come when conditions favor a new process of creation.

The United Nations was created in the mild political climate of the Moscow, Teheran, Yalta, and Potsdam conferences; collaboration between the United States, Great Britain, and the Soviet Union was personified in the Big Three, Roosevelt, Churchill, and Stalin. But it was not long before the illusion that unity created by a common enemy in war could also continue without this stimulation, was destroyed, so that the still tender green shoot came to unfold its first leaves in the climate of the cold war.

Nor is this East-West opposition the only one that has marked the conditions under which the United Nations has grown up. Another opposition, almost as important, has arisen in the course of time, which might be denominated by the other compass-axis, North–South. When the Charter was drawn up, the colonial system was, it is true, already under criticism and under liquidation, but nobody foresaw that this development would assume the explosive character it did. It has been important not only in that it has brought about new patterns in the formation of blocs and in voting in the Assembly, but also simply by virtue of the great increase in the number of states. Since the start, the number of member states has more than doubled, and may well be expected to continue to increase to 125 or 150, i.e. nearly thrice the original number. The mere increase in number cannot avoid creating unforeseen problems of organization and causing shifts in the inner balance of power in the Organization.

And then there is, of course, the atomic bomb—not only the comparatively primitive fission bomb (A-bomb) but the far more powerful fusion bomb (H-bomb). For the moment, at any rate, this new fantastic means of destruction has increased the tendency to alter the structure of the power situation toward a bipolarization with the two great atomic powers, the United States and the Soviet Union, as poles. All power relations now appear as the lines of force round the two poles of the magnet. All other states take up positions in this field of force, either orientated toward one or the other of the giants, or balancing in a neutral middle zone.

This chapter will describe how these changed conditions in the postwar world came to shape the United Nations in its growth, so that the organization as we know it today in the real world is fundamentally different from the one drawn on paper in the Charter. It will be shown how the security system that was modeled on the Concert of Europe never, in fact, worked, but has been replaced by a network of regional security arrangements. And we shall see how the center of gravity in the Organization has moved through various phases, from the Security Council to the General Assembly and thence to the Secretary-General, and may perhaps move back again toward the Security Council. It is also interesting to note that the part of the Charter that deals with the trusteeship system will soon be of merely historical importance. Finally, the manner in which this strange process of change has taken place will be explained.

1. The cold war

If one prefers, for the sake of simplicity, to divide into periods a development that in reality pursued its course continuously and gradually, then it may be said that the Cold War broke out in the summer of 1947. But even before then, there had been no lack of disagreements between East and West.

Experience shows that the coalition that has bound together a group of powers against a common enemy breaks down when victory has been won. The common aim is now replaced by competing interests, divergent ideals, and mutual distrust. And so it was after the last war: the common front of the Great Powers to resist the attack of the other states on the veto rule was the last demonstration of brotherly unity.

The first and greatest of the problems to be solved by the victorious powers at the end of the war was the conclusion of treaties of peace with the Axis Powers. It was a promising sign that in the course of a year or so, they were able to conclude, in common, treaties of peace with Bulgaria, Hungary, Roumania, Finland, and Italy (Feb. 10, 1947). But in the cases of Germany and Japan, which involved the greatest difficulty, it soon appeared that agreement was impossible. The problems were discussed at a conference of foreign ministers in London in September and October, but this ended without results and without an agreement on any further meetings.

No sooner had the General Assembly opened its first meeting (in London, Jan. 10, 1946) than the opposition between East and West broke out into disputes. As early as January 19, the Iranian situation was brought before the Security Council. Although agreement had been reached on the political independence of Iran and the speedy withdrawal of all troops stationed in the country during the war, and although the Western Powers had loyally fulfilled their obligations in this respect, the Russian troops remained, and negotiations with the West on this matter led to no result. So Iran complained to the Security Council and alleged that the Russians were exerting pressure on them to obtain oil concessions and were encouraging separatist tendencies in the Azerbaijan district. What was depressing was not so much that competing interests and friction should appear as that it soon became obvious that the Security Council was being used not as a forum for negotiation, mediation, and settlement, but as an instrument in the struggle, an arena for the cold war—a war that used all the techniques of propaganda and psychological warfare. Two days after the handing in of the Iranian complaint (taken by the Russians as a Western action), the Russians replied with what was obviously a reprisal—namely, a complaint of the presence of British troops in Greece.

In the course of 1946, it became clear that Russia would not respect the agreements on spheres of influence made with the Western Powers during the war. According to these, Greece was to have been a British sphere of influence, while Bulgaria, Hungary, and Rumania were acknowledged to belong to the Soviet sphere. When a Greek government had been formed with British support, Communist-led groups continued their war as a rebellion, supported by the neighboring Communist states (Albania, Bulgaria, and Yugoslavia) and thereby indirectly by the Soviet Union. At the beginning of 1947, economic difficulties compelled the British government to stop its economic and military support of the Greek government, and it looked as if the country, thus left to itself, would therefore fall a prey to Communist infiltration and seizure of control, as happened to Czechoslovakia a year later. It was in this situation that President Truman on March 12, 1947, issued his historic message to Congress, in which he laid down the political doctrine, later called by his name, that it must be the task of the United States to support free nations threatened with subjection by armed minorities within or pressures from without.

The gauntlet thrown down by the Russians was therefore taken up, and it became clear that the United States of America had assumed the leadership and the responsibility in the cold war between East and West. Any lingering doubt that the era of peaceful collaboration was over was dispelled by the Russian attitude to the Marshall Plan, proposed by the American Secretary of State, George Marshall, in June 1947. In a famous speech, delivered June 5, he urged the European states to work out plans in common for their economic reconstruction and promised American support. Russia refused, however, to take part in any such collaboration and also forbade its vassal states to take part.

Since then, the opposition between East and West, primarily between the Soviet Union and the United States, has settled into a permanent pattern, the very basic pattern of global politics, and the cold war has continued at varying temperatures. In 1948, Czechoslovakia was overrun from within under the threat of Russian military force. In the same year, the opposition sharpened in the Berlin crisis, which was successfully surmounted without recourse to military operations. On the other hand, Communist aggression, using the North Koreans as puppets, led to hot, though localized, war (1950-53). The revolts in East Germany (1953) and in Hungary (1956), both put down by Russian troops with an iron hand, made it clear that the Soviet Union would not tolerate any breach in its established positions.

From the Russian point of view, America's possession of the atomic bomb, used against Japan in August 1945, which, for the moment, gave the United States a unique monopoly and advantage in armament, had been a shock that did not encourage confidence. The existence of the bomb had been a secret, and the methods of its production were still secret. It is true that in the Baruch plan (based on the Acheson-Lilienthal report) America had made an unusually magnanimous and constructive offer. According to this plan, supreme control was to be vested in an international body that should have the monopoly of all raw materials for the production of atomic energy (thorium and uranium), and should itself operate all mines. The atomic authority would then distribute the usable material and allow the states, under the authority's control, to use it for the production of energy for peaceful purposes. When this point had been reached, the United States would be willing to destroy its stock of bombs and to hand over to the international organ all its scientific and technological knowledge of the production of atomic energy. On the other hand, it must be admitted that this plan, in spite of American magnanimity, suffered inevitably from the snag involved in every plan for atomic disarmament. So far, there is no known method of detecting a hidden store of atomic bombs or of material for their production. The plan, therefore, assumed that the Soviet Union would blindly rely on the United States loyally fulfilling its obligation, and keeping back neither stocks nor knowledge. Such confidence apparently goes beyond what can be expected between rival Great Powers in questions of survival.

It seems clear, therefore, that it was due neither to wickedness nor to stupidity that the atomic bomb was not, so to speak, strangled at birth. It followed from the given technical and psychological facts that no way of disarmament could be found that was acceptable to both sides. When, in September 1949, President Truman gave the world the news that the first Russian atomic bomb test had taken place, it was clear that Russia was about to catch up with America, and that the result, at first, at any rate, must be an atomic armaments race.

2. Anticolonialism and the new nationalism

Although the mandate system of the League of Nations arose, as we have seen, from mixed motives, and, for the colonial powers at all events, was perhaps only camouflage for their annexation of the former German colonies, yet it started a development that led to the total abolition of the colonial system.

At first it was liberal, humanitarian opinion, also among the peoples of the colonial powers themselves, that brought the system to public debate and demanded economic and political reforms to raise the standard of living and prepare the populations for self-govern-ment. It was such progressive, though relatively conservative, views —such as might be called the ideology of enlightened colonial rule— that prevailed when the United Nations agreed on the Charter and that characterized the provisions concerning trusteeship and the states' obligations toward all subject peoples. The exploitation of the colonies that had marked colonialism in the 19th century was in-creasingly replaced by active efforts to promote the welfare of the native populations. It was taken for granted that even though the final objective must be freedom—independence, or at all events a suitable degree of self-government—it would be a question of gener-ations, perhaps even centuries, before the white man could lay down his burden and his responsibility.

But the movement toward colonial liberation proceeded with a speed and an explosive violence nobody had ever dreamed of in 1945. To an increasing extent, the pressure and the drive now came from the colonial peoples themselves, as they realized the gulf be-tween the poor countries and the rich. It is never the poorest that rebel. Rebellion presumes a certain breadth of view, ability to make comparisons, and courage to doubt the right to rule of the ruling race or class. The war contributed powerfully toward this develop-ment. It opened the eyes of the dependent peoples to the great world and broke down emotional barriers in their relations with the white man. Not least in Asia, Japan's successful aggression and de-liberate humiliation of the Europeans, both military and civil, helped to destroy the belief in the white man's unchallengeable su-periority.

A liberating process of this kind, moreover, has a tendency to accelerate of itself. The circumstance that a number of colonial areas achieve existence as independent states is in itself an extremely pow-erful stimulus to demands for liberation from other colonial areas, where the native population may not yet have developed sufficiently, economically and politically, to be able to govern itself "under the strenuous conditions of the modern world." The urge to freedom, also stimulated by the propaganda that speculates in social poverty, unrest, and revolution, may come to violent emotional expression be-fore the people are sufficiently mature to make use of freedom. The task of the colonial power, then, is on the one hand to promote the economic and political development of the people, and on the other, not to let go the reins before the conditions necessary for self-government have been achieved. The unfortunate situation in the Congo after liberation in 1960 is a striking, but not the only, example of what can happen if liberation is not synchronized with economic, cultural, and political training for independence.

Newly gained independence characteristically brings with it a strongly developed and highly sensitive nationalism, and a hostile attitude to the colonial power under whose rule the people formerly lived. It takes time before, as now in India, hate yields to an understanding of the fact that the colonial administration also had its good points and that collaboration with the former colonial power is worth while, and perhaps even a necessity, for progress and development.

The liquidation of the colonial system has changed in several ways the conditions under which the United Nations functions and has thus helped to determine its inner development. The mere fact of the enormous increase in the number of members to more than double the original number—the liberation of the colonies accounts for most of the increase—is in itself a circumstance that gives rise to organizational consequences (demands for increased representation in the various Councils, in the Secretariat, and in the Court; change in relative weight of the various blocs in the General Assembly; and so on). The new states with a colonial past have, moreover, brought into the picture a clash of ideology and interest that has highly complicated the formation of groups in the General Assembly.

3. Bipolarization

At the time of the Congress of Vienna, there were five Great Powers, all European: Russia, Austria, Prussia, France, and Great Britain. In the course of the next hundred years, Italy joined them, and Prussia was replaced by Germany. Further, two non-European candidates for the title appeared—the United States and Japan.

The basis of the Concert of Europe and the balance of power in world politics was the fact that none of these five to eight powers was decidedly more powerful than the others. War starts only when one party, alone or allied with others, believes itself sufficiently superior to be able to win the war. The principle of the balance of power was to prevent this from happening, and the means were by varying groupings, understandings, and alliances, within the circle of the Great Powers and the more important of the lesser powers, to form a barrier to presumed aggressive tendencies. Alliances, ententes, and axes, could not, therefore, be stable but must be elastic and capable of adjustment when circumstances changed. That major political relations were based less on ideological connections or differences but were dictated, independently of these, by calculations of power politics, is illustrated by the fact that both Italy and Japan fought on opposite sides in the two world wars: and similarly by such a phenomenon as the Stalin-Hitler pact in 1939 (Chap. VIII.2).

The Charter of the United Nations builds on the continued existence of these conditions of power politics. But even while the Charter was being worked out, this assumption was no longer justified, and later developments have accentuated the difference from the many-centered pattern of the 19th century. The Charter recognizes five Great Powers: China, France, the United Kingdom, the Soviet Union, and the United States. China represents a greater mass of population than any other state, and has enormous development potential when its resources are exploited. But the admission of China to the oligarchy of the Great Powers must be considered a gesture of politeness. France came out of the war humiliated and weakened, and the painful readjustments after the loss of her overseas possessions, together with continued inner disunion, have not contributed to increase the country's weight in power politics. The United Kingdom came out of the war with all honor, and the liquidation of the Empire was conducted with greater wisdom and flexibility than on the other side of the Channel. But the country was so weakened economically as to be unable any longer to live up to the standard required to assume world-wide commitments and world political responsibilities.

Thus, when the United Nations was established, there were only two Great Powers, but each of these represented a power potential of an order hitherto unknown: the United States and the Soviet Union. This bipolarization of the field of force of high politics has, in the years that have elapsed since then, been further accentuated by two factors: developments in armaments and the ideological element

in the power groupings. The production of the modern "miracles"
of the technique of destruction, such as atomic bombs of various
sizes, long-distance rockets, atomic-powered submarines, supersonic
bombers and fighters, not to speak of sputniks and spaceships, requires such an industrial potential that only the very greatest states
can play a significant part. The ideological substratum of the opposition between East and West tends also to lock the positions taken up
in the cold war and hinders the approaches and regrouping that a
realistic estimation of the power political situation and of future possibilities would appear to demand.

4. The security system of the charter

The system of the Charter for the maintenance of international
peace and security is the expression of a new and bold construction
of a more realistic type than that of the League of Nations. The San
Francisco Conference realized clearly that the idea of automatic collective security (Chap. VIII.3), which Wilson had believed in and
which was the foundation of the peace system of the League, was an
illusion. In fact, the system had never worked. And it must be admitted that it was unreasonable to believe that states, simply by virtue
of a legal obligation and irrespective of national interests, would
each automatically apply sanctions—at any rate an economic boycott, perhaps military action—against every other state that violated
the peace. Instead, the Conference returned to the idea of a Concert
based on the hegemony of the Great Powers, that had functioned
satisfactorily for a hundred years. But what had then been a self-
created order, without institutional character, was now to be laid
down in paragraphs and given the juridical foundation of a treaty.

The security system of the United Nations for the maintenance of
peace builds on the idea that the system cannot be applied to relations between the five Great Powers—the power of veto secures each
of them against this—whereas the Big Five, when they are in agreement, have authority to make decisions binding on all members on
the measures of compulsion, economic or military, that shall be
taken to maintain peace and security. Article 24 states that the
members confer on the Security Council the primary responsibility
for the maintenance of peace and agree that the Security Council,

in carrying out its duties under this responsibility, acts on behalf of all. And in Article 25, the formulation is even sharper, stating that the members agree to accept and carry out the decisions of the Security Council in accordance with the Charter.

"The Security Council" in reality means the five Great Powers. It would have been more consistent if the Security Council had consisted exclusively of the Great Powers. As a concession to democratic ideas and the ambitions of the lesser powers, the lesser states, however, have been admitted to the Council, even as a majority, i.e. six. At the same times, though, by Article 27, the rules for voting have been prudently arranged so that the lesser states cannot carry any proposal against the will of a Great Power (the veto), while on the contrary the Great Powers when in agreement can in practice carry any proposal they wish. Since seven votes are required to carry a proposal, the united Great Powers can be stopped only by a group of five of the rest of the Council, a constellation that is hardly conceivable in practice.

The detailed rules for the powers of the Council for the securing of peace are to be found in Chapter VII of the Charter. The Council decides what measures are to be taken in the given circumstances, particularly whether economic boycott is sufficient or military action is to be used. It had been tacitly understood that just as it is the Great Powers that have the responsibility and exercise the authority, it is also they who normally shall bear the burden of carrying out military operations. This special position is clearly expressed in Article 47, which stipulates that the General Staff Committee, which is to advise the Security Council on all military questions, shall consist of the Chiefs of Staff (or their representatives) of the permanent members. Here, then, it was not considered necessary, even for the sake of appearances, to admit representatives of the lesser powers.

A security system on this pattern must appear extremely effective in the case of all threats to or violations of the peace of the type aimed at, i.e. such situations as involve none of the Great Powers directly or indirectly. When the united Great Powers order a boycott and direct military operations in common against the peace-breaker, it is difficult to imagine how any power in the world could resist. One can only wonder how, in concluding the Charter treaty, it was possible to get all the states outside the circle of the Great Powers to accept such a comprehensive obligation as that involved in Article 25 taken together with Chapter VII. This obligation cuts deep into the states' right of self-determination in foreign policy and even into the disposal of their military forces. The obligation to obey the directives of the Security Council implies such a fundamental interference with self-determination that normally it would be cried down as an intolerable infringement of what is called "sovereignty."

It would be incorrect to say that this security system has failed. It has simply never been realized or tested. It proved impossible, at San Francisco, to agree on the extent to which the Great Powers should put armed forces at the disposal of the Security Council. The question was therefore postponed and it was merely provided, in Article 43, that special agreements should be made between the Security Council and every single member on the extent to which the member should put armed forces at the disposal of the Organization, or merely provide help and facilities of other kinds, including the right of passage for troops operating on behalf of the Organization. These agreements, however, have never been concluded, and thus, as far as military operations are concerned, the whole of Chapter VII of the Charter has remained a dead letter.

But, of course, the real reason why the project remains merely a project lies deeper. The essential condition for the Concert system is precisely a concert, i.e. harmony between the leading powers. If that is lost, if the crucial political tensions and oppositions are between the Great Powers themselves, the system is worthless.

That it is this lack of concord, and not the lack of the Article 43 agreements as such, that is the real reason why the system has failed, appears also from the fact that the missing agreements would not exclude sanctions in the form of an economic boycott. Under Article 41 of the Charter, the Security Council can require members to break off, completely or in part, economic connection with a state breaking the peace, and also traffic and communications by rail, by sea, by air, by post, telegraph, and radio, as well as diplomatic relations. This is an extremely effective method of compulsion. That it has never been used, and probably cannot be expected to be used as long as the present political climate prevails in the world, is due to the lack of concord between East and West that paralyzes the Security Council in the exercise of its functions.

The view that it is the veto as such that makes the United Nations powerless is clearly a misunderstanding. Whether or not the veto should be excluded in certain matters may reasonably be discussed, but not where it is a question of taking measures of compulsion for the maintenance of peace. To apply sanctions either against a Great Power or against the will of a Great Power is not to secure peace, but to unleash war. The Great Power's right of veto is a realistic acknowledgment of the truth that without agreement between the Great Powers, no system for the maintenance of peace and security is possible.

The consequence is that as long as the split between East and West persists, it is impossible to look to the United Nations as the guardian of peace, or to base one's national security on reliance on this. The United Nations still has a function to perform in the preservation of peace, as a forum for world opinion. But when it comes to questions of existence, to situations where more is required than mere words, no state, great or small, can expect help from that quarter. The states realized long ago that they themselves must, in one way or another, make the arrangements necessary to secure their existence and freedom. This has been done, to a great extent, by the establishment of a series of regional arrangements in the nature of defensive alliances organized as institutions. These arrangements are grouped round the two dominating powers, the United States and the U.S.S.R.

The United States is the center of a system of pacts, supplemented by various bilateral agreements, whereby it is defensively allied to nearly forty other states in all parts of the world. The center of gravity of this system lies in the North Atlantic Treaty between the United States and Canada and 13 European countries. By the Rio Treaty, the United States is allied to all the Central and South American states (except Cuba); and in the ANZUS group, to Australia and New Zealand. On the other side, the Soviet Union is the center of a series of bilateral agreements allying it to Communist China, eastern Europe, and the other satellite states. Outside these systems of alliance, there are a number of unaligned states, including many of the young states formed by the liberation of colonies, which have found it advantageous to be able to negotiate with both sides. Among these unaligned states are Sweden and India and the two neutralized states, Switzerland and Austria.

5. Shifts in the center of gravity

The cold war, together with the great increase in the number of members, has also caused certain shifts in the center of gravity of the political working of the Organization. Roughly, it is possible to distinguish between various phases in this development: A first phase, in which the Security Council had the leading position envisaged for it under the Charter (1946 to about 1950); a second phase, marked by the General Assembly's supplanting of the Security Council as the center of the Organization's political activity (from about 1950 to about 1955); and a third phase, marked by the increasing tendency of the General Assembly to leave important political decisions to the Secretary-General. It may be that the death of Dag Hammarskjöld (1961) has brought this phase to an end, and that the present tendency is toward a renaissance of the Security Council's leadership.

In the period before the Korean conflict (June 1950) 13 cases of politically important conflict were brought before the Security Council. In those cases where the viewpoints of America and the Soviet Union more or less coincided, results of permanent value were achieved, for example the liberation of Indonesia from Holland, and in the Arab-Israeli conflict. But after the proclamation, in March 1947, of the Truman Doctrine, openly announcing the American determination to shore up against Communism, the Soviet attitude in the Security Council stiffened perceptibly. Now began that series of Soviet vetos that made the work of the Security Council impossible. Increasingly the attempt was made to by-pass this obstacle by bringing political questions before the General Assembly. One drawback of this procedure, however, was that the General Assembly, unlike the Security Council (Art. 21), was not in continuous session, but met only for its annual meetings. In order to overcome this difficulty, an Interim Committee (also called "the Little General Assembly") was formed in 1947. This was to have authority, between sessions, to deal with political questions, to investigate them, and to make recommendations to the General Assembly. Every member had the right to appoint a representative. While the Americans claimed that this was an auxiliary organ created under the authority of Article 22 of the Charter, the Russians refused to recognize the legality of the Committee on the ground that it was contrary to Article 7 of the Charter, as a new principal organ for weakening the position of the Security Council. The Soviet bloc refused to participate in the work of the Committee, which in practice never came to play the part earmarked for it.

The Korean war sharpened the opposition between East and West to such an extent that the chances of collaboration in the Security Council were correspondingly reduced. In other respects, the events at the outbreak of this war might, to a superficial observer, have given the impression that here was a case where the Security Council demonstrated its effectiveness and really brought the Charter's military sanctions system into use. It was, however, only the accident that since January 1950 the Soviet Union, in protest against Chinese representation on the Security Council, had been boycotting its meetings, that allowed the Council to function—without Soviet participation. Moreover, another circumstance contributed. When North Korea started its offensive, on June 24, 1950, a UN Observation Commission was on the spot, and was thus able to give a full report immediately. The Security Council was called together within 24 hours. Led by the United States, the Council passed three resolutions (June 25, and 27, and July 7, 1950) that formed the basis of the military operations. The Council *recommended* members to give the help necessary to resist the North Korean attack and *recommended* that they should place military contingents and other forms of aid at the disposal of a joint command, with General Douglas MacArthur as Commander-in-Chief. Since the Article 43 agreements had never been concluded, the Council could only recommend, but could not give a binding directive, nor apply actual sanctions under Chapter VII. The legal basis for the action must be sought in Article 51, laying down the right of self-defense, i.e. the right of every state to give assistance to the attacked party, whether or not there was a previously existing agreement to do so.

The recommendations of the Security Council were widely followed. About forty—that is to say, about two thirds of the members, including India—contributed to the action in one way or another. Besides the United States, 13 other states sent troops. Still, it was the United States that bore the main part (90-95%) of the burden in men and material. Denmark contributed a hospital ship and other forms of help.

The experience of the Korean conflict was encouraging in so far as it demonstrated the ability of the United Nations to improvise, on a voluntary basis, a concerted action against a manifest aggressor. But it was also clear that the part played by the Security Council on this occasion was a coup that could not be repeated. In August the Soviet Union, the wiser for the experience, resumed its seat on the Council (it was their turn to occupy the chair), and naturally the mice could no longer play.

When the General Assembly met in September 1950, it passed, on the proposal of the United States, a resolution that became famous as the "Uniting for Peace" resolution, No. 337 A (V) of November 3, 1950. The main idea was to put into permanent form the procedure for the restoration of peace that had been improvised in the Korean crisis—with the notable difference that the authority to brand the aggressor, apply and co-ordinate sanctions, should lie with the General Assembly, when the Security Council because of lack of unanimity of the permanent members, fails to exercise its primary responsibility for the maintenance of peace and security.

The resolution provided for:

(1) summoning (on the above condition) the General Assembly to an extraordinary Emergency Session within 24 hours after a request either from the Security Council (without veto!) or from a majority of the members of the United Nations;

(2) establishing a Peace Observation Commission (analogous to the Korean Observation Commission) to observe and report on the situation in any area where there exists international tension the continuance of which is likely to endanger the maintenance of international peace and security;

(3) inviting members to survey their resources in order to determine and inform the United Nations of the nature and scope of the assistance each will be able to place at the disposal of the United Nations for the restoration of peace and security, and a recommendation that special troop contingents should be kept in a state of readiness so that they could promptly be made available to the United Nations; and

(4) appointing a Collective Measures Committee, which, together with a staff of military experts, could co-ordinate the contributions and plan the concerted action.

The resolution was passed by a 52-5-2 vote (this customary way of giving the outcome of a vote means that 52 voted for, five against, and two abstained). Its validity was contested by the Russians, who relied on Article 11 (2) of the Charter, which states that any such question on which action (i.e. measures of enforcement under Chapter VII) is necessary shall be referred by the General Assembly to the Security Council (Chap. VI.2 of this book). This argument was rebutted by the argument that the measures that might be taken under the resolution have not the character of sanctions under Chapter VII, but are actions undertaken as collective self-defence under Article 51.

The Uniting for Peace resolution never gained the importance intended. The security forces that were to be placed voluntarily at the disposal of the General Assembly have no more become a reality than those that were to be placed obligatorily at the disposal of the Security Council under Article 43 of the Charter. On the other hand, the rules for summoning an Emergency Session of the General Assembly have been used several times—in 1956, in connection with Israel's attack on Egypt, and again because of the Soviet intervention in Hungary; in 1958, when the United States intervened in Lebanon; and in 1960 in connection with the operations in the Congo. It is interesting to note that the Uniting for Peace resolution, which was conceived as a move in the United States' anti-Communist policy of containment, in two of these four cases has been applied against America or its Western allies.

Even though the Uniting for Peace resolution did not achieve its object—to establish an organized security system under the authority of the General Assembly—it was a firm manifestation of the will to make the General Assembly, and not the Security Council, the body before which high political problems are brought. Practice has since been in accordance with this. Statistics show that the number of meetings of the Security Council and of political cases dealt with there has been small in recent years, compared with the first few years after the signing of the Charter, while, on the contrary, the number of political cases dealt with by the Assembly has been rising. That the Security Council has not been entirely put out of action is owing to the fact that it is, of course, a major and complicated matter to call the General Assembly to a Special Session or even to an Emergency Session. There is also a limit set in the provision in Article 12(1), under which the General Assembly is precluded from putting forward any recommendation with regard to a dispute or situation as long as the Security Council is exercising its functions in respect of the same case. It has proved possible, however, to limit to some extent the significance of this provision, by maintaining that it does not prevent the General Assembly from making recommendations concerning a case that is also on the agenda of the Security Council, when the two bodies are dealing with two different aspects of the case.

The year 1955 marks a turning point in the history of the United Nations. In the ten years that had elapsed since the birth of the organization, only nine new members had succeeded in joining, thereby bringing the number of members to 60. Many other states had sought admission, but all had hitherto failed because of the cold front between the United States and the U.S.S.R. Those applicants that were favored by one, the other refused to admit, and vice versa. But in 1955 the boil burst. A so-called "package-deal" was made, whereby 16 new members were admitted at once. This brought the number to 76. Since then there has been hardly any political opposition to new applicants, and the number of members has grown steadily, till it is now well over a hundred.

The majority of the members admitted since 1955 are young Afro-Asian states that have only recently grown out of colonial dependence and won independent existence as states. The Afro-Asian bloc altogether comprises half the votes in the Assembly. Most of them have not wished to be enrolled on either side of the cold war; they represent a numerically important third group, the neutralist. To them, the United Nations is primarily an instrument for fighting colonialism and defending nationalist or even tribal interests, for liberating the peoples that are still dependent, and for supporting the young states, which are having great difficulty in gaining their feet.

It is natural that these states should look on the General Assembly as the forum in which they can best make their views and interests heard. The increase in membership has therefore in the first instance served to confirm and to consolidate the shift in the organization's political center of gravity that has already occurred, to the advantage of the General Assembly. On the other hand, the increased and steadily growing number of members necessarily makes for a diminution in the efficiency of this body. The danger of using the rostrum in the General Assembly for propaganda has always been great, and naturally has not become less with the accession of the many new and politically more or less immature states. Moreover, the increase in numbers in an assembly that is not organized in parties, each with its spokesman, and that is without a strict parliamentary procedure must extremely complicate the carrying on of the business of the Assembly. The most serious consequence of the increase of numbers, to the advantage of the neutralist bloc, however, was that it might be difficult for any group in case of dispute to muster the two-thirds of members present and voting necessary, under Article 18(2) of the Charter, for passing resolutions in important questions.

These conditions may help to explain why, since 1955, the General Assembly, in several situations charged with political high tension, has come to exercise its powers by delegating authority to the Secretary-General. In 1953, Dag Hammarskjöld was chosen, with support from all quarters, as Trygve Lie's successor. During his tenure of office, the Secretary-General came to play a prominent political role as the man responsible for the direction of the United Nations Emergency Forces (in Egypt) and the United Nations Operations in the Congo. The zenith of his influence and responsibility was reached in 1960. Then was seen something that under the original plan of the Charter was wildly improbable, that it was the Secretary-General, not the Security Council or the General Staff Committee, who appointed the Commander-in-Chief of the Congo Forces and took the highest political decisions on the use to be made of these forces—naturally, within the framework of the authority and directives given by the Security Council. Since, however, this authority and these directives were to some extent imprecise, they left the Secretary-General a certain amount of latitude for interpretation and judgment. And since it was impossible, either in the Security Council (the veto) or in the General Assembly (two-thirds majority) to secure the adoption of further directives, it had to be mainly the Secretary-General who, as the Congo situation gradually developed with unforeseen aspects and perspectives, had to take the responsibility for adjusting the operations of the United Nations Forces to the changing conditions. Hammarskjöld was exposed to strong criticism, especially from the Russians, while at the same time proposals were put forward for reshaping the office in such a way as to make it decidedly weaker. It is possible that Hammarskjöld's tragic death while performing the duties of his office in the Congo, in 1961, also marked the end of the period in which the Secretary-General in fact personified the United Nations (Chap. VI.3).

At the time when, on American initiative, the Uniting for Peace resolution was passed, the number of members (60) and the composition of the General Assembly were such that the United States could, without difficulty, count on obtaining the necessary two-thirds majority for carrying through politically important decisions. The United Nations was mainly an instrument for American foreign policy. This picture has completely changed. With a membership of well over 100, of which half is composed of states that have not wished to engage in the opposition between East and West, the General Assembly is no longer so easy an instrument to play on. In particular, the General Assembly is unsuitable for dealing with acute political conflicts that require alert vigilance and decision from day to day. The Great Powers as such are naturally interested in having political questions dealt with in the Security Council. Should there come a relaxation of the tension between the United States and the U.S.S.R. in the questions concerning Berlin, disarmament, etc., these considerations make it conceivable, and perhaps even probable, that the Security Council will experience a renaissance as the political center of the Organization (Chap.XII.1).

Under this and the previous heading, we have mentioned two fundamental respects—the security system and the functions of the General Assembly—in which the United Nations as we know it today differs radically from the body agreed to in San Francisco after lengthy consideration and negotiation. These two points could be supplemented by a number of others of varying significance. The reservation on domestic jurisdiction, for example, in Article 2(7) has been watered down until it may seem to have lost its importance (Chap. III.3). The rule on voting in the Security Council (Art. 27.3) has been modified to the extent that if a permanent member abstains from voting or is not present, this is regarded as not preventing a resolution from being passed, although the clause requires the affirmative vote of every permanent member (Chap. V.2). Most of the deviations and new constructions have had the generality of opinion behind them, or have at any rate been supported by the dominant group led by the United States. In a few cases, an interpretation has been maintained and forced through against the views of the leading Western European powers. This was done, for example, in the case of the obviously stretched interpretation, forced through by the anticolonial states, of the obligation to report on non-self-governing areas (under Art. 73.e) that have not been put under Trusteeship (Chap. XI.2).

It would take us too far, however, in this general review of the developments from 1945 to the present, to go into detail on these matters, which will be dealt with at the appropriate place in the following chapters.

6. How did it happen?

In considering the more or less fundamental changes undergone by the United Nations, the question inevitably arises: How did this happen?

Article 108 of the Charter describes the procedure for amending the Charter. In the first place, any amendment requires a two-thirds majority of the members of the General Assembly (i.e. not merely of those present and voting); secondly, the amendment must be ratified by two-thirds of the members of the United Nations, including all the permanent members of the Security Council. This means that no change can be made unless these Great Powers all agree and the proposal is supported by the majority of the others. As long as the chasm between East and West exists, therefore, it will be difficult to make any change in the Charter.

No formal amendment to the Charter in accordance with these rules has been made. The adjustments that have taken place have been made in another way.

In constitutional law, it is well known that no constitution can be adequately described simply on the basis of the written laws in the rules laid down in a formerly adopted constitutional document. The constitution creates a number of organs and prescribes rules for the establishment and functioning of these organs. These rules are the rules of the game in which the political forces of the community meet, struggle, and unite on the political decisions that direct and shape the life of the community. But what the rules of the game are depends not only on the words of the constitution but also on the manner in which these words are in fact understood and followed in practice, i.e. the manner in which the game is actually played. Around every written constitution there grows up a set of understandings, conventions, and customs, to supplement or to change the written constitution. If this practice reflects the general conception of law and justice within the circle of the highest organs of state, there is said to be a custom or convention that supplements or changes the written constitution. If, on the other hand, opinion is divided between different organs or the individuals of which these are composed, then each organ must decide for itself. The outcome may be a political constitutional struggle, decided sooner or later by a political trial of strength. Or it may be that the conflict can be brought before some organ or other, e.g. a court of law, the decision of which is accepted as binding by all parties.

Briefly, then, it may be said that what a constitution really is depends on the manner in which its text is understood and followed, interpreted or misinterpreted by the competent authorities in practice. Metaphorically speaking, a constitution may be compared, not to a machine fixed once for all by particular laws and functions, but to a biological species, which, though determined by certain inherited factors, can develop and change by constant adaptation to changing conditions.

Thus also the Charter, which is the constitution of the United Nations. Certain of its provisions have remained a dead letter because they were based on conditions that have never been fulfilled. So it has been with the security system based on the condition that the members, or at all events the Great Powers, would be at one to conclude the agreements named in Article 43. Since this has proved imposible, the whole security system falls to the ground.

In most cases, adjustment has been made by interpretation of the provisions of the Charter—not infrequently an interpretation dictated by political considerations and beyond what can be regarded as permissible according to the usual juridical technique of interpretation.

Here the question arises: Who is competent to interpret the Charter? And what happens when several competent authorities maintain contradictory interpretations?

In the constitution of some international organizations, it is expressly provided that, in case of doubt or disagreement, any question of interpretation shall be referred for a binding decision to an international court, e.g. the Hague Court. During the discussions at San Francisco, various proposals in this direction were put forward. None was accepted, however, since it was feared that a court, bound by traditional legal principles, would not, in its interpretation, attach to political considerations the weight they ought to have in an organization so political in character as the United Nations. The competent committee, in its final (and accepted) report, made a statement on this. On this basis, and in accordance with the generally accepted principles in the interpretation of treaties, the legal position may be described as follows.

As there is no express provision in the Charter for the solution of problems of interpretation, it must be presumed in accordance with general principles, that each organ severally must decide the questions of interpretation that may arise in the exercise of its functions under the Charter. As a rule, the question of interpretation will not be put separately to a vote, but the decision will be implicit in the resolutions passed directly in the exercise of the organ's functions. For example, if the question concerns two ways of interpreting the reservation on domestic jurisdiction in Article 2(7), and one faction, but not the other, would rule the organ incompetent to deal with a certain case, the fact that the organ passes a resolution on the case tacitly implies a decision on the question of interpretation.

The interpretation on which a particular organ in fact bases its function is to that extent decisive for what actually happens. If it is acceptable to the general opinion, i.e. the great majority of states, including the Great Powers, then it becomes a customary law binding on all. If, on the contrary, it is not so acceptable, the interpretation is not legally binding, either for other organs or for the minority of states represented in the organ who may be of another opinion. This is to say, in the first place, that it is possible in fact for two organs to base themselves on two contradictory interpretations of the Charter; and in the second, that every state for its own part may refuse to accept the organ's interpretation and may demonstrate its refusal in action, e.g. by refusing to act in accordance with resolutions passed, by not attending meetings of the organ, by refusing to accept financial obligations that result from resolutions the state considers unlawful, or, in the last resort, even by leaving the Organization.

There are various judicial procedures that might be considered for dealing with contradictory interpretations. In particular, the main organs of the United Nations may request the International Court for an advisory opinion on the question. But even though many states would respect such an opinion, it is not legally binding. The same is true should the organ refer the question to an *ad hoc* legal committee. A legally binding decision is possible only in relations between two or more states, when these have agreed beforehand to seek a binding decision of the International Court or some other judicial body. This course of action is not very practical and has never been resorted to. Nor have the organs of the United Nations been particularly interested in obtaining advisory opinions on questions of interpretation. In the 15 years of the Organization's existence, it has been done in only 8 cases. There have, on the other hand, been innumerable cases where a reference to the Court has not been suggested at all, or, if so, where the proposal has been rejected.

This reserved attitude to the Court must be considered as due partly to the fact that many members of the United Nations—besides the Communist states, many of the new states with a colonial past—refuse in principle to accept the authority of the Court and the conception of law that it represents—partly, apparently, in the fear that the Court, bound by traditional legal principles, will not in its interpretations attach to political considerations the weight these ought to have in an organization so extremely political in character as the United Nations.

Jurists usually deplore this antijudicial attitude of the organs of the United Nations as an unfortunate break with the principle, otherwise acknowledged in the Western world, of the rule of law. Even though I am myself a jurist, I am inclined to dissent from this and to think that it is fortunate that political forces should be given the maximum of freedom to shape the development of the United Nations under changing conditions. To take an example: the Charter contains in Article 2(7) a reservation on domestic jurisdiction which, interpreted according to the text and the history of its origin, must lead to the conclusion that to a great extent the Organization must be considered incompetent in relation to matters of great international importance. In practice, this has been felt to be unreasonable, and the provision has been interpreted in such a way that it has been ignored in all situations where it was felt that the case involved the interests of other nations and therefore required the attention of the Organization. I consider this development fortunate, and I doubt if it would have been possible if the question of the interpretation of Article 2(7) had been brought before the Court for decision.

References

2. ANTI-COLONIALISM AND THE NEW NATIONALISM
    The various motives and compromises that lie behind the mandate system of the League of Nations and the trusteeship system of the United Nations are interestingly analyzed by Ernst B. Haas in two papers: "The Reconciliation of Conflicting Colonial Policy Aims: Acceptance of the League of Nations Mandate System," *International Organization* (1952), pp. 521-36, and "The Attempt to Terminate Colonialism: Acceptance of the United Nations Trusteeship System," *ibid.* (1953), pp. 1-21. See also Kenneth Robinson, "World Opinion and Colonial Status," *ibid.* (1954), pp. 468-83.

5. THE SHIFTING OF THE CENTER OF GRAVITY
    Hula Erich, "The United Nations in Crisis," *Social Research* (1960), pp. 387-420.
    Jackson, Elmore, "The Developing Role of the Secretary-General," *International Organization* (1957), pp. 431-45.
    Morgenthau, Hans J., "The New United Nations and the Revision of the Charter," *Review of Politics* (1954), pp. 3-21.
    On the Uniting for Peace Resolution and its application in practice, see Keith S. Petersen, "The Uses of the Uniting for Peace Resolution since 1950," *International Organization* (1952), pp. 219-32.

6. HOW DID IT HAPPEN?
    On interpretation of the Charter of the United Nations, see Pollux (Edward Hambro), "The Interpretation of the Charter," *British Yearbook of International Law* (1946), pp. 54-82.
    The eight cases in which the Court has been asked for an advisory opinion on the interpretation of the Charter are as follows: Admission of a state to the United Nations (1948), Reparation for injury suffered in the service of the United Nations (1949), Competence of the General Assembly for the admission of a state to the United Nations (1950), International status of South-West Africa (1950), Effect of awards of compensation made by the United Nations administrative tribunal (1954), Voting procedure on questions relating to reports and petitions concerning the territory of South-West Africa (1955), Admissibility of hearings of petitioners by the Committee on South-West Africa (1956), and Certain expenses of the United Nations (Art. 17. 2) (1962).

III ❀

ENDS,

FUNCTIONS,

PRINCIPLES

THE Charter of the United Nations includes, like every other constitution, provisions laying down what organs are to be found in the Organization and what functions these are to perform—for example, that there shall be a General Assembly, a Security Council, and so on. For each of these organs, these provisions may be divided into three groups, namely (1) those prescribing the composition and establishment of the organ, (2) those prescribing the procedure to be followed so that the organ may take valid decisions, and (3) those prescribing what the decisions may cover. Not until the conditions for the working of the organ have been laid down in all three directions can we decide how far a given resolution can be accepted as one that can be ascribed to the Organization.

But besides such provisions, dealing with the individual organs, the Charter also contains provisions that, without naming any individual organ, lay down in general terms the ends the Organization is to serve and the various ways in which these objectives shall be pursued. Similar "object" provisions do not appear in the constitutions of states, e.g. in Danish constitutional law, whereas it is a characteristic element in the constitutions of international organizations, as also in the rules of private societies and associations. The questions then arise: What is the reason for this difference? and, What is the significance of the "object" provisions of the Charter?

A state constitution contains no "object" provision because the state is not an organization set up for a particular, limited purpose, but is the all-inclusive framework of the life of a community. A club, on the other hand, a church, a commercial company, and all other associations of a nonstate character cover only certain aspects of the lives of those taking part, and therefore require a definition of the objective sought, thereby delimiting the sphere that the association is to serve.

Similarly with international organizations, including the United Nations. These organizations have all been established to look after certain interests that are common to all the participating states. One organization is concerned with combatting disease, another with promoting communications, a third with improving the social conditions of the workers, and so on. It is necessary to define the objective in order to delimit the organization's field of action.

The United Nations also was established to serve certain ends. But, as we shall see in this chapter, these ends are stated in such broad terms that they may be said to cover anything whatever that can be the subject of international collaboration. The United Nations may therefore be described as the *general* international organization, thereby saying that its field of action, without any limitation, covers everything that can lend itself to international collaboration. In the nature of things, there can be at any given time only one such organization embracing the whole world.

Hitherto I have spoken of the *end* of an organization as its special mark, by which its field of action is delimited. If, however, this delimitation is to be determined with any degree of precision, it is not enough simply to give the aim, i.e. the result in view. For example, if a town establishes a fire service, its sphere of action is not adequately delimited by the provision that its aim is to fight fires and to diminish the risk of fires starting. This aim might conceivably be realized in many ways, not only by establishing a fire brigade ready to act promptly, but also by means of building regulations, the dissemination of information on the danger of fire, prohibition of carelessness with fire and with inflammable materials, and so on. It must therefore be made clear by what measures the fire service has authority to promote the prescribed aim—in other words, what *functions* the fire service shall exercise to achieve its stated aim.

But even though it may be quite clear that an organization shall exercise certain functions in the pursuit of a certain end, this is not to say that these functions shall be exercised in all circumstances and at any cost. It is easy to see that a certain measure, besides serving the prescribed end, may also have other, and undesirable, side effects. There is no aim that is the only one of value in the world and may therefore be promoted by any means and at any cost. It would, for example, be an extremely effective measure to prevent fire in a town if the use of wood in buildings were forbidden. But it is conceivable that this would be considered too high a price to pay. A full delimitation of the field of action of an organization, therefore, requires a specification of the contrary considerations that are to be respected in exercising certain functions with the aim of attaining certain goals. As it will not ordinarily be possible to give these considerations in detail, they must be expressed as certain *principles* that must be respected by the organization in all its work.

Laying down the framework for the operations of an organization thus has a threefold aim: it gives an indication of (1) the end of the organization, (2) the functions to be exercised with this object, and (3) the principles to be observed in this connection. This pattern is shown in the provisions of the Charter, and the framework of the operation of the United Nations will be described accordingly in this chapter.

The significance of these provisions lies in the fact that they form the general background against which all the special rules of the Charter must be viewed and understood. The authority given to this or that organ must be understood with the limitation that it must be exercised as one of the accepted functions for the promotion of the given end, and with respect for the principles of the Organization.

Since end and functions are, as we shall see, so broadly defined, it is the principles that are particularly important.

1. Ends of the United Nations

In the formal introduction to the Charter (the Preamble) and in Articles 1 and 55, there are various pronouncements on the objectives of the Organization. These may be summarized by saying that the ultimate objects of the United Nations may be expressed in the slogan "Peace and Progress."

This duality corresponds to the two fundamental ways in which the relation between states may find expression. One kind of relationship arises out of opposing interests that lead to enmity, dispute, and perhaps to war. With regard to this side of international life, it is the task of the Organization to maintain international peace and security by repressing breaches of the peace, settling disputes that have arisen, and promoting friendly relations among the nations. But the relations between the states may also arise from joint interests and the desire to promote these in concert. With regard to this side of international life, it is the task of the United Nations to organize collaboration for the promotion of common interests, that is to say, to promote progress toward greater welfare for the citizens of the participating states. It is customary to describe the two objects, briefly expressed by the two words "peace and progress" as the *political* and the *economic and social* objects of the Organization. The latter of these expressions is actually too narrow. It must be understood as an abbreviation that covers all the interests and values of peaceful co-operation, especially those of cultural and humanistic character.

The political object of the United Nations is thus the maintenance of international peace and security. When "security" is named as an object alongside "peace," it is because it is not enough to keep war from the door, so to speak, from one day to another. The object is to create such conditions as will ensure that peace will not be broken, or at any rate, that any attempt to do so will be smothered at birth. Not until then will the human race be able to live securely and the "freedom from fear" proclaimed in the Atlantic Charter as one of the aims of humanity be realized.

It is only "international" peace and security that concerns the United Nations. This implies that civil war is an internal matter and that the organization, under the reservation in Article 2(7) concerning the domestic jurisdiction of the member states, is not entitled to take up the case.

It will often, however, be difficult to draw the line between civil war, i.e. an armed clash between groups within one and the same state, and international war, i.e. military action between two units that are both states, or at least independent entities under international law, i.e. units to which international law is applicable wholly or in part. If a group of insurgents succeeds in securing control of a certain part of the territory of the state, and there organizes itself with a government that can effectively maintain its authority in that part of the territory, such an organized group is given recognition as a local insurgent party as a partial subject of international law, and the struggle therefore assumes the character of an international war. Accordingly, it is clear that, for example, a war between Nationalist China on Formosa and the Communist republic on the mainland could not be regarded as a purely Chinese matter, a clash between two groups within the same state, that would fall outside the competence of the United Nations in maintaining peace. This must be so, whether or not it is assumed that Nationalist China has established itself as an independent state. The same held true when North Korea attacked South Korea. But in other situations, e.g. in the struggle between the Central Congolese government in Leopoldville and Moise Tshombe's government in Katanga, the case is not so clear, and it may be doubtful whether the conflict is to be considered an intranational or an international conflict. This doubt, however, will rarely concern the competence of the United Nations. For, if the conflict, even though in itself it has the character of an internal struggle, can, through its wider consequences in international politics, threaten international peace, it falls thereby within the sphere of competence of the United Nations. And in our day, this siutation will often arise, because interests are so interwoven that it is hard to imagine any clash of power politics of any importance in which the Great Powers would not also have some interest. It was because of such considerations, for example, that the Indonesian revolt against Holland (1947-49) and the Hungarian revolt (1956) were both regarded as matters of international concern, falling within the purview of the United Nations. Similarly, nobody doubts today that the troubles in the Congo cannot be classed as domestic matters of no concern to the United Nations.

In the economic and social sphere the object of the United Nations is progress, i.e. development of greater welfare within the states in every way that it is possible to promote this development by international co-operation. Article 55 of the Charter mentions in particular improvement of living conditions, full employment, and respect for human rights for all, irrespective of race, sex, language, or religion. Generally speaking, the object includes all collaboration for the promotion of economic, social, cultural, and humanitarian interests.

These interests are in themselves national, and their promotion is the object of national policy. The struggle against unemployment, sickness, and poverty, for example, are national concerns and form part of the policy of every state. But these questions assume an international aspect in so far as they can best be dealt with when every single country's efforts are co-ordinated with those of others in international collaboration.

The texts of Articles 1 and 55 imply that progress, as one object, is subordinate to peace, in the sense that greater welfare is sought because satisfactory socio-economic conditions make for peace. It is true enough, of course, that all forms of poverty, unrest, and need are likely to cause bitterness and hate that may well give rise to violent revolution and war. But if welfare is a source of peace, it is at any rate just as certain that peace is a source of welfare. To me, there is more sense in saying that welfare is the ultimate aim in itself, and that we seek to promote the cause of peace because war is the great destroyer of human happiness and welfare. But, provided we simply accept the value of both objects and their mutual dependence, the order of importance attached to them does not matter.

Peace and progress taken together form so inclusive an aim that it may seem as though the United Nations was intended to make all other international organizations unnecessary. Even though it is true that it is hardly possible to mention any international task that the United Nations would not be able to deal with, it has never been the intention that all international collaboration should be centralized in this one organization. The idea was, as appears from Article 57, that all existing or future organizations with wide international responsibilities in the social and economic sphere (taken in a broad sense) should be brought, by voluntary agreements, into relationship with the United Nations. And in the same manner, Chapter VIII of the Charter assumes that, though in the political sphere there may well be regional agreements or agencies for the maintenance of international peace and security, such local arrangements are to be subordinate to the authority of the Security Council. The idea is thus that all existing international organizations, whether political or nonpolitical, shall be included in one great system, the system of the United Nations, in which the United Nations is the central element, that coordinates and supplements the associated special agencies in the social and economic field and supervises and controls the subordinate regional arrangements in the political field. While the idea of a unity has been realized in the first of these (Chap. X.2.), the Organization's powerlessness in the political field means that the regional security arrangements are not subordinate to the authority of the Council (Chap. VIII.4).

2. Functions of the United Nations

The question is, by what means shall the United Nations seek to realize its two great aims, peace and progress? Here, this question will be answered only by brief outline of the functions of the United Nations. In later chapters, the individual functions will be discussed in more detail.

As far as peace is concerned, the Charter gives a fairly detailed answer. It gives three different types of measures, arranged stepwise according as the danger of a breach of the peace is more or less acute.

It appears from Article 1, taken together with Chapter VII, that when there is an act of aggression or other breach of the peace, or a threat to the peace, it is for the Security Council to take effective collective measures to suppress the breach or to repress the threat of a breach. This function, which may be called the function of maintaining peace, is dealt with in detail in Chapter VII of the Charter, where it is laid down in what these "effective" measures may consist. They namely concern economic boycott and military sanctions. It was explained in the last chapter that the agreements that are the necessary condition for building up an apparatus for military sanctions have never been concluded, and that the military security system, therefore, has never come into existence. Nor, because of lack of agreement among the five Great Powers, the permanent members of the Security Council, has the economic sanctions apparatus ever been brought into use. Above, Chapter II.5 describes how the attempt, by means of the Uniting for Peace resolution (1950), to organize a military sanctions apparatus under the authority of the General Assembly on a voluntary basis gave no result. Since the United Nations has thus proved incapable of guaranteeing the peace, the member states have sought security by organizing a network of regional defense arrangements and bilateral treaties of mutual assistance.

Prevention is better than cure. War arises from disputes between states, and it is therefore in the interests of peace that disputes, the continuance of which may seem to endanger peace, should be settled in time in a peaceful manner. Accordingly, Article 1(1) further stipulates that it is the task of the United Nations "by peaceful means and in conformity with the principles of justice and international law, to bring about adjustment or settlement of international disputes or situations which might lead to a breach of the peace." In Chapter VI of the Charter, there are more detailed provisions for the exercise of this function of settlement. It is assumed that this function will normally be performed by the Security Council (see Art. 24, where it is stated that it is the Security Council that has the primary responsibility for the maintenance of peace and security). Chapter II, above, describes how disagreement among the permanent members of the Council has paralyzed it and has caused the discussion of political disputes and situations to be largely taken over by the General Assembly under that body's subsidiary competence under Articles 10 to 12.

Finally, the Charter, in Article 1(2), prescribes the promotion of friendly relations among the nations, based on respect for the principle of equal rights and self-determination of peoples, and the taking of other appropriate measures to strengthen peace. This does not indicate any new, special function, but covers all efforts for securing peace not already covered by the first two functions, e.g. support for the progressive development of international law and its codification (Art. 13); efforts to achieve disarmament or the regulation of armaments (Art. 11, 62, and 47). Moreover, the results of everything the organization does to promote progress in the economic and social spheres may be viewed not only as good in themselves, but as measures that improve friendly relations between the nations and strengthen world peace.

On the other hand, with regard to the economic and social aims, progress and welfare, the Charter does not give directions on particular procedures or functions for the achievement of these objects. It confines itself, in Article 1(3) (see Chap. X) to stating that the aim shall be pursued by promoting international collaboration (the collaboration function). This is the same as to say that in this sphere the United Nations has neither international nor supranational authority.

The first means that in this sphere there is no organ in the United Nations that has power to issue orders to the member states that these have undertaken to comply with, as the Security Council has in the political sphere (see Art. 24 and 25). Thus the Organization cannot require any member state to take any measure for the promotion of progress in economic, social, cultural, or humanitarian matters. Everything here depends on free will and national autonomy. What the Organization can do is limited to information, advice, and the .pressure of public discussion and opinion to stimulate the states, severally or in co-operation based on treaties, to take steps to promote economic and social ends.

The other, the absence of supranational authority, means that there is no organ in the United Nations—in this or in any other sphere—that is empowered to act directly with legal authority in relation to the citizens of the member states. No "transfer of sovereignty" has been made, in the manner we are familiar with from the European communities, such as the Common Market. Thus Denmark could ratify the Charter of the United Nations without any amendment to the Danish Constitutional Law, and if the question arose today it could be done without reference to the rules of section 20 of the Constitutional Law of 1953.

The rules on the trusteeship system given in Chapter XII of the Charter can in all essentials be taken as a special function designed to promote the development of greater welfare.

3. Principles of the United Nations

A. RESPECT FOR DOMESTIC JURISDICTION

When the aims of an international organization are so comprehensive as is the case with the United Nations, it may be felt to be necessary to stress that naturally this competence must be exercised only in matter of international scope, and thus not in matters that can be considered as a particular state's "private" or "internal" affairs. For example, in Article 55 the Charter gives as an object of the United Nations the improvement of living conditions, the promotion of full employment, and the development of economic and social conditions in all member countries. It is obvious that the Organization has no authority to issue *instructions* in furtherance of this object to the member states, still less to *legislate* for their citizens. But ought the United Nations, by virtue of this object, to be competent to *discuss* Denmark's social legislation? Or Denmark's financial policy at a given moment? Or the plans for a bridge over the Great Belt? To investigate these subjects, or to advise on them, on the basis of whether they serve to promote progress toward welfare in the best way? It seems at once obvious that this cannot be the intention. Such power in the Organization, even though it were only a question of discussion, criticism, and advice, would be felt to be a violent infringement of the "sovereignty" of the states. There must be a limit, but it is not easy to see where it should be drawn. It is easy enough to agree on the formula that the Organization shall not intervene in matters within the domestic jurisdiction of a member state—but the question is how the terms "within the domestic jurisdiction" and "intervene" are to be understood.

The question presented itself for the first time when the Covenant of the League of Nations was being drafted. When President Wilson was leaving the Peace Conference in Paris and returning to the United States to work on American opinion, he observed that people were afraid that the draft as it stood would mean that the United States would have to submit to the authority of the Council if a dispute should arise on certain matters in which the Americans would not tolerate any interference. These were, in particular, such matters as immigration, labor conditions, tariffs, nationality questions, racial discrimination, and the distribution of raw materials. In order to meet this objection, Wilson got a provision inserted in the Covenant (Art. 15.8) that would preclude the Council from dealing with disputes concerning the domestic affairs of a state. Even so, he did not succeed, as is well known, in getting the Senate to approve the Covenant, and one of the Senate's objections, and perhaps the most serious, was in fact the belief that Article 15(8) did not adequately protect the United States against undesirable interference in questions such as those mentioned above.

In drafting the Charter of the United Nations, the Americans were naturally alert to the importance of this point. In the Dumbarton Oaks draft, a provision was inserted that was based on Article 15(8) of the Covenant but that made somewhat stronger the position of the state that objected to the intervention of the Organization. At the San Francisco Conference, the Great Powers, acting in concert, brought forward an amended version that gave the reservation on domestic jurisdiction considerably greater scope. This strengthening of the proviso in favor of domestic jurisdiction gained the adhesion of the great majority of the other states, who even considered that the provision did not go far enough in protecting the states against infringements of their "sovereignty." On the proposal of the Australian delegate, Dr. Evatt, the draft was amended so as to limit still further the competence of the Organization. At each of the three stages in the development of this provision taken over from the Covenant of the League of Nations, it has been stiffened in favor of respect for domestic jurisdiction.

Since it is important for the following discussion of the provisions in Article 2(7) of the Charter of the United Nations to have the text and also the previous versions at hand, they are all given below.

Article 15(8) of the Covenant of the League of Nations
If the dispute between the parties is claimed by one of them, and is found by the Council, to arise out of a matter which by international law is solely within the domestic jurisdiction of that party, the Council shall so report and shall make no recommendation as to its settlement.

Dumbarton Oaks draft of the United Nations Charter, Chapter VIII, A.7
The provisions of paragraphs 1 to 6 of Section A [provisions on peaceful settlement of disputes, corresponding to Chapter VI of the Charter]

should not apply to situations or disputes arising out of matters which by international law are solely within the domestic jurisdiction of the state concerned.

The Great Power's revised draft laid before the San Francisco Conference
Nothing in this Charter shall authorize the Organization to intervene in matters which are essentially within the domestic jurisdiction of the State concerned or shall require the members to submit such matters to settlement under this Charter; but this principle shall not prejudice the application of Chapter VIII, Section B [on measures against threats to peace, breaches of the peace, and aggressive acts, corresponding to Chapter VII of the Charter].

The Charter of the United Nations, Article 2(7)
Nothing contained in the present Charter shall authorize the United Nations to intervene in matters which are essentially within the domestic jurisdiction of any state, or shall require the members to submit such matters for settlement under the present Charter; but this principle shall not prejudice the application of enforcement measures under Chapter VII.

The question of interpretation raised by the principle of respect for the domestic jurisdiction of the states may be listed as follows:

(1) What is understood by a state's domestic (or internal) affairs?
(2) What is understood by "to intervene" in a state's domestic affairs?
(3) Who decides whether the objection to the competence of the Organization in a given case is valid or not?
(4) What is the scope of the exception provision in the last sentence of the section?

There is a wealth of practice that illuminates these questions. The competence of the United Nations to deal with a particular case is frequently impugned, with a reference to the principle of respect for domestic jurisdiction. But the objection is seldom, if ever, sustained. The study of the practice in this matter is facilitated—in this as in other questions—by the systematic tabulation and analysis undertaken by the Secretariat of the United Nations in that great work, *Repertory of Practice of United Nations Organs*, which is occasionally brought up to date.

This practice—first and foremost that of the General Assembly, then of the Security Council, and finally of the Economic and Social Council—very clearly shows that the principle has been interpreted by all organs very liberally in favor of the competence of the Organization. It may be said that without feeling themselves bound by any particular juridical interpretation of the various expressions in Article 2(7), these bodies have taken the line of rejecting objections as soon as they felt that political considerations justified their taking up the case. For example, the United Nations has in several cases, in spite of objections, felt competent to deal with cases concerning a state's internal form of government or administration, for example in the case of Franco's Fascist government in Spain (1946), the case of the Communist revolution in Czechoslovakia (1948), and the various questions concerning the government of Greece, including the postponement of sentences of death already pronounced (1946). The objection has often been made and rejected in questions concerning a colonial power's relations with non-self-governing territories subject to it. This appears from the General Assembly's routine practice of critically investigating conditions in such territories, whether or not they are under the trusteeship system (Chap. IX.2) and, further, from a number of prominent cases such as those concerned with conditions in Indonesia (1947-49), Morocco (1951), Tunis (1952-53), West New Guinea (1954), Cyprus (1954), and Algiers (1955). In other cases, the dispute has concerned the extent to which the United Nations can deal with questions of the infringement of human rights in relation to a state's own citizens. In spite of energetic protests from the Union of South Africa, the General Assembly has maintained its right to discuss and to express its opinion on the treatment of South African citizens of Indian descent (1946 and subsequently) and, in the same manner, on other racial discrimination within the Union (1952 and subsequently). Likewise, infringement of human rights in Bulgaria, Hungary, and Rumania (1949), and in the U.S.S.R. (1948), have been, in spite of protests, the subject of discussion and recommendations in the Organization.

Even though practice shows a clear and consistent tendency, this by no means implies that the attitude adopted by every member has been clear and consistent from case to case. Just because the interpretation has not been based on juridical arguments, but has been motivated by political considerations, the attitude of the individual member has often varied from case to case, and been determined by its interests. When an accusation is made against a state, it is not slow to protest indignantly against the case being taken up, claiming that the matter is within its domestic jurisdiction. As a rule, however, it will find itself alone or in a minority in this opinion, because, as has already been said, the general tendency among the noninterested is to maintain the competence of the Organization as soon as it is felt that the case is of importance to other states, and therefore to their common forum, the United Nations. There is therefore nothing to prevent a state that has itself objected in its own case from accepting the competence of the Organization when another state raises the same objection in another case that more or less resembles the first. But since, as has been said above, the interpretation is not based on juridical grounds, but on particular political considerations, it is hardly possible to speak of any real contradiction in the attitudes adopted from case to case, but rather that the changing attitude illustrates the well-known fact that general evaluations are not uninfluenced by the interests of the valuer at the time.

This tendency in practice in favor of the Organization's competence is in striking contrast to the estimates and ideas that prevailed while Article 2(7) was being drafted. Close study of the four texts given above will show that development from Article 15(8) of the Covenant of the League of Nations up to the present provision has clearly been in the direction of strengthening the reservation on domestic jurisdiction, both in the scope of the reservation and in the condition under which it may be appealed to. Dumbarton Oaks removed the provision in the Covenant of the League giving the decision to the Council. The revised draft of the Great Powers in the first place extended considerably the scope of the reservation by moving it up among the general principles of the Organization, so that it could be used not only against the Security Council, but against any organ of the United Nations. Then the conditions under which objection might be raised were eased, in that (1) the reference to international law was omitted, and (2) the requirement was limited to this: that the case, in essentials—not exclusively—should be within a state's domestic jurisdiction. At San Francisco, the majority of the lesser states shared the desire of the greater powers to protect their "sovereignty" against the interference of the Organization, with the result that the formulation was made even more strict: the exception in the last sentence came to apply only to compulsory measures under Chapter VII—i.e. not to the recommendations that may be made under Article 39 or to the temporary measures that may be taken under Article 40. The efforts to protect the members had thereby gone so far that many feared that in practice Article 2(7) would prove a serious hindrance to the working of the United Nations.

Practice has shown these fears to be groundless. It is interesting to note that the inner logic of things, under the pressure of the requirements of practical life, has quite overcome the considerations that were advanced as long as people sat around a conference table and discussed the problems as they imagined them to be. At that time, all were zealous to guard the members' "sovereignty." In practice, it soon became clear that if the Organization were to have any meaning and to function in accordance with its object, it would be necessary to interpret the principle in Article 2(7) with a certain elasticity in favor of the Organization. This contrast between theory and practice is strikingly illustrated by the role of the Australian delegation at San Francisco, and the attitude it adopted shortly afterwards, when the problem of the scope of the principle first arose in practice, in the discussion of the Spanish question in the General Assembly. It was the Australians who, at San Francisco, had carried through a stiffer formulation of the principle in defense of "sovereignty"; but it was also they, represented even by the same person, Evatt, who approved an interpretation under which the character of the Spanish government could not be considered a matter within its domestic jurisdiction, and thereby laid the foundation for the restrictive interpretation in favor of the Organization that came to prevail.

But even though it is easy enough to deduce from practice a general tendency not to accept the objection that by taking up a particular case the United Nations will be interfering in the domestic affairs of a state, it is very difficult, on the other hand, to say on what view this practice is based in regard to the two fundamental questions: What is understood by domestic (internal) affairs? and, What is understood by interference in these affairs? This is because the resolutions, whereby the competence of the Organization has been implicitly confirmed, have consistently neglected to give any reason for this competence. Close study of the debates leading up to these resolutions will show that they follow a typical course, thus: the state involved in the case maintains that certain proposed declarations or steps by the United Nations will mean an infringement of the principle of Article 2(7). This implies (1) that the case falls within its

domestic jurisdiction, and (2) that the measures proposed in the
case will mean an intervention in this domestic jurisdiction. An overwhelming majority opposes this view: some do so on the ground that
the matter in question is not a domestic matter: others on the ground
that the action proposed cannot be described as intervention. When
the resolution is then passed, it is impossible to say precisely on
which basis this has been done. Opinions have been divided. The
only thing they have agreed on is the result: that the Organization is
competent because at least one of the conditions to be fulfilled to
preclude competence was not fulfilled.

It may be thought that in these circumstances it is vain to attempt
to discuss how the above-mentioned questions of interpretation can
be answered, and that all that can be done is to state that in practice
the decision is taken on political grounds, and that the tendency is
clearly to maintain the Organization's competence against objections
on the basis of domestic jurisdiction. This cannot be accepted, however. It is useful to consider more closely what can reasonably be the
meaning of a provision like the one in Article 2(7) and to show that
the existing practice is not exclusively the outcome of political arbi-
trariness, but can be understood as expressing a possible and reasonable interpretation that has, presumably, not been consciously
present in the mind of anyone who has taken sides in these cases, but
that lies hidden, so to speak, in present practice. It is a matter of
deciphering a significance, of undertaking a rationalization after the
fact, that stands a chance of gaining acceptance as a correct expression of the more or less vaguely felt considerations that have under-
lain the development. I return, therefore, to the questions listed
above.

(1) What is understood by a state's domestic (internal) affairs?
This expression is not a technical term, with a meaning generally
accepted in the literature. The problem, therefore, must be to discover what the expression may reasonably be taken to mean when
used in the given context.

As stated above, it seems obvious that, in spite of the comprehensive object-provisions of the Charter, there must be certain matters
that an international organization is precluded from dealing with because they are of purely national or domestic character. It is always
wise to begin by considering the obvious cases—even though, just

because they are obvious, they are not practical. For example, nobody will doubt that it must lie outside the competence of the United Nations to interfere in the question of whom the King of Denmark wishes to appoint as Minister of Commerce, how many judges the Danish Supreme Court shall consist of, or whether two parishes shall be amalgamated into one on the Island of Funen. Nor is it hard to imagine matters that must obviously be "external" and thus suitable for discussion in an international forum—e.g., if the Danes decided to confiscate the property of all foreigners living in Denmark, or forbade foreign ships to sail in Danish waters and fired on all that did so. Somewhere between these obvious extremes, there must be a line dividing domestic from external affairs. But what is the criterion for this division? What is it that causes one in certain cases to feel justified in·saying, "This is no concern of other states or of any international organization," but not in other cases?

As far as I can see, there are two different considerations that, both in state and in ordinary human relations, may lie behind the claim that a certain matter is "internal" or "private," and so is no concern of others.

The first is that this matter does not concern others because it *does not affect their rights*. If, for example, my neighbor complains that I keep my garden badly, so that my weeds spread into his garden, I might conceivably reply,"I will not discuss this with you. I may keep my garden as I will. There is no law that forbids me, so that what I do with it does not concern you." Correspondingly, in relations between states, matters "within a state's domestic jurisdiction" may be taken to mean "such as are not subject to international legal regulation"—matters in which, therefore, one may refuse even to discuss the legality of a particular line of action. This sense is natural when it is a question of delimiting the competence of an organ for settling disputes on a legal basis.

The other consideration is that the matter does not affect the *interests* of others. It is clear that the scope of "internal" or "private" is much narrower in this sense than in the other. There are, of course, many circumstances that may affect people's interest though not their rights—while the contrary is inconceivable. Thus, from the viewpoint of interests, I cannot reject the complaint of my neighbor that my weeds spread to his garden and claim that this is a matter that does not concern him. Should he, on the other hand, attempt to advise me on whether I should marry or not, I may ask him not to interfere in matters that are no concern of his, affecting neither his rights nor his interests. It would be difficult enough to give examples of matters that can in no way interest others. In order to bring this conception within reasonable limits, a private or internal matter in this sense must be taken to be one that does not affect *essentially* the interests of others, who thus cannot, on the principles generally accepted, reasonably claim a moral right to discuss it with me. Similarly with relations between states. "Internal or domestic matters" will thus mean such matters as, in the first place, do not affect the rights of other states and, secondly, do not otherwise essentially affect their interests, so that they, in the prevailing state of political-moral opinion, cannot reasonably demand that they should be discussed in an international forum. Such an understanding of the position seems natural in the case of an international organization with political and socio-economic aims.

There can be no doubt that the expression "domestic jurisdiction" in Article 15(8) of the Covenant of the League of Nations, which, anyway, refers explicitly to international law, must be understood in the legal sense mentioned above. This is also stated in an opinion given by the Permanent Court of International Justice in 1923.* There are many good reasons, however, for interpreting the expression, when used in Article 2(7) of the Charter of the United Nations, in the second of the senses mentioned above, i.e. as concerning matters that essentially affect the interests of other states.

In the first place, the verbal change, the omission of the reference to international law, supports this view. It is true that the expressions used at the San Francisco Conference by John Foster Dulles, as spokesman for the powers that issued the invitations, are anything but clear. But he stressed that the proposed formulation should express a broad principle, and not a technical rule of law as in the corresponding provisions in the Covenant of the League of Nations, and that this difference is based on the fact that the United Nations has a much wider scope than the League of Nations had. Both these points tell in favor of the sense that takes "interest" as the determinant.

In the second place, the San Francisco Conference substituted the word "essentially" for the word "exclusively." This meant an exten-

* Tunis-Morocco Nationality Decrees, PCIJ, Series B, No. 4.

sion of the possibility of raising objections to the Organization's competence. It was no longer to be necessary that a case should be wholly within a state's domestic jurisdiction. It was enough for it to be essentially so.

In a report to President Roosevelt, Dulles gave as a reason for this, that a formulation with "exclusively" is too stringent, in view of the fact that under modern conditions what a state does internally will nearly always have at least some repercussions externally.

This change from "exclusively" to "essentially" has tormented those who have had to interpret the text. The point is that, if the concept of "matters within a state's domestic jurisdiction" is understood as referring to such matters as are not covered by international law, the change is obviously meaningless, and the reason given for it incomprehensible. If a case is subject, to some extent at any rate, to international law, it is quite incomprehensible why—at any rate, in so far as it is so subject—it should be excluded from international discussion. In a previous account of this matter, in which I based my discussion of the problem on a legal interpretation of the concept of "domestic jurisdiction," I therefore saw no alternative to declaring that the change is so unreasonable that it must simply be ignored, and "exclusively" replaced in the formulation of the text. These difficulties, however, completely disappear if the understanding that takes "interest" as the determinant is accepted. The expression "essentially" then expresses the point of view emphasized above, i.e. that not every effect on the interests of others can be considered, but only an effect that can be described as "essential." The reason given by Dulles then becomes comprehensible as the expression of precisely this point of view.

More important, however, than these textual arguments, is the consideration that an interpretation of Article 2(7) by which a state's domestic jurisdiction covers everything not regulated by international law, would be quite incompatible with the objects and functions of the United Nations. Such an interpretation would mean that the Organization was precluded from intervening in disputes of a nonlegal character that could not be brought under international law, and also from discussing and advising on matters that, though suitable for legal regulations, have not hitherto been the subject of international law. It is an obvious self-contradiction to set up an organization that (except for the Court) is to deal with political and socio-economic matters, and at the same time to enjoin the Organization to follow the principle of dealing only with matters that are regulated by international law. For the Court, there would be some meaning in such an injunction—aside from the fact that it would be unnecessary, since the function of the Court, by definition, is to settle disputes in accordance with international law. For the other organs of the Organization, however, with political, economic, and social functions, it would exclude all action that was not confined to the discussion of problems in abstract generalities, but was aimed at the circumstances of one or more particular states.

The only way to avoid so fatal a consequence seems to be to take the expression "to intervene" in a very narrow sense, so that it coincides with the technical term "intervention." In the next section it will be shown that this alternative is not open.

(2) *What is understood by "to intervene" in a state's domestic affairs?* In order to gain a clear view of the meaning in which the expression "to intervene" must be understood in this context, one should consider the obvious, though impractical, instances of "domestic jurisdiction"—e.g. the case in which the King of Denmark intends to appoint a certain person Minister of Commerce. This must be a purely domestic Danish matter. And in such a case, what is really meant by saying that the United Nations may not "intervene" in this? Obviously, that the Organization must not deal with the question at all: not only is it precluded from passing resolutions making recommendations to Denmark on this matter, but also even from discussing it, appointing a commission to inquire into it, or whatever other measures might come into question. It seems obvious that one cannot speak of intervening in the domestic jurisdiction of a particular state, if the action on the case is not aimed at the situation of that particular state. If the United Nations takes up some question or other, e.g. respect for human rights or the treatment of national minorities, and discusses it in general terms with the object of passing a resolution making general recommendations, or a declaration thereon, or a draft convention to be submitted to members for their accession, then of course no state can claim that this is a case of intervention in *its* domestic jurisdiction. Such a resolution in general terms does not concern the domestic jurisdiction of this or that state, but is of common concern.

If this interpretation of "to intervene" is accepted, it will mean that the application of Article 2(7) will come to depend exclusively on whether or not it is agreed that the case concerns a state's domestic jurisdiction. If this is the case, there can be neither discussion nor any other action, nor can the further question arise of how much or how little the Organization can do in a question of this kind. There is nothing, it seems to me, that tells against interpreting present practice in this way. As far as I know, there has been no case where it has been said: This case concerns a matter that comes within State A's domestic jurisdiction; nevertheless, we consider the Organization competent to deal with it (in such and such a manner). It is also understandable that the objection to the Organization's competence has so seldom, if ever, been upheld. The very fact that another state has taken the initiative to bring the case before one of the organs of the United Nations leads to an assumption that the case is of such international concern that it ought not to be rejected. On the other hand, practice does not compel the acceptance of this interpretation. As was explained above, it is impossible to deduce the extent to which confirmation of the competence of the Organization has been based on the claim either that the case did not concern a matter within the "domestic jurisdiction" of a certain state, or that the action taken did not have the character of "intervention."

Should there be hesitation in accepting the broad meaning of "intervene" defended here, there would appear to be only one other meaning that could come into question, if the expression is not to be interpreted quite arbitrarily. The words used by the Charter, "*intervene*" and "*intervenir*," point toward the well-known technical term "intervention." This means *dictatorial* interference in the concerns of another state, i.e. interference that (more or less openly or disguised) takes the form of demands accompanied by the threat of force.

It must be admitted that this linguistic circumstance may reasonably be taken as a sign that what the authors of the text had in mind was the technical concept of intervention. It is not difficult, however, to see that this possibility is unacceptable, since such an interpretation would make the passage quite meaningless. Why should the organs of the United Nations be enjoined not to meddle dictatorially in the domestic jurisdiction of the member states, when the Charter gives them no power of command at all? It is meaningless to emphasize that an organ must not command under threat of force, when that organ, by the provisions defining its functions, can do no more than discuss, appeal, recommend. Under the system of the Charter, there is only one exception to this: the Security Council can require the members to proceed to measures of enforcement against anyone who breaks the peace. But this very case is excepted in the last sentence of Article 2(7) from the prevalence of the principle.

The discussions at San Francisco throw no light on the question of what was intended by *"intervene."* Dulles said, and repeated, that what was meant was the simple principle that the Organization should negotiate with the states and not meddle directly in the internal life of the member states. But this merely shows that he did not understand what the question was about. According to his statement, the meaning of the principle was to enjoin the organs not to exercise direct supranational authority over the citizens of the member states. But according to the Charter, anything of this kind lies quite outside the competence of the Organization, so that any such injunction would be quite devoid of meaning. Dulles' understanding—or misunderstanding—would exclude the possibility of any state invoking the principle when the Organization merely addresses the state and does not directly interfere with its citizens. There is in the practice of the United Nations no trace of this interpretation's ever having been advanced by anybody.

The conclusion must be that the Organization is precluded from dealing in any way with a case that is acknowledged to be within a particular state's domestic jurisdiction. This does not mean, however, that the state in question can prevent the case from being put on the agenda. The very question of whether or not the case concerns domestic jurisdiction cannot be decided without being first discussed.

(3) *Who decides whether the objection to the competence of the Organization in a given case is valid or not?* It is clear from the discussion above that the decision on the question of whether or not the objection is justified rests on a moral and political judgment: Does this case affect so essentially the interests of other states that these may reasonably claim that it should be discussed in an international forum? So it is understandable that, where fixed criteria are wanting, a state will often try this objection; but it is equally understandable that as a rule it is rejected. As was pointed out above, the

very fact that another state brings the case before the Organization is prima-facie evidence of its international relevance.

It follows from the general rules for interpreting the Charter (Chap. II.6) that when the objection is raised before an organ it is for that organ itself to decide if the objection shall be accepted, but that this decision is not binding on the states that voted against the decision and, in particular, not on the state that raised the objection.

It has been proposed several times—also by the Union of South Africa, in connection with India's complaint of racial discrimination —to ask the Court for an advisory opinion on the validity of the objection. Without exception, these proposals, have all been rejected. This negative attitude has often been criticized by jurists. The Institute of International Law has thus, in one of its resolutions, declared that the question is particularly suitable for decision by an international judicial organ. This opinion would be well grounded, if the term "domestic jurisdiction" used in Article 2(7) of the Charter were to be taken as defined by reference to international law. As has been shown above, this is not the case, and obviously not the understanding on which the practice of the United Nations is based. According to this practice, the concept is determined, and thereby the scope of the objection, by a moral and political judgment, and it is thus quite in order that this judgment should be made by the world organization's politically composed organs, and not by a court of law.

(4) *What is the scope of the exception provision in the last sentence of the section?* According to the last sentence in Article 2(7), the principle of respect for domestic jurisdiction shall not prejudice the application of enforcement measures under Chapter VII. This formulation was due to an amendment made at the San Francisco Conference, whereby the words "enforcement measures" were inserted. This meant a limitation of the exception, and thus an increase in the protection given to domestic jurisdiction. According to this, the exception does not apply to other measures under Chapter VII, i.e. recommendations under Article 39 and temporary measures under Article 40. These measures, then, can be met by the objection.

It has been considered unreasonable that the Organization, when a breach of the peace occurs or threatens to occur and the dispute concerns a state's domestic affairs, should be unable to take the first steps—i.e., to recommend certain steps or to make temporary arrangements—but must stand idly by until the situation has become so serious that enforcement measures can be applied.

However, there is no reason to worry much about this. The whole exception provision is based on a misunderstanding and will never be of any practical importance—not, at any rate, on the assumptions on which practice is based in relation to the significance of the principle. The moment a case takes such a course that it involves or threatens to involve a breach of the peace, it is impossible, by definition, to regard it as coming essentially within a particular state's domestic jurisdiction. The competence of the Organization to deal with such a serious international situation cannot be called into question, and if the permanent members of the Security Council can agree, then all the powers under Chapter VII can be exercised.

B. RESPECT FOR THE SOVEREIGNTY OF THE STATES

According to Article 2(1) of the Charter, the Organization is based on the principle of the "sovereign equality" of all its members, which obviously means their equality as sovereign states.

This implies, in the first place, the requirement that the member's *sovereignty* shall be respected. (Equality is discussed in the next section.) This is an expression used often in international law and politics, but unfortunately it has no precise or clear meaning. On the other hand, it has long been colored by strong feelings of respect for the state as something august and sublime, the supreme source of political power on this earth. "Sovereignty" is a trumpet blast employed when it is required to emphasize the state's honor, independence, and grandeur. When a state does not wish to accept something under international law, or in connection with some international organization, it always sounds well to say that this would infringe on the state's sovereignty.

If "sovereignty" be taken in its original meaning, as something absolutely supreme and independent, then "sovereignty" is incompatible with every international law and every form of international organization, for these by their very nature imply that the state is bound by a superior order and is thus *not* absolutely independent or absolutely supreme. If the term is to be used meaningfully in international law and political theory—and not as a mere appeal to feelings of hostility to international law and instincts of national power politics—it must be so interpreted that it may be used to describe certain of the characteristics of the modern state in the international community. An analysis of the use made of the term shows that "sovereignty" is used to denote at least three of the characteristics of a well-developed state:

(1) that the state is *self-governing*, which means that it is the highest legal authority in direct relation to its citizens;

(2) that the state has *capacity for action*, which means that the state has authority to operate as an active entity in relation to other states, to enter into diplomatic relations with them, and to make agreements with them in the form of treaties and so on, under international law; and

(3) that the state has *extensive freedom of action*, which means that it is not, to an unusual extent, subject to international legal obligations, particularly concerning the disposal of its own territory and its own military apparatus.

A special case of limited freedom of action is that of a state that is subject to the orders of an international body. Such a case arises when an international organ is empowered to issue binding instructions to a state without that state's acquiescence being required in that particular case. (Thus there is also international authority, even where the state has once and for all agreed to the arrangement whereby the organ is empowered to give instructions.)

Correspondingly, when it is said that a particular arrangement infringes a state's sovereignty, it may mean one of three different things, but the expression is generally used without specifying which of the three meanings is, or are, intended. This causes great confusion, and it is therefore desirable in any theoretical discussion not to use this ambiguous and emotionally charged term, and, instead, to speak of "self-government," "capacity for action," and "extensive freedom of action."

The concept of sovereignty, as has been said, is so imprecise and ambiguous that it is impossible to deduce from the statement in Article 2(1) any exact delimitation of the competence of the Organization. The function of the statement is ideological—a respectful inclination to the magical principle of sovereignty, to assure the states that their supremacy is not at all impaired by membership of the Organization. It may well be asked, to what extent this is true when we resolve the moldering concept of sovereignty into the three descriptive terms given above.

As far as self-government is concerned, it is undoubtedly correct that none of the provisions of the Charter interferes with this by giving the Organization power to act directly as a legal authority for the citizens of the member states. The United Nations does not claim to be a super-state over and above the states, a federal state—as, e.g., the United States of America is a new and independent state over and above the constituent states, with an independent legislature, administration, and judicature in direct relations with its citizens, within the framework set by the constitution. There is nothing in the relations between the United Nations and its member states that corresponds to this. Nor does the United Nations claim to be a supranational authority like the European Communities. What is characteristic here is that although these organs do have a certain direct, legal authority over the citizens of the member states, the Community is not consolidated in such a way that it is natural to describe it as a super-state, a federal state.

The United Nations resembles none of these. The Organization is not above the international, or rather, the interstate level. Everything the United Nations can do—recommend, advise, or give legally binding instructions—is directed only at the member states. The states' self-government is thus respected absolutely.

The same is true of the capacity to act. There is nothing in the Charter that authorizes a limitation on, let alone a removal of, the capacity of the member states to appear as active entities in the international arena by exercising diplomatic functions and entering into international agreements and arrangements.

As for freedom of action, it is evident that no state can have unlimited freedom of action. Every international legal rule, every treaty a state has agreed to, means that it has accepted certain legal obligations and therefore a certain limitation of its legal freedom of action. It is therefore difficult to say when such a limitation has assumed such a far-reaching character that it is felt to be a limitation of "sovereignty." There can be no doubt, however, that the Charter of the United Nations implies certain obligations that are so far-reaching and unusual that, in the traditional view, they must be described as restrictions of sovereignty. In matters concerning the maintenance of peace, the Security Council is endowed, by Articles 24 and 25 of the Charter, with *international authority*. This authority to issue commands binding on the states is in itself something quite extraordinary, and the seriousness of the restriction is enhanced by the fact that this authority covers matters and functions of the most vital character—the application of economic boycott and of military force against other states.

On this basis, therefore, it is impossible to conceal that the United Nations, in spite of the proclamation in Article 2(1), involves limitations in the freedom of the member states, which, in the traditional view, must be described as restrictions of their sovereignty in one of the meanings of this term.

C. RESPECT FOR THE EQUALITY OF THE STATES

The Charter has proclaimed with particular care the principle of the equality of all member states irrespective of size. Such proclamation is found not only in the passage from Article 2(1) quoted in the previous section, but also in the Preamble and in Articles 1(2) and 78. This care may seem suspicious and the sign of an uneasy conscience, for it is obvious that the United Nations—as far as the Organization's most central function, i.e. the maintenance of peace, is concerned— is in fact founded on the principle of the special position of the Great Powers, their privileges as well as their special burdens and responsibilities, notwithstanding the repeated proclamation of the principle of equality. One may well wonder that it was even thought necessary, out of consideration for the vanity of the lesser states, to make a statement so obviously at variance with the truth.

This does not imply any criticism of the special position of the Great Powers. On the contrary, I consider this a sound and indispensable feature of an international organization for the maintenance of peace.

D. RESPECT FOR LAW AND JUSTICE

It is the function of the United Nations to maintain peace. Is this also the case if peace can be bought only at the expense of law and justice? "Munich" has become the symbol of the policy that recklessly threw a little state to the wolves, in the hope of thus buying "peace in our time." May the United Nations act in this way, or do law and justice set a limit to the price at which peace may be bought?

The question was clearly put and debated at the San Francisco Conference, and the answer was given by a distinction, expressed in Article 1(1) of the Charter. The *settlement* function shall be exercised in conformity with the principles of justice and international law, but this limitation of the Organization's freedom of action does not apply to the *maintenance of peace*.

The reason given for this distinction is that the two functions are said to differ in the same way as the respective functions of the police and of the law court. The function of the police is to maintain law and order. In the event of riots the police must intervene to separate and perhaps arrest the parties, and cannot be bound to consider which is guilty. This is a matter for the court to decide later. In the same way, it is said, if the peace is broken it is the function of the United Nations to restore peace by effective means without being bound to consider who, as the aggressor, is the guilty party. This implies two things: on the one hand, that the United Nations always has the right to apply enforcement measures to the aggressor, irrespective of whether he, in the particular dispute, was in the right or not; and, on the other hand, that the Organization is not obliged to direct its intervention against the aggressor, since the crucial point is simply that peace shall be restored. Enforcement measures under the Charter of the United Nations—unlike such measures under the Covenant of the League of Nations—are in principle not sanctions, i.e. intervention against the actual lawbreaker (peace-breaker). Maintenance of the peace thus follows the principle of effectiveness and not the principles of law and justice.

When, on the other hand, it is a question of settling a dispute, whether this happens before or without a breach of the peace, consideration of who is in the right cannot be neglected. Even though the Security Council (or the General Assembly) is not a judicial body, and not, therefore, bound strictly by international law, political settlement must be made with due respect for the principles of law and justice.

I shall return later to the analogy of the difference between the functions of police and law courts on which this distinction is based, and show that it does not hold and that it is hardly possible to conceive an action for the maintenance of peace being carried out without regard to which of the parties involved is taken to be in the right (Chap. VII.2).

E. RESPECT FOR THE RIGHT OF SELF-DETERMINATION OF PEOPLES

Finally, the Charter contains in Article 1(2) a provision that the friendly relations between the peoples, which it is the function of the United Nations to promote, shall be based on respect for the principle of the peoples' right of self-determination. What is meant by this is not clear, nor do the preparatory debates throw any light on the question.

The self-determination principle appears to be used with different meanings. It may mean that every people or ethnic group has a right to determine whether it shall be an independent state or be joined to another state. The principle is understood in this way, if an ethnic minority in any state (e.g. the people of the Faroes) demand the right to separate (here, from Denmark) and form their own state or join themselves to another state. It would seem that this can hardly be the meaning of the term in Article 1(2) of the Charter. This is partly because the principle understood in this way would provide an extremely poor basis on which to build friendly relations between the peoples. Experience shows that the demand for national self-determination is a source of difference, in that certain states invoke it to support separatist tendencies in another state. And, partly because it is impossible to give the principle a precise meaning and a reasonable delimitation in the face of opposed considerations. It is especially difficult to determine precisely what groups should have this right. Since the principle denies the right of the majority to maintain the community against the will of the minority, it must consequently follow that a minority within a minority must be conceded the same right. If, for example, Cyprus claims the right to separate on the principle of self-determination, then the Turkish minority on Cyprus must be conceded the same right. One could go on in this way, and, when the ethnic groups are not sharply divided territorially, the principle leads to anarchy. But even where the territorial grouping is more or less clear, the principle must be weighed against other considerations, e.g. geographical conditions of economic, traffic, or strategical importance, that may have great weight. A good example is the thorny question of Katanga's right to establish itself in independence of the rest of the Congo.

The principle of self-determination is also used in the sense of a people's right to decide on the constitution under which it desires to live. In this sense, it found expression in the French revolutionary Constitution of 1793, Article 33, which states that a people has the right to review, reform, or change its constitution at any time, and that no generation has the right to bind future generations by its laws. Consequently, on this interpretation, the principle must also mean that a people has the right to choose dictatorship and despotism. But here it clashes with respect for human rights and fundamental freedoms, which the Charter has made it the function of the United Nations to promote. The World Declaration on Human Rights, passed by the General Assembly December 10, 1948, states in Article 21(3): "The will of the people shall be the basis of the authority of the government: this shall be expressed in periodical and genuine elections taking place on the basis of universal and equal suffrage, and by secret ballot or other method of free vote."

It may well be that under these conditions the conclusion is that the principle of national self-determination is devoid of independent meaning and must be understood as merely a variant of the principle, in itself equally imprecise and ambiguous, of sovereignty.

References

3. A. RESPECT FOR DOMESTIC JURISDICTION
    The literature on this question is overwhelming. See, e.g., the lists in M. S. Rajan, *United Nations and Domestic Jurisdiction* (2nd ed., 1961), pp. 40ff. Majority opinion is probably in favor of defining "domestic jurisdiction" by reference to international law. Thus in 1954, the Institute of International Law passed a resolution, by a large majority, in this sense. (See the Institute's *Annuaire*, Vol. 45, II (1954), p. 292; cf. 198-99.)
    Alfred Verdross' paper "Die ausschliessliche Zuständigkeit der Staaten nach der Satzung der Vereinten Nationen," in *Scritti di Diritto Internazionale in Onere di T. Perassi* (1957), is against such an interpretation and essentially in harmony with the reasoning in this chapter. Verdross, however, in reference to the word "essentially" (*essentiellement*) in Article 2(7) considers that he can define "domestic affairs" as those that *by reason of their nature (essence)* are not and cannot be subject to international law. But this view is based on a linguistic misunderstanding ("essentially" means

simply "in the main" or "mainly") and a theoretical mare's nest (there are no such affairs). Moreover, there is no support for this interpretation in United Nations practice.

The origin of the reservation is fully discussed by Rajan, *United Nations and Domestic Jurisdiction*, Chap. II, with numerous references to UNCIO, *Documents*, Vol. I. A survey of the concept of domestic jurisdiction in United Nations' practice is found in Rosalyn Higgins, *The Development of International Law through the Political Organs of the United Nations* (1963), pp. 58-130.

See also the commentaries to Article 2(7) in *Repertory of Practice of United Nations Organs*, Vol. I and Supplement No. 1, Vol. I. The impossibility of deducing a precise view with regard to the definition of "domestic jurisdiction" and "intervene" appears from, e.g., Paras. 349, 350, 361, 373, and 426; cf. Paras. 80 and 162 of the main volume and Para. 132 of the Supplement. For placing on the agenda without regard to objection to the Organization's competence, see Paras. 454 and 455 in the main volume and Para. 174 in the Supplement.

3. B. RESPECT FOR THE SOVEREIGNTY OF THE STATES

On the concept of sovereignty, see Ross, *Lærebog i Folkeret* (4th ed., 1961; English ed., *Textbook on International Law*, 1947), Para. 3.

IV ❧

MEMBERSHIP IN
THE UNITED NATIONS

I n the previous chapters we discussed the distinction between a general and a specialized international organization. This distinction is based on the subject the organization deals with. The organization is called "general" when it unites, in principle, all international collaboration under one head—at any rate, to the extent that, as a central, superior instance, it supplements and co-ordinates the specialized organizations, each of which pursues a particular, limited object. The distinction thus refers to the degree to which it is sought to centralize international collaboration, with regard to its subject, in one comprehensive organization, or to divide it up into a series of specialized organizations.

The distinction between universal and regional organizations, to be discussed in this chapter, has another basis—the membership. An organization is called a "universal" or "world" organization when it aims, in principle, to include all the states of the world, and "regional" when the membership is limited beforehand by certain conditions.

It is easy to see that these two distinctions are independent of each other, and may therefore cross. An organization may very well aim, in regard to its subject, at comprehensive tasks, but be exclusive in regard to its membership—as, for example, the Organization of American States. Or, contrariwise, it may be limited, in regard to its subject, to a special function, while membership is open to all states —as is the case with specialized agencies that are connected with the United Nations.

The United Nations is both a general and a universal organization. This chapter begins with a discussion of some general problems in connection with the distinction between universalism and regionalism, and goes on to discuss the conditions for membership in the United Nations. It will be shown that there has been a development toward full universalism, so that today—with a few politically based exceptions—the Organization is open to all the states in the world. It must be presumed that the last limitations will disappear in the not very distant future. Closely connected with the question of membership is the question of which government, in a case of internal conflict, shall represent a state. Finally, the obligations involved in membership are described.

1. Regionalism–universalism

Strictly speaking, the term "regionalism" is not quite correct when used to describe all the international organizations in which membership is exclusive. The word indicates a geographical limitation, and even though it is typically geographical conditions that motivate the organization and limit its membership, this is not necessarily always the case. The motive for NATO, for example, is a common defense interest, but the membership, which stretches from Canada to Turkey, can hardly be said to form a region.

It is very common to set up "regionalism" against "universalism" as two contrary principles for international organization, and to discuss their respective advantages and disadvantages. The supporters of universalism maintain that the world of today is so much a unity that any international problem, political, economic, social, cultural, or humanitarian, is of world consequence and can be solved only by a world organization. The further technology progresses, the more closely interests and the conditions for welfare become interwoven in such a way that no single state or group of states can isolate itself, or solve its problems in regional seclusion. To this the supporters of regionalism reply that universalism in a highly one-sided way exaggerates a viewpoint that certainly contains some truth, but not the whole truth. Many problems are local problems and require for their adequate treatment and solution a real understanding of and contact with local interests, customs, and feelings of internal solidarity or hostility, not to be expected of an organization designed to deal with all the world's problems. Moreover, an international organization that is to be effective, able to turn wills and interests toward one another in a common effort, must be rooted not merely in objective common interests, but in a felt community of interest, in attitudes of solidarity and loyalty to the same ideals. Universalism is all too often before its time. It bases itself on purely rational considerations without paying the necessary attention to the conditions for human collaboration. Co-operativeness cannot be created by an order or a resolution, but must grow gradually, at the same pace as that at which the dividing emotional barriers are broken down and there develop more comprehensive attitudes of solidarity and a deeper understanding of the fact of solidarity—i.e., that in the long run our own interests are inextricably bound up with the welfare of everyone else on earth. (The agitation for increased help to the underdeveloped countries is a good example of how the international horizon is expanded by appeals to both humanitarian ideals of responsibility for our fellows and to self-interest—the fact of solidarity.)

This discussion, taking the matter as though it turned on a choice between two possibilities, is, in my opinion, fallacious. In most cases, regionalism and universalism are not two mutually exclusive alternatives, but, on the contrary, two methods that supplement each other. In other instances, the nature of the case will point so clearly to a particular solution that there is no problem to discuss: only in a few cases is there a choice that can give rise to considerations of the kind just described above.

It is well known how a state's national legislation and administration is supplemented by local self-government that deals partly with specifically local conditions and partly with local ramifications of those general matters that are the subject of the state's legislation and administration. In the same way, in international relations, regionalism and universalism will in most cases supplement each other, in that regional organs under a world-embracing superstructure will deal with special, local matters or with local aspects of universal problems. The same matters are at once the subject of world-embracing regulation in a universal union and of local regulation in closed, subordinate regional organizations. The Universal Postal Union, the International Telecommunication Union, the World Health Organization, the International Labor Organization, and many other world-embracing organizations, accordingly provide for the establishment of subordinate regional unions, conferences, and similar arrangements to deal with a region's particular business and interests, within the framework of the universal system. With regard to health matters, for example, certain diseases appear more commonly in particular areas, while in others they are almost unknown. Such diseases fall naturally into the province of a regional sub-organization. Similarly, regional conferences are held in the ILO and the International Civil Aviation Organization to deal with the region's particular problems within the framework of the world organization. There are, as is well known, regional postal arrangements within the framework of the UPU and regional radio unions subordinate to the ITU, and so on.

Thus, in these matters, universalism and regionalism go hand in hand, and the relation between them resembles that between central and local administrations. There is consequently no question of contrast or choice.

There are other spheres, too, where there is no problem. Regionalism arises of itself when the organization is created to deal exclusively with the interests of a particular group of states. With, e.g., the European Communities, the Scandinavian Council, and similar institutions it is meaningless to ask whether regionalism or universalism is the best way to achieve the desired object. The object is determined by exclusion: it is to promote the interests of a particular group of states, if not at the expense of, yet by the exclusion of, the interests of other states. This regionalism does not go hand in hand with universalism, but is contrary to it. It organizes interests peculiar to the region, not as a link in a universal community, but in opposition to other competing interests. It is based on a feeling of solidarity and a felt community of interest that does indeed bind the participating states together, but, on the other hand, sets them in opposition to those outside.

There are only a few, but extremely important, fields of international collaboration where universalism and regionalism are contrary possibilities, and where it is not obvious beforehand in which direction the problem must be solved. These are the political functions: the maintenance of peace and the settlement of disputes between states. The question is whether it is best to tackle these problems on a universal basis, i.e. that of the common interests of all states in maintaining peace, security, and harmony everywhere in the world, or on a regional basis, i.e. that of the special interests of a certain group of states in maintaining its own security externally and its own internal harmony.

Both the League of Nations and the United Nations based their program on universalism, though not quite in the same manner. Peace, it has been said, is one and indivisible, and every breach of peace is a threat to peace everywhere in the world. To defend the common interest in peace, every state must be willing to apply sanctions (also military sanctions, if necessary) against the peacebreaker, either automatically (the League of Nations) or on the decision of the Security Council. In both cases experience has shown that, in spite of the proclamation of this ideal, the states are unwilling to live up to it and to meet the requirements of collective security, when these conflict with their own interests. The feeling of international solidarity is not strong enough to make the states subject their national interests to it and risk their existence in a struggle that clashes with their national interests. In both cases the result has been that the provisions have become empty words, and in practice the maintenance of peace has been based on a network of alliances, highly organized and institutionalized (e.g., NATO). In this vital field, then, regionalism has supplanted universalism, and, be it noted, regionalism is of the type that does not go hand in hand with universalism, but is its negation, since it organizes opposing special interests and thereby divides the world into conflicting factions.

Under Chapter VIII, the Charter of the United Nations permits regional arrangements and institutions for the maintenance of peace, but only as subordinate links in the universal security system of the Charter. This is particularly evident in the provision in Article 53, whereby no enforcement measure may be taken by such regional institutions without the authority of the Security Council. It is clear that NATO and similar organizations are not of this type. They seek their formal legitimatization, not in Article 53, but in Article 51, on collective self-defence, a provision inserted with precisely this object in view.

As far as the settlement of disputes between states is concerned, it cannot be said that the United Nations' universal arrangements—political settlement by the Council (and the General Assembly) and judicial settlement by the Court—have correspondingly failed, but there is a strong tendency to supplant these by regional arrangements independent of the United Nations. The European Communities have their own Court, and under the Council of Europe there is another, that for human rights and fundamental freedoms. Conflicts between American states are very often brought before the Organization of American States and not before the world organization. It is probably partly the universal character of the International Court that has caused it to be so seldom frequented. Many states, especially the Communist ones and those that have grown out of former colonial status, do not regard traditional international law as the expression of *their* conception of law and justice, and have no confidence in a court that, in order to live up to the ideal of universalism, is composed so as to represent the world's main forms of civilization and principal legal systems. It will certainly be easier to get the states to accept regional courts with competence to decide disputes between the region's states. In that case, the International Court must be reserved for interregional disputes.

2. Conditions of membership

There are 51 original members of the United Nations, the 50 states that took part in the San Francisco Conference (and signed and ratified the Charter) and Poland. This state met the conditions for taking part in the conference as well as any, yet was not represented simply because, at the appropriate moment, it did not have a government that was recognized by all the inviting powers. As soon as this point was in order, Poland was allowed to sign as an original member.

The 51 original members were chosen as having participated in the alliance of states that had fought in the war against Germany and/or Japan. The "United Nations" was originally the name of the coalition of 26 states which on January 1, 1942, issued a Declaration whereby they confirmed the Atlantic Charter and undertook not to make a separate peace with the enemy. Those states that signed or later adhered to the Declaration and also declared war on Germany or Japan, were invited to the Conference. In all, 46 states fulfilled these conditions. At Yalta, Roosevelt agreed that two of the Soviet Republics, White Russia and the Ukraine, should be invited and recognized as members. At the Conference, it was further agreed to invite Denmark and Argentina.

Thus the United Nations, with some extensions, was originally an organization of the participants in an alliance for war—established even before the war was over. This origin marks the provisions of the Charter that deal with the conditions under which other states may be admitted as members of the Organization.

It was agreed at the Conference that an organization such as the United Nations, the object of which was to maintain the peace and promote the progress of the world, must in principle be universal, that is, be open to every state in the world. Yet certain elementary conditions were laid down in respect to membership. This was owing to the fact that the United Nations originated in a military alliance, and it was not desired, for the moment, to allow enemy states and their neutral sympathizers to enter.

Article 4(1) of the Charter was formulated on this basis. It provides that membership "is open to all other peace-loving states which accept the obligations contained in the present Charter and, in the judgment of the Organization, are able and willing to carry out these obligations."

This provision, viewed at the present time, has an unfortunate ring of pharisaic self-righteousness, justified least of all in international politics. We, the just, conclude this pact, and we will accept only others who likewise are just. This is indeed a strange attitude for an organization concerned with the maintenance of peace, for it was precisely the evil and bellicose states that needed to be admitted, to be subjected to the obligations of the Charter, and to be trained through fellowship with the peace-loving states!

Such provisions must be understood as the expression of wartime mentality. The enemy states are to be branded as war-loving, and the right of judging when they can be considered worthy of admission is to be reserved, presumably until peace has been made with them. The central point, therefore, came to lie in the second paragraph of the article that lays down how the Organization is to decide questions of admission. This states that admission "will be effected by a decision of the General Assembly upon the recommendation of the Security Council." Since the decision on admission is not, of course, a procedural question, this means that *each of the Great Powers, by virtue of its right of veto, can prevent the admission of a state.*

These provisions on admission, which, as stated above, were conceived with the Axis powers and their sympathizers in mind, became of much greater importance in practice. They found a use as weapons in the cold war. In the course of the first decade of the existence of the Organization, applications for admission to membership gave rise to continual political conflict between East and West. Purely political considerations, more or less camouflaged by the provisions of the Charter, decided the attitude of the parties. Applications from states on one side were voted down by the other side in the Security Council. During the first five years only nine applicants, of suitably neutral color, succeeded in getting in, whereby the number of members rose to 60. From 1950, when, because of the Korean crisis, the political climate deteriorated even further, admissions ceased altogether until 1955. Finally, with what was called "a package deal," the stalemate ended. There were applications from 18 states, and the parties were now willing to admit the whole "package" at once. At the last moment, China (Formosa) checked the compromise by vetoing the admission of Outer Mongolia. The whole deal was nearly wrecked, but was saved by a new compromise, whereby in compensation, Japan was excluded on the other side. The other 16 states were admitted, making now 76 members. Since then, there has been hardly any political conflict over the admission of new members. The number has grown steadily, and now it is more than double the original figure.

Growth of Membership in the United Nations

Original members,	1945	51
	1946	4
	1947	2
	1948	1
	1949	1
	1950	1
	1951-54	0
	1955	16
	1956	4
	1957	2
	1958	1
	1959	0
	1960	17
	1961	4
	1962	6
	1963	2
	1964	3
	1965	−1
	Total	114

There is little interest today in going into the details of the many years of tug-of-war over the admission of new members, or of the methods, political and legal, that were used to break the stalemate that prevailed. As a curiosity, however, I will give one example of how far casuistry was carried to break the opposition of the Soviet Union in the Security Council. Some of the states pointed out that while Article 4(2) does require "a recommendation" from the Security Council, it is nowhere stated that this must be favorable, and that the General Assembly must therefore be able to admit a member even though the Security Council had not given a favorable recommendation. Others considered that it must be possible to ignore the negative attitude of the Security Council when this was based on the exercise of the veto by a single member. Although these views did not find general support, the General Assembly did, however, agree to seek an advisory opinion from the Court on the question of whether the General Assembly can admit a state when there is no recommendation from the Security Council, whether this is due to the fact that the necessary majority cannot be found or that a permanent member has voted against admission. The Court replied in the negative by 10 votes to 2.*

After the great increase in membership, it is easier to say who is *not* a member of the United Nations. The only state that voluntarily remains outside is Switzerland, for this state considers the obligations involved by acceptance of the Charter to be incompatible with its traditional neutrality and the treaties acknowledging it. Early in 1965 Indonesia withdrew in protest against Malaysia's seat on the Security Council. The international political cold front runs through the middle of certain states, which are thus artificially divided. Until this situation is cleared up, political considerations will prevent their admission. These states are East and West Germany, North and South Korea, and North and South Vietnam. Outside are also, of course, the areas that have still not achieved independent existence as states, whether these are areas under trusteeship or otherwise non-self-governing. Except where these areas choose incorporation in the administering state or amalgamation with another state, they will all, sooner or later, be candidates for admission to membership in the United Nations. There is thus reason to believe that the number of members will still continue to increase for some years. Once full universality has been reached the number of members may increase or diminish only by amalgamation of two or more member states or by division of one state into two or more others. (See the accounts given in Chap. II. 5 and in Chap. XII.1 of the effect of the great increase in the number of members in complicating business in the General Assembly and in making the Assembly a less suitable forum in which to arrive at important political decisions.)

The Charter contains no provision for withdrawal. The question was discussed at the San Francisco Conference. The general opinion was that it must be possible to withdraw from the Organization, at all events under certain conditions. On the other hand, it was felt that express rules for withdrawal would disfigure the Charter. A declaration was therefore agreed on, stating how, in the absence of express provision, the Charter is to be interpreted. This states that it is the members' highest duty to continue to collaborate in the maintenance of international peace and security, but that if a member, be-

* Competence of Assembly regarding admission to United Nations, Advisory Opinion: ICJ *Reports,* 1950, 4.

cause of special circumstances, feels compelled to withdraw, it cannot be the task of the Organization to compel that member to continue to collaborate. Examples are given of circumstances that would justify withdrawal, especially where the Charter is changed and the state concerned has voted against the change and cannot accept it. The examples are not given as exhaustive.

Its vagueness notwithstanding, this declaration must mean that members are legally free to withdraw from the Organization, but that such a step must be morally disapproved of, unless special circumstances justify it. On the other hand, the Charter does contain provision for temporary suspension of the exercise of a member's rights and for expulsion from the Organization.

Under Article 5, suspension may be applied to a member against which the Security Council has taken preventive measures or enforcement measures under Chapter VII. Suspension concerns the exercise of a member's rights but does not release that member from its obligations. This means, in particular, that the member cannot be represented in the various organs composed of the member states. The decision on suspension is made by the General Assembly on the recommendation of the Security Council. The Security Council can revoke the suspension.

Article 19 prescribes a limited suspension, namely of the right to vote in the General Assembly. This takes effect automatically if a member is in arrears in the payment of its financial contributions to the Organization and the amount of its arrears equals or exceeds the amount of the contributions due from it for the preceding two full years. The General Assembly may, nevertheless, permit such a member to vote if it is satisfied that the failure to pay is due to conditions beyond the control of the member.

Under Article 6, expulsion can be applied to a member that has persistently violated the principles of the Charter. The decision is made by the General Assembly on the recommendation of the Security Council.

Up to the present, there has been only one withdrawal and no suspension or expulsion. Several states withdrew from the League of Nations, and one, the Soviet Union, was expelled in consequence of the aggression against Finland in 1939.

As distinct from the question of a state's membership there is the question of which government is entitled to represent the state and to appoint representatives on the various organs of the United Nations. Normally, there is no problem. When the delegation sent by the country's government arrives at the United Nations, its credentials are examined and approved. The examination is pure formality. But a *coup d'état,* civil war, or revolution may produce two governments, both claiming to represent the same state. In that case, which has the right to represent the state in the United Nations?

We have seen how a corresponding problem arose even at the San Francisco Conference. Poland was not represented there because the host powers could not agree on which of the two competing governments should be recognized as representing Poland. In the United Nations, the problem arose after the Communists succeeded, in 1949, in driving Chiang Kai-shek to Formosa and consolidating the People's Republic of China on the mainland. The Peking government demanded China's seat in the Security Council and all other Chinese representation in the United Nations. When the Council refused to accede to this demand, the Soviet Union left the Council in protest and took no further part in its meetings until the acts of the Council in connection with the Korean crisis had taught the Soviet Union how dangerous it can be to leave the game to one's opponents.

Even today, it is the Nationalist government on Formosa that represents China in the United Nations. Though it has gradually become evident to most people how unreasonable it is that the government in *de facto* control of the great majority of China's people and territory cannot exercise China's rights in the United Nations, the United States has so far managed to prevent a change of system. As long as the People's Republic of China was actually at war with the United Nations in Korea, it was reasonable, with the support of Article 5 of the Charter (suspension of rights), to oppose the Communists' taking over the representation of China. Now, however, both justice and political common sense speak for the necessity of drawing the obvious conclusion from the fact that it is the Peking government of Mao Tse-tung that rules China. That this has been resisted so obstinately and the discussion of the question so confused is owing (in part, at any rate) to confounding representation in the United Nations with political recognition. The policy of nonrecognition is an American invention, whereby one refuses to recognize the existence of facts of which one cannot morally and justly approve. This political fiction cannot but bring its own punishment, since nobody can deny facts with impunity. And so also in this case. Sooner or later, circumstances will compel the United States to recognize the existence of Communist China, (and of East Germany!) and to swallow the consequences thereof—with a considerable loss of prestige.

As early as 1950, the then Secretary-General Trygve Lie, drew up a Memorandum in which he showed that the question of representation and that of recognition ought to be kept separate. From the United Nations point of view, the crucial point must be that the obligations of a member can be met only by a government that in fact controls the resources of the state and leads the nation. This means that in the case of a revolution, the government that effectively exercises authority over the territory and is obeyed by the great mass of the people has the right to represent the state. But the Secretary-General was unable to gain support for this view.

For a long time, the United States succeeded not only in keeping the Peking government out, but even in preventing a debate on the matter in the General Assembly. At the 16th Assembly (1961-62), however, the question was placed on the agenda, but the United States managed once more to prevent a change. On American initiative, a resolution was first passed declaring that every proposal to change the representation of China is an important question, and therefore requires (Art. 18(3) of the Charter) a two-thirds majority to pass. A Soviet proposal to remove the representatives of "the Chiang Kai-shek clique" and to invite the People's Republic of China to send its representatives to the United Nations was rejected (36-48-20).

The change of representation is made more difficult by Russia's categorical refusal to see Nationalist China's continued representation in the United Nations. The same principle of effectiveness that supports the Peking government's demand must similarly apply to this governments' demand to represent Formosa also. Chiang Kai-shek's regime on this island is so well established that according to the normal rules of international law there can be no doubt that a new state has been established. That Chiang Kai-shek has never advanced this argument is, of course, due to the fact that he has thrived on the fiction that he represents China. If this fiction is now destroyed, he risks complete exclusion through another fiction, namely that there is one and only one China, represented by the Peking government. The danger will arise if the People's Republic should be granted its seat in the Security Council before the situation of Nationalist China has been put in order. As a new state, it would then apply for admission to the United Nations, and the People's Republic, by virtue of its veto in the Security Council, would be able to resist its admission. It is therefore desirable that the two problems should be settled at the same time.

3. *Obligations of membership*

Membership in the United Nations involves acceptance of a series of obligations. The most important of these may be summarized as follows. Members are obliged to:

(1) collaborate with the other members and with the organization to promote the objects of the United Nations (Art. 1, 2, and 56);

(2) settle their international disputes by peaceful means and in such a manner that neither international peace and security nor justice is endangered (Art. 2.3; cf. Art. 33);

(3) bring before the Security Council any dispute that the parties themselves cannot settle and that is likely, if allowed to continue, to endanger the maintenance of international peace and security (Art. 37);

(4) refrain in international relations from the threat of or use of force, whether against a state's territorial integrity or its political independence, or in any other manner inconsistent with the purposes of the United Nations (Art. 2.4); and

(5) assist the United Nations in every possible way in any action taken by the Organization in accordance with the Charter, and to refrain from assisting any state against which the United Nations takes preventive or enforcement measures (Art. 2.5). In particular, the states are bound to recognize and carry out the decisions of the Security Council, including those concerning the application of measures of enforcement (Art. 25; and Chapter VII of the Pact).

The first of these obligations is framed in such general terms, and leaves so much play for the judgment of every individual state, that it can hardly be recognized as an actual legal obligation. The remaining four, on the other hand, have a precisely expressed content; moreover, taken together with the provisions of the Charter concerning the United Nations' functions of maintaining peace and settling disputes, they form a whole, the scope of which it is most important to understand clearly. Not so much because an appeal to these obligations will probably be enough to bring a state that is in danger of forgetting them back to the narrow path of virtue, but rather because a clear understanding of these principles will help determine the moral and political judgment of world opinion on the actions of the states in the given circumstances and because this opinion, organized in the United Nations, is a not inconsiderable factor in the game of power politics.

The behavior pattern that is expected of the members and the Organization (according to the plan of the Charter) is briefly as follows. The members must try to settle their serious differences themselves, in the spirit of peace and justice. Article 33 gives examples of procedures for the attainment of this object: negotiation, inquiry, mediation, arbitration, judicial settlement, and resort to regional agencies or arrangements. If their attempt fails they are bound to bring the case before the Security Council (or, in practice, to the General Assembly). If a settlement is not brought about in this way either, neither of the parties may use force, or even the threat of force, to make good its claim. This prohibition is formal and absolute, i.e. it makes no difference how good or how bad is the material right claimed by the party in the case in dispute. Should one of the parties, in spite of everything, start an armed attack on the other, the party attacked has the right to defend itself, and other states the right to come to its assistance (individual and collective self-defense, Art. 51). Moreover, it is the function of the Organization to take effective measures to prevent threats to peace and to restore peace. With this in view, it is the duty of states outside the conflict to obey the instructions of the Security Council on the measures to be taken, and otherwise to assist the Organization, and to abstain from giving assistance to the state against which these measure are directed.

The central rule in this complex is the provision in Article 2(4), the absolute prohibition of the use of force or threat of force in any manner inconsistent with the purpose of the United Nations. This rule may also be expressed by saying that *self-help is unconditionally forbidden.* The use of force is permitted only in *self-defense* or as a contribution thereto, and as a *public exercise of force* authorized by the Security Council.

The prohibition of self-help is, as stated, absolute. This means that it is quite independent of the justification of the claim one state makes against another. It may be, for example, that State *A* acts with gross injustice toward the citizens of State *B*, detains *B*'s ships or refuses them access to waters where they may lawfully sail, or otherwise outrages and grossly provokes *B*. Or *A* may proclaim its determination to destroy *B*, and openly prepare an attack on *B*. Whatever the situation, it is the duty of *B*, according to Articles 2(4) and 51 of the Charter, to sit with folded hands until the moment that *A* crosses the frontier in an armed attack on *B*. This is the only sin that cannot be tolerated, that gives *B* the right of self-defense and the United Nations the duty to intervene with effective measures for the restoration of peace.

The prohibition in Article 2(4) applies not only to war but to every form of physical force, including military reprisals. It applies only to international conditions and thus not to internal disturbances and revolts. But if the struggle is over, and the rebel party has succeeded in establishing an effective authority over a certain territory, so that in fact a new state has arisen, then the prohibition comes into effect. Neither of the parties may attack the other, claiming that it is only continuing a civil war (as might be expected to happen with Communist and Nationalist China).

Article 2(4) is the culmination of a historical development of varying attitudes to the phenomenon of war. Classical international law, as developed by Grotius and his successors, took over from the Church Fathers and from the philosophy of the Middle Ages the theory of the *bellum justum,* the just war. According to this, war is permissible when it has a just reason (*causa justa*) and such a reason exists when war is necessary to resist an unjust attack (a war of defense) or to enforce a lawful claim (a war of execution). "Lawful" in this connection refers not merely to what we should call positive law, but also to the requirements of conscience or the sentiment of justice—what was called "the law of nature." With the waning of natural law and the rise of the positivist school at the end of the 18th century, the doctrine of *bellum justum* was referred to the moral sphere. Legally, war was accepted as a lawful instrument of a state's foreign policy and aspirations. The function of law, it was said, is not to forbid war but to regulate the manner in which it is waged. On this basis, the law of war and neutrality was developed, the function of which was partly to limit the extent of war (for neutrals, for civilians) and partly to humanize it by limiting the weapons and methods permitted. These attempts to civilize war, almost to a kind of noble duel, which might be bloody but not savage, culminated in the Hague Conventions of 1899 and 1907.

The Covenant of the League of Nations brought no break with this attitude. War as such was not criminalized, and the *reason* for the war was irrelevant to its lawfulness. On the other hand, it introduced certain rules for the *procedure* to be followed before war might be started. The dispute causing the trouble was to be submitted to one of several possible methods of reaching a peaceful settlement, and thereafter there should elapse a period of three months before any party might resort to war. This requirement, which, seen from the military point of view of our own day, is somewhat unrealistic, was based on the idea that in this "cooling-off" period the parties might come to reason.

A change did come, however, with the Kellogg-Briand Pact of 1928, signed or adhered to by most of the states of the world. In this the parties declared solemnly, in the name of their respective peoples, that they condemned recourse to war for the solution of international controversies and renounced it as an instrument of national policy in their relations with one another. It was assumed that self-defense and help to self-defense were permitted, but no effort was made to define the conditions for this in detail. No form of sanction was prescribed against the state that broke the peace. This document, which was hailed as a unique step forward in human history, is no more than an empty declaration, typical of the moralizing idealism of the years between the wars, which was more concerned with formulating high-sounding principles than with ensuring that there was a basis of political reality behind them. How close cynicism could lie to naïve idealism may be seen from the statement of one of the fathers of the Pact, the American Secretary of State, Frank B. Kellogg, who explained in the American Senate that war in self-defense included war in defense of rights—whereby in reality the door to aggressive war was kept open, for will not an aggressor always claim that he is making war in the name of justice?

Article 2(4), as stated, is the culmination of this development. It goes further than the Kellogg-Briand Pact in that it forbids not only war but also other use of force (military reprisals), and not only the use of force but even the threat of it. At the same time, it tightens up the prohibition. Under Article 51, the right of self-defense assumes that there is an armed attack, so that the concept of self-defense is more narrowly defined than is usual in traditional international law and even in the national legal systems, where it is a generally acknowledged principle that the right may be exercised not merely against an actual attack but also in the case of threatening (imminent) attack.

It is not hard to see that the peace system of the Charter is an attempt to transfer to the international community the principle on which is based the rule of law in the civil community in the state, i.e. the principle of *the authorities' monopoly of the exercise of physical force*. In the civil community, it is fundamental that private exercise of force is forbidden except in self-defense. The citizens must turn to the state for the settlement of disputes they cannot settle themselves, and it is the duty of the authorities to maintain the law by force where this is necessary.

Nobody would deny that it would be a great thing if it were possible to establish the rule of law in the community of states too. But it may be wondered if the actual physical and mental conditions in the two communities are not so different that it is not possible to transfer the idea of the monopoly of force to the international community. If this is the case, there is the risk that the proclaimed ideal is out of contact with the facts and, though treated with verbal respect, really gives more misdirection than guidance.

In the national legal system, the prohibition of self-help is justified by the state's putting its legal machinery at the disposal of the citizen who feels that his rights have been infringed. By going to law, the injured party has a good prospect of having his right acknowledged, and, if necessary, maintained by force. In the international community, there is nothing that corresponds to this—not according to the plan of the United Nations, and even less according to the system into which the United Nations has developed in the real world. The prohibition of self-help, therefore, has no foundation in political realities and is changed from a basic element in the rule of law to a high-flown ideal nobody can be expected to live up to.

Let us first consider the system as it looks on paper, as yet un-spotted by the disappointments of the real world. What can a state do, when it feels that its rights have been infringed or its vital inter-ests encroached on, without turning to self-help? It can bring the case before the Security Council. But this body has no authority to make a binding settlement. At most, it can recommend a certain so-lution, and consequently it cannot enforce compliance with this solu-tion. *The enforcement apparatus of the United Nations can be used only in case of a breach of the peace, not in case of contempt of law.* Only in the case of a legal dispute, and if the other party has ac-cepted the jurisdiction of the Court, can the Court make a binding settlement, and in that case, if the settlement is not complied with, it is possible for the Council, under Article 94(2) of the Charter, to decide on the application of measures of enforcement to execute the judgment of the Court.

From this it will be seen that, even according to the blueprint of the Charter, it is a predominant rule that there is no possibility of getting a right acknowledged and maintained by going to "the au-thorities." And under the conditions that actually exist, this applies even more clearly, since in reality the United Nations has no machin-ery of enforcement at all.

In brief, the analogy with national law on which is based the abso-lute prohibition of self-help in Article 2(4) will not hold. In the na-tional community, the resources of physical power are in fact monopolized by the state, while the citizens are disarmed. In a well-organized state, the individual has no chance of defying the appa-ratus of the state, and the injured party has a good prospect, by applying to the authorities, of having his right enforced. That the citizens are required to refrain from self-help is therefore both rea-sonable and practicable. In the international community, on the con-trary, the resources of power are far from being monopolized, and the states are not disarmed. There is nothing to prevent a state from defying "the authorities," and the injured party has no prospect, by applying to them, of getting its right enforced. The absolute prohibi-tion of self-help is therefore neither reasonable nor practicable.

There is no point in a distinguished author's trying to explain away the absolute prohibition of self-help by more or less astute argu-ments of interpretation. The wording is clear, and the debate at San Francisco leaves no possible doubt of its meaning. What *can* be done is to show that the prohibition is based on a false analogy, and that the judicial idea it expresses is before its time, as long as there is no monopoly of power—or, at any rate, a concentration of power—on which each individual state could rely to make certain that its rights were maintained.

The practice of international relations clearly reflects the truth of these considerations. Nobody seriously believes or expects that the states will respect the absolute prohibition of self-help in Article 2(4). Many states have disregarded it or declared themselves willing to do so if they could. If such violations have caused condemnation, as, for example, the action of India against the Portuguese colony of Goa, it has been feeble and based mainly on the ground that force was used before negotiation could be considered exhausted.

Under these circumstances, I am forced to conclude that it is a fiction to talk of the prohibition in the Charter of every form of self-help as though it were valid international law. A rule does not become valid law simply because it is written on paper. Article 2(4) is the expression of an idealistic aspiration that does not correspond to an effective conception of law and justice, and it is therefore unsuitable as a guide to a moral and legal judgment of the actions of a state. Naturally, I do not mean that a state that feels itself injured or threatened shall be able to turn to the use of force without more ado, but only that any judgment of such a state must be based on consideration of the circumstances in every single case. If by "aggressor" we mean the state that is guilty of starting a war, and against which public opinion and international sanctions (if these exist) should be directed, it is not possible to identify the aggressor with the state that, contrary to Article 2(4), has used force. It is certainly true that the judgment hereby loses the precision of the absolute prohibition, just as it has never been possible to define "the aggressor" by means of simple criteria. This means that such a judgment becomes more a moral than a legal one, and there is nothing to be done about that. A precise rule cannot be used. It is a fallacy to think it possible to set in motion the machinery of international sanctions on the basis of a precise rule that has not the backing of the moral judgment of world opinion.

It would be tempting to illustrate the problem by analyzing some of the cases in which, in recent years, a state has used force or the threat of force—for example, the Suez crisis (1956), India's action against the Portuguese colony of Goa (1962), and Indonesia's repeatedly declared intention of solving the conflict over West New Guinea by force (1961-62). However, I do not think it would serve any purpose. Simply because it is a question of judgment of a concrete case, the reader might well disagree with my view of these cases, and his attention would thus be distracted from the question of principle, namely, whether self-help ought to be condemned absolutely and irrespective of all provocation and other circumstances.

I can find only one argument of weight that tells in favor of an unconditional prohibition—namely, that all considerations of law, justice, and humanity, and whatever others may be adduced in a given case in favor of the necessity of putting an end to intolerable conditions, must yield to the opposite and supreme consideration: that every warlike act involves the risk of setting in motion forces that end in the great catastrophe, the total destruction of atomic war. I do not believe that the abstract danger of this can justify an unconditional prohibition. The imminence of the danger must be one of the factors considered in judging a particular case.

References

1. REGIONALISM–UNIVERSALISM
   Claude, Inis L., Jr., *Swords into Plowshares* (2nd ed., 1939), Chap. 6.
   Hill, Norman, *International Organization* (1952), pp. 85-112.
   Padelford, Norman J. and George A. Lincoln, *International Politics* (1954), Chap. XXI.
2. CONDITIONS OF MEMBERSHIP
   Briggs, Herbert W., "Chinese Representation in the United Nations," *International Organization* (1952), pp. 192-209.
   Secretary-General Trygve Lie's Memorandum on the representation problem is reprinted in *International Organization* (1950), pp. 356-60.
3. OBLIGATIONS OF MEMBERSHIP
   Stone, Julius, *Aggression and World Order* (1958), Chap. 5. My criticism of Article 2(4) of the Charter agrees in essentials with Stone's point of view.
   Cohen, Benjamin V., *The United Nations* (1961), pp. 38-63.
   Katz, Milton, *Proceedings of American Society of International Law* (1960), pp. 254-56.

V

THE APPARATUS OF
THE UNITED NATIONS

C HAPTER III gave an account of the ends the United Nations is to serve, the functions to be exercised in pursuit of these aims, and the principles to be observed in doing so. This gives the framework of its activities. Chapter IV dealt with the membership, and thereby with the source of energy that does the work. But an undertaking needs not only an objective and a source of energy but an *apparatus,* i.e. a set of organs that work in accordance with given rules on how they are to be composed, the procedure they are to follow, and what competence they have in their respective spheres to take decisions. The rules creating this apparatus form the constitutional law of the United Nations and are the subject to be dealt with in the present chapter.

I imagine there are many who are interested enough in the United Nations as far as the Organization's real contributions to peace and progress are concerned, but who find that the constitutional law of the Organization is a matter of formalities of no interest to them. For my part, I am willing to admit that a description of the apparatus is largely a technical, specialized matter, incapable of arousing the interest, extending the horizon, or increasing the understanding of the reader. On the other hand, it is undeniable that a certain knowledge of the way in which, technically, the work is organized is necessary, not merely to enable the active participant to play his part, but to enable the spectator to understand what goes on. Moreover, the organizational rules give rise, at a number of points, to problems of wide interest.

I have attempted to compromise between these contrary considerations by giving in this chapter a bare outline of the apparatus and of its manner of working, limited to what must be considered necessary for a general understanding of what goes on in the United Nations. In the next chapter, I shall discuss some problems of organization that are of more general interest.

Article 7 of the Charter states that six principal organs shall be established for the United Nations. These are the General Assembly, the Security Council, the Economic and Social Council, the Trusteeship Council, the International Court, and the Secretariat. The name "principal organs," however, does not imply that they are all of the same standing. In a sense, the General Assembly is the supreme organ, in so far as the Assembly may, under Article 10, discuss—and thus criticize—the powers and functions of all the others, for which purpose it is laid down that each of the three Councils shall periodically report to the Assembly (it is scarcely conceivable that the Assembly's critical authority should be exercised in relation to the Court). The Assembly also takes precedence over the Economic and Social Council and the Trusteeship Council in the sense that these two Councils act under the authority of the General Assembly, which means that the Assembly can give instructions to the Councils and can reverse their decisions. There is no such superior relation to the Security Council (nor, of course, to the Court). Within its own sphere of competence, maintenance of peace and settlement of disputes, the Security Council acts in complete independence, even though it reports to the General Assembly and even though the Assembly can make recommendations to the Council on both general principles and concrete cases.

Finally, the Secretariat is in the main a purely executive organ, serving all organs that make the decisions (except the Court). But certain independent powers of political importance have been given to the Secretary-General, and this is the reason why the Secretariat is listed among the Organization's principal organs.

1. The General Assembly

The General Assembly is the *central* organ of the United Nations. In the first place, because, as explained above, it has authority to exercise moral and, to some extent, legal supervision over all the other organs. In the second place, because it is the organ in which all member states are represented. And finally, because its authority covers all matters within the sphere of the Organization, with the single exception that the primary responsibility for the maintenance of international peace and security rests with the Security Council, so that in that particular field the General Assembly's authority has a subsidiary character (see Chap. VI).

The General Assembly is primarily the place where the major political debate takes place, the forum for world opinion, "the world's town meeting," as it has been called. Here assemble the delegates from practically all the states in the world, and each of these, the least as well as the greatest, can air its opinions and make its complaints and accusations. Here is forged the weapon called world opinion, which under present conditions, at any rate, is the most powerful weapon in the United Nations' armory.

In itself there is nothing new in states meeting in conference to discuss political questions. This has been called "conference diplomacy," in contrast to the more everyday diplomacy between state and state. But the debate at the United Nations is essentially different: partly because these assemblies are periodical meetings, where the agenda is open to all current problems, situations, and conflicts of international concern; and partly and especially because the debate is public and often results in proposals that are put to the vote, perhaps after being subjected to a number of amendments. The debate thus comes to resemble, to some extent, those that take place in the parliaments of democratic states, and it has therefore become common to call this type of diplomacy "parliamentary diplomacy."

This form of diplomacy undoubtedly has its value. President Wilson believed blindly in its mission to maintain peace. He was convinced that secret diplomacy led to plots and intrigues, and that an important cause of war would disappear when all international negotiation was carried on in the full light of day between democratically governed states. This has shown itself to be an exaggerated and one-sided view. The value of public diplomacy lies in the possibility of appealing to world opinion and in the resulting pressure to formulate a policy that can be expected to win the latter's approval. The drawback is the danger that the debate may degenerate in that the parties, instead of talking to each other in order to reach an understanding, will be "making a grandstand play" to win outside support. All the resources of agitation and propaganda are then used to blacken one's opponent and to present oneself in a favorable light and thereby win world opinion, or certain parts of it, for oneself. In this form, parliamentary diplomacy becomes a weapon in the cold war rather than a means of settling differences. Public debate is particularly unsuitable when it is a question of reaching an amicable settlement or a compromise. Things go far more easily when the parties concerned are allowed to sit around a table behind closed doors, and can discuss offers and concessions without the danger of these being utilized by the other side's propaganda machine. It is current experience that when the parties in a difficult controversial problem have reached a point where they are willing to find a solution, the crucial negotiation takes place behind closed doors.

The importance of the General Assembly, however, is not limited to the fact that it is the forum where parliamentary democracy is practiced in a blaze of publicity. While the high political play is being presented on the stage of the General Assembly with violent language and dramatic effects, there is going on behind the scenes, i.e. in hotel suites and corridors, in restaurants and bars, at cocktail parties and other social arrangements, what is called "corridor diplomacy." The parties concerned take soundings among other delegates and try, with all means available in interstate relations, to persuade or press them for support. Or perhaps the parties seek direct contact to negotiate or bargain. Both language and tone are different from those in the Assembly. The appeal is less to ideals and principles, more to interests and facts.

The importance of the United Nations as a nerve center, where connections are easily made between the agents in the game of high-level politics and informal contacts and communications easily established, is not confined to the relatively short period during which the Assembly meets. It has become customary for the member states to maintain, besides the delegation sent to attend the meetings of the Assembly, a permanent diplomatic mission to the United Nations, the head of which is termed the state's "permanent representative at the United Nations." There are even several states, not members of the Organization, that maintain permanent observers in New York in order to keep in touch with what goes on at the United Nations, also behind the scenes. There is thus always in New York a diplomatic corps of more than 600 people prepared to engage at any moment, like a permanent diplomatic conference, in formal or informal diplomatic activity in cases concerning the United Nations. This permanent apparatus is of great importance. It creates valuable continuity in the work, and is a valuable support to the delegations, the personnel of which often changes from year to year. To many of the young and small states that cannot maintain diplomatic missions all over the world, the permanent missions at the United Nations offer an easy way of contacting over 100 governments. Between states that have not exchanged diplomatic missions or have broken off diplomatic relations, they make possible informal discussion.

Composition. The General Assembly consists of all the members of the United Nations. Each member is represented by a delegation that may have up to five representatives and five alternate representatives, and as many advisers, experts, and assistants as may be desired. The reason a member state may send a large delegation is simply that it would be impossible for a single person, or a few persons, to do simultaneously all the work required in plenary session and in a series of committees. An alternate representative may, at the discretion of the leader of the delegation, act as a representative. Advisers and experts of various kinds may, also at the discretion of the leader, act as members of committees—without, however, being eligible for positions such as chairman, vice-chairman, or *rapporteur* (Rules of Procedure 25, 26, 102, and 103).

Powers. While the original intention was that there should be a clear demarcation between the functions of the General Assembly and those of the Security Council, the line of demarcation was blurred at the San Francisco Conference. The idea that the Security Council should have the main responsibility for the maintenance of peace and security was maintained. But, moved by the fear of the Security Council's being paralyzed by the veto, Australia, with the support of a number of other states, carried amendments to Article 10, 11, and 12 with the object of securing for the General Assembly, too, a certain subsidiary authority in this field. It was laid down that the Assembly has an absolute right to discuss every matter falling within the sphere of the Charter, and consequently also security matters. Moreover, the Assembly's right to make recommendations in political questions was also recognized, though only with certain reservations in favor of the primary responsibility of the Security Council (Chap. VI.2).

In the economic and social sphere, on the other hand, the authority of the General Assembly is unlimited. The responsibility for the exercise of these functions lies with the Assembly, and the Economic and Social Council and the Trusteeship Council are completely subject to it.

The General Assembly, in the exercise of its functions, can in no case invest its resolutions with higher authority than that of recommendations. The Assembly can initiate *investigations* into actual circumstances, and declare in a resolution what, in its opinion, the findings are; and the Assembly can *discuss* both the actual situation and the solution of a conflict; and finally, it can *make recommendations* both to the members and to the Security Council. On the other hand, its resolutions are never legally binding. The Assembly has power neither to legislate nor to give instructions: it can only appeal, propose, recommend.

Further, the Assembly has various internal, organizational functions, and its resolutions on these matters are legally binding. These include, e.g., participation in the admission or the expulsion of members, the suspension of rights, the appointment of the Secretary-

General, election of members of the various organs of the United Nations, amendment of the Charter, and instructions to and control of subordinate organs.

Voting. Under Article 18(1), every member (i.e. every state) has one vote. The Great Powers thus have no voting privilege. The General Assembly is based on the principle of equality, both in composition and in voting power.

Moreover, Article 18(2) provides that decisions on *important questions* require a two-thirds majority of the members present and voting, and it lists a series of categories of questions covered by this rule. The last paragraph of the Article states that decisions on *other questions,* including the determination of additional categories of questions to be decided by a two-thirds majority, can be made by a majority of the members present and voting.

Rule of Procedure 88 states that the phrase "members present and voting" means "members casting an affirmative or negative vote" and that members abstaining are not counted. The voting is usually cited in the form of three figures, x, y, and z, where x is the number of "Ayes," y the number of "Noes," and z the number of abstentions. Rule 88 thus means that a proposal is carried by a simple majority when x is greater than y, and by a two-thirds majority when x is equal to (or more than) twice y. This is a sensible rule. If the abstentions were also to be counted, their presence would in fact work against the passing of the proposal, since they would increase the number of votes (simple majority or two-thirds majority) necessary. To avoid this, it would be necessary for the delegations abstaining to leave the chamber. The desire for neutrality is respected in a simpler way by not counting those that abstain.

It is most natural to interpret Article 18(2 and 3) as giving an exhaustive list of matters that require a two-thirds majority, so that these cases include, and include only, (1) those categories of questions listed in Paragraph 2, and (2) the additional categories that the General Assembly has decided, under Paragraph 3, to add to the list.

It is possible, however, to construe these paragraphs in another way: as though the list of important questions in Paragraph 2 were not exhaustive, but a series of examples, so that in dealing with a particular question, it would be possible to qualify it as "important," whereby it would come under the two-thirds majority rule. Where there is disagreement on whether a question is "important" or not, it must be possible to decide this by simple majority under Paragraph 3, which applies generally to all questions other than those listed under Paragraph 2.

Both views have been maintained in debate in the General Assembly, but it is impossible to deduce a definite attitude from the voting to date. In certain cases, a particular question has been voted "important" in view of Article 18(2)—but without any clear indication whether this has been justified by considering that it fell into one of the categories listed, or whether it was considered important directly and in itself. Other cases have been more indeterminate, in that the question put was simply whether a simple or a qualified majority was required.

This absence of a definite attitude to the interpretation of Article 18 is probably not unconnected with the fact that in later years the question has been of almost no practical consequence. From the systematic analysis of the practice of the General Assembly (*Repertory of Practice*) which covers the period up to August 31, 1959, it appears that out of 1380 resolutions passed up to that date, 1362 were passed by majorities of two-thirds or more, and only 18 by simple majority, and moreover, that only about 46 proposals were not passed because they did not get the necessary two-thirds majority. This means, then, that the grouping in the General Assembly, except in a few cases, has been such that the majority has likewise been a majority of two-thirds or more. The question whether a particular proposal needs one or the other kind of majority has consequently been of almost no interest.

There is reason to believe that this will change. The enormous increases in the number of members in the last few years, and the unwillingness of many of the new members to enroll in the existing groups, have made it increasingly difficult for either party to muster two-thirds of the votes. Under these conditions there will probably be an increasing interest in a more precise interpretation of Article 18.

When a proposal requires a two-thirds majority, this may make it impossible to arrive at a decision. This result may be fatal in cases where a positive decision is necessary if the Unite Nations is to function according to plan, e.g. in the election of members to the various organs, especially the Security Council. It has repeatedly happened that in elections to the Security Council it has been impossible for any of the candidates to obtain the necessary majority, in spite of a long series of votes punctuated by informal negotiations. So far, however, a solution has always been found at last by agreements on special arrangements. It was thus, for example, in the election in 1959, when Poland and Turkey, supported by the East and the West respectively, competed for a seat that had become vacant. Voting began on October 12 and continued for two whole months. There were 52 votes—an average of one each working day—before it was possible to obtain a two-thirds majority for Poland. This result was achieved by an agreement to the effect that Poland should vacate the seat at the end of 1960, and that Turkey should then be proposed as the only candidate.

Procedure. The General Assembly is not a permanently functioning organ. It assembles automatically on the third Tuesday in September for its regular annual session. When special reasons require it, the Security Council or a majority of the members of the Assembly can demand that the assembly be called together for a special session within 15 days. Moreover, on the same initiative, the Assembly can be called at 24-hour notice to an emergency special session, in accordance with the rules in Resolution 377 A (V), the Uniting for Peace resolution discussed in Chapter II.5. The point is that in this case the decision of the Security Council is taken without the Great Power veto. In the same chapter, we gave an account of the Interim Committee that was established in 1947 with the task of dealing with political questions in the interval between sessions and making recommendations to the Assembly. It was the first of the steps taken with the object of shifting the center of gravity in dealing with political cases from the veto-paralyzed Security Council to the General Assembly. The Committee was considered illegal by the Eastern states, which refused to take part in its work. It still exists, but has never come to play the part earmarked for it.

Every session opens and closes with a request from the President that the delegates observe one minute's silence for prayer or meditation.

Immediately after the opening, the Assembly elects its President for the coming year. Traditionally, he must not be the representative

of one of the Great Powers. The main committees are also constituted.

One of the first things to be done is to approve the agenda. A
provisional agenda is drafted by the Secretary-General and sent to
the members at least 60 days before the opening of the session.
Every item proposed by any member must be included. In the time
before the opening there is limited access to add supplementary
items. The provisional agenda is considered by the General Committee, which reports to the General Assembly, which takes the final
decision on its form. In both the General Committee and the General
Assembly itself, there is often a heated debate on whether or not a
particular item is to be included. Objections based on domestic jurisdiction under Article 2(7) are frequent. There is a firm rule that this
objection cannot prevent the case from being discussed in order to
decide whether or not it shall be placed on the agenda. Discussion of
the agenda is often continued far into the session, but of course this
does not prevent the Assembly from dealing with the items that are
agreed upon.

There is a tradition that when the formalities have been got
through, the meeting begins with a general debate, in which the
members, unconfined by the agenda, may freely present their views
on anything that falls within the sphere of the United Nations. The
great majority of the members make use of this right, with the result
that the general debate takes up a relatively large part of the pre-
cious time—in later years, nearly a month. The debate, which is
rather a series of monologues, ranges over a broad field of political
and philosophical considerations, even though there are usually some
main topics on which attention is especially concentrated. Its chief
value lies in the welcome opportunity it gives to many of the lesser
states, which normally find it difficult to assert themselves, to come
forward and draw the attention of the whole world to their problems, their complaints, and their accusations. It has long been known
that the mere fact of getting the opportunity to air a complaint may
be enough to ease the pressure in the boiler. Still, it seems to me
doubtful if it is defensible to be so generous with the time taken up
by the general debate.

Organization. The General Assembly is, of course, a rather cumbrous apparatus. It has been compared to a herd of grazing cattle

that move slowly along, heads down. It is therefore the rule that the items of the agenda are prepared in a Committee before they are laid before the Assembly, which itself, as distinct from its committees, is called the plenum or plenary Assembly.

Under the Rules of Procedure, the Assembly may set up such committees as it deems necessary for performing its functions. Moreover, the Rules of Procedure directly authorize a series of regular committees that form a permanent apparatus for the performance of particular functions. There are 11 such committees:

(1-7) The seven main committees. Each of these is a "committee of the whole," as every member is represented by one person in each main committee. Their task is to prepare the cases that are to be discussed in plenary session and perhaps to draft a resolution. The topics are distributed among the seven main committees as follows: political and security questions, including the regulation of armaments (First Committee); special political questions (Special Political Committee); economic and financial matters (Second Committee); social, humanitarian, and cultural matters (Third Committee); trusteeship matters and matters concerning non-self-governing territories (Fourth Committee); administrative and budgetary matters (Fifth Committee); and legal matters (Sixth Committee). The somewhat peculiar numbering is due to the fact that originally there were only six main committees and that later, after the numbering of the committees had become familiar, it was found necessary to divide the First Committee into two.

(8) The Credentials Committee, consisting of nine members, chosen at the beginning of each session, with the task of examining the credentials of the delegates.

(9) The General Committee, consisting of the President of the General Assembly, the thirteen vice-presidents, and the Chairmen of the seven main committees. They make recommendations to the plenary Assembly concerning the drawing up of the agenda and the closing date of the session, and also assist the President in the general conduct of the work of the Assembly.

(10) The Advisory Committee on Administrative and Budgetary

Questions, consisting of nine members, chosen by the General
Assembly for three years. Its task is to make an expert review
of the budget and to assist the Fifth Committee.

(11) Committee on Contributions, consisting of ten members
elected for three years. Its task is to submit proposals to the
General Assembly on the apportionment of expenses among
the member states.

As already mentioned, the General Assembly can also set up such
committees as it deems appropriate. It has often availed itself of this
right in order to set up *ad hoc* committees, i.e. committees for dealing with individual problems, e.g. the Committee on South-West Africa, the Committee on the Peaceful Uses of Outer Space, and the
Conciliation Commission for Palestine. There are, at the moment,
more than a score of such committees, each with a certain number of
members.

Under Article 22 of the Charter, the General Assembly may also
"establish such subsidiary organs as it deems necessary for the performance of its functions." The expression "subsidiary organ" is
sometimes used to designate the committees mentioned above, consisting of all or some of the members of the Organization, but the
essential point is that the concept is wider than this, since it extends
also to organs that do not consist exclusively of member states. A
good example is the International Law Commission, which consists
of 21 distinguished jurists of recognized competence in the field of
international law, representing the main forms of civilization and the
principal legal systems of the world, whose task is to promote the
progressive development of international law and its codification.

2. The Security Council

The Security Council may be said to be intended as a combination of
a police force and a board of conciliation. Under Article 24, it has the
primary responsibility for the maintenance of international peace
and security. This implies that, on the one hand, the Council must
intervene with effective measures in case of a breach of the peace or
the threat thereof (Chap. VII of the Charter); and, on the other

hand, that the Council—with this authority behind it—must work for the peaceful settlement of such disputes as may be considered to endanger peace if allowed to continue (Chap. VI of the Charter). Under the system, the Security Council has no force directly at its disposal for the maintenance of peace, but it can instruct the members to take the necessary measures. This, however, is conditional upon the conclusion of specific agreements between the Organization and each individual member on the forces and other forms of assistance the particular state is to place at the disposal of the Security Council.

Chapter II explains how it is that this plan has never been realized. Lack of agreement among the Great Powers has prevented the conclusion of the intended agreements under Article 43, which means that the Security Council cannot require the members to take military measures for the maintenance of peace. This lack of agreement has also, to a large extent, prevented the Security Council from exercising its authority in other ways for the solution of political conflicts and situations, and has therefore caused the center of gravity in the work of the United Nations to move more and more toward the General Assembly and the Secretary-General. Since, however, the enormous increase in its membership makes the General Assembly a somewhat unwieldy body, where it can be difficult for any party to collect the necessary two-thirds majority, it is not improbable that the Security Council will experience a renaissance, particularly if there is a *détente* between East and West.

Composition. The system of the Charter for the maintenance of peace is, as stated above, an institutionalization of the idea of a concert based on the hegemony of the Great Powers. It would have been consistent with this idea to have confined membership of the Council to the five Great Powers, China, France, the Soviet Union, the United Kingdom, and the United States of America. As a concession to "democratic" ideas concerning the representation of the lesser states also, the membership was expanded to eleven states: the five Great Powers as permanent members plus six other members of the United Nations as nonpermanent members elected by the General Assembly for a period of two years. The nonpermanent members thus constitute the majority of the Council, which, however, because of the rules of voting, is of no great importance. The veto power of the permanent members ensures that no decision opposed by even one of them can be taken. On the other hand, if the Great Powers agree, a common front of five of the other members is required to block a decision desired by the Great Powers, which in practice is an unlikely constellation.

The Charter states that the choice of the six nonpermanent members shall be made in the first place with special regard for their contribution to the maintenance of international peace and security and to the other purposes of the Organization, and, in the second, to an equitable geographical distribution.

The first of these considerations points mainly to the members' military resources as the principal yardstick, and then to their influence and importance in other respects, especially economic. These extremely vague references have not, in practice, had much influence, while decisive weight, on the other hand, has been given to geographical distribution. As early as the first meeting of the General Assembly, in 1946, the Great Powers came to a gentlemen's agreement on a definite geographical distribution, and in essentials this has been kept to in subsequent elections. The six nonpermanent seats in the Council are distributed as follows: Latin America, 2; Western Europe, 1; Commonwealth, 1; Eastern Europe, 1; and the Middle East (Asia, Africa), 1. There has been a running disagreement between the Soviet Union and the United States as to whether this agreement is still binding. Several times the elections have given rise to vehement and protracted differences, especially over the representation of Eastern Europe. There have been conflicts over the question of which states ought to be counted as belonging to this group, and whether the choice is free or is bound to be a state that is supported by a majority of the states in the area (i.e., a Communist state faithful to the Soviet). A dispute has sometimes got into a deadlock, in that a long series of votes have not given one of the candidates the necessary two-thirds majority. It has then been possible to break the deadlock only by agreement on special arrangements.

In 1946, when this geographical distribution was settled, it was more or less in proportion to the number of members in the various geographical areas, though the Afro-Asian group even then was underrepresented in proportion to its size. Later, the enormous growth in membership, which has increased particularly the Afro-Asian group, has very much accentuated the underrepresentation, as is clearly shown by the accompanying table.

Nonpermanent Membership of the Security Council

	Seats	No. of states 1946	No. of states 1962
Latin America	2	20	22
Western Europe	1	5	12
Commonwealth	1	4	4
Eastern Europe	1	7	13
Middle East (Asia, Africa)	1	10	56

Against this background, it is not surprising that the Afro-Asian group has laid claim to increased representation on the Security Council. Since any interference with the representation of the other groups would meet with violent resistance, the only possibility seems to be to increase the number of members of the Council. In December 1963 the General Assembly passed a resolution that the number of elected members of the Security Council should be increased from six to ten, enlarging the total membership to 15. Further, it was decided that the ten nonpermanent members should be elected according to the following pattern: five from African and Asian states, one from eastern European states, two from Latin American states, and two from western European and other states. This amendment of the Charter will, according to Article 108, come into force when it has been ratified by two-thirds of the member states of the United Nations, including all the permanent members of the Security Council. As of May 31, 1965, 72 member states, including one permanent member of the Security Council, have ratified the amendment. With the present membership, two-thirds of the members amounts to 76 members. As two of the permanent members (France and Russia) voted against the resolution and two others (United Kingdom and United States) abstained, the chances of the amendment's entering into force appear rather small. The Secretary-General, however, in a report dated May 31, 1965, has said that there is every reason to hope that the amendment will come into force before long.

The election of a nonpermanent member to the Security Council is for two years. A retiring member cannot be re-elected at once. This prevents the arrangement, familiar from League of Nations practice, whereby certain medium-sized states were regularly re-elected as "semipermanent members."

Powers. The authority of the Security Council is confined to matters that come within the scope of the United Nations' political objectives, but within these limits it includes both the function of maintaining peace and that of settling disputes—dealt with in the Charter in Chapters VII and VI, respectively. For its relation to the competing competence of the General Assembly in this field, reference should be made to the next chapter.

Decisions of the Council have various degrees of authority. When it is a question of taking measures under Chapter VII against threats to or breaches of the peace, the decisions of the Council are legally binding on the members, since by Article 25 they have agreed to recognize and carry out these decisions in accordance with the Charter. Since the special agreements under Article 43 have never been concluded, the Council cannot require the members to participate in military measures. On the other hand, the Council has full authority with regard to nonmilitary measures. Because of the schism between the Great Powers, however, this authority has never been exercised.

When, however, it is a question of the Security Council's settlement function, under Chapter VI, the Council has no authority to prescribe a settlement of the dispute binding on the parties. It can never do more than advance a recommendation.

It may seem paradoxical that the Charter gives the Council wide authority to issue instructions once the conflict has gone so far that peace is in danger, while in the early stages of the conflict it gives the Council no corresponding authority and thus compels the Organization to refrain from any authoritative intervention until the breaking point has been reached. It has been said that this paradox reflects the fact that the states are readier, in the last resort, to accept a policeman than to submit in time to a judge. And this is probably true. But it must also be understood that in questions concerning the peaceful settlement of disputes, the recommendations of the Security Council, in spite of the fact that they are not formally binding, have greater weight than the form would imply. The passage of a resolution recommending a solution of a political dispute would mean that the Great Powers were agreed on it. If one party refuses to follow the recommendation, and the result is a breach of the peace or even merely the threat of a breach, then the party that refused must be prepared for the worst. For now the Council has authority to take effective measures, including military sanctions, and it can be foreseen that these must necessarily be directed against the party that has turned a deaf ear to the Council's recommendation.

Even though the Council's recommendations on the peaceful settlement of disputes are not binding on the parties, they do have a certain authority in relation to the members. These have declared in Article 24 that they lay the primary responsibility for the maintenance of international peace and security on the Security Council and agree that the Security Council, in performing the duties that this responsibility requires of it, is acting on behalf of the members. While it can be said of any organ that it acts on behalf of the Organization, it is not usual to say, as here, that it is acting *on behalf of the individual members.* This can only mean that the members are bound to respect the recommendations of the Security Council, and have thus debarred themselves from opposing the solution of a conflict approved by the Council, whether by criticizing it or taking political measures.

Voting. Article 27 of the Charter contains three different rules for voting necessary to pass a resolution in the Council. The rules vary according to the content of the resolution. All three prescribe that seven affirmative votes are required, each member having one vote. This means that in no case can a resolution be passed with less than seven affirmative votes.

The first rule states that in procedural matters nothing is required beyond the seven affirmative votes mentioned above.

The second rule states that in all other matters it is further required, as a principal rule, that the seven affirmative votes shall include the concurring votes of the permanent members. This is the rule of the Great Powers' veto.

To this, however, there is an exception, based on the general maxim that nobody is entitled to vote on his own case. This limitation of the veto is not, however, carried out in full. If it is a question of a resolution on measures of enforcement under Chapter VII, the right of the veto is valid without limitation, i.e. also to the advantage of a permanent member accused of a breach of the peace. Sanctions can therefore never be applied against a permanent member. If, on the other hand, it is a question of the peaceful settlement of a dispute under Chapter VI, the state or states that are parties to the dispute must abstain from voting. The third voting rule in such cases means that only members that have no part in the dispute can vote on it. The requirement of seven affirmative votes stands unchanged, and these, moreover, shall include the concurring votes of those permanent members that are entitled to vote on the question.

Scarcely any other article in the Charter has caused so much discussion or so many controversies in the practice of the United Nations, and attracted so much notice and criticism in wider circles outside, as Article 27, especially the veto rule. A general discussion of the right of veto is postponed to the next chapter. Here an account will be given of the problems of interpretation the article raises and of the manner in which these problems have been dealt with in practice.

In all other cases than those concerning procedure—for the sake of simplicity, let us speak of *material* as opposed to *procedural* cases— Article 27(3) requires that all permanent members shall vote "Aye" for a resolution to be adopted. This seems to leave no possibility for a permanent member that cannot vote for a particular proposal but does not, on the other hand, wish to prevent a decision by exercising its right of veto, to achieve the desired result by simply *abstaining* from voting. This result, however, would be quite unreasonable. Everywhere else where voting takes place, the practice is that those entitled to vote may choose among three different ways of reacting to a proposal. Besides saying "Aye" or "No," they may abstain from voting at all. This indicates that the voter concerned does not wish to take any responsibility for a decision one way or the other, but intends to be neutral. Technically, this attitude has an effect that lies midway between that of the affirmative and the negative votes. There is no reason why the permanent members of the Security Council should not be able to adopt a neutral attitude in this manner, and the provision has accordingly been taken in this sense in practice. And this practice is quite unambiguous. There have been many decisions where a resolution has been considered to have been adopted, in spite of the fact that one or more of the permanent members have abstained from voting. All the permanent members are agreed on this interpretation, nor has there been any criticism worth mentioning from other members of the United Nations.

Similar reasoning cannot be applied to a member's nonattendance. While it is obvious that a member that abstains from voting has no wish to prevent the adoption of a proposal, it is not possible to interpret nonattendance in the same sense without more ado. The point is of no great importance in practice. The situation has arisen only twice and is not likely to be repeated. In 1946 the Soviet Union left the Council in protest against the way the Council dealt with the Iranian question and was not represented at three of its meetings. Since only procedural questions came up in this period, the question was not driven to its logical conclusion. This did happen, however, when the Soviet boycotted the Council for the second time, from January 4 to July 31, 1950, in protest against the continuation of the Formosa government's representation of China. In this period occurred the aggression against South Korea, and, notwithstanding the absence of Russia, the Council passed the important resolutions of June 25 and 27 that provided the basis for the action in Korea. The justification given was that membership in the Security Council not only grants the right but imposes a duty to take the responsibility for the maintenance of peace that the other members of the Organization laid upon the Council when the Charter was agreed upon. A member shall not, by abandoning its responsibilities, be able to put the Council (which, under Article 28 of the Charter, must function continuously) out of action. However that may be, the Soviet Union quickly realized its tactical error and resumed its seat on the Council on August 1, 1950. After this experience, it is unlikely that such a situation will arise again.

The veto rule comes into the picture as soon as a case concerns other than procedural matters. Hence the central question in the interpretation of Article 27 is to determine how this expression is to be understood.

It is natural to assume that the expression "procedure" is used in a precise, generally accepted juridical sense, so that one has a firm basis on which to interpret the article. And the expression has, indeed, such a sense. It is common for collectively composed organs to conduct their business in accordance with rules of procedure, usually determined by the organ itself—for example, how the organ is to be called together, where it is to meet, how the meeting is to be conducted, the election of the chairman, other officials and committees, the language to be used, the hearing of witnesses or the undertaking of other investigations, invitation of other interested parties to be present and so forth. In accordance with this, "procedure" means the procedure that is laid down by ordinary rules of procedure; and a "case concerning procedural matters" is a case in which it is a question either of making a change in the rules of procedure, or of correctly interpreting them in the light of an actual situation, or of making a decision or taking a step of purely administrative nature—i.e. without bearing on the proceedings of any particular case, such as, e.g., election of the chairman and other officials, the establishment of chambers, and decisions in secretarial matters.

Taken in this sense, the term "procedure" gains a clear and definite meaning. Any step that is part of the process of *dealing with a concrete case* falls outside the concept of procedural matters. If, for example, it is a matter of appointing a commission of investigation, this is a part of a process of dealing with the case, and not a question of procedure. If a case is to be described as a procedural matter simply because it involves taking a step in accordance with the rules of procedure, the result would be that *all* cases could be so described. On the other hand, the case does concern procedural matters if the question arises how far the rules of procedure authorize such a step, or how far the method used in appointing the commission is in accordance with the rules of procedure for such matters.

An interpretation of Article 27 based on this distinction would draw a clear line between decisions in the Security Council that depend on the veto and those that do not, even though this would not, of course, exclude the possibility of doubtful, borderline cases arising in practice.

Such an interpretation, however, is definitely impossible to uphold, for it is quite evident from the negotiations at the San Francisco Conference that the intention was to extend the veto-free area to include also decisions on the taking of certain steps as part of the process of dealing with a concrete case. At the Conference, the veto rule was subjected to strong and sustained criticism by the invited powers. Many proposals were put forward for material changes in the wording proposed by the hosts, the Great Powers. As there was no prospect of carrying such limiting amendments, efforts were made to gain approval of an interpretation that limited the sphere in which the veto might be applied.

A list of 23 questions was drawn up, to **which** a clear answer was requested, as to whether the veto applied or not. It became apparent that the Great Powers, which stood fast in agreement on the proposed formulation (the "Yalta Formula"), did not agree among themselves on its interpretation in concrete cases. The debate on the sphere of application of the veto was on the point of producing a crisis in the Conference. After a couple of weeks of deadlock, the four host Great Powers (China, the Soviet Union, the United Kingdom, and the United States of America) agreed on a Common Statement of June 7, 1945, on voting in the Security Council. The Declaration was later acceded to by France. It was strongly criticized in many quarters, but the Great Powers refused to move from their position that the Yalta Formula (in the given interpretation) must be accepted, or there would be no Charter. Even though the Common Statement has never been subscribed to by the other states, and formally is thus not legally binding, it would be quite unrealistic to deny its decisive importance for the interpretation of Article 27.

The Common Statement gives the expression "procedural matters" —and therefore the sphere of veto-free voting—an extension that goes beyond the definition given above. The distinction between the two methods of voting is now in principle based on whether the decision concerns measures according to Chapter VII or, at any rate, steps that may start a *chain of events* that may *lead to* a decision on such measures. The veto-free voting rule, therefore, according to the Common Statement, finds application not only in cases concerning procedural matters as defined above, but also where it is a question of various steps in dealing with a concrete case. For example, mention is made of the invitation to a state that is a party to a dispute to participate in the discussion when the Council deals with the case. Similarly, no member, by means of the veto, shall be able to prevent the Council from considering and discussing a dispute or a situation, or from hearing the parties to it. Nor can the veto be used against a decision to remind the members of their general obligations under the Charter. But steps that go beyond this come, in accordance with the point regarding the "chain of events," under the veto rule. The decision to order an investigation is given as an example. The results of an investigation may be such as to oblige the Council to take further steps to maintain peace.

The result of the different negotiations at San Francisco was, then, that the Great Powers would not budge from the Yalta Formula that

had cost them such efforts to arrive at, but, under the heavy pressure
of criticism, they agreed to an interpretation of the formula that considerably limited the sphere of the veto. If one is an opponent of the
veto (which I am not) one may find this result laudable, but it is
undeniable that it had its price, and this was that the limitation of
the sphere of application of the veto has become arbitrary and not
based on any principle. The principle of the "chain of events" gives
no guidance. This chain has neither beginning nor end. Why set the
beginning at the appointment of a commission of inquiry? There is
nothing to prevent the discussion or the hearing of the parties from
being considered as parts of the chain, too.

With this background, it is not to be wondered at that the voting
rules in Article 27 have been a continual source of conflict and tug-of-
war—and, be it noted, a conflict fought by the parties in good faith,
in most cases. As the dividing line is not drawn on any principle, and
objectivity is impossible, each of the parties can defend its view with
full conviction.

An analytic examination of the Council's practice shows that no
attempt has ever been made to follow a criterion based on principle.
The result is purely enumerative, i.e. it is possible to list a series of
matters on which it is agreed that seven affirmative votes, no matter which, are sufficient to pass a resolution, and likewise, another
series where it is a matter of dispute whether the veto can be applied or not. On this, reference should be made to the *Repertory of
Practice*. Only one point of dispute will be given as an illustration.

It has been disputed several times whether the veto can be applied
against a decision to appoint a commission of inquiry in connection
with a complaint about a threat to peace. As stated above, the Common Statement mentions precisely this, the ordering of an investigation, as an example of a step that can start a chain of events and
therefore comes under the veto rule. One party appeals to this. The
other refers to an earlier paragraph in the Statement, which names
the setting up of a subsidiary organ as an example of a case in which
a positive decision may be taken by seven affirmative votes, no matter which. In my opinion, the first-mentioned view is the correct one.
The Statement's detailed account of starting an investigation leaves
no room for doubt. That the Statement in an earlier paragraph mentions the setting up of a subsidiary organ as an example of a case
concerning procedure does not invalidate this interpretation; this

paragraph simply cites the matters dealt with in Articles 28 to 32 of the Charter under the heading of "Procedure." In doing so, the authors of the Common Statement have not understood what I pointed out above, namely that a case does not concern procedure merely because it concerns a step taken *in accordance with* the rules of procedure.

Because of the lack of a principle and the opposing views and interests—often burning interests—that are involved in the question of whether the veto may be used or not, the rules about how the question is to be decided in case of disagreement assume great importance. Unfortunately, these rules themselves are not clear and undisputed. The problems may be set up in this order:

Question 1. Shall a commission of inquiry be appointed in this case as proposed in a draft resolution?
Question 2. In voting on this proposal, can the veto be used?
Question 3. In case of disagreement over question 2, how is this to be decided?

The starting point for answering question 3 is a pronouncement on this matter in the Common Statement of June 7, 1945. With astonishing lack of imagination it is said that it is unlikely that there will arise in the future any matters of great importance on which a decision will have to be made as to whether a procedural vote would apply. However, should such a matter arise, the decision regarding the preliminary question as to whether or not such a matter is procedural must be taken by a vote of seven members of the Security Council, including the concurring votes of the permanent members. That is to say, Question 2, the question of whether the veto may be used or not in deciding Question 1, is itself to be decided by voting under the veto rule. But what does this lead to in practice?

A study of this shows that two diametrically opposite methods of decision have established themselves—methods that, although no one seems to have acted consciously on this view, can be traced back to different understandings of the pronouncement just cited.

The first view is as follows. If doubt arises as to whether the decision of Question 1 comes under the veto rule, then the party that claims that it is a procedural matter must propose a resolution to this effect. According to the Common Statement the vote on this proposal must be taken under the veto rule. Then if one of the Great Powers votes "No," *this decides that Question 1 does not concern a procedural matter, and that consequently the veto rule applies in Question 1.* This voting technique is called "double veto." If a Great Power uses this ruthlessly, it can secure for itself the power of veto in any case whatever. Should its right to do so be disputed, it need only use its veto in the next round of voting on the proposal that the veto cannot be used. The double veto, has, in fact, been used in a number of cases by the Soviet Union, and in one case by France. This method of proceeding has caused irritation because it makes it possible for a Great Power to behave with unrestrained high-handedness if it is determined, in a given case, to resist the passing of a resolution at all costs.

The other view, which has not been clearly expressed, but which by rationalization after the event can be deduced from the attitudes taken up, denies the statements in italics above. If a resolution declaring that Question 1 is a procedural matter is rejected (by use of the veto), it must, of course, be admitted that it *has not been decided that the matter is of procedural character. But this is not the same as saying that it has been decided that it is of the opposite character.* There can be no doubt that if a resolution had been proposed declaring this, this would also have been rejected. If the view criticized is followed, the result becomes completely dependent upon which of the parties puts forward the proposal. The real situation is that the Council has not been able to decide on the answer to Question 2 in either direction. In these circumstances it must fall to the President, in accordance with Rule of Procedure 30, to decide whether by voting on Question 1 a valid resolution has been produced, irrespective of a permanent member's "No." Here the President must be guided by his conscience. His ruling, however, is not definitive. Under Rule 30, its correctness can be challenged by every member of the Council. He shall then submit it to the vote of the Council directly, "and it shall stand, unless it be overruled." A positive rejection is thus required to upset the President's decision, which thus means that at least seven members must vote for its rejection.

This method of proceeding, which may be called "the Presidential decision method," means that the definitive decision of the question of whether or not the veto may be used in any particular case comes to depend on what seven members of the Council can agree on. This method, too, can be misused if the seven members are willing to force through an arbitrary decision. To illustrate the point, two actual cases will be given, in one of which it was used to stop misuses of the double veto, and the other in which it was itself misused.

The first situation arose in September 1950, in connection with the case of a threatened attack on Formosa. At the 506th meeting of the Council, a proposal was made to invite a representative of the People's Republic of China to be present at the discussion in the Council. A resolution to this effect was put to the vote (Question 1), and the result was 7-3-1. Among the 3 negatives were the votes of 2 permanent members, the United States and Nationalist China. The President declared the resolution carried, obviously considering that the question was a "procedural matter" and therefore outside the scope of the veto. This view was also well grounded, as the Common Statement expressly mentions such an invitation as lying within the field of decision on procedural matters. China, however, had no wish to see its antagonist's representative in the Council and obviously counted on being able to prevent this by using the double veto, which up to that time had been successfully used in the Council three times. China therefore protested against the President's decision on the ground that the case was not a procedural matter and the decision was thus subject to the veto. At the next meeting, therefore, the question whether it was a procedural matter or not (Question 2) was put to the vote, with the result of 9-1-1. The vote against was China's, which had thus exercised the double veto. Hereby the resolution declaring that this was a procedural matter stranded. But the President did not conclude from this that the question was of a material character. Since a formal decision by the Council was lacking, the President, using his own judgment, ruled that the question of an invitation to communist China *was* a procedural matter (see the Common Statement) and that the resolution on the invitation was therefore duly carried. China protested against this ruling, which was then put to the vote and not rejected—rejection would have required the votes of seven members. Thus China's attempt to exploit the double veto technique was defeated. It should be remembered that here the other four permanent members were agreed on the procedural character of the decision (East and West agreed, for once) and that the permanent member that tried the double veto maneuver was China.

The other situation arose in September 1959, during a case concerning an aggression against Laos. A proposal was made to set up a commission of inquiry (Question 1), but before the resolution was put to the vote, disagreement arose over the character of the case and the type of voting. The Americans maintained that it was a procedural matter and that the resolution could be passed by seven affirmative votes, no matter which. The Soviet Union protested against this, invoking with justification the terms of the Common Statement, in which the decision to order an investigation is given as an example that comes under the veto rule. The question of whether the proposed resolution was a procedural matter (Question 2) was then put to the vote, with the result that ten voted for and one, the Soviet Union, against. Hereby the positive proposal to designate the case as a procedural matter was defeated, but the President did not conclude from this that it was of the opposite character. He exercised his judgment independently and declared that the case concerned a procedural matter. The Soviet Union protested against this, saying that the decision was illegal and invalid, but did not formally contest its validity—knowing very well that it would be impossible to muster the seven votes necessary to reject the ruling. The resolution itself was then put to the vote. Ten voted for, and one (the U.S.S.R.) against. The President declared the resolution carried. In this way, in spite of the opposition of the Soviet Union, the appointment of a commission of inquiry was forced through, a proceeding that, in my opinion, was obviously contrary to the rules of the Common Statement.

Similar problems can present themselves and similar tactics can be used when the question arises whether a permanent member is bound to abstain from voting. According to the last provision of Article 27, such an obligation exists in the case of decisions under Chapter VI (on peaceful settlement) if the case concerns a dispute in which a (permanent) member is involved. There may be a preliminary question of whether the case concerns a dispute or only *a situation,* and, again, the still more preliminary question, how to decide whether it is the one or the other. Since these problems are quite analogous with those already discussed, and have not been particularly important in practice, I shall not discuss them further.

Procedure. Unlike the General Assembly, the Security Council is an organ in permanent function (Art. 28). It is in continuous session and ready to meet at short notice. The Charter envisages periodic meetings of special importance, marked by the members being represented at government level, but the relevant provisions have never been carried out in practice.

Organization. The Security Council may set up such subsidiary organs as it considers necessary for the performance of its functions. Further, it can, of course, appoint committees or commissions from among its members. Because of the limited size of the Council, these have not played the same important part as in the General Assembly.

3. The Economic and Social Council

Even though in the Charter the Economic and Social Council is included in the list of the Organization's principal organs, it is not a supreme organ, as are the General Assembly and the Security Council, each in its own sphere. ECOSOC, as the Council is called in the language of abbreviation, exercises its functions under the authority of the General Assembly, which means that it is subject to the Assembly's orders and supervision. Nevertheless, the Charter allows the Council scope for independent initiative at a number of points. The operations of the Council are confined to the sphere of nonpolitical objectives. The Council has nothing to do with the problems of peace and security—or at any rate, only indirectly, in that social progress also serves the cause of peace. Apart from the special questions that come within the competence of the Trusteeship Council, there are no limits to ECOSOC's activities in nonpolitical international collaboration. This is not to say, however, that this 18-man Council is to perform directly all the manifold functions of the enormously extensive international collaboration. Such a thing would be quite impossible. As has already been mentioned, there are a considerable number of specialized international organizations, each with its extensive field of operations. It was not intended that the Economic and Social Council should supplant these, but that by means of various kinds of agreement they should be brought into an organized collaboration with the United Nations, especially with ECOSOC. It is then the task of this Council to deal with all fields not covered by the special institutions. But even these remaining areas are so variegated that it would be impossible for the Council to occupy itself directly with the actual work. This must be done mainly by means of subsidiary organs (Commissions) established by the Council. There remains as the Council's own field of direct operations: (1) a rather vaguely defined activity as the superior central organ for planning, co-ordinating, and controlling the work carried out by a large number of more or less subordinate special organs—I say "more or less subordinate" because the specialized organizations which have their own constitutions in treaties independent of the United Nations, zealously guard their own independence (as far as they are concerned, it is more accurate to speak of co-operation on a voluntary basis than of an organic superior-subordinate relation); and (2) a vague area covering tasks the Council has found it necessary to take up directly, either on its own initiative or in continuation of the work of a Commission.

Composition. The Council consists of 18 members of the United Nations, elected by the General Assembly (by a two-thirds majority). Each member has one representative on the Council, besides deputies and technical advisers. The Charter does not provide for permanent seats for the Great Powers, but these were expected, nonetheless, to be elected regularly. By providing that a retiring member may be re-elected at once, it has left open the possibility that certain states can in fact occupy the position of quasi-permanent members. In practice, too, the five states that are permanent members of the Security Council have been elected, and constantly re-elected, members of the Economic and Social Council. A break in this custom, however, occurred in 1960, when China could not gain the necessary two-thirds of the votes in the General Assembly. The seat remained vacant until, in 1961, it proved possible to elect Italy. It must be remembered that the China that was rejected was the Nationalist government on Formosa, which many of the member states do not accept as the valid representative of China.

As with the Security Council, the great increase in the number of members, which has especially added to the number of Afro-Asian members, has led to a strong demand for increased representation of this group. From the beginning, elections to the Council have kept to a more or less fixed pattern of geographical distribution of the seats, under which the Afro-Asian group has always had four of the 18 seats. Since this group now accounts for about half the member countries, it considers itself seriously underrepresented. There is more reality in this demand than in the corresponding one for more representation in the Security Council. Many undeveloped, newly formed states, who will never be more than pawns in the Security Council, have vital interests in the economic and social assistance programs of the United Nations. Their wish for more representation on ECOSOC is therefore not just a matter of vanity.

In December 1963 the General Assembly passed a resolution that the membership of ECOSOC should be increased from 18 to 27 members. Further, it was decided that, without prejudice to the present distribution of seats, the nine additional members would be elected according to the following pattern: seven from African and Asian states, one from Latin American states, and one from western European and other states. This amendment of the Charter will, according to Article 108, come into force when it has been ratified by two-thirds of the member states of the United Nations, including all the permanent members of the Security Council. As of May 31, 1965, 72 member states, including one permanent member of the Security Council, have ratified the amendment; with present membership, 76 votes are needed. As France and Russia voted against the resolution and the United Kingdom and the United States abstained, there seems little chance that the amendment will enter into force.

Powers. The Charter's description of the functions and powers of the Council is wordy but not precise. It is as if the politicians who drafted the Charter did not take this aspect of the Organization's work quite as seriously as the political side. The aims (see Chapter III) are stated in such general and comprehensive terms—improvement of living conditions, progress and development in economic and social conditions, solution of international problems in all spheres, respect for human rights—that they could almost as well have said, "To make the world a better place." On the other hand, the Charter is not generous with indications of how this is to happen, i.e. what functions the Council is to perform in pursuance of these comprehensive objectives.

It is axiomatic that the Council has no power to give instructions. It can inform, guide, coax, recommend—never order. Its most powerful weapon is the criticism of public opinion, the moral condemnation of world opinion. As with the General Assembly, it is possible to distinguish between three different phases or modalities in the work of the Council: investigation, discussion and criticism, and recommendation. *Investigation* is the collecting and digesting of information of every possible kind (historical, statistical, demographic, scientific, etc.) for the illumination and understanding of economic and social conditions all over the world. This work is limitless. If agreement cannot be achieved on anything else, it is always possible to set up a committee of investigation to study the particular problem—and, as far as this Council is concerned, there is no question of a veto. The innumerable reports that have been thus produced in the lifetime of the United Nations offers an enormous mass of varied material, often of great value—not only to the Council and its affiliated international institutions but to everyone who has anything to do with the problems arising in this wide field, whether as a practical politician or as a theoretical research worker. Never before have living conditions in the world been mapped out so extensively and in such detail—and the work continues. This map-making is of the same order of importance in its field, as geographical map-making for the world's traffic. The first prerequisite for dealing with a problem is to know it, and the mere act of presenting the naked facts is often the strongest of all arguments. Even though the facts often speak for themselves, this does not of course render unnecessary *discussion* and *criticism*, which brings us to the second phase of the work. Criticism in itself has weight because, without further appeals or advice, it can often cause a reform of policy. But often it is aimed at the passing of a resolution, in which the Council's judgment of the existing conditions can be given precise expression, together with advice on how these ought to be changed. The *proposals* and *recommendations* of the Council may be addressed to the General Assembly, to the members of the United Nations, or to the specialized agencies. There is express authority for giving the recommendation the form of a draft convention to be submitted to the General Assembly, and for the Council, on its own authority, to call international conferences for the discussion (which may result in a treaty) of matters within the scope of its authority.

Voting. Each member of the Council has one vote, and decisions are taken by simple majority of members present and voting. In this nonpolitical sphere, it has not been found necessary, as in the Security Council, to assure the Great Powers any voting privilege (the power of veto) nor, as in the Security Council and, when important matters are concerned, in the General Assembly also, to require a qualified majority for the taking of decisions in certain categories.

Procedure. The Council normally has two ordinary meetings a year, one in New York in April, and one in Geneva in July. The rules of procedure give the detailed rules for these, for the summoning of extraordinary meetings, for invitations to attend a meeting without vote, etc.

Organization. The extent of the Council's field of work makes it necessary that the special tasks should be dealt with by a number of subsidiary organs created for this purpose, the members of which are not limited to the 18 members with seats on the Council. These organs created by the Council itself are called Commissions. There are 12 of these, 8 functional and 4 regional. Further, the Council collaborates with 14 specialized agencies, which have their own independent existence based on a constitution embodied in a treaty, but are linked to the United Nations by agreements. The so-called special bodies, which have their own legal basis but, through this, are subject to a certain degree of control by ECOSOC, occupy an intermediate position. A long list of private, international organizations have achieved recognition with "consultative status," which means that they can send observers to the public meetings of the Council and have some possibility of making oral or written representations. On the other hand, committees, i.e. bodies composed of the Council's own members, are much less used than in the General Assembly.

The following list of the many bodies the Council is in contact with, either as a superior body or as partner in an agreement, will give some idea of the extent and the ramifications of the Council's work.

A. *Standing Committees:*
1. Technical Assistance Committee (TAC), which directs the assistance program of the United Nations
2. Committee for Industrial Development
3. Interim Committee on Program of Conferences
4. Committee on Nongovernmental Organizations
B. *Commissions* (12), of which 8 are functional:
1. Statistical Commission
2. Population Commission
3. Social Commission
4. Commission on Human Rights, with
5. Sub-commission on Prevention of Discrimination and Protection of Minorities
6. Commission on the Status of Women
7. Commission on Narcotic Drugs
8. Commission on International Commodity Trade
   and 4 regional:
1. Economic Commission for Europe (ECE)
2. Economic Commission for Asia and the Far East (ECAFE)
3. Economic Commission for Latin America (ECLA)
4. Economic Commission for Africa (ECA)
C. *Specialized Agencies:*
1. International Atomic Energy Agency (IAEA), which formally does not have the status of a "specialized agency"
2. International Labor Organization (ILO)
3. Food and Agriculture Organization of the United Nations (FAO)
4. United Nations Educational, Scientific, and Cultural Organization (UNESCO)
5. World Health Organization (WHO)
6. International Bank for Reconstruction and Development (BANK)
7. International Finance Corporation (IFC)
8. International Development Association (IDA)
9. International Monetary Fund (FUND)
10. International Civil Aviation Organization (ICAO)
11. International Telecommunication Union (ITU)
12. Universal Postal Union (UPU)
13. World Meteorological Organization (WMO)
14. Inter-Governmental Maritime Consultative Organization (IMCO)
D. A number of *Special Bodies,* including
Permanent Central Opium Board
United Nations Children's Fund (UNICEF)
Technical Assistance Board (TAB)
United Nations Special Fund
E. About 400 *private international organizations,* divided into three categories. The first includes organizations of particular representative importance, interested in most of the Council's fields of action.

At present there are only 10 such organizations, e.g. the International Chamber of Commerce. The second category, which includes about 100 organizations, comprises those with more specialized competence. Finally, nearly 200 other international organizations are registered for occasional consultation.

4. The Trusteeship Council

Since this Council will soon be of only historical interest, the account of it given here will be brief. The colonial system has undergone liquidation with a speed and an impetus no one expected when the Charter of the United Nations was drafted. Demands for independent existence as a national state are put forward with such impatience that the danger today is that the control and guidance of the colonial power should be relinquished too early rather than too late. Experience has shown that if the colonial people have not managed to develop a feeling of national unity transcending local tribal divisions and to gain a certain training in government and administration, the result of liberation may easily be bloody tribal feuds, administrative corruption, and dictatorial rule for the benefit of a clique.

The driving force in this avalanche-like development has been the awakening national consciousness of the dependent peoples themselves, stimulated by the widening of their horizon caused by the war and modern means of communication. But once this movement has started, it has a tendency to accelerate of itself. The new states that have been established have become members of the United Nations, and there they have zealously urged the continuance and acceleration of the liberation of other colonial peoples. Another important element in the situation has been the fact that the demand for liberation appeals to ideas that have deep roots in the democratic states of the West, not least in the United States of America. As with other great social evolutions—or revolutions—the struggle against those in power has been fought out primarily in the minds of those in power. Who believes today in Kipling's myth of the white man's burden? Everyone knows that, for good or ill, the days of colonialism are gone, and the only problem now is finding the best method of disposing of the remains. And this problem is not, of course, made any easier by the fact that colonial liberation has become a pawn in the game of high politics. Although the Soviet Union is the only really imperialistic power in the world today, ruling with an iron hand over a number of subject peoples, it never neglects an opportunity to exploit anticolonial feelings to stimulate ill-will and hate against the old colonial powers, or to promote disorder and revolution in which the seed of Communism can be sown.

When the Charter of the United Nations was signed, in 1945, over two hundred million people were still living under colonial rule. The Charter proclaimed that one of the objectives of the Organization was to bring this system to an end by leading the dependent peoples forward to self-government and perhaps independence. The Trusteeship Council was created as part of the work of the Organization for this purpose. It was expected that the existing mandated territories, at any rate, would continue as trust territories. The task of the Council was to be that of supervising the trustee states' administration of these territories to ensure that this, in the spirit of the Charter, would be carried on so as to improve the social conditions of the dependent peoples and to promote their development toward self-government or independence. But that nobody had imagined that this development would occur with such speed that the role of the Council would soon be finished, is perhaps most strikingly shown by the fact that the rules for the composition of the Council were so formulated that it is simply impossible to comply with them when the number of administering states seriously diminishes. This point was not discussed at San Francisco. The Preparatory Commission noticed it, but the question was not seriously discussed, obviously because it was considered to be a problem that would not arise for some considerable time.

Composition. The Trusteeship Council's activities may be considered to fall mainly under the economic and social objectives of the United Nations. In so far as it is a matter of promoting development toward independence, its work has a political character also. The same is true where a trust territory, as with the Pacific islands, is declared a strategic area. This political element is reflected in the composition of the Council, in that seats on the Council are assured to the five permanent members of the Security Council. The rules for the composition of the Council are based on a combination of two ideas: (1) that, because of the political importance of the Council,

the five Great Powers must have permanent seats on it, and (2) that
the Council must be so composed that there is numerical equality
between the administering and the nonadministering states, which
will prevent one of the parties, by a simple majority, from forcing
through its point of view at the expense of the other. These two ideas
have been embodied in the rules, so that the Council must consist of
(1) those members of the United Nations that administer trust territories, (2) those permanent members of the Security Council that do
not administer such territories, and (3) as many other members,
elected by the General Assembly, as may be necessary to ensure that
the total number of members is equally divided between administering and nonadministering states. This can also be expressed by saying that a state is an ex officio member of the Council both in its
capacity as a trustee and in its capacity as a Great Power. Thereafter,
the membership must be supplemented by election in such a manner
that there is parity in number between the administering and the
nonadministering states.

These rules are based on the assumption that the number of administering states is greater than the number of Great Powers that
do not administer any trust territory. If this assumption does not
hold, there is of course no need of any election to supplement the
number of nonadministering power. But if the number of administering states should become even less than the number of nonadministering Great Powers, it is impossible to provide the equality required.

The requirement of equality means that the Council must have
twice as many members as there are trustee states. At the establishment of the Council, there were five trustee states, (Australia, Belgium, France, New Zealand, and the United Kingdom), and the
Council consequently had ten members. Later, two other trustee
states (Italy and the United States) were added, whereby the Council was increased to 14 members. This was the composition of the
Council until 1960, when France and Italy ceased to be administering states following the liberation of the French Cameroons, Togoland, and Italian Somaliland. This should have reduced the Council's
membership to 10. Since Italy automatically went out, while France
as a Great Power remained, three of the elected members should
have gone out too. However, as there was no provision for bringing a
state's membership to an end, the Council continued with this un-

equal composition, comforting itself with the thought that the end of the election period would restore the balance. This balance was not, however, achieved, since, as early as 1962, the continuing process of liberation left only two administering powers, Australia and the United States. Even though all the elected members will go in the course of time, it will still be impossible to keep to the principle of equality, since the Council will come to consist of two administering states (Australia and the U.S.) on one side, and the four nonadministering Great Powers, (China, France, the U.S.S.R., and the United Kingdom) on the other.

This definitely puts the rule of equality out of action and destroys a crucial prerequisite for the trusteeship system. The administering states may reasonably refuse further to recognize the Council's authority to exercise its functions under the Charter. Unless some new arrangement is made by a formal amendment to the Charter, the most reasonable solution would seem to be to allow the Council to disappear and the General Assembly (or the Security Council in the case of the Pacific islands, a strategic area) to exercise direct supervision. To create a new Trusteeship Council merely to supervise the last two trust territories, New Guinea and the Pacific islands, seems to be a measure out of all proportion to its object. Each of the two remaining territories presents very special conditions that make the approach to independence difficult: in New Guinea, the population is at the lowest stage of civilization, and the Pacific trust territory consists of innumerable small islands, scattered over an area the size of the Australian continent. But even so, a solution that will bring the trusteeship system to an end at a date not far distant will certainly be found.

Powers. The Trusteeship Council, like the Economic and Social Council, is a subordinate organ. It exercises its functions under the authority of the General Assembly (for strategic trust territories, that of the Security Council). Its task is to see that these territories are administered in accordance with the principles of the Charter. For that purpose, the Council has authority to investigate and to inspect what goes on in these territories, partly by requiring the Trustees to furnish periodic reports, partly by organizing periodic visits and receiving petitions from the peoples of the territories. On the basis of these, the Council can discuss and criticize the administration and make recommendations. The Council has no authority to issue instructions in any circumstances.

Voting. The Great Powers, as stated above, are automatically members of the Council, but they have no voting privileges, for these would be contrary to the idea of equality between the administering and the nonadministering states, on which the Council's composition is founded. Each member has one vote; decisions are taken by a majority of the members present and voting.

Procedure. The Council meets regularly for two sessions a year, in January and July.

Organization. The Council may set up such committees of its own members as may seem necessary but has no authority to create subsidiary organs.

5. The International Court of Justice

When the Charter of the United Nations was drafted, an international court with general competence was already in existence. It was the Permanent Court of International Justice, established in 1920, connected with the League of Nations without actually being an organ of that organization. During the discussions at Dumbarton Oaks between the Big Four, it was an open question whether to reorganize the existing court or create a new one. At the San Francisco Conference the second alternative was chosen. A new court, named the International Court of Justice, was set up as one of the six principal organs of the United Nations. Its Statute forms an integral part of the Charter of the United Nations, which means in particular that it can be changed only by the same procedure as for amending the Charter itself. Although, however, the Court is formally a new creation, it is in reality a continuation of the old one, since the Statute governing its operation is identical, in essentials, with the old one.

The Court consists of 15 judges, elected by the General Assembly and the Security Council, voting independently of each other. To be elected, a candidate must have obtained an absolute majority of votes in each of the two bodies, without the permanent members of the Security Council having any voting privilege; the candidate that gains 6 of the Council's 11 votes is elected. The detailed rules for voting are based on, to some extent, disparate considerations. On one side, they are based on the idea that a judge is elected not as representative of a state, but because of his personal qualifications as expert in international law. In accordance with this point of view, it is prescribed that the judges are to be chosen without regard to their nationality and that the choice shall be made on the basis of a list of candidates drawn up, not by the states themselves, but by each country's group of judges in the Permanent Court of Arbitration. Every such group may nominate up to four candidates, of whom not more than two may be of the group's own nationality. This idea of independence of nationality, however, is not followed with complete consistency. In the first place, it is also provided that there must not be two judges who are nationals of the same state; and, in the second place, that at every election the electors shall bear in mind not only that the persons to be elected should individually possess the qualifications required, but also that in the body as a whole the representation of the main forms of civilization and of the principal legal systems of the world should be assured.

These last expressions are vague. I find it difficult to connect any idea with the phrase "main forms of civilization." There is no definite accepted grouping of "the principal legal systems of the world." One conceivable grouping is as follows:

(1) *Common law:* those systems of law that have developed from the Anglo-Saxon tradition, and are now represented all over the world where legal development has been under English influence, thus especially in the countries of the Commonwealth.

(2) Roman law (*Civil law*): those systems that have developed under the influence of Roman law, and are now represented in those countries where legal development has been under the influence of French law (Napoleon's *Code Civil*, 1804) and Germanic law (*Bürgerliches Gesetzbuch*, 1897).

(3) Law inspired by Communism.

(4) Islamic law.

(5) Indian law.

(6) Chinese law.

These rather vague directives for election have not prevented political considerations from playing a part. There has even been a case in which the election of a particular judge formed part of a bargain for the election of a particular state to the Security Council. In order to take politics out of the atmosphere in which the elections are held, the Institute for International Law has suggested that they should take place at a different time from those for the other organs of the United Nations.

The Great Powers have no statutory right to be represented in the Court, but hitherto it has been the generally accepted practice to ensure that there is always a citizen of each of them sitting on the bench.

Since the Court, as stated above, is one of the organs of the United Nations, and the Statute an integral part of the United Nations Charter, every member of the Organization is, as such, a participant in the Statute. This means that every member of the United Nations is entitled to the benefits and must accept the obligations of the Statute, more particularly, the right to make use of the Court and the obligation to contribute to the expenses of maintaining it. On the other hand, this does not mean that a member state as such is subject to the jurisdiction of the Court, i.e. bound to appear before it and to acknowledge its authority if another state should summon it before the Court. The Statute gives no authority for this, as it was clear that otherwise the majority of the states would not have accepted it.

The obligation to accept the authority of the Court to decide a particular case must have a special basis other than the Statute. Under Article 36 of the Statute, this basis may be either (1) an agreement between the contending parties to bring this particular case before the Court, or (2) an existing general agreement (treaty) between two or more states that all future cases of a certain kind shall be capable of being brought before the Court, or (3) a unilateral declaration, deposited with the Secretary General, that the state concerned will accept the judicial authority of the Court in all legal disputes with any other state that accepts the same obligation, without any further agreement or treaty. In practice, it is assumed that this declaration may be made with reservations as to certain types of disputes. In such a case, the principle of mutuality implies that other states may automatically plead corresponding reservations in relation to the state that made the reservations.

Thus the principle is that the authority of the Court to settle a dispute between two states unconditionally assumes that both states have accepted it by mutual agreement. But this can be brought about in different ways. The third method described above provides an easy way whereby states can acknowledge the Court's authority in general, without having to conclude treaties with a large number of states.

A state that is not a member of the United Nations can also participate in the Statute, and thereby gain access to the Court and take part in the election of the judges. The conditions are that the state concerned should declare that it subscribes to the Statute, undertakes to comply with the decisions of the Court in any case to which it is a party, and bears its share of the expenses of the Court. Switzerland, Liechtenstein, and San Marino have become participants in the Statute in this way. States that are not participants in the Statute can also, on certain conditions, bring a case before the Court.

This court is an excellent organ for settling disputes between states on the basis of international law, whether the states are members of the United Nations or not. But it is for the states themselves to decide to what extent they will make use of it, particularly whether they will bind themselves beforehand to accept the Court's jurisdiction.

Before judging the extent to which the states have shown themselves willing to do this, it is necessary to have a definite idea of what may reasonably be expected of an international court. It is a not uncommon view that if only respect for the law were great enough then all differences between states could be settled in court, and that the ideal to be pursued would be that each state should acknowledge the authority of the Court in all disputes or conflicts with another state. When this ideal had been realized, the rule of law in international relations would prevail in the same way as in those between individuals in a state, and thus peace would be secured.

In my opinion, this view is based on a misunderstanding and sets up an illusion as an ideal. It rests on too narrow a conception of the function of law in a well-organized community. It wrongly identifies this function with that of the courts, whose task it is to decide comparatively small conflicts on the basis of the established order and its rules for the distribution of wealth, power, advantages, and burdens. But the law is more than this essentially static function of the maintenance of the established order of things. It is also the framework of political life—i.e., law organizes the procedure by which the various groups in the community press and struggle for changes in the social order. The way of law here is legislation, and in the struggle over legislation, the relatively important, politically dynamic conflicts in the community are solved. When, for example, it is a question of whether agriculture shall be given financial help or not, whether a purchase tax shall be levied or not, and whether, in that case, the poor shall be compensated or direct taxation eased, these disputed questions are settled not in the law courts but in the legislature, since they concern disputes not over what the law *is* but over what the law *ought to be*. Such disputes are called political. The legislature is the arena prescribed by the law for the peaceful settlement of political disputes.

If this view is now applied to the relations between states in the international community, it will be seen that an international court, just like the national courts, is a suitable instrument for solving the comparatively unimportant disputes between states that are of a legal and not political character, i.e. static conflicts over the rights, under the existing order, of one or other of the parties; but that an international court, on the contrary, is not suitable for deciding political conflicts, i.e. those arising out of the demands of certain states or groups of states for a change in the existing order. When a state demands that a treaty, no longer appropriate, shall be annulled; that its territories be extended; that it be given a share in technological progress and economic development and access to raw materials; that threatening bases from which an attack could be launched should be removed; and so on, it would be meaningless to bring such demands before a court, of which the function is to say what *is* legal according to the existing order of things. For the very point of these demands is a change in the existing order. If these problems are to be solved by legal methods, what is required is something analogous to legislative procedure in the national community, and the appropriate organ must be a political representation of the states, not a court of persons skilled in law.

Against this background, it is clear that the yardstick by which the Court's success is to be measured cannot be an expectation that the states should have subjected themselves to its authority in all international disputes, whether political or legal. The most that can be hoped for is that the states will accept the Court's jurisdiction in disputes of a purely legal character, that is, those concerned exclusively with the parties' rights and obligations under the existing order of things.

Measured even by this yardstick, the result is disappointing. Of the over one hundred members of the United Nations, less than forty have made the declaration mentioned above, that they will recognize as compulsory the jurisdiction of the Court in all legal disputes with other states. Moreover, many of these declarations are hedged about with such reservations as make them more or less illusory. In 1946 the United States set a bad example by making a reservation with regard to matters that, *in the opinion of the United States,* come within the domestic jurisdiction of the United States. The words italicized mean that the United States has reserved for itself the right to exclude, by unilateral declaration, any case from the competence of the Court. This example was later followed by France, Liberia, Mexico, the Sudan, and the Union of South Africa. France, however, has since modified its reservation. The United Kingdom and Portugal have made use of a formula that is roughly as extensive. This, apart from a number of special reservations, reserves the right to introduce, with immediate effect, new special reservations by giving the Secretary-General notice of them. It is thus only to a limited extent and often with extensive safeguards that the states have been willing to submit beforehand to the jurisdiction of the Court. Moreover, it cannot be said that the states, within this framework, have shown great eagerness to use the Court. The number of cases, compared with the years between the wars, has been declining. In about half the cases the accused state has questioned the competence of the Court, so that there has often had to be lengthy argument on this question. Finally, it has repeatedly happened that the losing party has simply refused to obey the Court's decision.

All things considered, this is a depressing picture, not least because confidence in the administration of justice seems to have been diminishing as compared with the period before the establishment of the new Court. Part of the explanation, perhaps, is that international law is in a transitional period, in which it has not yet adapted itself to the changed conditions for international relations. Many states, particularly the Communist ones and those recently emerged from former colonial territories, are suspicious of current international law, to the development of which they have not themselves contributed and which they consider to be formed to promote the interests of imperialistic and capitalistic colonial powers. It may seem strange that it is just the small and weak states that have hesitated to accept international administration of justice, for hitherto the accepted view has been that for a small and weak state, reliance on the law was the best means of maintaining its rights in its relations with stronger states. When even states such as England, France, and the United States, which represent the leading powers in the system of classical international law, show great reserve in their attitude to the International Court and are reluctant to submit themselves to its decisions, this may well be due to a corresponding skepticism and lack of confidence in international law as it is developing under the pressure of the new states. While in the old court, the judges from Western European civilization were in the majority, this is no longer the case. There are at present only 4 such judges among the Court's 15, to whom must be added one from the Commonwealth and one from the United States. Of the other nine judges, two come from Communist states, three from Afro-Asian countries, and four from Latin America. This variegated composition is in conformity with the idea of the Court, since, as a world court, it must reflect all conceptions of law. But it is undeniable that in an age of conflicting conceptions and beliefs it creates great uncertainty as to how the Court will interpret and develop international law, an uncertainty that explains why also the countries with a background in classical international law view the Court with considerable reserve.

If the members have been thus restrained in their use of the Court, it cannot be said that the United Nations as an organization has set them a good example. The Charter provides that the General Assembly and the Security Council, and such other of the organs of the Organization as are authorized to do so by the General Assembly, may request the Court to give an advisory opinion on legal questions. Authority to do so has now been given to the two other Councils and all the specialized agencies. This authorization, however, has been seldom used, for, in the first 15 years of its existence the Court has given only half a score of advisory opinions. It was stated above (Chap. III.3) that the various organs of the United Nations have consistently refused to bring before the Court the important question of the interpretation of Article 2(7), apparently fearing that the

Court would not leave enough play for political considerations in the interpretation of the Charter. The same attitude has been shown with regard to other questions that have arisen in practice, regarding the interpretation of the Charter or other juridical matters.

The United Nations Charter has, as an innovation, introduced a certain possibility of applying international measures of enforcement to execute a judgment of the Court. Article 94(2) states that if a party to a case fails to perform the obligations incumbent upon it under a judgment rendered by the Court, the other party may have recourse to the Security Council, which may, if it deems necessary, make recommendations or decide upon measures to be taken to give effect to the judgment.

If the losing party refuses to comply with the judgment and the winning party then takes to arms to enforce its rights itself, the question discussed in Chapter IV.3 above arises, whether this is unlawful self-help, contrary to the obligation under Article 2(4) of the Charter to refrain from all use of force that is incompatible with the purposes of the United Nations. However that may be, it is inconceivable that military sanctions should be applied against a state that has taken to arms to enforce its rights under a judgment of the International Court. Cambodia recently won a case against Thailand and had its sovereignty over the disputed Preah Vihear temple acknowledged. Thailand accepted the judgment. But suppose that Thailand had refused to evacuate the temple district, and that Cambodia had taken possession of it by force. Then the situation mentioned above would have arisen, and it is inconceivable that military measures would have been taken against Cambodia to drive that state out of the area legally awarded to it, and to replace Thailand in unlawful possession.

6. *The Secretariat*

The idea of an international secretariat, i.e. a staff of "civil servants" who, irrespective of the individual's nationality, are responsible only to the head of the staff, the Secretary-General, and through him to the organization and who are to be guided in their work solely by loyalty to the organization as such and by their devotion to the objects and ideals it stands for, raises a series of problems, which will be discussed in the next chapter. Here, an account will be given of the provisions of the Charter that concern the Secretariat and the Secretary-General.

At first sight, it may seem astonishing that the Charter in Article 7 includes the Secretariat among the six principal organs of the United Nations. If the Secretariat of the United Nations were simply a staff of clerks serving the various organs of the Organization by doing office work, translation, and other technical services necessary for holding the meetings the term would be incorrect. But this is not the case. The Secretariat, which consists of the Secretary-General and the staff appointed by him, has much wider functions according to the Charter. These may be divided into three groups.

By Article 97, the Secretary-General is the Organization's highest *administrative* official. The administrative functions of the Secretariat cover all operations that, without being part of the functions determined by the aims of the Organization, are necessary for the working of the machine. This covers, first of all, the services needed for the meetings, such as the preparation and distribution of the working papers; the interpreting and translating services, arranging for simultaneous interpretation into the five working languages and translation into the "official languages" (English and French); recording and distributing records of meetings; filing of innumerable documents; library service, information, and many other forms of assistance for the individual delegates.

Also under administrative services come the collection and preparation by experts of information of many kinds, the necessary basis for dealing with any problem. Such studies are often undertaken at the request of the organ concerned, and this assumes that the Secretariat has at its disposal a staff of experts of the highest caliber. Just as the civil service in a country, because of the technical expertise at its disposal, exercises a considerable influence on the country's legislation, so the Secretariat leaves its mark on the work of the various organs of the United Nations. To a certain extent, especially on fiscal and financial matters, the Secretariat, at the request of ECOSOC, advises the members' governments and the specialized agencies also.

It is very important that the public all over the world should be kept informed about the work of the United Nations and be able to obtain further information without difficulty. For this purpose the

Secretariat maintains an extensive information service through regular use of modern media of mass communication, preparation of a variety of publications, and the establishment and maintenance of a considerable number (at present 49) of Information Centers all over the world.

To operate the Secretariat, which comprises about 5,000 persons, is, of course, in itself a comprehensive administrative task that gives rise to many problems of appointment, promotion, salaries, discipline, etc.

Under Article 98 of the Charter, the Secretary-General shall perform such functions as are entrusted to him by the various organs of the United Nations (with the exception of the Court). This provision is the basis for the Secretary-General's *executive authority*. This authority makes it possible for the Secretary-General and thereby the Secretariat to participate directly in the exercise of the real functions of the United Nations, including those of a high political nature. Since the directives given to the Secretary-General are often framed in extremely general terms, expressing only that minimum on which agreement could be reached in the organ concerned, the Secretary-General will often have considerable latitude, in executive action, for independent political judgment and decision. In particular, it may happen that the directives are inadequate because the assumptions on which they are based no longer hold good. If, furthermore, it is politically impossible to get the members of the competent organ to agree on supplementary directives, the Secretary-General is faced with the task of interpreting the directives on his own responsibility, in the light of the general aims and principles of the United Nations. One example of such development was the Secretary-General's executive action in the Congo as Chief of the United Nations Forces in the Congo. The Security Council passed a resolution July 13, 1960, authorizing the Secretary-General, in consultation with the government of the Republic of the Congo, to give military support to this government until it considered itself capable of exercising its authority without such help. When, however, the situation changed, in that Katanga broke away and the Central Government in Leopoldville began to disintegrate, the directive contained in the resolution of July 13 gave little guidance in these chaotic conditions. The Secretary-General asked in vain for more precise guidance from the Security Council. In these circumstances, he was forced to carry on the operation alone as well as he could and inevitably was exposed to strong criticism, now from one side, now from the other.

The competent organs themselves are free to determine the extent to which they wish to make use of the Secretary-General by delegating authority to him. It is understandable that the urge to turn to this expedient has increased since the General Assembly has become the main forum in which political matters are dealt with. In the period in which Trygve Lie was Secretary-General (1946-53), such authority was hardly ever given. In Dag Hammarskjöld's period of office (1953-61), however, things were otherwise. The new practice began when, in 1954, the General Assembly authorized him to take the steps most appropriate, in his judgment, to obtain the release of eleven American airmen held prisoner in China—a task he succeeded in performing satisfactorily. Then followed, in 1956, first, authority to bring into force the truce agreement in Palestine and, later, authority to take all the necessary administrative and executive steps to organize the United Nations Emergency Force and send it to Egypt. In 1958 the Secretary-General was given the responsibility of sending a group of observers to Lebanon and authorized to make such practical arrangements as might be necessary to maintain the objects and principles of the Charter in the relations between Lebanon and Jordan. The culmination of this development was reached with the 1960 resolution mentioned above, by which the Council gave the Secretary-General the direction of the Congo Force and the responsibility for its operations. The same pattern was followed in the Council's resolution of March 4, 1964, concerning the establishment of a United Nations peace-keeping force on Cyprus.

Article 99 of the Charter opens yet another prospect for the work of the Secretary-General, in that it gives him authority for *independent diplomatic and political action*. It is stated in this article that he may draw the attention of the Security Council to any matter that, in his opinion, may threaten the maintenance of international peace and security. It is obvious that the right to take such an initiative at the very center of the Organization's sphere of operations assumes that, to prepare such an initiative, the Secretary-General can, of his own accord, make investigations and open diplomatic negotiations in which he acts as a spokesman for the United Nations.

This authority for independent political initiative and decisions was used more by Trygve Lie than by Dag Hammarskjöld, though with little success. As early as 1946, when the Iranian question arose, Lie of his own accord maintained, without success, that the case should be removed from the agenda of the Security Council after the Russian troops had left Iran. As mentioned above, in Chapter IV.2, he drafted a Memorandum in 1950 defending Mao's right to represent China at the United Nations. His most important initiative was his great peace mission, which culminated in his ten-point peace program, published June 6, 1950—in the same month, unfortunately, in which the Korean conflict broke out. At the Security Council's meeting on June 25, 1950, Lie branded North Korea as an aggressor and maintained the competence and the duty of the Security Council to resist the aggression. This, and his subsequent support of the Korea operation and the Uniting for Peace resolution, drew on him the anger of the Soviet Union. The Soviet vetoed his re-election in 1951. The General Assembly decided that he should "remain in office" for three years more, but the opposition and criticism of the Soviet Union made his position so difficult that he preferred to resign in 1952.

Although Dag Hammarskjöld's political activity was, as we have seen, of an executive character (based on specific authority) he, too, did not escape the Soviet Union's extreme anger, malice, and attacks, and nobody can tell how the situation would have developed had not his career been so tragically cut short. Experience seems to show that active participation by the Secretary-General in the political functions of the United Nations involves great danger of conflict with one of the Great Powers, of so serious a nature as to make it difficult for the Secretary-General to continue in office.

Even without getting into the limelight, the Secretary-General has good opportunities to exercise his influence. If he is able to win confidence, his office can become a place where unofficial but important negotiations can take place. Thus it is known that during the Suez crisis Dag Hammarskjöld negotiated with the parties concerned, and that it was he who formulated the principles for the solution of the crisis that were later accepted by the Security Council.

The Secretary-General is thus other and more than a *chef de bureau*. His high position is reflected in the rules for his appointment, which is made by resolution of the General Assembly on the recommendation of the Security Council—i.e., under the exercise of the veto of the Great Powers.

The staff of the Secretariat is appointed by the Secretary-General; its international character is reflected in both its composition and its responsibility. Under the terms of the Charter the paramount consideration in the employment of the staff and in the determination of the conditions of service shall be the necessity of the highest standards of efficiency, competence, and integrity. Due regard shall be paid also to the importance of recruiting the staff on as wide a geographical basis as possible. (Art. 101). These rules apply to about 1,500 posts in the Secretariat. The Secretary-General is under strong pressure from many states to appoint their citizens, so that the geographical distribution almost becomes a quota system at the expense of what ought to be the paramount consideration. The proportion in which the member states contribute to the Organization's finances is taken, in practice, as a guide for their representation in the Secretariat, though with the possibility of adjusting the quota up or down within certain limits. For many of the untrained young states, which have no surplus of qualified personnel and sorely need what they have, it has become a matter of prestige to demand their share in the posts in the Secretariat, a demand that may well clash with the Secretariat's demand for quality.

The Secretary-General may also come under pressure in individual appointments. It may be tempting for a member state to try to censor an appointment, e.g. to prevent a person considered nationally unreliable from coming in, or perhaps to use these appointments to get rid of less-qualified individuals in their national administrations. The situation of the Secretary-General can be difficult, since he can hardly avoid, in procuring information about an applicant, some dealing with his home state.

It is quite in accordance with the idea of a neutral, supernational Secretariat, whose way of thinking is dictated not by national interests and prejudices but by common views and standards, that some consideration should be given to geographical distribution in the composition of the staff. Only by an appropriate blending of national elements can the universality in expertise, ideas, and influence be achieved that is the prerequisite for objectivity and neutrality. But when this consideration for universality deteriorates into a quota system it has run off the rails and is contrary to the basic standpoint, since the appointment is now bound to the particular nationality, instead of being raised above it and freed of this tie.

The Charter contains, in Article 100, two important rules for the promotion and protection of the independence of view and way of thinking, which, more than its composition, is what creates a Secretariat that can stand as the exponent of the United Nations as an institution raised above its component parts and symbolizing and incorporating in itself the ideas and objectives of the international community. The first makes it the duty of the Secretary-General and the staff to perform their functions in complete independence of every government or other authority outside the United Nations itself. What is meant here, of course, is primarily independence from the home state of the particular official, but also from international, ideological organizations of a political or religious kind that might exercise an undue influence. All who are appointed to the Secretariat are forbidden to seek or to receive instructions from such authorities, and they are enjoined to refrain from every activity which might reflect on their position as international officials responsible only to the Organization they serve. The second rule places an obligation on the member states to respect this independence, which means that they are forbidden to try to influence the manner in which the international civil servants perform their duties. In addition, it is provided in Article 105(2), that the officials of the Organization shall enjoy such privileges and immunities as are necessary for the independent exercise of their functions in the service of the Organization. These privileges and immunities are given in detail in a general convention.

The future role of the Secretary-General in the Organization is uncertain. Dag Hammarskjöld, until the situation in the Congo reached a stalemate, had achieved a position that will perhaps come to stand as the culmination, for the time, of the prestige, influence, and responsibility of the office. The powerful attacks directed against Hammarskjöld toward the end of his tenure of office by the Soviet Union were aimed not only at his person but also at the office as such. It was the Russian Prime Minister, Khrushchev, who, in the General Assembly in September 1960, personally proposed the so-called troika plan for reforming the office. According to this plan, the Secretary-General was to be replaced by a triumvirate of Directors representing the Communist, the capitalist, and the neutral states. It was further demanded that the personnel of the Secretariat should be so recruited that these three groups should be proportionally represented in it. Although on the face of it, this plan must be attractive to the many small neutral states, it met with support only from the Communists. For the intention was not difficult to understand—to draw the only tooth that had at last grown in the mouth of the United Nations in the form of the Secretary-General. To replace him by a troika of three would be tantamount to introducing the power of veto into the office of Secretary-General also. And to recruit the Secretariat in such a way as to reflect the three factions would be to destroy its international character and responsibility. Shortly before his death, Hammarskjöld published the report of a committee on a reorganization of the direction of the Secretariat, with his own comments. His sudden death, just as the 16th Session of the General Assembly was about to begin in September 1961, gave a sharp turn to the conflict over the office. It took seven weeks of informal negotiations to appoint the Burmese Ambassador, U Thant, as temporary Secretary-General for the remainder of the period of office, i.e. until April 10, 1963. On November 30, 1962, U Thant was elected Secretary-General, his period of office to run out on November 3, 1966, five years after his original temporary appointment. He was elected unanimously, both in the Security Council and in the General Assembly. Apparently, the Russian demands for the reorganization of the Secretariat must hereby be considered as shelved, for the moment, at any rate.

References

1. THE GENERAL ASSEMBLY

Bailey, Sidney D., *The General Assembly of the United Nations* (1960).

Ball, M. Margaret, "Bloc Voting in the General Assembly," *International Organization* (1951), pp. 3-31.

Brugiere, Pierre-F., *Les Pouvoirs de l'assemblée générale des Nations Unies en matière politique et de securité* (1955).

Haviland, H. Field, *The Political Role of the General Assembly* (1951).

Hovey, Allan, Jr., "Voting Procedure in the General Assembly," *International Organization* (1950), pp. 412-27.

Nicolas, H. G., *The United Nations as a Political Institution* (1959), Chap. V.

2. THE SECURITY COUNCIL

Aréchaga, Eduardo Jiménez de, *Voting and the Handling of Disputes in the Security Council* (1950).

Cheever, Daniel S. and H. Field Haviland, Jr., *Organizing for Peace* (1954), pp. 132-58.

Day, Georges, *Le droit de veto dans l'organisation des Nations Unies* (1952).

Emerson, Rupert and Inis L. Claude, Jr., "The Soviet Union and the United Nations," *International Organization* (1952), pp. 1-26.

Gross, Leo, "The Question of Laos and the Double Veto in the Security Council," *American Journal of International Law* (1960), pp. 118-31; "Voting in the Security Council: Abstention from Voting and Absence from Meetings," *The Yale Law Journal* (1951), pp. 209-57.

Leonard, L. Larry, *International Organization* (1951), pp. 196-224.

Moldaver, Arlette, "Repertoire of the Veto in the Security Council, 1946-1956," *International Organization* (1957), pp. 261-74.

3. THE ECONOMIC AND SOCIAL COUNCIL

Asher, Robert E. et al., *The United Nations and Promotion of the General Welfare* (1957), pp. 40-107.

Cheever, Daniel S. and H. Field Haviland, Jr., *Organizing for Peace* (1954), pp. 187-226.

Leonard, L. Larry, *International Organization* (1951), pp. 358-80.

Loveday, A., "Suggestions for the Reform of the United Nations Economic and Social Machinery," *International Organization* (1953), pp. 325-41.

Padelford, Norman J., "Politics and the Future of ECOSOC," *International Organization* (1961), pp. 564-80.

4. THE TRUSTEESHIP COUNCIL

Asher, Robert E. et al., *The United Nations and Promotion of the General Welfare* (1957), pp. 934-1020.

Baily, Sidney D., "The Future Composition of the Trusteeship Council," *International Organization* (1959), pp. 412-30.

5. THE INTERNATIONAL COURT OF JUSTICE

Castañeda, Jorge, "The Underdeveloped Nations and the Development of International Law," *International Organization* (1961), pp. 38-48.

Gross, Leo, "Some Observations on the International Court of Justice," *American Journal of International Law* (1962), pp. 33-62.

Lissitzyn, Oliver J., *The International Court* (1951).

Sørensen, Max, "The International Court of Justice: Its Role in Contemporary International Relations," *International Organization* (1960), pp. 261-76.

Full information on the composition of the Court, the legal basis of its competence, meetings, and judgments in the course of the year, its finances, etc. are to be found in the Yearbook published by the Court. The Court's decisions are published in the annual *Reports of Judgments, Advisory Opinions, and Orders.*

6. THE SECRETARIAT

Bailey, Sidney D., "The Troika and the Future of the UN," *International Organization* (May 1962).

Claude, Inis L., Jr., *Swords into Plowshares* (2nd ed., 1961), pp. 193-215.

Lengyel, Peter, "Some Trends in the International Civil Service," *International Organization* (1959), pp. 520-37.

Friedmann, Wolfgang and Arghyrios A. Fatouros, "The United Nations Administrative Tribunal," *International Organization* (1957), pp. 13-29.

Hammarskjöld, Dag, "The International Civil Service (address at Oxford University), May 30, 1961, *Current Notes on International Affairs*, Vol.

32, No. 6, pp. 39-51. Idem., "Two Differing Concepts of the United Nations Assayed," *International Organization* (1961), pp. 549-63.

Jackson, Elmore, "The Developing Role of the Secretary General," *International Organization* (1957), pp. 431-45.

Swift, Richard N., "Personnel Problems and the United Nations Secretariat," *International Organization* (1957), pp. 228-47.

Virally, Michel "Vers une réforme du secrétariat des Nations Unies?," *International Organization* (1961), pp. 236-55.

VI ❧

POLITICAL POWER
AND INFLUENCE
BEHIND THE APPARATUS

A constitution is an attempt to canalize into the forms of law the forces that shape and determine the life of a community. If the attempt succeeds, if, that is, the constitution becomes effectively established, this means that procedures are created by which individuals or groups of individuals can assert their interests, and which result in important decisions, determining the development of the life of the community. In a democratic society, the road that must be followed to achieve political decisions is long. It assumes, particularly, that there has been an election to a legislature, and that in this body there has been debate and voting in accordance with certain rules. The rules for election and voting are essential elements in the apparatus through which "the general will" finds expression. The constitution thus creates the legal framework for the political struggle in which the various groups in the community assert their interests. Under normal conditions, election, debate, and voting replace physical violence and other means of compulsion.

It is an essential condition, however, for such a legal canalizing of the clash of interests and ideas, that the formal ways of the constitution more or less accurately reflect the forces and sources of power in the community. If the tension between the legal form and the social forces that are to be pressed into this form becomes too great, there is an explosion. Dissatisfaction finds expression in violence, in the form of revolution, revolt, *coups d' état,* political strikes, and similar disorders aimed at forcing through a change in the constitution.

I adduce these commonplaces because it is important to keep them in mind in discussing some of the problems that have arisen in connection with the constitution of the United Nations. If the forces of power politics that determine the mutual relations of states are left out of account, and it is believed that rules for elections and voting in the United Nations can be based simply on abstract ideas of peace and justice, the result is a set of unreal constructions, worthless as a practical program of action. Indeed, the determinant social factors must be regarded as particularly important, especially in international relations. In national communities, the authorities have the monopoly of physical force. It is therefore difficult for the dissatisfied to organize resistance, and it will often be possible to maintain a constitution and to carry out decisions under it in spite of widespread discontent. The pressure in the community's boiler must rise to a considerable height before it explodes in revolution. In the international community it is otherwise. Here there is no monopoly of physical force. On the contrary, this is distributed among precisely those units, the states, that are subject to the rule of international law, particularly the constitution of the United Nations. Therefore, if the decisions that are taken in accordance with the organizational rules in the Charter of the United Nations for the composition and voting of the organs do not reflect in essentials the existing power relations, they will be of no practical consequence. The result may be that the Organization breaks up or that a number of its members leave it. It is unlikely, however, that rules for voting that do not harmonize with political power relations would ever be used in this way. The political forces will make themselves felt also before the vote is taken and will influence it. The voting rules make possible a certain play, just as, for example, the rules of chess determine the possibilities of the game. But how the game will in fact be played within this framework depends upon the political influence to which the players are subjected.

Too much importance, therefore, must not be attached to the voting procedures. However the rules may be formulated, it will not be possible to direct world politics by passing resolutions that are not in harmony with the actual power relations. It must be understood that the United Nations, however the organizational rules may be formulated, can never be anything but an instrument for the policies of the Great Powers, a forum that makes possible particular forms of political influence and diplomatic strategy. The idea that the United Nations, if only the procedural rules were suitably altered—for example, by abolishing the right of veto—could bring power politics to an end is infinitely naïve. On the contrary, the result would be that power politics would make an end of the United Nations. It is misleading to set up politics through the United Nations as the opposite of power politics, for there is no other kind of politics than power politics. The United Nations can be understood only as an integral part of international power politics. The most important function of the Organization is to be the anvil on which public opinion in world politics is hammered out and finds expression, so that it becomes one of the factors in the struggle of power politics.

Against this background, this chapter will discuss some questions of organization to which recent trends have lent immediate interest. These are, first of all, the various Great Power privileges in conflict with the principle of the "sovereign equality" of the states, especially the right of veto of the permanent members of the Security Council, and, in connection with this, certain recurrent questions on the application of the majority principle; then, the division of functions between the Security Council and the General Assembly, and the change in relative power to the advantage of the latter that has taken place as part of the actual exploitation of the United Nations apparatus by the Western Powers; and finally, the Secretary-General's position as an organ symbolizing the idea of the international order and independent of the conflicting forces.

1. Great Power privileges and the majority principle

The Charter of the United Nations proclaims, in Article 2, that the Organization is based on the principle of the sovereign equality of all its members. As I stated in Chapter II, sections 4 and 5, this is simply not true. On essential points the Charter violates both the principle of sovereignty and the principle of equality as these have been generally understood. But so great is the emotional aura that has surrounded these ideas from time immemorial, so important are they for the vanity of the states (especially the smaller ones), that it was considered advisable to cover up reality with this confession of faith in the time-honored principles.

In accordance with the principles of sovereignty and equality, the traditional rule of voting in conferences of states is the "unanimity principle," together with the rule that each state has one and only one vote irrespective of its size. To give greater weight to the votes of the greater states would offend against the principle of equality; and to acknowledge any form of majority decision would conflict with the principle of sovereignty, since this would subject the state to international authority.

The principle of unanimity, or the principle of a veto for each, was not only the principle of state conferences but also the foundation of the League of Nations. The Covenant of the League of Nations provided, in Article 5, that where the Covenant had not made a special exception, the agreement of all the members represented at the meeting was required for a valid decision, both in the Assembly and in the Council. In practice, however, this rule was modified in various ways. On the one hand, the custom developed of distinguishing between actual decisions and "recommendations" (voeux) so that only an ordinary majority was required to pass the latter. On the other hand, the pressure of circumstances caused individual states that could not vote for a particular resolution to refrain from exercising a veto by refraining from voting. It must be remembered that under the Covenant of the League of Nations resolutions were never formally binding.

The Charter of the United Nations deviates widely and glaringly from the principle of equality by giving the Great Powers a privileged position, partly in the rules for the composition of the organs and partly in the voting rules. By thus institutionalizing the dominating position of the Great Powers, the legal apparatus is brought closer to the political realities, and the possibility of utilizing the apparatus for passing effective resolutions is increased.

It is interesting to note that the privileges of the Great Powers are naturally related to the importance of the decisions to be taken. They are therefore greatest in the Security Council, as the organ specially created to deal with the high political questions of peace and security: the Great Powers have both permanent seats and the power of veto (with certain limitations). On the Trusteeship Council, which also deals with matters of political importance, the Great Powers have assured permanent seats but no voting privilege. In the election of the Secretary-General, each of the Great Powers has the right of veto, in that he is appointed by the General Assembly on the recommendation of the Security Council, voting without the matter being considered as merely procedural. In the election of judges to the International Court the Great Powers exercise special influence, since for the election of every single judge an absolute majority is required both in the General Assembly and in the Security Council. The election in the Security Council thus requires six affirmative votes, which means that the Great Powers have no individual right of veto in these elections. When we come to the Economic and Social Council and the General Assembly, which, according to the plan of the Charter, are to deal exclusively or at any rate mainly with nonpolitical matters, and which, in principle, have no power to pass legally binding resolutions, the Great Powers are given no advantage either in seats or in voting. It may be noted, however, that it is normal practice for the five permanent members of the Security Council always to have seats on the Economic and Social Council.

Among these privileges of the Great Powers the power of veto in the Security Council is the most important, the most discussed, and the most misunderstood. The rules for voting given in Article 27 of the Charter and the use in practice of the veto rule were discussed in the previous chapter. Here, we will deal with some points of principle on the importance and the justification of the rule.

It is generally conceded that it is not unreasonable to require the agreement of the Great Powers to the application of sanctions against a state. In any case it will be they who come to bear the main burden; and their disagreement among themselves on the question of whether such measures were opportune could very well start a major war. Criticism is directed at two points in particular: that the veto can be used not only when it is a question of measures of enforcement, but also in matters concerned with the peaceful settlement of a dispute; and that the veto can be used when it is a question of applying sanctions against the Great Power concerned itself.

As for the first point, the answer lies in the notion of the "chain of events." Once the Security Council, without the Great Powers being in agreement, has become involved in a political dispute between two states, and one of the parties will not obey the orders of the Council, the situation may very easily develop in such a way that it is difficult for those of the Great Powers that voted for these orders not to go further and furnish political, and perhaps military, support for the other party, thus preparing the way for a conflict between the Great Powers.

As for the second point, it can be said that on abstract principles of justice and equality it is unjust and unreasonable that the great, by using their own veto, should be able to shelter themselves from the responsibility that can overtake the small. This is to hang the little thieves and let the big ones go. On this subject, Finn I. B. Friis writes: "There is no doubt that this is an injustice and a shortcoming in the system of the Charter." And he quotes the old protagonist of the League of Nations, Lord Robert Cecil, as having said that there is nobody who will maintain that a policeman who breaks the law ought not to be compelled to keep it. Such remarks are textbook examples of a lack of understanding of the connection between justice and social realities. Such emotional reactions of disapproval and resentment are understandable, but if they are directed against the system of the Charter they are wrongly addressed. All criticism of the Charter on this point is unsound in view of the simple, though regrettable, fact that the application of sanctions against a Great Power would mean, in most cases, not the maintenance of peace but the opening of a world war.

It is true enough that the power of veto has largely paralyzed the Security Council and prevented it from performing the function intended for it under the system of the Charter. But it is superficial to blame the veto rule for this. The veto only registers the chasm between the two world powers; it is not the reason for it. The Charter of the United Nations is based, in accordance with political realities, on the idea that peace can be built only on the concert of the Great Powers. If this collapses, the system breaks down. All efforts must then be directed toward restoring harmony, not toward abolishing the veto. For the veto is only the honest and candid acknowledgment of the fact that without agreement among the Great Powers, and especially the two giant states of the Atomic Age, no political leadership of world politics for guaranteeing peace is possible.

It is seemingly a widespread belief that the veto rule is a Russian invention, which, in the secret discussions before Yalta, was forced through by Stalin against a more liberal and progressive Western view. This, however, is a myth that has arisen, presumably, because in practice in the United Nations it has been mainly the Soviet Union that has used the veto in opposition to American interests. It has nothing to do with historic reality. It appears from accounts given by men such as Cordell Hull and Edward Stettinius that, while the Russians constantly held the view that the power of veto should apply in all matters, i.e. also in cases in which the Great Power itself was a party, various and varying views prevailed among the American and English statesmen. Roosevelt personally strongly maintained that a state could not use the veto in its own case, because that would be contrary to a fundamental principle of justice imbedded in American law by our forefathers. He sent several personal messages about this to Stalin. The British negotiators originally held the same view, but later leading statesmen, such as Churchill and Sir Richard Stafford Cripps, drew very near to the Russian view. The planners in the American State Department oscillated between various opinions, but the result was their adoption of precisely the proposal that was adopted at Yalta and later embodied in the Charter, i.e. the rule that the veto in one's own case is excluded in questions of the peaceful settlement of a dispute, but can be used against proposals for the application of measures of enforcement. It is therefore impossible to maintain that the veto rule as it now stands in Article 27 of the Charter is a Russian product forced through against American wishes. On the contrary, it precisely expresses the view the Americans at length decided on, and it was Stalin who on this point gave way and accepted the American formula.

It is a fact that in the great majority of cases it is the Soviet Union that has prevented the passing of resolutions in the Security Council by voting against. It is a favorite occupation of the Western press to count up the number of Russian vetoes. This statistical information is a cheap move in the propaganda war—a move intended, by continually demonstrating the Russian *Nyet,* to give the impression that it is always the Russians who are recalcitrant and uncompromising and who exploit and misuse the voting rules of the Charter. It is hardly to be expected that people in general should be able to understand that the reason it is the Russians and not the Western powers that in practice use the veto is simply and solely that only the Western powers have been able to muster the seven votes in the Security Council required to pass a resolution. The rejection of a Russian proposal has not needed a veto: the proposal does not go through simply because it has not obtained the necessary seven affirmative votes. Should the picture change in this respect one day, the veto statistics will surely change also.

There are probably some who, though they can accept the veto rule in principle, think that Russia has misused the power of veto. In my opinion, it is difficult to draw the line between use and misuse in a field so strongly marked by conflicts of high political interests. The Russians, especially since the Korean conflict, have considered the United Nations to be an instrument of Western policy, in which the Soviet Union, and the Eastern bloc as a whole, found itself in a permanent minority. The Security Council soon developed into a theater of the cold war. In this situation, the Soviet Union is hardly to be blamed for making the most of the rules of voting to block political moves by its opponents. True, there have been cases where the Russians, especially in the double veto maneuver, have used the voting rules in a manner incompatible with good faith. But it is just as true that there have been cases in which the Western powers have made use, just as ruthlessly, of the power of the President under the rules of procedure to force through a high-handed decision (see the example in Chap. V.2).

While the privileges of the Great Powers, and especially the power of veto, means a breach of the time-honored principle of equality, the rules for voting in the General Assembly and the various Councils, providing as they do that a resolution can be passed by either a simple or a qualified majority, are a breach with the idea of sovereignty on which the unanimity principle is based. I would here remind the reader that in the General Assembly a two-thirds majority is required to pass a resolution on important questions, a simple majority on other questions. In the Economic and Social Council, as in the Trusteeship Council, a simple majority is always sufficient. In the Security Council, a resolution requires that 7 of the Council's 11 members have voted for it, whether the veto is applicable or not.

Apart from the Great Powers in the Security Council, these rules for voting mean that a state, even a Great Power, must acknowledge the validity of a resolution whether or not the state concerned has voted against. One may perhaps wonder that the Great Powers have agreed to acknowledge a majority principle whereby they may have to accept resolutions they cannot approve of, and see in this a proof that the states, even the mightiest, are willing, though within certain limits, to write off their sovereign independence and give way to the rule of law. I do not think that great weight should be attached to such views. Various factors explain why the leading powers have been able to agree to these rules for voting without fearing that in really important matters they would be bound by majority decisions dictating a course of action contrary, in their view, to their national interests.

In the first place, the resolutions on which a Great Power risks being outvoted are not legally binding. The resolutions of the General Assembly, the Economic and Social Council, and the Trusteeship Council have only the force of not legally binding recommendations. Organized world opinion is certainly not without importance, especially for the governments of the Western democracies. But that is a factor that must be taken into account, even without any formal passing of a resolution in one of the organs of the United Nations. On the other hand, however, majority decisions can be legally binding and can concern matters of great importance—especially the various organizational decisions taken by the General Assembly, such as the election of the Secretary-General and of the judges, election of members to the Councils, admission of members, establishment of auxiliary organs, and so on. But in the most important of these cases, the Great Powers have also made sure of the power of veto by a rule that such decisions require the consent of the Security Council.

In the second place, the Great Powers, when the Charter was being drafted, undoubtedly reasoned that resolutions passed against the vote of a Great Power in the General Assembly, the Economic and Social Council, and the Trusteeship Council could in any case concern only the nonpolitical aspects of the work of the Organization, that is, economic, social, cultural, and humanitarian matters that do not crucially affect the vital interests of the Great Powers. Once the Great Powers had secured the power of veto in the Security Council as the organ responsible for the maintenance of peace and security, there was no harm in the other powers obtaining an important say in the work of the Organization in the nonpolitical sphere.

Developments since 1945, however, have shown that this view is no longer quite justified. The General Assembly has come to deal with concrete questions of great political importance to a much greater extent than was foreseen. This is partly due to the shift, described in Chapter II, in the political center of gravity of the Organization from the Security Council to the General Assembly, engineered deliberately as part of the Western strategy to enable resolutions to be carried unhindered by a Soviet veto, and partly to the fact that the liquidation of the colonial system came to proceed so much faster than was expected, so that trusteeship questions and assistance to the underdeveloped young states—which, of course, via the subordinate councils come under the General Assembly—have become topics of high political moment, for example, the Congo crisis and the conflict over West New Guinea (West Irian). The Russians have naturally not been pleased to be deprived of the power of veto in this way, and have denounced the shift of power as contrary to the Charter. Incidentally, the Soviet Union, in consequence of the latest developments, is regaining a kind of power of veto in the General Assembly. In important questions, the passing of a resolution can be prevented by a third of the members present and voting. With a membership of over a hundred, it is becoming increasingly difficult for the Western powers to muster the two-thirds majority required to pass a resolution, and thus correspondingly easier for the Eastern bloc to gather the third of the votes necessary to block passage.

In the third place, the general considerations emphasized at the beginning of this chapter must be kept in mind: the formal rules for voting must not be taken too seriously, since these rules cannot disguise the fact that debate and voting take place in a political field of force, where the participants act not in abstract, celestial freedom, but under the influence of the enticements and pressures under which all international diplomacy is exerted. Even if you call it a free vote in the General Assembly of the United Nations, the way State X votes is still a step among other steps in its foreign policy—a step motivated, like any other decision in foreign policy, by considerations and deliberations, calculations, fears, and hopes. All diplomacy consists in exercising *influence* on other states 'courses of action. One aspect of this is the argumentation appealing to common interests and common ideals that is carried on in public from the rostra of the United Nations. Another aspect, and perhaps the most effective, is the appeal to the other party's special interests made behind the scenes, or quite outside the framework of the United Nations, and which, put bluntly, means offering advantages and threatening trouble. I say "put bluntly," for a diplomat would not be a diplomat if he could not disguise his actions in forms that spare the other side's vanity.

It is in the light of these considerations that the plans that have often been proposed, especially in recent years after the enormous growth in membership, for introducing voting rules in the General Assembly that take more account of the varying "weight" of the various members, should be judged. It is usual to speak of "weighted voting." These reform plans arise from the obvious unreasonableness of the principle of "one state, one vote," e.g. that a state such as Iceland, with a few hundred thousand inhabitants, can vote with the same weight as giant states such as the United States or the U.S.S.R. The advent of the many new, small states, which, considered as states, are still fledglings, has made the point even more obvious. The possible objection, that it would be undemocratic to make any difference between the weights of the votes of the large states and the small ones, is rejected. In the civil community, it may be reasonable to disregard individual differences, but in the international community the differences are too great to be overlooked. It may also be pointed out that weighted voting has already been introduced in a number of international organizations. In the International Bank and the International Monetary Fund, for example, voting power is weighted in proportion to the financial contributions of the members. In the Assemblies of the Council of Europe and the European Communities, the participating states are represented by a number of delegates roughly proportional to the size of their populations. In other cases, where maritime or commercial interests are involved, the rules of voting take account of the commercial tonnage or the balance between import and export interests. The United Nations is not unfamiliar with the idea of giving institutional expression to differences in the size and influence of the states, as is evident from the Great Power privileges discussed above. Weighted voting is only intended to carry this idea, true to reality, further.

Such are, roughly, the arguments for a reform of the rules for voting. Behind these may lie a strategic consideration with a longer view. Those who believe it possible to develop the United Nations gradually into a world government regard the introduction of weighted voting as a necessary preliminary for building up the authority of the General Assembly. Not until the distribution of votes becomes a reasonable reflection of the relative importance of nations can the demand be raised that the Assembly be given the power of political decision.

It is clear that there will be very great difficulty in securing agreement on the criteria on which the calculation of weight is to be based. Size of population, military strength, industrial capacity, culture, and elementary skills (ability to read), have all been suggested as factors to be taken into account in the calculation of each single state's coefficient of weight. It is hard, however, to imagine it possible to achieve agreement on any definite method of calculation. Moreover, there will hardly be any particular interest in or will to overcome these difficulties, since it is not at all clear what would be gained by doing so. As long as the General Assembly can only discuss, criticize, and recommend, and its importance continues to lie in the canalizing of world opinion that takes place in this forum, the formal rules for voting are, as stated, of subordinate importance. If the many small states misuse—as they have done—their voting power to force through resolutions that do not have the general support of the larger states, they will very soon find that such resolutions are of no effect and only serve to squander the prestige of the General Assembly. The idea of weighted voting has real interest and meaning only on the implied assumption that the General Assembly shall be given simultaneously the authority to take decisions.

But this assumption is something far beyond what can be considered a practical political objective that has the ghost of a chance of being realized in the foreseeable future. It would mean that the Great Powers would give up their right of vote in questions concerning the maintenance of international peace and security, and that they would bind themselves to allow their foreign policy to be determined by formal resolutions and not by the facts of the balance of power. Even in the long view, as a project for a new and better world, this idea is, in my view, abortive. That it should be possible, one day, to ensure peace by the introduction of the democratic principle of majority decision in the international community of the states, I do not believe. I can more readily believe that the way lies through dictatorship of the Great Powers (the idea of the Concert). My reason for this is that the background that gives meaning to the majority principle in a democratic state and makes it workable is lacking in the international community.

The theorists of democracy have often emphasized that the democratic ideology, if it is to function, assumes a certain agreement on fundamental values. That the individual feels the majority's decision as law and is willing to accept it is conditional upon his feeling solidarity with the other members of the group in spite of differences of opinion. However difficult it is to define, there must be a certain background of moral and cultural fellowship, a certain harmony in the final objectives, which makes an understanding possible. The individual must be able to identify himself with the group in order to feel its decisions as binding and as the expression of his own autonomy. A person who found himself among a company of bandits would never, in that company, be able to acknowledge the right of the majority.

Under normal conditions in a firmly established state this condition is fulfilled, approximately at any rate. Common standards and the historically conditioned feeling of solidarity here create the framework that, in spite of all differences, integrates majority and minority into a whole and gives the majority decision its meaning and its limitation.

In the international community, on the other hand, this condition is not fulfilled, thus excluding the possibility that the majority principle might be applied in reaching important political decisions. As long as the leading powers stand opposed to one another in hostile blocs, radically divided on economic, political, and religious ideology and prepared to destroy one another with the frightful weapons of mass destruction, it is contrary to the most elementary laws of political life to believe that in this community important decisions can conceivably be taken democratically by voting in a representative assembly. If we can imagine, for example, that the United States should succeed in mustering the necessary majority for a resolution requiring the Soviet Union to abandon its occupation of the border states in eastern Europe, it is difficult to understand what could motivate the Russians to comply with this resolution if they considered that such a withdrawal would weaken their security.

2. *General Assembly versus Security Council*

How the political center of gravity has moved, especially since the Korean crisis in 1950, from the Security Council to the General Assembly (and the Secretary-General) has been described previously (Chap. II.5). This development, which was aimed at bypassing the paralyzing Russian veto in the Security Council, has taken place to the accompaniment of constant protests by the Soviet Union. The Russians have maintained that the establishment of the Interim Commission, the Uniting for Peace resolution, and similar steps whereby the General Assembly has assumed authority to discuss and advise on questions concerning the maintenance of peace, involve a breach of the Charter by the illegal transfer to the General Assembly of functions whose exercise is exclusively the province of the Security Council. Even though this development must now be regarded as a *fait accompli*, the discussion of its justification is not closed, among other reasons, because the proper delimitation of the competence of the General Assembly has an important bearing on the thorny question of the members' obligation to share the past and present costs of the United Nations Emergency Forces in the Gaza area and in the Congo (Chap. VII.3). It is therefore not without interest to examine the rules of the Charter on the relation between the competence of the two organs.

It is undeniable that the role the General Assembly has come to play in political questions lies beyond what the authors conceived when the Charter was drafted. But it does not follow from this that this role is contrary to the Charter. For it must be remembered, on the other hand, that the Charter clearly and unambiguously gives the Assembly a certain authority also in political questions; and this authority was considerably extended during the proceedings at San Francisco, to allow for the possibility that disagreement among the Great Powers might paralyze the Security Council. On this last point, reference should be made to the discussion in Chapter I.5, of the contribution of the Australian delegate, Dr. Herbert Evatt.

Under Article 24 of the Charter, the members have given the primary responsibility (*responsabilité principale*) for the maintenance of peace to the Security Council. This clearly implies that the responsibility of the Council is not exclusive, but that other organs, particularly the General Assembly, must have a joint responsibility, though of a certain subordinate or subsidiary character. This also appears clear from Articles 10-17, which deal with the functions and powers of the Assembly. Especially noteworthy is Article 11(2), under which the General Assembly may *discuss* any questions relating to the maintenance of international peace and security brought before it by any member of the United Nations, by the Security Council, or, in accordance with Article 35, by a state that is not a member of the Organization; noteworthy, too, are Article 11(2) (in continuation of that just quoted) and Article 14, whereby the Assembly may *make recommendations*, not only in situations like those just mentioned, where the case has been brought before the Assembly from outside, but also on its own initiative, in regard to any situation, regardless of origin, which it deems likely to impair the general welfare or friendly relations among nations.

It is thus incontestable that the General Assembly has a certain authority in questions of peace and security both to discuss and to recommend on these matters. It is also clear that this authority is in a way subsidiary in relation to the principal authority or primary responsibility of the Security Council. The question is, therefore: In what way does the General Assembly's authority fall short of that of the Security Council? In two respects the Charter gives a clear answer to this question. In a third respect the wording is obscure and the whole conflict between East and West depends on which of two possible interpretations is chosen.

The two (or three) limitations to the authority of the Assembly all concern its authority to *make recommendations*. There are absolutely no limitations to its authority to *discuss*.

The General Assembly's authority to make recommendations concerning any dispute or situation is, in the first place, incontestably limited by Article 12(1) of the Charter, to which the statements quoted above, both in Article 11(2) and in Article 14, expressly refer. Article 12(1) provides that the General Assembly, while the Security Council is exercising, in respect of any dispute or situation, the functions assigned to it in the Charter, shall not make any recommendation with regard to that dispute or situation unless the Security Council so requests. In order that the General Assembly may be clear as to precisely when its competence is limited and when the limitation is removed, the second paragraph of the Article provides that the Secretary-General, with the consent of the Security Council, shall notify the General Assembly at each session of any matters relative to the maintenance of international peace and security which are being dealt with by the Security Council, and shall similarly notify the General Assembly or, if this is not in session, the members of the United Nations as soon as the Security Council ceases to deal with such matters.

The intention of this provision is clear enough. It does not prevent the same case from being discussed in both bodies. But as soon as a case is laid before the Security Council, the General Assembly must refrain from making proposals: it would not do to have conflicting proposals made in the two bodies. This clearness about what is meant does not, of course, exclude the possibility that doubtful borderline cases may arise in applying it. There may be doubt, for example, about whether it is the same dispute or situation that is being dealt with by the two organs.

Since the General Assembly is not competent to make proposals as long as the case is on the agenda of the Security Council, the question of what is the voting rule for the Council's decision to remove a case from the agenda assumes great practical importance. It has become an undisputed rule that this decision can be taken by any seven affirmative votes, i.e. without the exercise of the power of veto. A single great power cannot, therefore, prevent the way being opened for the General Assembly, if it becomes impossible to reach agreement in the Council.

Another undoubted limitation in the authority of the General Assembly follows from the fact that nowhere does the Charter give that organ power to take decisions that bind the members, whereas the Security Council can, under Chapter VII of the Charter, take binding decisions on the measures that the members are to take for the maintenance of peace. Even though the conditions necessary under Article 43 for the imposition of military sanctions have never been brought about, the power of the Council under Article 41 to order a boycott against a member remains unchallenged. On the other hand, as far as the General Assembly is concerned, there can be no question of anything but recommendations, which are not binding.

The doubtful question is whether there is also a third limitation of the competence of the General Assembly, i.e. that it is precluded from recommending such measures for the maintenance of peace as are dealt with in Chapter VII of the Charter and may make recommendations only for the peaceful settlement of disputes (Chap. VI of the Charter). The dispute on this point concerns the interpretation of an obscure provision in Article 11(2).

Article 11(2) contains, as explained above, first a provision that the Assembly can *discuss* any question of peace and security that is brought before it. Then follows a provision that it can also *make recommendations* in such questions, in continuation of which it is said: "Any such question on which action is necessary shall be referred to the Security Council by the General Assembly either before or after discussion." The problem is: What is to be understood by "a question on which action is necessary"? This phrase may be understood in one of two ways:

(1) After it has been laid down in the previous part of Article 11(2) that the Assembly can *discuss* political questions brought before it and *make recommendations* concerning such questions, it is now said that should it become necessary to go further and to *impose* on the members the duty to take measures of enforcement dealt with in Chapter VII, then the case must be referred to the Security Council.

(2) After it has been laid down that the General Assembly can make recommendations concerning political questions brought before it, the provision limits this competence by stipulating that the recommendations of the General Assembly must not concern measures for the maintenance of peace dealt with in Chapter VII. If measures of that kind are required, the case must be referred to the Security Council.

The first of these interpretations, then, means that the competence of the General Assembly is not limited beyond what follows from Article 12 and its lack of power to bind the members. The second interpretation means, on the other hand, that a third and very important limitation is introduced: the General Assembly is precluded from making proposals for measures for the maintenance of peace. The Assembly cannot, therefore, act as did the Security Council during the Korean crisis. Consequently, the Uniting for Peace resolution, which aims at organizing precisely such leadership in the Assembly, is illegal.

In my opinion it is possible to argue reasonably, in conformity with the usually accepted technique of interpretation, in support of each of the views mentioned. It cannot be maintained that either of the parties, in their attitudes to this question, has exceeded the bounds prescribed by good faith.

In support of the first interpretation—that is, the one the Western powers have followed in practice—it can be said that the Charter contains in Article 10 a general provision, formulated in very broad terms, concerning the powers of the General Assembly, which is undoubtedly so comprehensive that it also includes authority to make proposals for the maintenance of peace. The intention of Article 11 is to give various concrete specifications of this power, not to limit the general compass of Article 10. This last is expressly stated in Article 11(4). It is consequently impossible to deduce the alleged limitation from the words in Article 11(2). Article 14, too, contains comprehensive authority for the powers of the General Assembly. It is true that on this interpretation the disputed provision in Article 11(2) is unnecessary, in that it already follows from the lack of positive authority to do so that the General Assembly cannot impose on the members a duty to carry out measures for the maintenance of peace. The Charter is not, however, formulated with such logical stringency that any conclusion can safely be drawn from this. The provision stands as an example of what is usually called *ex tuto*, which means that one states something, for the sake of clarity and coherence, that is strictly speaking superfluous, since it can be deduced from other provisions. Thus, here the context makes it natural, after having spoken of the General Assembly's authority to discuss and make recommendations, to add that if the case requires further decisions, especially on *imposing obligations to take measures*, it must be referred to the Security Council.

In support of the other view, that defended by the Eastern bloc, it may be urged that the provision will otherwise be unnecessary and meaningless, and that it is a general principle of interpretation to read such a meaning into the text that no part of it comes to stand as superfluous. The weight of this argument is weakened in practice by the fact that the Eastern powers, before the dispute over the Uniting for Peace resolution, had themselves been party to proposing, in accordance with Article 41, a resolution in the General Assembly recommending the members to institute a boycott of Spain, just as they have also, since then, voted for the resolution of November 6, 1962, for the application of sanctions against the Union of South Africa (Chap. VII.2).

In the debate on the Uniting for Peace resolution, the Western powers further maintained that the measures contemplated under this resolution are not sanctions under Chapter VII of the Charter, but acts of collective self-defense under Article 51 of the Charter.

In later years, the interpretation of Article 11(2) has received renewed interest as a central point in the discussion of the legality of United Nations so-called peace-keeping operations, such as the United Nations Emergency Force (UNEF) operating between Suez and Gaza, the United Nations Operation in Congo (ONUC), and the United Nations Force in Cyprus (UNFICYP) (Chap. VII.3). The question of legality is a central point in the financial dispute that in January 1965 threatened to blow the Organization to pieces and made it necessary to adjourn the 19th session of the General Assembly until September 1, 1965. To sustain their refusal to participate in the expenses incurred by these and similar operations, the Eastern powers maintain that Article 11(2) precludes the General Assembly from making recommendations not only with regard to enforcement measures under Chapter VII of the Charter, but also with regard to any operation involving the use of armed forces. A brief account of the still unsettled financial dispute is given in Chapter VII (3).

3. *The neutrality of the Secretary-General*

The Secretariat, and first and foremost its head, the Secretary-General, is the organ of the United Nations that is the most concrete embodiment of the idea of the United Nations as something more than the sum of a series of conferences of states: an institution with continuous existence and an individuality determined by its constitution and the set of aims, principles, and ideals expressed in it. Of course, the other organs also represent the Organization and speak on its behalf. But these are mixed organs composed of individuals, each of whom is also bound by loyalty to his own state. The Secretary-General, on the other hand, is not bound by loyalty to any single state but only to the Organization, the United Nations. When functioning as Secretary-General, he must forget his home country and free himself from all ideological, cultural, or political ties that might, in view of his upbringing, tradition, and personal religion, incline him more to one party in a dispute than to the other. The debate on interests and ideas that takes place in the General Assembly and the other collective organs must also go on in the Secretary-General's mind and be exclusively directed by objective respect for the supranational principles and ideals of the United Nations.

This program raises problems. Is it psychologically possible to carry it out? Is it really possible for a man to achieve such neutrality? Is it politically possible—i.e., is it possible for the Secretary-General to live up to this standard without being crushed between two Great Powers, each of which will make conflicting demands on his objectivity or simply refuse to acknowledge the possibility of it? The importance of the question corresponds to the extent to which the Secretary-General is effectively entrusted with politically important executive tasks (Art. 98) or to which he himself takes political initiatives (Art. 99). As mentioned in earlier chapters (II.5 and V.6), developments have brought it about that in later years the Secretary-General has come to play a central part in the political activities of the United Nations. The question is therefore of topical importance. The late Secretary-General, Hammarskjöld, saw this very clearly and wrestled with the problem in deep seriousness, both as a matter of conscience and as a question of the functions of the Secretary-General according to the principles of the Charter. The office of Secretary-General is still in a state of crisis, although latent, and the problem of the neutrality of the Secretary-General may be expected to be raised again at any moment.

The Charter of the United Nations is based on the principle that measures for the maintenance of international peace and security assume agreement among the five permanent members of the Security Council. Considering the Secretary-General's possibility of making political decisions of great importance, it is natural that his election should require the agreement of the five Great Powers. Nobody can be elected who does not, at the time of the election, enjoy "parliamentary" confidence in this sense. On the other hand, the Charter says nothing about the continuance of this confidence being a condition for the Secretary-General's remaining in office. It is not possible to pass a resolution of "no confidence" that would cause the Secretary-General to go. But if he is seriously criticized by one of the Great Powers, the difficult question arises of how, in that case, he is to interpret his obligations to himself and to the Organization.

Trygve Lie, the first Secretary-General of the United Nations, drew on himself the wrath of the Soviet Union because of his attitude during the Korean crisis. When his period of office expired, in February 1951, the Soviet Union refused to vote for his re-election. It regarded the resolution extending his period of office as illegal and refused to recognize him as Secretary-General. The boycott was complete to the last detail. Correspondence was no longer addressed to the Secretary-General but to the Secretariat, invitations from Lie were not answered, just as, of course, he received no invitations from the Eastern states. Lie has described in his Memoirs the considerations that caused him to decide in the first place to continue, but to give up after two years and resign. This decision was primarily due to his feeling that the persistent opposition of the Russians made it impossible to perform the functions of his office with the authority required.

In the long run, his successor, Dag Hammarskjöld, had no better fortune. His prestige increased steadily for a number of years. Again and again he was given executive tasks that laid great responsibilities on his shoulders and that he succeeded in performing, not without criticism, of course, but without anyone doubting his loyalty and neutrality in relation to the various conflicts. A climax was reached in the summer of 1960, when he stood as leader of the action in the Congo, which had gone well up to then. As, however, the situation in the Congo gradually became more and more thorny, because of the internal struggle for power among the various pretenders and the outer effects of this struggle on outside interests, Hammarskjöld was exposed to violent criticism and gross personal attacks in the autumn of 1960 by the Soviet Union and its vassals. He was accused of having exceeded his powers and of having used them in a partial manner to favor the interests of the colonial powers. Khrushchev personally led these attacks during the general debate in 1960. He declared that the Secretary-General no longer enjoyed the confidence of the Soviet Union and demanded his resignation. The arrest and murder of Patrice Lumumba poured oil on the flames, and in a document dated February 14, 1961, the Soviet declared that they no longer recognized Hammarskjöld as Secretary-General and would no longer have any communication with him. In connection with these attacks on the Secretary-General personally, a proposal was made for a reform of his office, so that the Secretariat should be headed by a triumvirate of Secretaries-General representing the Western, the Eastern, and the neutral powers.

The accusation of partiality undoubtedly cut Hammarskjöld to the quick. Sprung as he was from a long line of civil servants in Sweden, brought up in the faith of the loyalty of the civil servant to the state he serves, but neutral in his relation to the changing governments of various political complexions, he must have felt Khrushchev's accusation in the very nerve of his professional faith and morality. He returned to the problem of neutrality again and again. In an address given at the University of Oxford, May 30, 1961, he took as his text a remark of Khrushchev, that there may very well be neutral countries but not neutral persons. His answer to this was that this may be true, if "neutrality" means complete absence of any political view. But such a neutrality in the Secretary-General would be contrary to the Charter of the United Nations. What is required of him is that in exercising his functions where a political decision is required, he shall be completely unaffected by national interests and the ideologies that divide men and be guided exclusively by the principles and objects of the Charter, juridical doctrines, and directives passed by the organs of the United Nations. Such a neutrality, Hammarskjöld claimed, is possible when the international civil servant keeps a watchful eye on himself and has the necessary will to maintain his integrity. In his introduction to the Secretary-General's annual report, 1960-61, he came back to this point:

While it may be said that no man is neutral in the sense that he is without opinions or ideals, it is just as true that, in spite of this, a neutral Secretariat is possible. Anyone of integrity, not subjected to undue pressure, can, regardless of his own views, readily act in an "exclusively international" spirit and can be guided in his actions on behalf of the Organization solely by its interests and principles, and by the instructions of its organs.

It seems to me as fascinating as it is illuminating, to study this clash between two personalities, which are the very incarnations of such different traditions of culture and ideas. To Khrushchev, Hammarskjöld's speech must, at best, have seemed naïve self-deception. As a Marxist, he must have assumed that in political questions there is no such thing as objectivity, since every human being is necessarily an exponent of a particular historical milieu, and that Hammarskjöld's doctrine of objectivity is nothing but an ideological superstructure, part of the doctrine whereby the capitalistic bureaucracy justifies itself and cements its rule. Hammarskjöld may very well believe in his own neutrality, but in a crucial situation, his ties with the Western, capitalist society will come out. It is not a question of personal honesty, but of sociological, historical necessity.

Which is right? Hammarskjöld was steeped in the ideals of objectivity that are the hallmark of the highly cultivated civil servant, especially in Scandinavia and England. For my part, I have no doubt that these ideals are a real force culminating in the professional ethics of the judiciary. But this objectivity or neutrality does not imply an attitude entirely free of preconceived ideas. It is possible only because these civil servants, and especially the judges, have a firm basis for their decisions in an inherited tradition of law and culture and the judicial system in which it has crystallized. Objectivity means, not a balancing of interests *in vacuo* but a balancing in the light of the standards and evaluations that, historically, have been accepted as the cultural inheritance of the community. Hammarskjöld did realize that this objectivity (neutrality) of the international civil servant must be rooted in a corresponding set of international community values, and here he pointed to the principles and ideas embodied in the Charter of the United Nations. But do these express realities comparable to the cultural tradition underlying the national communities of the West, or are they rather only the proclamation of ideals as desirable aims for the future? With all due respect for Hammarskjöld's unimpeachable integrity and for the tradition of which he was the very incarnation, I am inclined to agree with Khrushchev. In international relations, neutrality is inconceivable while the common ground in the cultural basis of the international community is as limited as it is at present.

The lesson to be drawn from the experiences of Lie and Hammarskjöld seems to me to be this: that a Secretary-General who tries to play the part of a political exponent of the principles of the United Nations must expect to meet with such violent criticism and opposition from one side or the other that he will fall victim to the cold war. The prominent role the Secretary-General has come to play since about 1955 is, as explained earlier, the natural consequence of the shifting of the political center of gravity from the Security Council to the General Assembly and the necessity for this large and cumbrous body to delegate extensive powers to the Secretary-General. There has been, as one might say, an experimental constitutional evolution that has revealed the difficulties involved in exaggerating the power and responsibility of the Secretary-General. In reality, a Secretary-General with great executive powers is a superior political entity whereby the Great Powers' right of veto is cancelled. The anger of the Soviet Union must be understood from this point of view, and the Soviet proposal that the office of the Secretary-General should be reorganized and his functions exercised by a triumvirate representing the Eastern, the Western, and the neutral states is framed in accordance with this view and is, in substance, a proposal to introduce the veto into the office of the Secretary-General also.

Problems have also arisen concerning the staff, since the member states find it difficult to live up to the principle that the members of the Secretariat are international civil servants, responsible only to the United Nations in the performance of their duties. It is the Secretary-General who appoints and dismisses the personnel, but in practice it is hardly possible for him to avoid reference to the applicant's home state in order to procure the necessary information. This consultation may easily be misused to put pressure on the Secretary-General to appoint only persons whom the state concerned considers nationally reliable. If this tendency were to prevail, the Secretariat would lose its international character and become a conglomerate of national factions.

Such a national check has been attempted by several states. The climax was reached in connection with the hysteria that seized the United States at the beginning of the 1950's, fed by the fear of Communism and whipped up by demagogues like Senator Joseph McCarthy. From the beginning, the American government had taken the opposite attitude: from fear of improperly interfering it had flatly refused to express any opinion on American candidates for posts in the Secretariat. Trygve Lie describes how, when he arrived in New York in 1946, he found boxes containing tens of thousands of American applications without any kind of sorting or comment by the American government.

Under the pressure of the feeling that had been whipped up, this attitude was reversed. The inquisition of the Senate subcommittee that McCarthy headed was directed also against the American citizens holding appointments in the Secretariat. There were about 1,800 of them. The fantastic stories about the Russians using the Secretariat as a bridgehead for spying proved to be baseless. Of the 1,800, the conflict centered on 18 men, who, appealing to the Fifth Amendment to the American Constitution, refused to answer questions by the Senate's permanent investigations subcommittee. On the principles on which the witch hunt was conducted, this appeal to a constitutional right (not to give evidence that might tend to incriminate oneself) should lead to instant dismissal. Trygve Lie was in doubt whether he ought to yield to American opinion. He gave the persons concerned provisional leave, and in the autumn of 1952 appointed three jurists as a committee on the problem. The main conclusion of this committee (which agreed with Trygve Lie's own opinion) was that refusal of the 18 to answer the questions put to them constituted a breach of duty under the Staff Regulations that justified dismissal. All 18 were thereupon dismissed—but this was far from being the end of the matter. Eleven of them were holders of permanent appointments, and they brought the question before the Administrative Tribunal that had been set up in 1949 to decide questions of appointment. The tribunal declared the dismissals illegal under the staff regulations and awarded compensation ($179,420) to those dismissed. Excited American opinion, however, would not accept this decision of the tribunal, which, it was maintained, the General Assembly must be allowed to reject as incorrect. The result was that the General Assembly resolved to ask the International Court for its opinion on whether the General Assembly had the right to refuse to give effect to the award of the tribunal. The reply of the Court, given July 13, 1954, was in the negative, and the General Assembly thereupon resolved to uphold the tribunal's decision.

In the meantime, the American government and the Secretary-General had arrived at a *modus vivendi*. The government formally acknowledged the sovereignty of the Secretary-General in personnel questions, while he, in reality, accepted the demands for investigations and the evidence resulting from these. Trygve Lie even went so far as to allow American police into the international territory of the Headquarters.

Today, it may look as though Trygve Lie did not adequately defend his staff's international status and independence from their national government. We, who remember how severe was the storm of mass hysteria, will be somewhat reserved in our judgment of events we did not ourselves experience. It is not improbable that, by not adopting an uncompromising attitude, Trygve Lie achieved the best result possible in the circumstances: to keep up appearances and to avoid intervention, which might have been catastrophic.

References

1. GREAT POWER PRIVILEGES AND THE MAJORITY PRINCIPLE
    Bailey, Sidney D., *The General Assembly of the United Nations* (1960), Chap. 2: Coalitions, Groups, and Blocs in the Assembly.
    Ball, M. Margaret, "Bloc Voting in the General Assembly," *International Organization* (1951), pp. 3-31.
    Claude, Inis L., Jr., *Swords into Plowshares* (2nd ed., 1961), Chap. 7 and 8.
    Goodrich, Leland M., *The United Nations* (1960), Chap VI: The Structure of Power and Influence.
    Moldaver, Arlette, "Repertoire of the Veto in the Security Council, 1946-1956," *International Organization* (1957), pp. 261-74.
    Schücking, Walther and Hans Wehberg, *Die Satzung des Völkerbundes* (1931), pp. 307 et seq.
2. GENERAL ASSEMBLY VERSUS SECURITY COUNCIL
    The International Court, in an advisory opinion of July 22, 1962, (*Certain Expenses of the United Nations*) has considered the question of the interpretation of Article 11(2) of the Charter (see pp. 163-65, 172, and 177), but it is not possible from this to draw precise conclusions on the question of interpretation discussed in this section of the chapter. For the question laid before the Court, it was sufficient to declare that the word "action" in Article 11(2) refers to enforcement measures under Chapter VII, and that the actions carried out by the UN Emergency Forces do not have that character. The Court therefore did not need to decide whether the General Assembly can lawfully *recommend* the taking of measures under Chapter VII.
3. THE NEUTRALITY OF THE SECRETARY-GENERAL
    Hammarskjöld, Dag, "Two Differing Concepts of United Nations Assayed," *International Organization* (1961), pp. 549-63.

———— "The International Civil Service" (address at Oxford University, May 30, 1961), *Current Notes on International Affairs,* Vol. 32, No. 6 (June 1961), pp. 39-51.

Jackson, Elmore, "The Developing Role of the Secretary-General," *International Organization* (1957), pp. 431-45.

Lie, Trygve, *In the Cause for Peace* (1954).

VII ❀

SETTLEMENT
OF DISPUTES
AND MAINTENANCE OF PEACE

T HE political objective of the United Nations is the maintenance of peace and security among the states. If matters have gone so far that there is an open breach of the peace, or a situation threatening to develop into one, the task of the Organization is to take effective measures to restore or to ensure peace. But prevention is better than cure. The direct cause of war is always a dispute between states—even though, fortunately, not all disputes lead to war. The settlement function is therefore connected with the function of maintaining peace. The two functions are closely connected, and the rules concerning them in Chapters VI and VII of the Charter must be viewed together.

Under Article 24 it is the Security Council that has the primary responsibility for the maintenance of international peace and security. As explained previously (especially in Chapter VI), the Charter also gives the General Assembly subsidiary authority in this matter, and the disunity of the Great Powers, which has hindered the Security Council in fulfilling its responsibility, has caused the General Assembly to exercise political functions to an extent nobody had expected when the Charter was being drafted. In the following discussion, when I consistently, for the sake of simplicity, speak of the Security Council's authority to settle disputes, the reader is asked to remember that the same applies to the General Assembly, in so far as that body is competent to deal with the case under the reservation in Article 12 of the Charter (While the Security Council is exercising in respect of any dispute or situation its functions under the Charter, the General Assembly cannot make recommendations concerning that dispute or situation except at the request of the Security Council.) and with the proviso that the General Assembly has no authority to instruct the members to take measures for the maintenance of peace, but can at most make recommendations, not binding on anyone, on the case.

The rules in Chapters VI and VII concerning intervention by the Organization must be seen in connection with the principle proclaimed in Article 2, by which the members shall refrain from the use of force and threats thereof in international relations, and, similarly, with the traditional system of procedures and institutions for the settlement of disputes. It is not at all the intention of the Charter that these should be rendered superfluous by the intervention of the United Nations. On the contrary, the normal sequence is that the states shall first try to settle their differences themselves by the traditional methods. So far, the United Nations comes in only to the extent that, by the establishment of the International Court, the Organization has created yet another institution which the states, if they so choose, can use in their efforts to resolve conflicts. Only when the parties give up and acknowledge that they cannot agree on a solution themselves does the mission of the United Nations begin. It begins at the point where the parties gave up, in that the special "parliamentary diplomacy" before the organs of the United Nations takes over instead of the traditional diplomacy directly between the parties. It may be said that the case is removed from the "private" to the "public" sphere. A dispute that the parties cannot settle is—when its continuance can be taken to endanger international peace and security—no longer a case that concerns only the parties in conflict, but a case that concerns the whole world. The United Nations has both the right and the duty to intervene for the purpose of settling the dispute, and every member state has the right of action—i.e., to draw the attention of the Security Council (the General Assembly) to the dispute.

In this chapter, the United Nations' functions for the settlement of disputes and for the maintenance of peace will be discussed on the basis of the provisions of the Charter as these have been understood in practice. Apart from the little-used power of the Security Council to dictate enforcement measures for the maintenance of peace, what goes on in the Security Council or the General Assembly has the character of formalized politico-diplomatic activity that appears in the form of resolutions, the effectiveness of which depends entirely upon the moral and political authority behind them. The Articles of Chapters VI and VII give the detailed rules for this activity. It is understandable that neither the Security Council nor the General Assembly has shown any tendency to clarify the legal authority for the steps they take (as would be natural for a court), but have been more interested in their political appropriateness and have regarded the juridical arguments as weapons in the political struggle for or against a proposed resolution. Only in exceptional cases are existing resolutions decided on their legal bases or on disputed questions of interpretation. Any account of this matter must naturally conform to this fact. There is no point in discussing distinctions and subtle interpretations that are ignored in practice.

It is well known that nothing came of the Charter's plan for the establishment of a United Nations army composed of national contingents put at the disposal of the Security Council for the maintenance of peace and security. Yet the United Nations has several times made actual use of armed forces. These Emergency Forces will be discussed in more detail, and it will be shown that their task is not to apply measures of enforcement to any state and that they cannot therefore be seen as the germ of the missing United Nations army.

The lack of effective means of compulsion and of unity among the Great Powers has prevented the United Nations from performing its most important task, that of guaranteeing the lesser states against attack. The last section of this chapter will describe how the states, recognizing this, have created, outside the United Nations, a complicated set of regional defense arrangements for their own security.

1. Settlement of disputes

The provisions of the Charter dealing with this subject can be understood only when their relation to the traditional procedures and institutions of international law for this purpose are made clear. In the course of time, a number of different methods have been developed that states may utilize for the settlement of a dispute. It is customary to distinguish between the procedures aiming at a legal decision, therefore carried out by jurists and normally binding on the parties, and procedures aiming at a solution politically acceptable by both parties, therefore undertaken by persons with political training and insight, and normally not binding on the parties.

To the first group, the legal procedures, belong *arbitration* (undertaken by an arbitration tribunal especially appointed for the particular case, and composed of arbitrators chosen by the parties) and *adjudication* (pronounced by a permanently organized court). To the second group belong *diplomatic negotiation* between the parties, *mediation* (undertaken by a third state, and working with the authority represented by the mediating state), *conciliation* (undertaken by a conciliation commission), and *inquiry* (undertaken by a commission of inquiry). There are political methods side by side with the legal ones because many interstate disputes are by their very nature unsuitable for submission to a court (Chap. V.5).

Apart from the obvious rule that a state is bound to seek a solution by negotiation before resorting to force, it is true of all these procedures, both the legal and the political, that they are voluntary in the sense that they can never be undertaken in a dispute unless both parties have agreed thereto. But one state may agree beforehand with other states that certain types of dispute arising in the future shall be submitted to a particular settlement procedure. In that case, it is voluntary in the above sense, but compulsory or obligatory in respect to a dispute that falls within the scope of the agreement.

Spread all over the world today is an extremely wide network of agreements, some bilateral, some multilateral, whereby states have undertaken the obligation to submit certain types of dispute to settlement procedures of one kind or another. The first principle for understanding the settlement apparatus of the United Nations states that the Charter *assumes the existence of these agreements* and the institutions established in connection with them (courts, arbitration arrangements, standing commissions of conciliation, and so on), but *does not in any way increase the duty of the states to seek to settle disputes by any particular procedure.* Article 2 proclaims the general duty of members to settle their disputes peacefully, and Article 33 repeats this, listing the usual settlement procedures as possible means of doing so. But the members are quite free to choose which method they will use. If the parties cannot agree on this, and if, outside the Charter, there is no previous agreement on the point, neither of the parties has any obligation to submit the case to any form of settlement—beyond the obvious minimum that a demand for usual diplomatic negotiations must not be rejected. Article 37 might seem to lay an obligation on the parties, when they cannot settle a dispute themselves, to bring it before the Security Council. There is no question, however, of anything but a moral exhortation. If the parties agree, they can always say that they have not yet given up hope of finding a solution themselves.

The essence of the Charter, the point where it definitely breaks with the rules of traditional international law, is that it establishes the principle that *every dispute* (the continuance of which is likely to endanger the maintenance of international peace and security) *is a public matter,* so that whether the parties wish it or not, they must accept the fact that the dispute may be debated in the Security Council (General Assembly), if that organ considers such debate to be in the interests of peace. The parties are not obliged to seek the assistance of the Organization, but they are obliged to put up with its intervention. Under ordinary international law, it is for the parties themselves to decide if they will accept the offer of other states to help in settling the conflict, especially in the form of mediation. It is laid down in the Hague Conventions that an offer to mediate must never be taken as an unfriendly act, but also that the parties to a dispute are not obliged to accept such an offer. They can always say that the dispute is a matter that concerns only them. The Charter, on the other hand, considers that every dispute (the continuance of which is likely to endanger the maintenance of international peace and security) is a matter that concerns all states, since the maintenance of peace is a matter that concerns the whole world. This implies (1) that any member state and either of the parties in dispute, whether it is a member or not, can bring the matter before the Security Council or the General Assembly, and (2) that either of these organs can take up the case if it deems this expedient.

I have here put the condition—that the continuance of the dispute is likely to endanger the maintenance of peace and security—in parentheses, because it does not really limit the competence of the United Nations. The condition is entirely a question of judgment and must be considered as met by the very fact that the world organization finds it appropriate to spend time and energy on the case. Practice is in accordance with this: there is normally no formal discussion and declaration on the question of whether a dispute brought before the organ fulfills the condition of endangering the peace.

The third principle for the work of the United Nations in settling disputes is that it *does not intend to supplant or reduce the efforts of the parties to settle the dispute by traditional methods.* It is not intended, of course, that every diplomatic entanglement should be automatically transferred to the United Nations. There is no clearly defined limit, beyond which a case is "ripe" for the forum of the United Nations, but Chapter VI clearly assumes that it is desirable that the parties shall, as far as possible, reach agreement themselves, and that the task of the Organization is mainly limited to persuading them to do so, or to advising them to follow this or that procedure for achieving a peaceful solution.

Accordingly, it is customary for a state bringing its own case before the Organization to attach an account of its efforts to achieve an understanding with the other side. The debate on the question of whether or not to put the case on the agenda often turns on the question of whether the parties have exhausted the possibilities of negotiation. And, in many cases, the result of the Council's deliberations is an exhortation to the parties to resume or to continue their negotiations.

Finally, the efforts to settle disputes that can be made by the United Nations are in their nature similar to all other kinds of diplomatic activity. Neither the Security Council nor the General Assembly has authority to decide a dispute. Resolutions can never do more than remind, recommend, advise, request. In brief, the United Nations has the right under the Charter to *exercise mediation* (which thus cannot be rejected), *but not to act as a (political) tribunal of arbitration.*

It may seem paradoxical that, when peace has been broken, or is threatened, the Organization has been granted extensive authority to impose on the members the obligation to take measures, even military ones, for the maintenance of peace, while similar authority is denied it in dealing with a dispute that may be a step toward war. It may seem strange that the United Nations is thus precluded from effective intervention before the crisis has become acute. The explanation is to be found in the inner connection between Chapter VI and Chapter VII. The recommendations that can be made under Chapter VI derive special weight and significance from the fact that the party that ignores them runs the risk that its refusal may create a tense situation which will be regarded as a threat to peace and arouse measures under Chapter VII directed against him as the recalcitrant party.

Within the framework of these principles, Chapter VI gives in detail the steps that can be taken by the Security Council. They include investigation, appeal in general terms to the parties to settle their dispute peacefully, recommendation of particular procedures or methods that the parties should follow in their search for a solution, and recommendation of conditions for the settlement of the actual dispute.

In spite of the fact that the expressions used in this chapter may give rise to doubt, in practice they have been taken to mean that the Security Council, using its own judgment of what is politically appropriate, may at any stage of a dispute resolve to take any of these steps. Taking Article 37(2) in connection with 37(1) and contrary to 36(1), one might be tempted by a purely linguistic interpretation to conclude that the power of the Council to recommend conditions for the settlement of the dispute must be conditional on the parties themselves having brought the case before the Council. It must, however, be considered unreasonable that one of the parties, by refusing to carry out its obligations under Article 37(1), should be able to deprive the Council of its competence under Article 37(2). If this is accepted, there seems to be no reason for making any distinction between a case submitted by one of the parties and one brought before the Council by a third state. In practice, no importance has been attached to the question of who submitted the case. A case may be brought before the Security Council in many ways: by the parties themselves or by one of the parties, by any member state, by the General Assembly, by the Secretary-General, or on the Council's own initiative, without this having any influence on the scope of the Council's competence or the method of dealing with it.

Even though, in accordance with the principle of publicity, any member of the United Nations is entitled by Article 35 to draw the attention of the Security Council or the General Assembly to the dispute, this does not mean that such a member can demand that the case be put on the agenda. The Council or the General Assembly will itself decide whether or not to take up a case. The circumstance that neither of the parties to the dispute has applied to the Organization, perhaps even that they agree in *not* desiring its interference, may be a factor militating against forcing the case forward in spite of this as being politically unwise. It is also a fact that the great majority of the questions of conflict dealt with in the United Nations have been laid before the Organization by one of the parties to the dispute.

While the states have shown great reluctance to submit their juridical differences to the International Court, they have on the whole been very willing to make use of the Organization's mediatory powers in their political disputes. In some cases, it may well be thought that this willingness has been excessive, in so far as there has seemed to be a tendency to give up and run to the United Nations before it could reasonably be claimed that the parties had done everything they could to arrive at a solution themselves. On the other hand, there are also conflicts, and very serious conflicts, that neither of the parties concerned has wanted discussed in the United Nations, and to which no other state has found cause to draw the Organization's attention. This applies, for example, to the Berlin crisis (apart from the Russian attempt to blockade the city in 1948) and other burning questions concerning the two Germanies. In approaching the most delicate of the questions at issue between the East and the West, it seems to be a well-founded view that nothing is to be gained by appealing to public opinion in the world organization. It is very likely that a public discussion will only help to build up the war of propaganda and accentuate ideological differences, and that there is a better chance of finding a solution if the parties can agree to meet quietly around a table and negotiate.

In the previous pages, I have consistently spoken of "disputes" between states. The rules in Chapter VI also apply to what are called "situations" when they are of such a nature that their continuance is likely to endanger international peace and security. A situation is distinguished from a dispute by the fact that clearly formulated questions at issue between the parties have not (as yet) crystallized, but no clear line can be drawn between the two. When the Spanish question was discussed in the Security Council in 1946, Franco's dictatorial and fascist regime was described as a "situation" containing a threat to peace. The same was the case when the Russian blockade of Berlin in 1948 was brought before the Security Council. Although the Charter distinguishes between "disputes" and "situations" and attaches importance to the distinction in various ways, no particular importance has been attached to it in practice. There appears to be a tendency, when a state brings a case before the United Nations, to prefer the more moderate and neutral expression "situation."

Both the General Assembly and the Security Council have often, either for the preparation or the implementation of a decision, resorted to the expedient of appointing a committee or creating a special subsidiary organ. This has especially been the case with commissions to investigate conditions on the spot, to mediate between the parties, or to see that truce conditions are observed. In some cases, such commissions have consisted of member states (representatives of these), in other cases of persons chosen in their personal capacity. An important task is sometimes entrusted to a single person; thus Count Folke Bernadotte (and after his death, Dr. Ralph Bunche) was given the task of mediating between Israel and the Arab states, in order to promote a peaceful arrangement of the situation in Palestine.

2. Maintenance of peace

An unsettled dispute need not lead to war. Many disputes are preserved as old enmities and form a permanent element in the pattern of the foreign policy of the various states. It is by no means impossible, even, that one of the parties (perhaps both) does not really want a settlement, since it would thereby lose a card that can be played in its home politics. The idea of a foreign enemy and his threatening plots is often useful to stimulate national unity and to divert the attention of the people from the government's unfortunate mistakes and fiascoes in internal politics.

If, however, a dispute should lead or threaten to lead to open conflict between two or more states—whether the parties call their actions "war" or use a term that sounds better—the United Nations is presented with the new task of maintaining or restoring international peace and security. This function differs from that of settlement, but is often performed side by side with it. Efforts are made to maintain peace and to settle the conflict simultaneously.

The rules for the action of the United Nations to maintain peace are to be found in Chapter VII of the Charter. They are modeled on the corresponding rules in the Covenant of the League of Nations, but differ considerably from these in their basic principles. In the first place, while the Covenant of the League of Nations was based on the idea of collective security, and gave the Council only a modest advisory authority for the co-ordination of the members' military operations, the Charter of the United Nations returns to the older pattern known as the concert and hegemony of the Great Powers. According to Article 16 of the Covenant of the League of Nations, if any member state resorts to war in disregard of the provisions of the Covenant, every other member of the Leauge should automatically institute an economic boycott of the aggressor. Whether or not the crucial conditions for this were present and which of the parties was guilty of breaking the peace were left to the judgment of the individual members. The role of the Council was limited to making recommendations on the military force the members should contribute to the joint military actions for the protection of the state attacked. It was soon evident that such a system could not work in practice, and, in the years that followed, efforts were concentrated on improving it by supplementary arrangements and agreements.

Taught by experience, the framers of the United Nations Charter gave up the attractive but illusory idea of the democratic equality of all members in the maintenance of peace, and realistically acknowledged that capacity (power), responsibility, and authority ought to go together. Responsibility without power is almost as unfortunate as power without responsibility. In reality, it is only the Great Powers that have the necessary power should it be necessary to set in motion measures of enforcement in case of a breach of the peace, and it is also they who must bear the responsibility for this and have the authority to take decisions binding on the other members. Accordingly, the Charter allots the authority to decide on such matters to the Security Council, and, in view of the right of veto, this means the five concurring permanent members of the Council. Thus, in institutional forms, the pattern known as the Concert of Europe has returned.

Another difference is bound up with this. According to the philosophy of collective security that inspired the Covenant of the League of Nations, aggression is an international crime, and the steps that could be taken by the League were sanctions—that is, a legal consequence similar to punishment directed against the party that has been found guilty. These collective steps assume, therefore, in principle a legal decision on the question of who, in a given case, is guilty. The Charter of the United Nations has abandoned the idea of a breach of the law and sanctions. Maintenance of peace is seen from the point of view of effectiveness. The crucial point is effective intervention so that fighting is stopped, and the question of right and guilt can be discussed afterwards. This is why the Charter, in describing the circumstances that release the reaction provided for in Chapter VII, speaks not only of an act of aggression but also of a breach of the peace. While the first of these expressions assumes the ascription of guilt, the second is neutral in this respect. This is why the Charter in Article 1 confines the requirement of respect for justice and international law to the settlement function, unlike the function of maintaining peace.

To illustrate this point, it is often said that the idea in the Charter is that the Security Council shall act like the police, and not like the law courts. The duty of the police is to maintain peace and order. Should disturbances and brawls arise, the task of the police is to intervene, separate the combatants, and bring the disturbance to an end, without first investigating and deciding who was guilty of an attack and who was only exercising his legal right of self-defense. These questions must fall to a law court to decide. During a police action, blows and arrests may be shared by both the innocent and the guilty. The police do not join in the fight on the side of those who are in the right but simply to separate the combatants and restore peace and order.

If anyone should think that it is possible for the Security Council in a given case to act on the same neutral principles of order as the police, we have an example of how dangerous it can be to translate conceptions from the life of the civil community to the sphere of international relations. It is, perhaps, conceivable that economic boycott, embargo on weapons, and similar measures might be undertaken against the parties to the conflict without discrimination. But when it comes to military operations, a similar neutral attitude is impracticable for both military and psychological reasons. With regard to the first, it is difficult to imagine how the United Nations troops could force their way into the front between the combatants and fire at both sides. As to the second, it is obvious that men cannot be sent into action with orders to fire against both sides without regard to the question of right and wrong, friend or foe. Try, for example, to imagine a Korean action in this style. To go to war is to stake your life on a cause. It is not possible to require such a stake for an abstract principle of order, while the political judgment of the rights, demands, and interests of the combatants is postponed till the fighting is over. My conclusion is that the divergence from the League of Nations system on this point is more of a theoretical than a practical nature. Should it ever come to collective military operations for the maintenance of peace, these will undoubtedly, like the Korean action, have the character of sanctions directed against the party branded as guilty of aggression.

It is clear that a security system that, like that of the Charter, is founded on the concert of the Great Powers, has a limited scope from the start. It has given up beforehand every attempt to apply the principle of collective security against a Great Power. This is formally excluded by the veto rule. This implies further that sanctions against a small state that one of the Great Powers wishes to protect, whether a vassal state or an ally in the cold war, are also excluded. In brief, as soon as the Great Powers disagree, as soon as their interests in the field of high politics clash, the apparatus for the maintenance of peace is out of order. And, it may be added, if the Great Powers agree, it should hardly be necessary to set up so great an apparatus to maintain peace. To sum up: when the Great Powers disagree, the system is useless; when they agree, it is superfluous.

This view, even though sharply formulated, is on the whole correct. But it would not be correct, on this basis, to blame the architects of the United Nations for having equipped the Organization with so unsatisfactory a sanctions apparatus, and particularly to criticize the unanimity rule (the veto rule) that enables a permanent member of the Security Council to protect itself and its friends against just sanctions. Nor do I think it justifiable to scorn the fathers of the Charter for naïvely assuming that the collaboration in unity (at any rate, approximate unity) achieved in war should be capable of being continued in the interests of peace. In my opinion, the Charter is based on the realities of political life. To prescribe sanctions against a Great Power, e.g. the Soviet Union, is not to maintain peace but to start a world war. The Charter was not based on any assumption of how politics would develop after the war. The assumption it *is* based on is that it is possible to organize peace only when the Great Powers, in unity, lead the way. The rules are based on this realistic principle, acknowledging that this is the only possible basis and leaving it to the future to show if this necessary assumption can be realized or not. The point of view of the Charter is simply this, that there is no better alternative. It must be accepted, not because of an uncritical belief that the Great Powers will certainly agree, but in resigned acceptance of the fact that this the only possibility, and in the hope that there may be a chance of realizing it.

At the San Francisco Conference it was agreed that the Security Council should be empowered to give orders to the members to take part not only in economic boycott but also in military action against the state that broke the peace (see Articles 25 and 42). The idea was that military forces composed of contingents from the member states should be placed at the disposal of the Security Council. During the previous American discussions, this point had raised constitutional doubts. It was foreseen that American military forces might have to go into action in pursuance of a resolution in the Security Council. Even though the American representative must necessarily have voted for the resolution, this would be in conflict with the American constitution, according to which only Congress has the power to declare war. To avoid these difficulties, the American representatives at Dumbarton Oaks proposed that after the Charter had been established, special agreements should be concluded between the Security Council and every single member on the extent to which the state concerned would undertake to put armed forces at the disposal of the Organization or give other forms of assistance, including the right of the passage of troops across its territory. Such an arrangement, in connection with an American federal law authorizing the President to make such an agreement, would, it was thought, settle the doubts expressed in certain circles. This proposal met with general agreement at Dumbarton Oaks and also at San Francisco. Apart from the special American considerations, it was certainly a relief to be excused from the burden of working out in the Charter itself detailed rules for the extent of the members' obligations.

The result was Article 43, which refers the military obligations of the members to the conclusion of special agreements, with the consequence that no specific claim can be made of any state until such an agreement has been concluded with it. Thus a central point concerning the functions of the Organization, the establishment of military forces, was deliberately left blank, and a check was drawn on the future in that this point was to be dealt with by later agreements. I find it hard to accept that anyone seriously believed in the possibility of achieving agreement on these extremely delicate questions later on, without the pressure of the need to get the Charter accepted. It seems to me more likely that it was decided to postpone the problem, knowing full well that the United Nations military apparatus would never be more than a dream.

Immediately after the Security Council had assembled for its first session, in February 1946, it ordered the General Staff Committee (which consists of the Chiefs of Staff of the Great Powers or their representatives) to work out directives for the agreements on the extent and character of the military assistance envisaged in Article 43. After having negotiated for over a year, the Committee was compelled to report that it had proved impossible to agree on various important points. Certain general principles had been agreed on, such as that the forces should be adequate in size and readiness to permit the Security Council to take immediate action, and that they must be supplied primarily by the Great Powers. It was also agreed that the forces to be held in readiness for the United Nations should remain under national command, but that in case of action they should be put under a Commander-in-Chief appointed by the Security Council.

On the other hand, it had proved impossible to achieve agreement on the size and distribution of these forces. While the Soviet Union wanted them to be small and to be distributed equally among the Great Powers, the United States wanted them to be considerably larger, and the distribution to be proportional to the capacities of the various countries in regard to the various arms. Among the undecided questions were: where the forces should be stationed when not in action, and whether the United Nations should have bases in the territories of the members. Although the most marked disagreement was between the Soviet Union and the other members of the Committee, there was also disagreement among the Western powers. In the course of 1947, relations between East and West deteriorated, and the chances of achieving agreement faded accordingly. In the summer of 1948, negotiations ceased and have not been resumed since.

This failure means that the United Nations has never been equipped with the military apparatus planned for the maintenance of peace. There is no reason to take too seriously, however, the fact that the agreements envisaged in Article 43 have never been made, since, even if they had been made, the apparatus would have been of no importance as long as the schism between East and West existed.

The consequence is that as long as this is the case, it is idle to recommend that any nation base its security on the United Nations. The most that a state in distress can expect is the sympathy of public opinion, which, for example, was so generously given to Hungary in 1956. If a state feels that it is not able to ensure its defense with its own forces, it must seek strength by collaboration with other states in defensive alliances. As is well known, the states have sought security, to a great extent, in a series of regional arrangements grouped around the two dominant powers, the United States and the Soviet Union. The most important of these is the North Atlantic Treaty Organization (NATO), comprising the United States and Canada and 13 European states.

Even though under present conditions Chapter VII is of no practical importance, it is necessary to give a brief account of the provisions of the chapter on the organization of the maintenance of peace.

The basic condition for applying the provisions of the chapter is that there should exist an acute conflict or situation: a threat to the peace, a breach of the peace, or an act of aggression. A reading of Article 39 must give the impression that it is the duty of the Security Council to declare formally whether this condition is met or not; or that at any rate such a positive declaration is a necessary condition for all further steps taken under this chapter. In practice, however, the Council has not felt itself bound by this. Only rarely has the Council, as in the Palestine and Korea cases, expressly declared that there existed a threat to the peace or a breach of the peace (aggression), though this has not prevented resolutions being proposed, and passed, on measures that must be understood as being taken in accordance with the rules of Chapter VII. The explanation is, I submit, that it is often undiplomatic to begin by gripping the nettle so firmly. Negotiations are facilitated by leaving open, for the moment, the question of whether the situation is being dealt with in accordance with Chapter VI or Chapter VII.

The steps that can be taken under Chapter VII are (1) making recommendations, (2) branding the aggressor, (3) prescribing provisional measures, (4) instituting an economic and diplomatic boycott, and (5) instituting military sanctions.

The fact that the situation has become acute, as assumed in Chapter VII, does not, of course, signify that the Council cannot, while maintaining peace, also seek to settle the conflict by means of the methods dealt with in Chapter VI. This is quite natural, especially when there is still only a threat to the peace, and not an open breach. This is what Article 39 means when it says that the Council can "make recommendations."

That one of the parties should be branded as the aggressor is not a necessary condition for applying Chapter VII. But as previously stated, it is hardly conceivable that military measures could be taken without their being given the character of sanctions directed against the party found guilty of aggression.

In order to prevent an aggravation of the situation, the Security Council may, under Article 40, call upon the parties concerned to comply with such provisional measures as it deems necessary or desirable, as for example the immediate cessation of hostilities, withdrawal of troops behind a certain demarcation line, establishment of international control over certain areas. Measures of this kind have been prescribed in a large number of cases, sometimes without any formal claim to be acting under the authority of Article 40. In this article, it is further laid down that such measures shall be without prejudice to the rights, claims, or position of the parties concerned, but that the Security Council shall duly take account of failure to comply with such provisional measures. The intention is that these provisional measures shall aim only at maintaining or restoring peace, and not at deciding the conflict. If, for example, one party is enjoined to evacuate a certain territory, this has no reference to the question of whether this party has a justified claim to the possession of this territory. The parties can therefore obey the Council's injunctions without any risk of compromising the final decision, and neglect to do so is a factor militating in favor of taking more extensive steps, in accordance with Chapter VII, against the recalcitrant party. Considering the very poor guarantee the United Nations can give that a justified claim will be enforced, it is not surprising that the parties involved often have shown extreme reluctance to evacuate positions once won.

Under Article 41, the Security Council may decide on a boycott, and may enjoin the members to take measures for this purpose. These may include complete or partial interruption of economic relations and of rail, sea, air, postal, telegraphic, radio, and other means of communication, and the severance of diplomatic relations. There is no doubt that such a boycott, if consistently and universally carried out, would be an extremely powerful weapon, which would bring even a power of considerable size to its knees. On the other hand, it is extremely difficult to organize and carry out so comprehensive a boycott. An illuminating example of this is the attempt made in 1935 to counter Italy's attack on Ethiopia by economic sanctions. The Council branded Italy as an aggressor and recommended that the Assembly should assist the members to organize economic sanctions against Italy. Nearly all the members of the League of Nations agreed. Only a few, some of Italy's neighbors (Albania, Austria, and Hungary) felt it wiser to hold aloof, and Switzerland pleaded its traditional neutrality. That the action failed in spite of this (Italy had carried through its conquest of Ethiopia by May 1936.) was owing to the fact that the blockade was only half-hearted, and more of a demonstration than a serious effort to subdue Italy. The blockade did not cover oil, which was of vital importance to Italy, nor was the Suez Canal closed. The explanation must be sought in the conflicting political and commercial interests involved. England, especially, was anxious about breaking off friendly relations with Mussolini, in whom she saw an ally against the rising power of Hitler in Germany. The United States stood outside the League. An embargo on oil would involve the risk that the market would go to American companies, and an enforcement of the blockade would involve the risk of a collision with the United States.

In 1946, it was proposed in the Security Council of the United Nations that the members should be enjoined to break off diplomatic relations with Spain as a sanction against Franco's fascist dictatorship. The proposal failed. After the matter had been referred to the General Assembly, this body resolved to recommend members to recall their ambassadors and ministers from Madrid. The recommendation was followed by nearly all the members. It was withdrawn in 1950.

On November 6, 1962, the General Assembly passed a resolution on the apartheid policy of the Union of South Africa. After stating that a continuation of this policy was a serious threat to international peace and security, the resolution requested the members to break off diplomatic relations with the Union, and to set in motion a comprehensive boycott by breaking off all trade and traffic with the Union by sea and by air. It was thus a clear call for sanctions under Chapter VII of the Charter. The boycott was doomed to fail from the start, because the resolution was forced through by the Afro-Asian members and the Eastern bloc in spite of the opposition of the states whose collaboration was a necessary condition for its success (67-16-23). Many of the states that were unable to vote for the resolution, including Denmark, explained that their attitude was not the expression of unwillingness to condemn apartheid, but of doubt of the use of recommending sanctions when it was known that the states most involved would not take part. Adopting a policy foredoomed to failure can only damage the prestige of the United Nations.

Measures of economic boycott suffer from the drawback that they may also involve consequences for states other than the one they are directed against. It is therefore provided in the Charter that any state, whether a member of the United Nations or not, which finds itself confronted with special economic problems arising from the carrying out of such measures, shall have the right to consult the Security Council with regard to a solution of those problems, which must mean that the innocent state that suffers damage may receive some form of compensation.

If the Security Council considers that economic measures would be or have proved to be inadequate, it may decide to use military forces to maintain or restore peace. The steps that can be taken include demonstrations, blockade, and other operations by air, sea, or land forces of members of the United Nations.

It is worth noting that the Charter of the United Nations does not envisage the establishment of an international army, i.e. an army in which the members owe obedience and loyalty only to the Organization, as with the members of the Secretariat. Military sanctions are decided on and planned by the Organization, but they are carried out by the members by means of their national troops, who remain under national command and discipline (see Art. 45, 47, 48, and 49).

Co-ordination of the military forces of the various members for carrying out a collective action for the maintenance of peace naturally requires a certain central control. It is therefore provided that the Security Council shall make plans for the use of armed force in a collective action. This is done with the help of the General Staff Committee, consisting of the Chiefs of Staff of the permanent members or their representatives. This exclusively Great Power committee is to be responsible for the strategic direction of the armed forces placed at the disposal of the Security Council. Questions relating to the command of such forces, says Article 47(3), shall be worked out subsequently. During the discussions of the General Staff Committee in 1946, it was agreed that in case of action, these troop contingents should be put under a common Commander-in-Chief. This does not affect the national character of the troops: the orders of the Commander-in-Chief do not become effective until they have passed the national command; the troops owe obedience only to officers of their own nation and are responsible only to their national authorities.

3. The United Nations Emergency Forces

Although the military apparatus of the Charter has never been realized, there are at present a not inconsiderable number of armed men under the command of the United Nations. Along the demarcation line of the truce between Israel and Egypt stands the United Nations Emergency Force (UNEF), over 5,000 strong, and in the Congo there was, until recently, the United Nations Force in the Congo

(ONUC), once 20,000 strong. It would be a misunderstanding, however, to see in these forces the modest beginning of the formation of the military forces envisaged in the Charter as standing at the disposal of the Security Council for the maintenance of peace. In order to prevent this misunderstanding, it is worth looking more closely at the origin, objective, and nature of these forces.

As early as 1948, during the Palestine crisis, the Secretary-General, Trygve Lie, suggested that a corps of 5,000 to 10,000 men should be established for the maintenance of the authority of the United Nations in Palestine. When the UN mediator, Count Bernadotte, was assassinated in Jerusalem, Lie made a proposal to this effect at the 3rd General Assembly. The proposal met with a cool reception, and the result was the establishment of the United Nations Field Service, which is not a military force but a section of the Secretariat specially trained in transport, guard, and other duties in areas where observers, conciliation commissions, and similar United Nations organs are working.

It was disturbances in the same political field of tension that, a few years later, gave the impetus to the establishment of UNEF. During the Suez crisis, in October and November 1956, Egypt was attacked by land by Israeli troops, and from the sea by combined Franco-British squadrons. This action, however, came to nothing, mainly because the United States and the Soviet Union, though moved by different motives, agreed that it should not be allowed to continue. The establishment of the United Nations Emergency Force was an improvisation of genius. Its immediate effect was as a face-saving arrangement that allowed France and the United Kingdom to back out of their unsuccessful venture; in the long term, it proved to be a useful arrangement for the maintenance of peace in the area, since it permitted Egypt to refrain, with honor, from the oft-proclaimed war to destroy Israel.

It was the Canadian delegate, Lester Pearson, who proposed, at an evening meeting of the General Assembly on November 3, 1956, a resolution requesting the Secretary-General to submit to it within 48 hours a plan for the setting up, with the consent of the nations concerned, of an international United Nations force to ensure and supervise the cessation of hostilities in accordance with the Assembly's resolution of November 2. The resolution was passed in the early morning of November 4, and the very same day the Secretary-

General presented his first report, which was followed by a second and final report on November 6. These two reports, approved by resolutions of the General Assembly on November 5 and 7 respectively, laid down the principles for the composition, tasks, command, etc. of the force. These plans were carried out with astonishing speed and efficiency. An agreement was arrived at with Egypt, and the first troop transports were able to sail on November 15; before Christmas the withdrawal of Anglo-French troops was completed. Israel was at first unresponsive, but in March 1957 agreed to withdraw its troops from the Gaza and Sharm el-Sheikh areas. On the other hand, Israel still refuses UNEF units access to its territory. The United Nations Emergency Force has manned the 170 mile-long demarcation line to this very day.

On the basis of the resolutions of the General Assembly, the reports of the Secretary-General, the agreement with Egypt, and the directives for the Force issued by the Secretary-General as authorized, it can be stated incontrovertibly that in all essential respects the Emergency Forces are clearly different from such military forces as are envisaged in Chapter VII of the Charter.

First and foremost it is not their intent to use force against any state. In the Secretary-General's second report (point 12) the aim of the emergency force is described as follows:

to enter Egyptian territory with the consent of the Egyptian Government, in order to help maintain quiet during and after the withdrawal of non-Egyptian troops, and to secure compliance with the other terms established in the resolution of 2 November 1956.

Thus nothing is said about using force against Egypt or the invading powers or their troops in Egypt. From the legal point of view, UNEF is regarded as a subsidiary organ set up in accordance with Article 22 of the Charter with powers delegated to the Secretary-General in conformity with Article 98. In an advisory opinion dated July 20, 1962, the International Court of Justice agreed with this view.

In keeping with the purpose of this force, the latter's composition and command differ from those of the enforcement action force. While it was assumed that the primary responsibility for the force envisaged in Chapter VII fell to the major powers, in the case of UNEF it is provided that both the officers and other ranks shall be recruited from member states which are not permanent members of the Security Council. In this way an effort has been made to keep the order-restoring forces clear of any competing major power interests. Recruiting is carried out by the Commander-in-Chief, not on an individual basis but in the form of national contingents negotiated with the state concerned. Twenty-four states offered their services, and ten, including the three Scandinavian countries, were accepted.

The force's Commander-in-Chief is appointed directly by the General Assembly, but it is the Secretary-General who, with the assistance of an advisory committee, lays down all the regulations and instructions required to ensure the effective functioning of the force. It is significant that the main responsibility rests with the Secretary-General and not with the Military Staff Committee of the major powers provided for in Articles 46 and 47 of the Charter.

It is of some interest that UNEF has a more international character than the enforcement action force would have had if they had been formed in accordance with the rules of Chapter VII (see above at the end of section 2). It is provided in the regulations that the members of the force, although remaining in their national service, are international personnel under the authority of the United Nations and subject to the instructions of the Commander-in-Chief through the chain of command. The functions of the force are exclusively international, and its members shall discharge these functions and regulate their conduct with the interest only of the United Nations in view. From the point of view of discipline, the members of this force are, in the last resort, under the authority of the Commander-in-Chief, but the national commander is directly responsible for maintaining order. In the event of criminal behavior, members can only be brought before their own domestic courts.

Thus it will be seen that even though these regulations do not go, in this respect, quite so far as in the case of the Secretariat, whose members owe allegiance to the United Nations alone, national loyalty during the period of service yields to a large extent to international loyalty toward the United Nations. The fact that the members of the force remain in their country's service means that they can be recalled at any time. But so long as their country has not ordered them back home, their allegiance to their country is suspended and replaced by a loyalty toward the Organization.

UNEF is not a permanent institution but a provisionally created body, which will cease to exist as soon as it has fulfilled its purpose.

ONUC (United Nations Operation in the Congo) was not an extension of UNEF but a new, independent institution, created in response to a certain situation and, from the legal point of view, like UNEF, a subsidiary organ administered by the Secretary-General, with far-reaching powers.

The Congo force was set up by a resolution adopted by the Security Council on July 14, 1960, and constituted on the basis of principles that closely followed those laid down for the creation of UNEF. Here, also, the idea was to establish a force that, with the consent and agreement of a government (in this case, that of the Congo), was to assist that government in the performance of certain tasks (in this case, the maintenance of law and order in the newly created republic) until the government felt able to do so on its own. The main factors causing unrest were the continued presence of Belgian troops, Katanga's claim to independence, and other separatist movements and disputes between different tribes. If nothing was done there was a danger that conditions in the young state would deteriorate into chaos and civil war, as a result of which certain major powers might be tempted to intervene in order to safeguard their economic or political interests. This might easily have endangered world peace. The United Nations intervention was motivated by the wish to avert this danger by filling a vacuum that would otherwise have aroused the conflicting ambitions of power politics. The composition and command of the force was organized in the same way as in the previous case, but with the not unimportant difference that the Commander-in-Chief was not appointed directly by the Security Council (General Assembly) but by the Secretary-General, whose supreme responsibility and authority were accordingly accentuated.

Thus the Secretary-General's authority was based on the prerequisite of the existence of a Congolese central government, which the United Nations force was to assist without interfering in the republic's internal disputes. Its exclusive task was to ensure the preservation of law and order so as to create conditions that would enable the Congolese to strengthen their government without any of the Great Powers taking advantage of a political vacuum as a pretext for intervening in the Congo. Arms could only be used in self-defense. As is known, events in the Congo developed in such a chaotic fashion that this assumption no longer held true. Hammarskjöld's mandate thus remained in suspense, and a number of attempts made to redefine it at the General Assembly in December 1960 failed, as the relevant resolution could not secure the necessary two-thirds majority. The Secretary-General was therefore obliged to "interpret" his mandate on his own responsibility, and he gradually found himself actively drawn into the internal political disputes in the Congo between groups represented by such men as Lumumba, Kasavubu, Mobutu, Gizenga, and Tshombe. The Security Council's resolutions of February 21 and April 15, 1961, were along similar lines. The use of armed force was authorized not only for self-defense but also as an ultimate means of preventing civil war. After Hammarskjöld's death (Sept. 1961), the Security Council passed a resolution on November 24, 1961, which went the whole way. Now an open intervention in the Congo's internal problems took place in order to support the Central Government in its struggle against Katanga's claims to independence, and military force was further authorized not only as a last resort for preventing civil war but also for seizing all foreign military and para military personnel and political advisers.

Although ONUC has left, the Congo chapter is not yet closed, and it is not my intention to discuss the many problems arising at that particular stage of the United Nations' existence. I shall confine myself to a few aspects of this question.

Originally, the legal ground for the United Nations' intervention in the Congo was a request to this effect from that country's "lawful government." It is a generally recognized principle of international law that it is lawful for a state, or an organization of states, to intervene in another state's internal disputes *at the request of that country's lawful government.* I regard this as one of the most unfortunate principles of international law of our time. It opens the way for infiltration and camouflaged invasions. Thus it would be sufficient for a clever major power to help establish a friendly government, which could then in a given situation request that major power's friendly help. On the basis of this principle, the Soviet Union, for instance, was able, in accordance with formal law, to put down the Hungarian people's revolt after the country's "lawful government" had requested Russian help. In my opinion it would be wiser to establish a strict nonintervention principle regardless of any requests for help. So long as such a principle has not been effectively established it may still, under certain conditions, be advisable to allow the United Nations to intervene in order to maintain law and order, so as to prevent any of the rival Great Powers from taking advantage of the situation. Under circumstances such as those existing in the Congo, a United Nations Action cannot be said to conflict with the provisions of the Charter's Article 2(7) as regards intervention in domestic affairs. This clause must yield to any request from the state concerned. Furthermore civil war and unrest cannot be regarded as "domestic matters" when the situation, as in the Congo, is loaded with international dynamite (Chap. III.1 and 3). But, as developments in the Congo have shown, such intervention can easily lead to the Organization taking sides in internal disputes behind which there are conflicting Great Powers interests. The United Nations would thus be acting contrary to its own fundamental principle, which is not to take any action without the unanimous agreement of the five permanent members of the Security Council. In that event the policy of the United Nations may help to sharpen the conflicts between the Great Powers instead of doing away with them. I think that in the future there will be great reluctance to allow the United Nations to engage in such military interventions as that in the Congo.

Dag Hammarskjöld's major idea—the idea of acting as an intermediary in the pursuit of an objective neutral policy on behalf of the United Nations dictated exclusively by that Organization's principles and ideas—must, I am afraid, be regarded as having died with him. Although no one could have been better fitted than he, from the point of view of character and culture, to bring such a task to a successful conclusion, he was subjected to violent and vicious criticism from the Soviet Union, coupled with personal attacks and humiliations when his Congo action did not develop as the Russians had wished. As a result he created a precarious situation not only for himself but also for the office of the Secretary-General. The British, too, strongly criticized the Secretary-General's use of the powers granted him. These attacks show how difficult it is to break free from the tight noose of the veto by granting certain powers to the Secretary-General.

The Congo action was attacked in many other quarters—not least in the quarters which were otherwise friendly toward the United Nations—because they could not see what justification or necessity there was for using military force against Tshombe's administration in Katanga. Many idealists and peace-loving persons felt disturbed at seeing the United Nations involved in military operations that would drag on for years. I do not share these views, for such operations are not at variance with the Charter's idea that peace should, where necessary, be preserved by using armed force. On the contrary, the justification and, indeed, the duty to act in this fashion is the fundamental principle on which the Charter's system for the maintenance of freedom is based. Unfortunately, the United Nations propaganda services lacked the courage to admit that the operations in the Congo had developed into an action against Tshombe because this was necessary in order to avert a serious threat to peace. The open sophistries to which the United Nations resorted, in trying to explain that the advances and capture of a number of positions and towns by the United Nations forces had been carried out in pure self-defense, were merely clumsy, comical, and in bad taste.

The Eastern bloc availed itself of the opportunity to create an economic crisis for the United Nations. Contending that the UNEF and ONUC actions were contrary to the United Nations Charter, they refused to contribute to the considerable expenses entailed by these operations. On December 20, 1961, the General Assembly decided to ask the International Court of Justice for an advisory opinion on this question. The Court's reply was given on July 20, 1962. It was to the effect that the expenditure in question was to be regarded as "expenses of the Organization" within the meaning of Article 17 of the Charter, which means that they shall be borne by the members as apportioned by the General Assembly. In a resolution dated December 19, 1962, the General Assembly approved the Court's advisory opinion. Seventeen states, including those of the Eastern bloc, voted against it.

This negative attitude to the opinion of the Court must be taken as a sign of the unabated unwillingness of these powers to pay their share of the expenses and as a warning of a gathering storm. Subsequent events have confirmed fully this view. The dispute must become acute when the apportioned, unpaid contributions reach such a proportion that Article 19 of the Charter applies. According to this article, a member of the United Nations who is in arrears in the payment of its financial contributions to the Organization shall have no vote in the General Assembly if the amount of its arrears equals or exceeds the amount of the contributions due from it for the preceding two full years. This critical stage was reached at the 19th session of the General Assembly. In a report of January 18, 1965, the

Secretary-General stated that 16 member states "should be considered to be in arrears, as at January 17, 1965, in the payment of their contributions to the United Nations, in amounts in excess of the amounts of their assessed contributions for the preceding two full years, namely 1963 and 1964." The member states listed in the Secretary-General's report were: Albania, Belgium, Bolivia, Byelorussian S.S.R. (White Russia), Cuba, Czechoslovakia, France, Haiti, Hungary, Paraguay, Poland, Rumania, South Africa, Ukrainian S.S.R., U.S.S.R., and Yemen.

For reasons having nothing to do with the financial dispute, the opening of the 19th session of the General Assembly had been postponed until December 1, 1964. Previous consultations with several delegations undertaken by the Secretary-General had made it clear that any vote in the Assembly would lead to a confrontation of the two opposing contentions—a confrontation that, whatever the immediate outcome of the dispute, must bring about disastrous consequences for the Organization. If a vote took place, the United States would be bound to challenge the participation of Russia and the other states in arrears as invalid under Article 19. If this challenge should be upheld by the Assembly, a situation would be created leaving the disenfranchised nations hardly any choice but to leave or to boycott the Organization. In the opposite case, the United States would be in a correspondingly difficult situation, and the logical reaction would seem to be to stop its own contributions to the Organization. In both cases the outcome would be a complete disintegration, if not the death, of the United Nations.

At the very beginning of the session, on December 1, 1964, the Secretary-General addressed the Assembly, saying that he had found among the delegations a common understanding to the effect that issues other than those that could be disposed of without objection would not be raised while the general debate proceeded. The Assembly agreed without objection to this procedure. The general debate accordingly proceeded without incidents. On December 23, the meetings were adjourned until January 18, 1965, in the hope that an agreement would be reached in the meantime. This hope, however, was not fulfilled. When the General Assembly resumed its nineteenth session on January 18, the general debate was continued on the same basis the remaining part of the month. On February 1, the Secretary-General pointed out that now that the general debate was over, the

Assembly had to decide on the procedure to be followed. He added that to his knowledge all members still were agreed that a confrontation on the applicability of Article 19 should be avoided at the present session of the Assembly. No one objected to this. After a week's adjournment, two meetings, on February 8 and 10, were held without incidents.

At the following meeting, on January 16, a remote-controlled bomb exploded. Halim Budo, representative of Albania, stated that the "no objection" procedure had been meant to apply only during the period of the general debate and formally requested that the Assembly immediately embark on its normal work in accordance with the Charter. He claimed priority for his proposal over any other question and he asked that the Assembly should take an immediate decision on the matter by a roll-call vote. The object of this proposal could only be to force a decision of the dispute in an open fight, with all its disastrous consequences for the United Nations and for the relations between the United States and the Soviet Union. It was not difficult to see that it was Communist China who, acting through a marionette, tried to upset the game. Completely unprepared, the President and the Assembly had some difficulty in repelling the attack. A hair-splitting fight over the rules of procedure took place. As a first step to find a way out of the impasse the President, on a somewhat dubious authority in Rule 35, on his own power adjourned the meeting for two days. When the Assembly met again, on the 18th, it was impossible any longer to evade a vote. The President ruled that there was a consensus against reconsidering the Assembly's previous decision as to the procedure to be followed. Mr. Budo challenged this ruling, which then was put to the vote in the Assembly. Mr. Budo thus had his way—but without the intended effects. In the meantime an understanding was obtained. Adlai Stevenson, representative of the United States, said that in order that the overwhelming majority might not be frustrated by one member, the United States would raise no objection to the procedural vote but would consider that such a vote would not involve or prejudice the question of the applicability of Article 19. The challenge to the President's ruling was then voted on by roll call and was rejected by 2 in favor (Albania, Mauritania) to 97 against, with 13 abstentions.

On the same day (Jan. 18, 1965) it was decided without objection to reconvene the Assembly on September 1. A resolution was adopted, also without objection, inviting the Secretary-General and the President of the General Assembly to undertake appropriate consultation on the whole question of peace-keeping operations in all their aspects, including ways of overcoming the present financial difficulties of the Organization, and authorizing the President of the General Assembly to establish a Special Committee on Peace-keeping Operations to undertake (taking into account the above-mentioned consultations) a comprehensive review of the whole question. In its report of June 15, 1965, the Special Committee merely stated that more time was required to complete the consideration of the matters covered by its mandate and that it had decided to continue its work. It is reasonable to assume that the Committee will concentrate on the immediate and urgent tasks, namely (1) to ensure the normal functioning of the Assembly when it resumes in September, and (2) to restore the solvency of the Organization by voluntary contributions by the entire membership, it being understood that this arrangement should not be construed as any change in the basic position of any individual member—and leave the far-reaching general problem of the peace-keeping operations in all its aspects to subsequent comprehensive studies and negotiations.

The issues of the financial crisis evidently reach far beyond purely economic interests. The Russian position fundamentally is a struggle for the re-establishment of the Security Council in its powers and functions according to the Charter. Legally the dispute centers around two questions: (1) Have the disputed peace-keeping operations been decided on and executed legally according to the Charter? and (2) If so, do the expenses relating to these operations constitute "expenses of the Organization" within the meaning of Article 17(2)? If either of these two questions is answered in the negative, the Russian position, from a legal point of view, is unimpeachable.

The question of the legality of the peace-keeping operations is related to the question of the distribution of power between the Security Council and the General Assembly (dealt with in Chap. VI.2). The central point in this case, however, is not an interpretation of Article 11(2). This paragraph deals with the power of the Assembly to make recommendations to the states and to the Security Council. No such recommendation is involved in the peace-keeping operations; they legally must be construed as organizational activity, conducted by the Secretary-General as functions entrusted to him in accordance with Article 98 and executed, in some cases, through "subsidiary organs" established under Articles 22 or 29. The International Court in its opinion of July 20, 1962 (Certain Expenses of the United Nations), has found the peace-keeping operations legal even when they were decided on by the General Assembly. From a legalistic point of view, this opinion, of course, is well founded as based in recognized methods of text interpretation. From a political point of view, however, there is, in my opinion, much to be said for the Russian contention that it is contrary to the spirit and general philosophy of the Charter if a decision on the use of armed force in order to maintain international peace and security could be made by any other organ than the Security Council.

The opinion of the Court with regard to the second question is, in my eyes, equally lacking in political wisdom. Based essentially on a linguistic interpretation of Article 17, the Court finds that there is no justification for limiting the term "expenses of the Organization" to expenses according to its administrative or regular budget; and that the General Assembly therefore has authority to apportion also operational expenses, on the condition that the operations are undertaken in accordance with the purposes and functions of the United Nations. This view is politically unsound because it divides the power to decide from the obligation to pay. It implies consequences which hardly can be accepted by any of the important financial contributors to the Organization, least of all by the United States. The principle that operational expenses are "expenses of the Organization" must, of course, apply analogously to financial operations within the purposes of the United Nations. The way then is open for the General Assembly, dominated by the many new states in need of economic assistance, to decide the setting-up of new institutions to carry out large-scale financial operations to further economic growth and development. As this is clearly within the purposes of the Organization, the expenses incurred in financing such operations, in the view of the Court and of the United States, are "expenses of the Organization" to be apportioned by the Assembly and paid for by the essential contributors to the Organization.

The opinion of the Court in this case seems to me to confirm the apprehension, felt by many in United Nations circles, that the Court is no suitable instrument for the interpretation of the Charter because it is necessarily dominated by legalistic points of view, neglecting or not understanding political-pragmatic considerations essential for the functioning of the United Nations.

To me it is hard to understand why the United States has bound itself up with this interpretation of the Charter and a policy that seems to lead inevitably to an impasse. It is difficult to imagine any way out other than to accept the proposals of the Soviet Union: To leave the question of the applicability of Article 19 alone and to solve the financial difficulties by means of voluntary contributions, without any prejudice to positions of principle.

The financial crisis of the United Nations, which is not without histrionic aspects, would grow into a real tragedy if it should prevent that *rapprochement* between the two big atomic powers which more than anything else is needed today to save our world from an atomic war.

4. Regional arrangements

In Chapter IV.1, which outlines the conflict between universalism and regionalism, it is said that this conflict raises particular problems as regards the maintenance of peace. The question is whether the organization of peace is best undertaken on a universal basis—i.e., on the basis of the common interest of all states that there should be peace throughout the world—or on a regional basis—i.e., on the basis of the special interest of a given group of states in preserving peace and security within their own group and in relation to other groups. As Cordell Hull states in his memoirs, Churchill and Roosevelt were firm supporters of a regional system. They considered that the world should be divided up into a number of areas organized to ensure the maintenance of peace within each of them. The universal international organization would rest on these pillars, and its task would be essentially limited to co-ordinating the regional systems. Cordell Hull, however, strongly urged that a powerful world organization be created for the maintenance of peace and that regional organizations should be tolerated only if they were organized in such a way that they would not lessen the authority or effectiveness of the universal organization. As is known, it was Cordell Hull's views that prevailed.

Chapter VIII of the Charter contains a number of articles on regional arrangements or institutions intended to deal with matters concerning the maintenance of international peace and security—in other words, political questions of the kind dealt with in Chapter VI (settlement of disputes) and Chapter VII (measures for the enforcement of peace). The idea underlying these articles is that such arrangements are welcome as a supplement to the United Nations' activities in so far as their aim is to ensure the *peaceful settlement* of disputes within the regions concerned. It is even said that the Security Council shall encourage a settlement along these lines and that members entering into such arrangements shall endeavor to settle their disputes in this manner before referring them to the Security Council. The United Nations does not seek in any way to control these regional settlements or lay down any requirements as to their organization and operation. Here the idea is simply: "If you can come to an arrangement among yourselves, so much the better!" If, however, the regional organization also intends to apply *enforcement measures for the maintenance of peace and security* (i.e. the measures described in Arts. 41 and 42 of the Charter), it is required that such an organization shall submit to the control of the United Nations in this matter: no enforcement action may take place without the authorization of the Security Council (certain exceptions to this rule are outlined below).

This distinction is quite understandable. There is no reasonable ground on which the world organization could claim a monopoly in the settlement of disputes. On the contrary, the idea, as we have already seen, is to encourage the members in their duty to settle their disputes themselves as far as possible with the help of the procedures and institutions of which they can avail themselves under traditional international law, namely negotiation, inquiry, mediation, conciliation, arbitration, and judicial settlement. The fact that the member states have set up regional institutions for the settlement of disputes can therefore only be welcomed in so far as such arrangements can only contribute to the achievement of the proclaimed objective, namely that disputes shall be settled without the parties having recourse to the United Nations. In Article 33, which emphasizes the duty of member states to seek a solution to their disputes without any outside help, express reference is made to "regional agencies or arrangements" in addition to the other means mentioned above. This juxtaposition is, however, erroneous, in that the resort to a regional agency is not comparable with the other means (negotiation etc.) but is only a special way of using one or more of those means.

It is a different matter when it comes to the application of enforcement measures. Here a choice must be made; authority and responsibility must be vested either in the regional or the central organization. The United Nations Charter has opted for centralization. The theory underlying the Charter is that peace is one and indivisible and that responsibility for its maintenance cannot be divided up among a number of local authorities but must be vested in the executive organ of the world organization, i.e. the Security Council. It follows that the regional organizations are completely under the authority of the world organization: no enforcement action can be taken without the authorization of the Security Council. This is clearly stated in Article 53 and means that regional organizations can never be more than tools in the hands of the Security Council, without any responsibility of their own.

The draft of the United Nations Charter, which was unanimously agreed on at Dumbarton Oaks, closely followed the above-mentioned pattern. At the San Francisco Conference the proposal for a strict application of the universality principle met with resistance, particularly from those states that had already concluded regional arrangements. This was especially the case with the American states, which at the Mexico City Conference in February and March, 1945 (that is, just before the San Francisco Conference), had adopted the "Chapultepec Act." This set forth provisional rules concerning mutual help in the event of an attack of any of the signatory states and recommended that as soon as possible after the end of the war a permanent treaty should be concluded concerning the organized execution of enforcement measures with respect to breaches of or threats to the peace. Similarly, in March 1944 a number of Arab states founded a league, known as the Arab League, with provision for collective security. It was clear that the arrangements in question could not be reconciled with the principle formulated at Dumbarton Oaks as regards the Security Council's absolute monopoly over any enforcement measures for the maintenance of peace. The result was a compromise between universalism and regionalism. While adhering formally to the rule that the taking of regional enforcement measures required the Security Council's authorization (with unanimity among the permanent members), this rule was to a large extent waived in Article 51, which confirms *the inherent right of individual or collective self-defense if an armed attack occurs against any member state*, until the Security Council has taken the measures necessary to maintain peace. The important point here is collective self-defense whereby other states, possibly on the basis of a previous agreement, can lawfully come to the aid of an attacked state.

By virtue of this article, member states of the United Nations can without violating the Charter, enter into regional agreements whereby they undertake, in the event of an *armed attack* on one of the parties to the agreement, to resort to joint enforcement measures, including military action against the aggressor. Thus it is possible to conclude defensive alliances, and there is nothing to prevent these from being institutionalized in such a way as to provide for far-reaching preparations for the co-ordination of the armed forces, against the day when collective self-defense against an attack may be necessary.

On the other hand, Article 53 hampers the application of any enforcement measures without the Security Council's authorization before an armed aggression has actually occurred—in other words, in the event of *other forms of aggression or of mere threats to peace*.

Article 53 allows for yet another exception to the rule concerning the absolute authority of the Security Council, in that it provides that the authorization of the Security Council shall not be necessary in respect of regional arrangements directed against renewal of aggressive policy on the part of an "enemy state," which term is more closely defined as any state that, during the Second World War, was an enemy of any signatory of the Charter, i.e. first and foremost Germany.

As the cold war developed, it soon became clear that owing to the disunity among the major powers, the United Nations were not in a position to provide the member states, especially the smaller countries, with the security they had hoped for. There could be no question of military sanctions, since the necessary agreements referred to in Article 43 of the Charter had not been concluded. Nor could economic measures be envisaged because of the Security Council's inertia. All that was left was the "parliamentary" diplomatic press, namely resolutions expressing criticism or sympathy. Although such expressions of opinion are not without real value, no state can base its existence and security on such lofty principles. It was bound to follow as a logical consequence of these circumstances that the states would build up a security system through regional arrangements outside the United Nations.

That is what actually happened and, by virtue of the safeguard clauses contained in Articles 51 and 53, this process could take place in full agreement with the formal letter of the Charter, even if, in reality, this meant abandoning the idea of giving life to the Charter in so far as the United Nations had been conceived as an institution responsible for the enforcement of peace and security. The formal legality of this development is, of course, of secondary importance, for it would have taken place even if it could not have been justified on legal grounds.

Today the world is covered by a network of regional arrangements based on an agreement on mutual assistance in the event of an armed attack on one of the partners and more or less organized on the institutional side by organs responsible for the preparation and co-ordination of collective defense measures. Most of these arrangements are centered around the United States and Russia, the two centers of gravity whereby the many arrangements are united into a system. The Western system, in which the United States is the central power, comprises the following regional arrangements:

(1) *The Rio Pact,* i.e. the *Inter-American Treaty of Reciprocal Assistance* of September 2, 1947. This arrangement forms part of the *Organization of American States* (OAS) set up by the Bogotá Charter of April 29, 1948. This organization's aim is co-operation in the economic, social, and cultural fields, the settlement of members' disputes, and collective security against armed attack. In other words, its aim is as far-reaching as that of the United Nations; thus this organization may be regarded as a corresponding organization for the American continent, associating the 20 South and Central American states (excluding Cuba after 1962) with the United States (and not including Canada). This organization has a well-developed set of organs which are broadly similar to those of the United Nations. The leading organ (corresponding to the General Assembly) is the *Inter-American Conference,* which meets regularly every 5 years. The *Meeting of Consultation of Ministers of Foreign Affairs* is devoted to political questions and can to some extent be compared with the UN Security Council, just as the Council of the OAS is

roughly equivalent to the Economic and Social Council of the United Nations. Under the Council are various specialized organs, namely the *Inter-American Economic and Social Council,* the *Inter-American Cultural Council,* and the *Inter-American Council of Jurists.* The permanent secretariat is known as the *Pan-American Union.*

The OAS's settlement system is set out in a special treaty known as the Bogotá Treaty, adopted on the same day as the Bogotá Charter.

The organization's security system is, as already mentioned, set out in the Rio Pact. Its chief provision is that an armed attack on any American state shall be regarded as an attack on all American states and that each of the partners accordingly undertake to meet such an attack by making use of its inherent right of individual or collective self-defense as recognized in the United Nations Charter (Art. 51). The Meeting of Consultation of Ministers of Foreign Affairs can, on the basis of a two-thirds majority, take binding decisions regarding the measures to be adopted to meet an attack, but no state shall be required to use armed force without its consent.

The OAS has so far concerned itself more with the settlement of disputes and the development of co-operation on a regional basis than with protecting itself from an attack from outside. It has in fact succeeded, in a number of cases, in settling conflicts. It has, however, proved very difficult to co-ordinate and integrate defense preparations, presumably on account of the United States' overwhelming armed strength, which is regarded as sufficient to protect the continent.

(2) *The North Atlantic Treaty* of April 4, 1949. Under this treaty, the United States is linked with Canada and 13 European nations (Belgium, Denmark, France, the Federal Republic of (West) Germany, Greece, Holland, Iceland, Italy, Luxembourg, Norway, Portugal, Turkey, and the United Kingdom) under a defense association known as the *North Atlantic Treaty Organization* (NATO).

The provision concerning mutual assistance is to be found in Article 5 of the Treaty, whose wording is very similar to that of the corresponding provision in the Rio Pact: the parties agree that an armed attack against one or more of them shall be considered an attack against them all and agree that if such an attack occurs they will assist the party or parties so attacked in accordance with Article 51 of the Charter of the United Nations. There is, however, a difference in that the North Atlantic Treaty does not contain any provision to the effect that an authority operating on the majority principle can take binding decisions as to the measures to be adopted by each of the states concerned. Thus, each of these states must, on its own responsibility, determine how far the relevant conditions exist and what steps it should take to fulfill its assistance pledge. This formal legal difference is, however, of minor importance. The parties to the North Atlantic Treaty are bound together by something stronger than treaty provisions, namely by the solidarity resulting from the integration of the members' armed forces in a common defense system. Thus Article 3 says that the parties, separately and jointly, by means of mutual aid, will maintain and develop their individual and collective capacity to resist armed attack. In practice, this means that the United States has spent enormous sums on the building up of Western Europe's defenses in the form of arms, supplies, and military installations of various kinds (airfields, radar installations, communications, oil pipelines, depots, etc. commonly known as "infrastructure"). This assistance has been given under conditions that have encouraged the recipients to increase their own efforts.

Under Denmark's Constitution, Article 19(2), the authorization of the Folketing (Danish parliament) is required before armed force can be used against any foreign state, except in the case of an armed attack on Danish territory or against Danish forces. The actual text of this provision reflects the agreed view that this means only individual self-defense (i.e., defense against a direct attack launched against Danish territory or Danish forces abroad) and not collective self-defense as outlined in Article 51 of the United Nations Charter (i.e., the giving of armed assistance to another state undergoing a direct armed aggression). This applies even though Denmark, under NATO, has undertaken to regard an attack against a foreign state as an attack against Denmark also. The fact that Article 19(2) of the Constitution does not provide for collective self-defense should not, of course, be taken to mean that Denmark does not intend to fulfill its obligations under the treaty but only that the Folketing's approval must be obtained before the Danish government can use armed force against the aggressor. This is understandable, for in many cases it is a matter of political judgment whether the conditions justifying fulfillment of the assistance obligation exist. It goes without saying that such a fateful decision could only be taken by the Folketing.

Another point is that if NATO ever comes under armed attack the situation will probably develop so quickly that it will be practically impossible to wait for the Folketing's authorization. In the case of an open attack which clearly and unmistakably corresponds to one of several well-defined types of situations, there will not even be time to consult the NATO Council, and it will be for SACEUR and SACLANT to handle the situation by virtue of their standing powers.

From the organizational point of view a distinction should be drawn between NATO's political and military organs. Supreme power is vested in the *Council,* which is made up of the representatives of each of the 15 member governments. The Council can meet either at the level of the Ministers or that of the permanent representatives. The Ministers usually meet about twice a year. In the intervals between these meetings, the permanent representatives can be required to meet at short notice. The Council's task is to take the relevant political decisions on which the military authorities can base their work. One of its most important tasks is to strike a balance between military requirements and the economic resources of the member states. An Annual Review is prepared every year, which contains plans for the coming and the two following years. These plans fix the military targets in respect of the development of the armed forces, having regard to the economic and financial situation in the individual countries, and form a basis for recommendations as to improvements in the national armed forces. The Council also apportions the expenditure arising out of the joint measures. Its work is carried out to a large extent through a series of subordinate organs. All its decisions must be unanimous. In the absence of unanimity, negotiations continue until unanimity is in fact achieved or the decision is postponed. This formal power of veto, enjoyed by each of the member countries, does not really mean that the opinion of the smallest state carries as much weight as that of the largest.

The Council is assisted in its work by an international secretariat headed by a secretary-general.

The supreme military authority is vested with the *Military Committee,* which is made up of the Chief of Staff, or his deputy, of each member country. It meets regularly twice a year in order to take up a position on the problems concerning the organization's military policy. This is a concession to the principle of equality which cannot, however, conceal the fact that the real influence is exercised through a working party known as the *Standing Group,* made up of the Chiefs-of-Staff of France, the United Kingdom, and the United States. It is this organ that issues strategic instructions to the various NATO commands and co-ordinates the defense plans prepared by them. Under the authority of the Standing Group are a series of commands, of which the most important is the *Supreme Allied Commander in Europe* (SACEUR), whose headquarters, known as SHAPE (Supreme Headquarters Allied Powers Europe) are at Rocquencourt, between Paris and Versailles, and the *Supreme Allied Commander Atlantic* (SACLANT), with headquarters at Norfolk, Virginia. SACEUR has five European commands under it. SACLANT also is split up into a series of subcommands.

NATO was set up at a time when the Soviet Union had shown that it did not intend to relinquish its rule over the oppressed Eastern European peoples but, on the contrary, as demonstrated by the fate of Czechoslovakia, might well be tempted to move the Iron Curtain further west. The Soviet Union's expansion, which had started already during the war with the annexation of Estonia, Latvia, and Lithuania, now also covered Finland, East Germany, Czechoslovakia, Poland, Hungary, Bulgaria, Rumania, and Albania, forming a Soviet colonial territory inhabited by 90 million non-Russians. During those years, Russian armed might on the continent was of overwhelming strength, and Western Europe's security rested solely on the American monopoly of the atomic bomb. It was clear that this monopoly would not last long and that it was therefore necessary to restore the balance in Europe. Even if this aim has not been completely realized, it has nevertheless proved possible, thanks to NATO, to build up a defense system that would make any attack a risky venture. NATO has restored confidence in Western Europe and stimulated European awareness, while at the same time reaching out toward a larger Atlantic community.

Historically speaking, NATO was not the first step in the organization of Europe's defense. Already during the preceding year, the United Kingdom, France, and the Benelux countries had concluded the Brussels Treaty of March 17, 1948, on economic, social, and cultural co-operation and collective self-defense. This led to the creation of the *Western European Union's* defense organization. This organization is still in existence, but, in the main, it has been rendered superfluous by NATO. Two of the NATO states, namely Greece and Turkey, concluded with Yugoslavia on August 9, 1954, a treaty, the *Balkan Pact*, on mutual assistance in the event of an armed attack. This does not, however, signify that an attack on Yugoslavia carries any obligation for the other NATO members to come to the assistance of that country.

(3) *The ANZUS Pact* of September 1, 1951, whereby the United States entered into joint defense undertakings with Australia and New Zealand.

(4) *The South-East Asia Treaty* of September 8, 1954, whereby the United States entered into an undertaking with Australia, France, New Zealand, Pakistan, the Philippines, Thailand, and the United Kingdom for the joint defense of South-East Asia. The organization set up for this purpose is known as SEATO (South-East Asia Collective Defense Treaty Organization).

(5) *Mutual Defense Treaty* of August 30, 1951, between the United States and the Philippines.

(6) *Similar treaties with Japan* (Sept. 8, 1951, and Jan. 19, 1960).

(7) *Similar treaty with Korea* (Oct. 1, 1953).

(8) *Treaty with China (Formosa)* (Dec. 2, 1954).

The United States has never been formally associated with the *Baghdad Pact* of February 24, 1955, providing for mutual defense undertakings between Iraq, Iran, Pakistan, Turkey, and the United Kingdom, but has in various ways demonstrated its interest by giving its support to this Western-oriented Middle-Eastern association. As a result of political developments, however, the Baghdad Pact has virtually fallen apart.

Through this network of treaties, the United States is linked as regards defense matters with 42 other states. None of the arrangements mentioned under headings 3 to 8 are comparable in importance with the Rio Pact or the North Atlantic Treaty. They are not as firmly based on tradition and common interest and do not involve a co-ordination of armed forces as is the case with NATO, which is by far the most important of all the defense arrangements.

The Eastern treaty system, pivoting around the Soviet Union as the central power, consists mainly of a great number of bilateral agreements on mutual assistance concluded partly between the U.S.S.R. and the individual satellite countries and partly between the latter among themselves. Added to these, there is the *Warsaw Pact* of May 14, 1955, concluded between Albania, Bulgaria, Czechoslovakia, the (East) German Democratic Republic, Hungary, Poland, and Rumania.

Outside the two major blocs, mention may be made of the *Cairo Treaty* on mutual assistance concluded between the Arab League states on April 12, 1950. The *Arab League* is a regional association created in 1945 by seven Arab states—Egypt, Iraq, Jordan, Lebanon, Saudi Arabia, Syria, and Yemen—as an attempt to organize the Arab world under Egyptian leadership. The League was subsequently also joined by Libya, Morocco, Sudan, and Tunisia. Internal disputes, in particular between Egypt, Syria, and Iraq, have had a disturbing effect on the League and rendered it of doubtful value as a defense arrangement.

References

1. SETTLEMENT OF DISPUTES
    For the general rules of international law concerning the settlement of disputes, reference may be made to current textbooks of international law. For more detailed treatment, see:
    Goodrich, Leland M. and Anne P. Simons, *The United Nations and the Maintenance of International Peace and Security* (1955), Parts II and III.
    Stone, Julius, *Legal Controls of International Conflicts* (1954), Book II.
2. MAINTENANCE OF PEACE
    Goodrich, Leland M. and Anne P. Simons, *The United Nations and the Maintenance of International Peace and Security* (1955), Part IV.
3. THE UNITED NATIONS EMERGENCY FORCES
    Frye, William R. A., *United Nations Peace Force* (1957).
    Goodrich, Leland M. and Rosner, Gabriella E., "The United Nations Emergency Force," *International Organization* (1957), pp. 413-30.
    Hoffmann, Stanley, "In Search of a Thread: The UN in the Congo Labyrinth," *International Organization* (1962), pp. 331-61.

O'Brien, Conor Cruise, *To Katanga and Back* (1962).

Seyersted, Finn, "Can the United Nations Establish Military Forces and Perform Other Acts Without Specific Basis in the Charter?", *Österr. Zeitschrift für öffentliches Recht* XII (1952), 188-229.

The United Nations Emergency Force: Basic Documents. A collection prepared by E. Lauterpacht (1960).

4. REGIONAL ARRANGEMENTS

Cheever, Daniel S. and H. Field Haviland, Jr., *Organizing for Peace* (1954), Part IV.

Ismay, Hastings Lionel I., *NATO: The First Five Years, 1949-1954* (1955).

NATO: Facts about the North Atlantic Treaty Organization, NATO Information Service (1962).

Padelford, Norman J. and George A. Lincoln, *International Politics* (1954), Chap. 21.

VIII ❧

BALANCE OF POWER,
COLLECTIVE SECURITY,
WORLD STATE

OR thousands of years war was regarded as an inevitable part of mankind's destiny. Some honored it, regarding it as a crucible in which a nation's power could be purified, but most men regarded it as a misfortune comparable with the plague, famine, and natural disasters. This fatalism was in some cases supported by religious ideas about war being a visitation by God, who used it as a means of testing mankind. There were also scientific theories to the effect that fighting and warfare were inseparably bound up with human society because man was provided by nature from the outset with a warlike instinct. Freud even spoke of a death-instinct (Thanatos) as the counterpart of the life and love instinct (Eros).

Although through the ages there have been a few thinkers and statesmen who have studied the problem of war and devised plans for achieving lasting peace on earth, it is only in the present century that a really serious effort has been made, both in theory and in practice, to study the question of the prevention and the ultimate elimination of war. It is not denied that war, like all other aspects of human behavior, may, in some respects, be rooted in human nature. But this does not mean that war is an inevitable part of man's fate. Illness, too, is bound up with human nature, but this does not mean that the fight against illness is in vain or that doctors are useless.

The fight against war must be carried out along the same lines as the fight against illness. Just as medical science first endeavors to determine the laws governing the occurrence and development of an illness—i.e., the conditions, existing partly in the human body and partly in the environment, that cause disease—and then devises its methods of treatment accordingly, so, also, the prevention of war requires an insight into the internal and external causes for war on the basis of which the appropriate methods of treatment must be worked out.

Medical treatment consists in acting on the internal or external circumstances and forces that are thought to be the causes of the disease. This process must, of course, take place in harmony with the laws of nature. If, for example, in a given case it is found that an illness is caused by the presence of a stone in the gall bladder, one must indicate specific methods of removing the stone. We found out a long time ago that no purpose was served by threatening the stone or begging it to disappear. A doctor can show how it is possible, in harmony with chemical and physiological laws, to get rid of the stone by administering a certain medicine, or how the same result can be achieved in accordance with physical laws, by surgical methods.

It is important to understand that this analogy holds true in respect of the fight against war. If the conclusion is reached that war is caused by, among other things, certain traits in human nature, for example egoism and the will to power, and that it is therefore desirable to alter these traits, a definite technique that has stood the test of time for achieving this result should be devised accordingly. Just as in the case of the gallstone, the problem of war cannot be solved with admonitions and incantations. Experience has shown that there is a genetic (hereditary) basis of human nature and that we are not equipped with the means to alter it. However, this genetic basis can develop in different ways under the pressure of the individual's experience. One talks about adaption and learning processes in the teaching and upbringing of young individuals. Experience has shown that verbal appeals—that is, exhortations and sermons—play only a very modest role in the learning processes and that under no circumstance are they capable of influencing the genetic factor.

In other words, certain pacifists are laboring under a delusion when they think that war can be abolished and the world made a better place by preaching nonviolence, tolerance, brotherly love, and respect for human rights. Pacifists are unexceptionable as long as they confine themselves to expressing and propagating these ideals and refusing to take up arms under any circumstances. If, however, in addition to this, they claim that their example and agitation is the way to peace, they are not only expressing a personal attitude but are also putting forward a theory—as it happens, an erroneous theory contrary to the fundamental principle that psychological facts are as real as physical facts and just as little amenable to efforts to alter them arbitrarily, yielding only to techniques based on experience.

It is not only the would-be world-improving pacifist who sins against what I would call the "rational technique principle." This also applies to those who think that the problem of peace can be solved by the creation of a body of law. Just as the pacifists believe that human nature can be altered arbitrarily, the others, whom I would call the "legalists," believe that they can alter the present state of the law by a free decision of will. This, too, is a delusion. Law cannot be created arbitrarily; it grows out of a set of social and sociopsychological conditions. To ask for a radical change in the state of the law without first altering these conditions is like believing in the primitive witchcraft of the medicine man.

The efforts made by the United Nations to prevent war must, like all other efforts of this kind, be judged in the light of theories on the causes of war. The study of this problem is still only in its infancy but should be pursued energetically, for only an understanding of the reasons for war can provide a rational basis for our search for the way to permanent peace and security. Within the present context, of course, there can be no question of dealing in greater detail with this extremely far-reaching problem, which I am not, in any case, qualified to do. I shall therefore confine myself in the present chapter, by way of an introduction, to outlining a reasonable approach to the problem of the causes of war. This will show that the chances of war or peace depend on a large series of factors—among others, on the type of law governing relations between states. I shall then proceed to analyze more closely the relevance of this legal factor. This analysis will be based on three different ways in which relations between states have been or could be regulated by law. They are customarily referred to as the *balance of power, collective security,* and the *world state.*

1. The causes of war

In his major work, *Study of War,* Quincy Wright points out that various authors have found a whole variety of different causes for the outbreak of the First World War: namely, Russian or German mobilization; the Austrian ultimatum; the assassination at Sarajevo; the ambitions of the Emperor, Poincaré, and other leading statesmen; France's desire to recover Alsace-Lorraine and Austria's desire to dominate the Balkans; the European alliance system; the interests of arms manufacturers and of international financiers; the lack of a European organization; rearmament; colonial rivalry; trade policy; nationalism; the concept of sovereignty; expansionism; the unequal distribution of population and resources; the law of diminishing returns; the valuation of war as a means of achieving national solidarity; group prejudice and group egoism; man's mental frailty—and many other factors.

Thus it is clear that the expression "causes of war" can give rise to a host of different interpretations and bring up a whole variety of problems. To illustrate this point it might be useful to compare the problem of the causes of war with another and similar problem that has been under study for a long time, namely the problem of the causes of crime.

When a criminal offense, a murder, has been committed, we can ask about the causes of such an act in the sense that we ask for an explanation of the psychological situation which culminated in the murder, regarded as an act of the human will. How did the perpetrator come to a decision to act? Was the murder committed on an impulse or in blind anger? Or was it premeditated, in cold blood? If so, what were the motives for the murder?

When the psychological reasons for the act are laid bare, one can go further and ask in what way this act is rooted in the perpetrator's personality. In other words, an effort is made to understand and explain the murder in terms of the murderer's previous history. The isolated act is considered in relation to the murderer's "character," which is regarded as the result of his life pattern. This might be defined as the interplay between inborn, inherited dispositions and a variety of personal experiences (for example, illness or misfortunes), and environmental factors, in particular the conditions in which the murderer grew up (birth, home conditions, social milieu, economic conditions, school, friends, etc.), and his subsequent way of life (marriage, etc.).

Up to this point, the investigation has been "historic," i.e. we have considered a specific offense and a specific offender with his individual life history—in other words, phenomena of a unique and individual nature. In moving from the particular to the general we adopt a "theoretical" approach. It is then no longer a question of determining the causes of a given criminal offense but of crime in general, i.e. those factors that generally act as a stimulus to crime. The branch of knowledge that concerns itself with such matters is known as criminology. Here a distinction is usually made between the psychology (or biology) of crime and the sociology of crime. The former deals with the causes of crime in terms of man's psycho-physical nature and endeavors to discover traits in man's personality that predispose him to crime. The latter investigates those environmental factors that are likely to release such dispositions. There may be a great variety of such factors, and the term "sociology of crime" must therefore be understood in a very broad sense. It covers not only conditions which, in a restricted sense, are described as sociological (family relationships and other group relationships) but also economic, political, and ideological factors and possibly even climatic and other physical environmental factors.

When crime is thus understood as being the resultant of an interplay between psychological dispositions and environmental conditions, it follows that the expression "the causes of crime" must be handled with some care. It can be misleading in so far as it may indicate a necessary relation between cause and effect. For instance, if poverty and need in the home are described as one of the causes of crime this does not mean that a child born under such conditions will necessarily end up as a criminal. Nor does it mean that a child born in a prosperous home cannot become a criminal. In other words we are dealing here with *statistical* probabilities. More children born under conditions of poverty and need will, all other things being equal, become criminals than children who grow up under more favorable circumstances. Hence it is more appropriate to speak of factors conducive to crime than of factors causing crime.

The problem of the causes of war must be approached in the same way. The historian's task is to describe the motives and circumstances that led to the outbreak of a given war, and the background to it. The task of the theoretical sociologist is to determine and describe those factors that are generally conducive to war. As "war" denotes a particular development (that is, involving the use of armed force) of particular conflicts (namely, between states) the causes of war should be studied within a very broad context, namely that of social conflicts, their origin, development, and termination. The branch of knowledge dealing with this question is known as "conflict research." This may, like criminology, be divided up into two main branches, the "psychology of conflict" and the "sociology of conflict." The former deals with social conflicts in terms of human nature, in other words those psychological and physical traits in man's character that lead to conflicts and violence. The second branch, the sociology of conflict, is concerned with the environmental factors likely to trigger the psychological predispositions to conflict and war.

In this connection, too, the word "sociology" is employed in a broad sense. The factors making for conflict may be of many different kinds and can be classified in many ways. Research in this field is still in its infancy, and no definite models have yet emerged. I would say, however, that the most appropriate classification would be one based on the various disciplines involved in the study of these factors. Thus a distinction could be made between the legal-political, the economic, the cultural, the ideological, and other factors conducive to war, and the sociology of conflict could accordingly be subdivided into these aspects.

Here also the concept of "causes" does not imply any necessary connection but only a statistical trend. Conflict and war must be

viewed as the result of the interplay of many factors, both psychological and social, each of which displays a tendency to lead either to
conflict and war or to peace and co-operation. All theories based on
the singling out of one specific factor, for example an inborn instinct
or a specific economic system, as the actual or true cause of war,
must be dismissed at once as arbitrary constructions at variance with
the principles of empirical research.

In the rest of this chapter I shall deal at greater length with certain
of the legal-political conditions that must be regarded as important
in connection with the question of war and peace. For the moment I
shall touch quite briefly on some of the other problems arising in
conflict research.

The psychology of conflict, as already said, aims at investigating
the psychological reasons for conflict and war. It already makes a
considerable contribution in a negative sense by eradicating certain
popular or pseudoscientific errors, for example, the view that war
cannot be abolished because it springs from a warlike instinct inherent in human nature. Psychologists are agreed that human behavior
is not instinctive, if by that are meant stereotyped reactions triggered
by specific stimuli. True, human behavior is the result of inborn instincts or drives, but what characterizes human conduct is the flexibility of these dispositions and their development through education.
Even if man is genetically inclined to self-assertion and aggressiveness, this is no reason for arguing that with appropriate education
under favorable social conditions this inclination cannot be adjusted
("conditioned") in such a way as to ensure the prevention of war.

The task of the psychology of conflict should be to make a closer
analysis of the concept and origins of conflict. Are all conflicts clashes
of interest, or should a distinction be drawn between these and ideological conflicts?

A conflict of interests can be broken down into objective and subjective factors. The objective factor is the external fact that the interests or needs of different individuals cannot be reconciled in the
sense that they cannot all be satisfied, for instance, on account of a
scarcity of material goods, or because a danger threatening a number
of them can only be averted by the sacrifice of one. Such an objective
incompatibility of interests need not, however, necessarily be regarded subjectively as a conflict. Two persons who find themselves in
such a situation can react either as friends (fellows) or as enemies

(rivals). In the former case the two partners try to co-operate in making the best of the situation. Co-operation can consist in one of the parties *helping* the other, sometimes to the point of *self-sacrifice*. In the other case, the clash of interest is conducive to *aggression* and *struggle*. It may, however, happen that the parties concerned will, instead, agree to *compose* their differences, just as it is conceivable that an active conflict may be averted by one of the parties choosing *flight* or *capitulation*. It may be the task of the psychology of conflict to investigate more thoroughly these different possibilities and the individual or group psychological dispositions and conditions that tend to call forth one or other of these different reactions.

As is known, psychologists have dealt at great length with aggressiveness, regarding it as a spontaneous behavior reaction stimulated by what is known as "frustration." Aggressiveness is often directed at that which is thought to be responsible for the frustration but can also shift to other objects (scapegoats) or, when the emotional pressure (anger, irritation) is strong, be unleashed at the first likely object that comes into view. To a large extent, group conflicts or group struggles have been explained along these lines. In support of this view, it has been pointed out that the education and socialization of the individual as a member of society results in a constant frustration of the individual's instincts, a frustration that carries a latent aggressiveness which the group tries to channel by unleashing it at other groups. Frustration due to poverty and need likewise create an aggressiveness, which those in power can easily exploit by turning it against external enemies.

It is doubtful, however, how far the psychology of war can be explained in this way. It must not be forgotten that the use of force is not always an expression of aggressiveness viewed as a spontaneous behavior reaction. It can also be a simple rational means, a technique like any other, for achieving certain aims. Here the driving force is the need that it is aimed to satisfy, not aggressiveness as an emotion. I believe that the decision of those in power to resort to war is not usually an expression of emotional aggressiveness but must be understood as being based on rational considerations concerning what they expect to achieve thereby. Aggressiveness in international relations is something different from what psychologists mean when they employ that term. What characterizes aggressiveness in international politics—for example, Hitler's aggressive policy—is that war is employed as a means of satisfying a craving for power, self-aggrandizement, or prestige. Its special feature is that it concerns things that can only be secured through struggle and war. Material goods and territory can also be obtained through negotiation and agreement, but victory can only be won through a fight. Here aggressiveness can be defined as the will to fight in order to satisfy the desire for victory.

If war is a means of achieving certain aims, the questions then arise: What is a typical war-aim? By what interests (or ideas) is war motivated? What needs is war usually supposed to satisfy?

It is in itself a problem whether these questions can be formulated in such a way as to be given a precise meaning and can be answered by systematic investigation. Whose motives or needs are actually involved? Can motives be ascribed to the state or the people or only to private individuals? Is it the leader's motives, or the motives by which the broad mass of the people are actuated? What ways are there of determining objectively which motives (in one or the other sense of the term) are operative?

These questions, too, belong to the psychology of conflict. For the present, owing to the lack of fundamental studies in this field, we must be satisfied with more intuitive explanations, and the reply must no doubt be that wars are waged mainly for material gains and power.

From time immemorial, war has been synonymous with plunder: one went to war to seize cattle, women, land, and other goods. Venice's and Genoa's prosperity was based on the plundering of the Byzantine Empire and the Levant. Spain's plundering in Central America and Peru set a pattern for many subsequent colonial wars. The same get-rich motive is still manifest in our own day but to a lesser extent. The destructiveness of war has become so terrifying, also for the attacker, that it can hardly be regarded as a suitable means of material gain. Particularly in a liberal world economy which provides opportunities for the "export" of surplus population and the import of capital and raw materials, there are usually better ways for a people to raise its standard of living than by going to war. If, in certain cases, a state attaches decisive importance to the occupation or control of certain territories, sea areas, or communications, the explanation usually lies in power politics—in other words, these territories etc. are desired for their strategic value.

The desire for riches was hardly a decisive reason for the efforts of

Alexander the Great or the Romans to create a world empire. Nor were the Vikings' raids purely and simply plunder expeditions, for the Vikings also wanted adventure, glory, and fame. Hitler's desire for the territorial expansion of Germany by annexing the Ukraine and half of Europe and by recovering its former colonies had nothing to do with improving the living conditions of the German people. His only purpose was to consolidate his power and greatness and to exploit Germany's victory by imposing German rule on the Slavs and other "inferior" people. If I were asked to single out one motive which, more than any other, makes for war, I would, in my interpretation of man and history, point to the desire to wield power and the fear of being subjected to another's power. Added to this is, in some cases, the aggressive desire for the glory and honor that are the fruit of victory and can therefore only be secured through fighting and war. The attributes of greatness that the Christians ascribe to their God—the Kingdom, the Power, and the Glory—are what man craves most of all and for which he is prepared to go to war.

Unfortunately, these benefits are indivisible. So long as a rival exists, no power can be complete and there can be no freedom from fear. The basic motive for war will therefore continue to exist so long as there are sovereign states. Hence world dominion has always been the final goal of the great conquerors.

I am doubtful as to how far, in addition to the desire for riches and power, belief in an idea can be regarded as an important motive for going to war. One could, for instance, point to the Crusaders, the Moslems' holy war, and the Marxist theory concerning the inevitable collapse of the capitalist states and the communization of the world. I am still, however, inclined to think that closer analysis would show that in these cases, too, the true motive was the desire for power.

As already stated, there is nothing in man's nature that predisposes him to enmity and war. Objective clashes of interests can produce either co-operative or hostile reactions. Man is the animal with the fewest inborn and immutable response patterns (reflexes, stereotyped instincts) and the greatest capacity for learning. Man can be taught to engage in enmity and fighting just as he can learn fellowship and co-operation. It is the task of the psychology of conflict as a science of group relations, in particular international relations, to determine appropriate methods for getting rid of fear, mistrust, and hate between groups and to strengthen the feeling of fellowship and co-operation. As fear often springs from ignorance or prejudice regarding the qualities, aims, and ways of life of other groups, one of the methods of combating war should be to overcome such ignorance and prejudice through education and the free movement across all frontiers of persons, information, and ideas. This is the idea underlying the United Nations Educational, Scientific, and Cultural Organization (UNESCO). In the introduction to the UNESCO Constitution is said:

that since wars begin in the minds of men, it is in the minds of men that the defences of peace must be constructed;
that ignorance of each other's ways and lives has been a common cause, throughout the history of mankind, of that suspicion and mistrust between the peoples of the world through which their differences have all too often broken into war;

.   .   .   .

For these reasons the States party to this Constitution, believing in full and equal opportunities for education for all, in the unrestricted pursuit of objective truth, and in the free exchange of ideas and knowledge are agreed and determined to develop and to increase the means of communication between their peoples and to employ these means for the purpose of mutual understanding and a truer and more perfect knowledge of each other's lives.

Conflicts will, of course, always be with us, but our aim should be to ensure that, in every case, they are settled without resorting to violence, i.e. through negotiation or settlement of one kind or another. It will be for jurists, politicians, and diplomats to devise the different methods of peaceful settlement and see to it that they are applied in practice. But the psychology of conflict may make a valuable contribution to the preparation and application of such methods, for instance with regard to the selection and training of diplomats, and meeting and negotiation techniques, especially with a view to avoiding misunderstandings, unintentional slights, blocking of negotiations for prestige reasons, and other similar psychological obstacles to the successful course of negotiations.

As already said, the "sociology of conflict" is an attempt to discover some objective pattern in the way different social factors, taken in the broadest sense, are conducive to war or to peace. It is a generally accepted fact that economic conditions are important in this respect. It seems self-evident that poverty and need, and the illness, distress, and insecurity bound up with it, cause dissatisfaction and unrest, which can lead to revolution and war. This applies, at any rate, where the distressed peoples have begun to realize the possibilities of improving their living conditions and have discovered that other peoples are rich and prosperous. It is this development that characterizes most underdeveloped peoples today and confirms the old argument that it is not the most wretched who cause unrest but the groups that have moved a step up in the world and have acquired a taste for further progress. Taken in conjunction with the political liberation of the colonial peoples, fiery nationalism, and the lack of political maturity, economic dissatisfaction arouses an aggressive spirit which breaks out into quarrels and war. Thus it seems obvious that the desire of the Congolese Central Government to rule over Katanga is motivated by the wish to share in Katanga's considerable natural resources and industrial development.

According to Marxist doctrine, as interpreted by Lenin and Stalin, the major reason for war is not economic need but the capitalist production system. The capitalist exploitation of the workers, it is claimed, makes it impossible for a state to dispose of its whole production on the home market. The capitalist countries therefore have to look for foreign markets where they can sell their goods and invest surplus capital. The rivalry that arises in this connection leads to imperialist wars. Capitalism is doomed because historical necessity will lead to the proletarian revolution and to war in which the capitalist countries will eat each other up, like the tigers in the well-known tale of *Little Black Sambo*. This theory—like other Marxist doctrines—assumes a certain situation typical of capitalist society around the middle of the 19th century and claims general validity for it. It should hardly be necessary today to disprove this theory and point out that the wars threatening at the present time, for instance between China and India or between Israel and the Arab countries, to say nothing of a world war between East and West, cannot be regarded as a struggle for markets.

In the light of the foregoing psychological considerations it seems unlikely that economic conditions are among the circumstances that are particularly conducive to war. Economics are, in the final analysis, man's struggle against a common enemy, nature, and therefore calls for co-operation. This is the way our modern society is developing. Today it is more usual for economic advantages to be received as gifts than to be secured through war. It is political interests and the will to power that are inherently conducive to conflict and war, because political benefits—the Kingdom, the Power, and the Glory—are indivisible and can only be secured by overcoming every rival.

If we accept the fact that, through his environment, man can learn to live in enmity and war just as he can learn to live in fellowship and co-operation, it is not improbable that the cultural pattern in which an individual grows up is important as an influence on his behavior in one or another direction and can stamp a group as predominantly warlike or peaceful.

Ruth Benedict, the world-famous cultural anthropologist, has tried to prove the existence of a profound difference in this respect in the ideals and standards found in various cultural patterns. In her studies of the American Indians she has pointed to fundamental contradictions between what, using expressions taken from Nietzsche, she calls the Dionysian and the Apollonian attitudes. The former is most widespread and finds perhaps its purest expression among the Kwakiutl Indians, who are still living on Vancouver Island and whose culture is known and has been described in detail. The pattern that runs through the institutions and human relations of this culture is rivalry. Rivalry is a struggle, not for real tangible benefits but only for victory over an opponent. The desire for superiority is expressed in the most unrestrained ways, for instance in hymns of self-glorification and the mocking of strangers. Their whole economy is bent to the service of this obsession. There are two ways in which a chief can gain the victory and glory he desires. One way is to shame his rival by overwhelming him with so many presents that the recipient is unable to make any return. The other is to indulge in spectacular destruction of his own economic assets. The Kwakiutl even go so far as to burn their riches at their feasts in order to outshine their guests, who must then try to match them by casting their own goods to the flames in equal or even greater amounts. These contrast with the Apollonian Pueblo Indians in the southwestern United States. According to the standards of this particular culture, the ideal man is a person of dignity and affability who never tries to impress. He must display reluctance to accept any official positions or exercise leadership. Any conflict he is involved in, even though he is in the right, is counted against him. In contests of skill such as footraces, a man who wins habitually is debarred from running. The Pueblo are interested in a game that a number can play with even chances and not in individual top performances. Moderation is regarded as a virtue, and violence is condemned.

If this theory of fixed cultural patterns, difficult to alter, is correct, the conclusion is a pessimistic one. The Apollonian culture of the Pueblo Indians is, unfortunately, an exception. In any case, Western culture, which to a growing extent is spreading the world over, does not in any way conform to the gentle pattern of the Pueblo culture. Our culture is closer to that of the Kwakiutl Indians, even if we protest that the picture they present is a caricature of ourselves. Our culture too is based on self-assertion, competition, and success as central values. It would be a mistake to think that this applies only to the capitalist world, where economic competition is so obvious, as compared with the socialist countries, where life is based to a greater extent on the ideals of fellowship and co-operation. The truth is that competition and rivalry there have merely taken other forms. High performances and victory are as highly valued in the one system as in the other. In the Soviet Union, no one would dream of excluding a superior athlete from a race and, indeed, that country contributes lavishly to the destruction of other values in the vain race for space.

Ideological factors, unlike cultural patterns, are not based on deeply rooted customs and judgments but are doctrinaire systems concerned with politics and attitudes to life, e.g. Christianity, Communism, liberalism, capitalism, and many other "isms." The question is: What will happen if the political opposition between rival states also has an ideological content? Investigation of this question is yet another task for the sociology of conflict. Offhand, one would say that ideological opposition makes it more difficult for two opponents to come to an agreement. One can come to an agreement with a competitor but not with the devil himself. When it is a question of clashes of interests or influence, it is possible to bargain, compromise, and mark out zones of influence, but when belief and conscience are involved this cannot be done. Holy war knows no compromise.

If it is true to say that foremost among the mainsprings of war are the craving for honor and glory, the will to power and dreams of dominion, it follows accordingly that among the external determining factors the legal-political forms, in which states compete for power and influence, must be of decisive importance.

In this connection, one idea has dominated all thinking about peace from the time of the creation of the League of Nations down to the present day, namely the simple inference that since, in a national context, it has been possible to establish an order based on the rule of law—i.e., to secure peace through law—so the problem in *international* relations, too, must be to replace power politics by the rule of law. The League of Nations was established with great enthusiasm in the belief that it would once and for all put a stop to the unlawful rule of might. Unfortunately, experience showed that the rule of law was powerless. This did not, however, kill the belief that peace between states could be achieved through law. But the nature of this ideal underwent a change. Many thought that if previous efforts had failed, it was because the wrong sort of law had been set up as a standard for relations between states as a means of doing away with the rule of might. The law on which the League of Nations and later the United Nations were founded was international law, i.e. international agreements and international organization. But, it was reasoned, international law is not "real law"—only an extremely imperfect law, which differs from real law, that is, domestic or national law, in that it lacks legislative, judicial, and law-enforcing organs, in other words everything that makes state law a factor of power capable of competing with and overcoming the rule of force. It is not the bloodless idea of law inherent in international law but only a law similar to national law that will be capable of putting an end to the rule of brute force and bring the states together into a law-abiding and nonviolent community. Thus, to sum up, peace cannot be secured by international organizations such as the League of Nations or United Nations but only by the creation of a world state where the constituent states are subject to the authority of a system of laws backed by legislative, judicial, and law-enforcement organs, in the same way as an individual is subject to the law of his state. An international organization such as the United Nations is of value only as a modest first step toward one world.

Thus the program: the preservation of peace through law has been financed by a check drawn on the future. The question is whether this check is likely to be honored.

As a basis for the ensuing discussion on the importance of legal-political international relations as a factor making for peace or for war, we can suggest three ways in which a state's foreign policy can be directed toward the preservation of peace:

(1) The balance of power, i.e., a situation characterized by the fundamental absence of the rule of law, where it is sought to preserve peace by political and diplomatic means and by skillfully manipulating the power factors in such a way that no state will have anything to gain by starting a war.

(2) Collective security, i.e., an international arrangement whereby all states, while preserving their capacity for resorting to violence, undertake under international law (that is, by agreement and without any law-enforcing authority) to act in solidarity against anyone breaking the peace.

(3) The world state, i.e., a system whereby states are subject to a legal order, in the same way as we are now subject to domestic law, in other words, a legal order equipped with law-enforcing power. This implies that the organs of the world state must enjoy a monopoly of the physical means of violence and that there must be a corresponding disarmament by the national states.

I shall now proceed to make a closer analysis of these three models and assess their value as instruments for the preservation of peace.

2. *The balance of power*

The expression "balance of power" can denote either a given state of affairs or a given political principle. In the former case it means the factual distribution of power, existing at a given moment, between the agents active within an international political system. Today, the world has shrunk to such an extent and mutual dependence has become so great that there is only one international political system in existence, namely the global system. In the latter case, this term denotes the principle according to which the aim of the foreign policy of any state should be to ensure such a distribution of power that no state or group of states can count on being so superior in power to its potential enemies as to have a chance of winning a war. If such a balance of power can be achieved and if states behave rationally in relation to their own interests, war will be eliminated.

As the principle of the balance of power refers to the notions of power and the distribution of power, it is necessary first to give a brief explanation on this point.

In general, the term "power" (in human relations) denotes the capacity of rulers to persuade their subjects to act in accordance with their (the rulers') wishes. How is that possible? And what is the technique of the exercise of power? The answer is that fundamentally this technique is similar to that which enables us to direct the forces of nature in accordance with our own wishes. Let us say, for example, that we wish to alter the course of a river. How do we set about it? We build dams, dig canals, and so forth. We cannot alter the force and laws of nature themselves, but when we know these forces and laws we can adjust conditions in such a way as to make nature do exactly what we want it to. The same holds true when it comes to exercising power over human beings. The behavior of those over whom this power is being exercised is and remains their own behavior as determined by the normal forces and motives of human behavior. All that rulers can do is to adjust internal and external conditions in such a way that their subjects are motivated to behave as they want them to. The ruler must always appeal to some motive capable of impressing his subjects, and, to that extent, the source of all rule can be said to lie with the subjects rather than with the ruler.

Depending on the motive and the means employed for exploiting it, the exercise of power can take the most varied forms. One of these forms is compulsory force, playing on the subject's fear through the threat that evil (or punishment) will befall him if he does not do what is asked of him. A prerequisite for the effectiveness of the threat is that the ruler possesses such overwhelming power resources that he can enforce the sanction, if necessary, by overcoming any resistance on the part of his subjects.

Again, compulsory force can be either violent or nonviolent. In the former case, the punishment threatened takes the form of personal injury. The use of force is nonviolent when the punishment, e.g., consists in disclosing a secret (extortion) or refusing to co-operate (strike).

The kind of force that is involved in international politics, particularly in the politics of the balance of power, is violent force, i.e., the power to impose one's will on other states owing to the ability, where necessary, to cause deprivation and inconvenience to the refractory —and even destruction, mutilation, and annihilation.

The magnitude of the power a state is capable of exercising (its power volume or capacity) is determined by a series of factors known as "power resources." Just as production factors can be subdivided into land, capital, and labor, so power resources can be subdivided into:

(1) territory, i.e., the geographical area, including particular bases, available to the state, which is important both as production factor and as starting point for military operations;

(2) technical machinery and technical means of various kinds, which directly or indirectly facilitate the exercise of power: in particular, a military apparatus and an industrial apparatus that can be converted to war production, means of self-supply, civil defense, etc; and

(3) the population, the importance of which depends not only on its size but also on its moral and educational level and its national homogeneity, as well as on the effectiveness of its political organization.

This is, of course, only a rough outline, which would have to be filled in with many details in any close analysis. It is, however, sufficient to bring out two facts that play a very important role in the theory and practice of the balance of power. In the first place, the volume of power enjoyed by a state can increase or diminish in ways other than the most evident (i.e., through the acquisition or giving up of territory and by rearmament or disarmament)—for instance, through the development of industrial capacity and flexibility; by training the population or imbuing it with an aggressive ideology (Nazi race theory, Communist philosophy of history); through the development of infrastructures, the strengthening of self-supply capacity, etc. Secondly, the actual volume of power involved in the balance of power, both as a descriptive concept and as a political idea, can be assessed only approximately by means of statistical and similar methods of evaluation, while an adequate estimate requires a comprehensive assessment of the situation as a whole and an over-all political judgment.

The balance of power as a descriptive concept denotes the distribution of power existing at any given moment, viewed as a "power constellation," assuming that a war is started by one of the states belonging to the system. This presupposes political relations of friendship or enmity between states and that in the event of war, depending on who was the aggressor, these relations will crystallize in different ways so that the states concerned will fall into three groups: those who wish to join the aggressor, those who wish to fight him, and those who wish to stay neutral.

The balance of power as a political idea cannot take the form of a well-defined doctrine. It is not an invention or a system but, rather, an obvious pattern or natural rule of foreign policy when the latter is regarded as *a game where a number of sovereign agents, whose only law is that of self-interest, fight for power by using power.* In such a game the goal of each of the contestants, in positive terms, is to secure the maximum amount of power and, in negative terms, to prevent any other player from gaining such a position of strength within a given power constellation as to be able to start a war with any prospect of success. After victory, the power position of this player would be further strengthened and present an increased danger to the other players and perhaps even open the way to final victory, namely world domination.

In order to achieve this negative aim it is necessary first to alter the political relations of friendship or enmity in such a way that a potential aggressor will find himself faced with a power constellation capable of putting up a tremendous resistance or which, at any rate, will not give him the necessary superiority to be able to start a war with any chance of success. To put it in a more concrete way, the purpose of a balance of power policy is to create, through shifting, flexible, and defensive alliances, a common front against the state which at any given time and in a given area is regarded as a probable aggressor. If, for example, states A and B (say, France and Germany) stand in historic opposition to one another and are rivals for supremacy in a given area, the idea of the balance of power would mean that other powerful states belonging to the same political system should turn the balance in favor of the weaker of the two rival states (England's traditional Continental policy).

Alliances are the diplomatic instrument of the balance of power. Military strength also is important in this context. Minor military operations, in particular against the system's smaller powers are resorted to in order to adjust the balance of power and thereby prevent the outbreak of a major war between the main powers in the system.

Historically this pattern has occurred wherever the necessary conditions, namely the existence of a number of sovereign states within the framework of a given system, have been present, for example in the case of the Greek city-states. It is only later that it was formulated as a definite political principle by the English philosopher David Hume.

In the theoretical model used to illustrate the principle of the balance of power we assumed that the ultimate and positive aim of each of the players in this game ws to secure as much power as possible—in the final instance a total power monopoly within the system, in other words, world domination. Under favorable conditions the system can develop in such a way that the idea of world domination recedes and the negative aim, i.e. the preservation of the balance of power with all the players becoming members of a community, becomes an aim in itself.

This is what happened in 19th-century Europe after the defeat of Napoleon's attempt to achieve world domination. The number of major powers was so large (five to eight) and their mutual power relations so well balanced, that it would not have been possible for any one of them to overcome the joint resistance of all the rest. The fear of hegemony by a single state, in conjunction with the awakening of nationalism, produced a legal-political ideology whereby every people was entitled to an independent national existence, an ideology which also restricted the ambitions of the major powers. Moreover, there were no far-reaching ideological divergences. With various nuances, all the participants shared the same Christian beliefs and the idea of constitutional monarchy. No state was the mortal enemy of another. Each state recognized the right of any other to its own existence and, indeed, the fundamental necessity of such existence in order to be able to preserve a flexible and multipolar balance of power.

This attitude found expression as early as during the peace negotiations after the Napoleonic Wars. There was no intention of crippling France or reducing it to the rank of a second-class power. Talleyrand was a leading spirit at the Vienna Congress, and only a few years later France was formally admitted as the fifth major power. There were few wars within the European system up to 1914, and none of them was aimed at the annihilation or subjection of the other side.

The balance of power is amoral in that it requires flexible shifts and groupings in alliances solely in accordance with the needs of the balance of power itself and unhampered by any ideological-moral bond or any other political purpose. This is the attitude that was reflected in Lord Palmerston's famous remark that England knew neither unshakable friendships nor natural enemies but only eternal interests (1848). If the power configuration is disturbed because definite political oppositions arise on moral-emotional, sentimental grounds, the system does not work.

It would take us too far if we analyzed the circumstances that led to the collapse of the system during the First World War, its disappointing performance between the wars, and its renewed collapse during the Second World War. I should like, however, to mention one fact that contains an important lesson for us today.

Compare the Versailles Treaty with the Vienna Peace of 1815! How was it possible for Europe's statesmen so completely to forget the fundamental principles of the balance of power as to humiliate Germany, cripple her, reduce her to the rank of a power without power, create chaos in Europe, and leave the minds of the German people in a state receptive to the hysterical dreams of revenge and greatness of a frustrated psychopath, leading at length to another world war? In my opinion the explanation lies, at least partly, in the illusion created by Wilsonian idealism.

Europe's statesmen wittingly allowed themselves to be led by this American, an academic ideologist without training in foreign policy, to ignore the principles of the balance of power in favor of the loudly proclaimed belief that henceforth the rule of law would take the place of might. On January 22, 1917, Wilson said, "Mankind is now looking for freedom of life, not for equipoises of power." What was needed, he continued, was "not a balance of power, but a community of power; not organized rivalries, but an organized common peace." It is on these principles that the Versailles Treaty and the League of Nations were based, thereby unknowingly paving the way for a new world war. In my opinion it is difficult to say who, in the long run, represents the greater danger to mankind: the criminal (Hitler) who, with his cynical grasp of the technique of political power, leads men astray by appealing to their baser instincts; or the ideologist (Wilson) who, full of good will and appealing to all that is noblest in man—the dream of law and justice—deludes people through his illusory conceptions of law and justice and their function in international politics.

In the world of today, conditions have undergone such a decisive change that the balance of power pattern has taken on a very different appearance, so different in fact that various authors refrain from employing the term "balance of power" in international relations but instead speak of bipolarity. I personally prefer to use the term *bipolar balance of power* as opposed to *multipolar balance of power*.

The most characteristic feature of the new situation is, as the corresponding terminology shows, first and foremost, the fact that in the power constellation overwhelming power is concentrated in the hands of two giant powers, and the power-political field is therefore stably and unambiguously centered on these two poles, which, unlike the magnetic poles, are referred to as East and West. This system comprises three types of states: (1) the two pole or "planet" states; (2) satellite states, which, for one reason or another and more or less of their own free will, are allied with one or other of the two pole states; and (3) the neutral or "comet" states which (as yet) have not been drawn into the gravitational field of one of the planet states but travel in a free orbit.

Another major difference that characterizes the bipolar system of today (but not necessarily every such system) is a profound ideological gulf between the two main protagonists. It is significant that, whereas one of these ideologies claims only the right to existence for itself and freedom of choice for every people, the other ideology, like the Christian religion, claims absolute authority, which, unlike the Christianity of today, is to be secured, if necessary, by force.

It will be readily understood that within such a system there are only limited possibilities for the flexible groupings that were the most important feature of the multipolar balance of power. As there are only two dominant states, there is no longer any room for a multiplicity of constellations against a potential aggressor. Alliances now tend to be permanent and to develop on institutional lines. In this way, the opposition between the two leading powers becomes an opposition between blocs. So long as there are still neutral states of any importance, the two blocs will compete with each other, using political, economic, or ideological means in an attempt to attract or scare them into joining one or the other system.

The principle of the balance of power still functions in a locked bloc system, inasmuch as each of the parties zealously sees to it that the other party's power volume does not grow to give him decisive

superiority. But the possibility of achieving this aim by flexible ma-
neuvering no longer exists. If one of the parties is considered by the
other to have gained a lead, the balance can only be restored by
means of a corresponding increase in the power of the bloc that has
fallen behind. As it is not possible to achieve security through *new
power combinations,* i.e. alliances, the only way left open is to *increase* one's power. First and foremost, this implies a military and
industrial arms race. It is difficult to halt this process by dividing the
world into zones of interest, because of the ideological differences.
There can be no compromise with evil. The prospect therefore seems
to be a race without end—or with a frightful end.

The backbone of a balance of power policy is self-interest free
from any ideological or legal ties. This requirement was fulfilled in
the 19th century. International law recognized the right of any state
to employ armed force against another state, in the form of war or
military reprisals, once it judged that such action was required. In
this way, minor military operations could be carried out, unhindered
by any legal considerations, in order to preserve the balance of
power and thereby avert a major war. This requirement, which ensures the flexibility of the balance of power policy, ceased to be met
once it became increasingly accepted in the Covenant of the League
of Nations, the Kellogg-Briand Pact, and the Charter of the United
Nations that all use of force is prohibited that is not lawfully authorized by the international community as a measure to enforce peace.
Even if this legal obligation has never been taken seriously by any
state capable of effective use of power, it has to some extent stood in
the way of a speedy and flexible adjustment of the balance.

As the basis of the balance of power is the state's self-interest and
natural desire for power, it does not require any organizing or other
form of legal system. But there is nothing to prevent balance of
power diplomacy from being conducted within fixed frameworks, for
instance by means of regular or occasional consultation between the
leading powers as mentioned in connection with the European Concert (Chapter I.1). The balance principle, then, is concerned first
and foremost with the direct relations between the participating
major powers. But their joint interventions in the relations of other
states in order to preserve peace must also be viewed in terms of the
indirect importance of such action to the balance of power between
the chief powers.

The balance of power is not, of course, an infallible means of preserving peace, as indeed is demonstrated all too clearly by history. The (relatively) best results were achieved during the century that elapsed between the end of the Napoleonic Wars and the beginning of the First World War. During that period various conflicts still took place for the consolidation and regulation of certain power positions, but there was no major war aimed at a radical alteration of the *status quo*.

The balance of power is a diplomatic art or skill which, like any other, requires training and ability if it is to be practiced successfully. Lack of vigilance or understanding can cause a disturbance in the balance. This policy is based on an assessment of the power-capacity and the power–political intentions of the protagonists. A lack of information, or inaccurate evaluations and interpretations of the available information, can have the result of allowing a potential aggressor to get his way unhindered so long that he can no longer be stopped. Such was the erroneous assessment that allowed Hitler to march into the Rhineland and, together with Mussolini, to intervene in the Spanish Civil War. Through a series of concessions induced by fear and appeasement, this road led to Munich and the Second World War.

Within a bipolar political system the difficulties of applying such a policy are multiplied tenfold. At the same time, the existence of nuclear weapons has made the abyss over which the powers balance a thousand times deeper. Under these circumstances it is more important than ever that, as soon as a situation becomes critical, every possible effort should be made to settle the dispute without loss of face for any of the parties involved. In this respect the United Nations and the neutral powers have a definite task to perform. But it is becoming increasingly difficult to perform this function as nations of all sizes are drawn into one or the other bloc. Hence it is in everyone's interest that a fairly substantial group of secondary states remain outside the alliance systems. There is no shortage of such states, but mere numbers are not enough. The question is, rather, whether the great number of newly independent states that are now swelling the General Assembly of the United Nations may not create the risk of delay and confusion over any peace-making initiative taken at a critical moment.

3. Collective security (or peace through international law)

The term "collective security" is often employed, naturally enough, in a loose and general sense so that it includes all cases in which a group of states jointly seek to ensure their security by means of collective arrangements, such as, for example, is the case in NATO and other similar defensive alliances. This is not, however, the sense in which this expression is employed here. In political theory, this term has been used to describe peace preserving arrangements of the kind that was attempted for the first time through the League of Nations Covenant, and it is in this narrower sense that the term is used here.

The central fact in the idea of collective security as opposed to the principle of the balance of power is that peace is to be preserved through a set of legal obligations, instead of the unrestrained self-interest and free exercise of power that, as we have seen, lie at the heart of the balance of power. The philosophy of collective security puts international society on the same footing as a firmly established national society organized into a state. States have, by and large, succeeded in putting a stop to the violent settlement of conflicts between individuals or groups of individuals within the state, thereby ensuring a peaceful society. As individuals we have learned—say the proponents of this philosophy—to submit our disputes to a court and to accept the court's ruling. We have learned to respect the law that says that no one shall take the law into his own hands, particularly when it comes to using force. And if anyone insufficiently imbued with such respect tries to use violence in an effort to oppose the rule of law, society, by legal means, takes the appropriate steps including, if necessary, force, to overcome his resistance. The knowledge that society will, with overwhelming might, punish the individual who violates the law and breaks the peace supplies a strong, selfish reason for refraining from doing so.

Thus the idea is that if peace is to be secured also in the international community of nations, states, too, must learn to refrain from using violence against each other and to accept instead the legal settlement of all conflicts (compulsory and unrestricted arbitration or adjudication). A state that violates the peace and opposes the rule of law must be met by sanctions applied with overwhelming force. The knowledge that this will happen will provide a motive of self-interest for refraining from aggression. Such sanctions shall be carried out through all states undertaking to join forces against the state that has been guilty of a breach of peace. Acting in solidarity, they will punish the guilty party by means of an economic boycott and, if necessary, joint military action.

Thus the central tenet of collective security consists of the following two legal rules: (1) a *prohibition* of resorting to war or any other form of violence as a means of furthering the national interests of a state, and (2) a *command* that all states shall jointly apply sanctions against any violator of the prohibition mentioned. Such sanctions can take the form of a boycott and/or the use of armed force. There are two exceptions to the prohibition of the use of violence: (a) an attacked state is permitted to defend itself, and (b) any state has the right and, if need be, the duty to use force as a sanction against an aggressor.

If one compares this with the balance of power system, it will be seen that they are similar in that both aim at a system whereby a state that is thinking of going to war must expect to meet with overwhelming resistance and will therefore act reasonably and refrain from carrying out its aggressive plans. The main difference between the two is that whereas the policy of balance of power is based on the fact that the enlightened self-interest of the leading powers, reflected in shifting alliances, will lead to the desired result, the system of collective security seeks to achieve the same result through each state entering into a legal undertaking to join with all the others in resisting the state that breaks the peace.

Collective security knows no alliances. An alliance denotes a given group of states who jointly seek to strengthen their own special security, usually against a specific threat. An alliance therefore has a special and concrete aim. Collective security is both universal and abstract. It is designed to protect the security of all against any danger regardless of where it stems from. Its aim is universal and anonymous: sanctions are applied against anyone, whether friend or enemy, who has violated the peace.

The practical implementation of the collective security program raises many problems. As regards the first point in the program, namely the prohibition of resorting to war or other forms of violence, there are no great difficulties in formulating such a prohibition. In the League of Nations Covenant this prohibition was set out in a limited form. In Article 10, the members undertook to respect the territorial integrity and political independence of the other members, but this did not imply any absolute prohibition of resorting to war. This appeared in Articles 12, 13, and 15, which laid down definite rules as to the circumstances under which war was permitted or forbidden. The main rule was the "cooling-off rule" whereby it was forbidden to resort to war until the dispute had been submitted to arbitration, judicial settlement, or to inquiry by the Council of the League and a period of three months had elapsed after the award by the arbitrators or the judicial decision of the report by the Council. Subsequently, in the Kellogg-Briand Pact of 1928, this prohibition was extended in that the parties thereto frankly renounced war as an instrument of national policy. This prohibition, however, applied only to war and not to other forms of violence, even armed force and, in particular, military reprisals. In the United Nations Charter the prohibition was extended to include other forms of violence. The Charter provides that all members shall refrain in their international relations from the threat or use of force in any manner inconsistent with the purposes of the United Nations.

On the other hand, great difficulties arise when it comes to defining more closely the actual content of the prohibition and the practical measures to be taken against a country that has failed to observe it. The point is that it has always been accepted as a matter of course —and this is now explicitly provided for in Article 51 of the United Nations Charter—that the attacked party has the right to defend itself. The prohibition to resort to war consequently applies only to a *war of aggression,* and the actual meaning of such prohibition therefore depends on a closer definition of aggression, assuming that a politically acceptable definition is at all possible.

If a war of aggression is to give rise to sanctions and, more particularly, it is intended that such sanctions shall be applied automatically, it is very important to be able to define aggression so closely on the basis of objective factors that, in practice, when the actual facts have been established, there will be no doubt about to whom the sanctions will be applied.

In the years between the two world wars many efforts were made to define the terms "aggression" and "aggressor" but without success.

One particularly well-known definition is that worked out by a committee headed by Nicholas Politis in connection with the 1933 disarmament conference in Geneva. According to this definition a state should be considered an aggressor if it was the first to commit any of the following acts:

(1) declaration of war upon another State;
(2) invasion by its armed forces, with or without a declaration of war, on the territory of another State;
(3) attack by its land, naval, or air forces, with or without a declaration of war, on the territory, vessels, or aircraft of another State;
(4) naval blockade of the coasts or ports of another State;
(5) provision of support to armed bands formed in its territory which have invaded the territory of another State, or refusal, notwithstanding the request of the invaded State, to take in its own territory all the measures in its power to deprive those bands of all assistance or protection.

It was added that no political, military, economic, or other grounds could be invoked as a reason for aggression and that the definition given was to be observed regardless of what wrong had been done to the attacking state. Thus no form of provocation was to be accepted as an excuse for committing an aggression.

Neither this nor any other "objective" definition has won general support, and this is quite understandable. The reason is that in this respect one is faced with an insoluble dilemma. The stricter the definition, the less acceptable it is, for no strict rule can allow for the political and moral considerations that necessarily arise in practice when it is a question of taking the drastic step of applying sanctions against a state. It is quite unthinkable that a decision of such political scope should be made automatic and, in particular, that no account should be taken of underlying interests and legal factors. On the other hand, the more flexible the definition, in particular in so far as it can also take into account provocations, underlying interests, and legal factors, the less it will serve its stated purpose, which is to avoid estimates, doubt, and subjectivity when applied in practice. The truth of the matter is that this aim cannot be fulfilled.

In view of these considerations, others have adopted the viewpoint that sanctions should be applied quite regardless of whether the state in question was guilty or not, in the same way as the police act to stop a riot. Thus they are no longer sanctions in the proper sense of the term. As already stated in Chapter VII.2, this method does not work in practice either.

The United Nations Charter refrains from giving any definition of the term "aggression." But by limiting the right of self-defense to cases of *armed* attack (Article 51) it implies indirectly that no provocation or underlying interests or legal factors can justify the use of force. It has already been explained that this far-reaching prohibition has lost its meaning because the assumption on which it rests, namely that the United Nations is able to protect the interests and rights of the injured party, has turned out to be an illusion (Chapter IV.3).

As regards the second main rule of collective security, concerning everyone's duty to take part in the sanctions against the aggressor, the question arises as to how this duty is to be defined and by what conditions it is to be governed. Under the Covenant of the League of Nations this duty was direct and automatic, i.e., the mere fact that a member resorted to war in violation of the Covenant meant, *eo ipso*, that it was the duty of every other member immediately to apply sanctions, at any rate in the form of a boycott. Each individual member was to use its own judgment in deciding to what extent the Covenant had been violated. The Council of the League of Nations had no authority to take any binding decision on this question but could only give advice as regards the joint application of military sanctions.

It is not difficult to imagine the chaos that would have ensued if the states had actually tried to apply this system in practice. It was only to be expected that there would be differences of opinion concerning any given breach of peace, with the result that some states would have applied sanctions to one party and others to the other party. Furthermore, military sanctions applied by one state to another would have been regarded as an aggression and, accordingly, would have given rise to more sanctions and so on.

It is understandable, therefore, that in the years after 1920 various attempts were made, by means of additional agreements, to bring some order and system into the application of sanctions. However, none of these attempts succeeded.

Realizing that a decentralized and automatic system was impossible, the United Nations Charter adopted a system whereby the Security Council is authorized to take the decision binding upon all as to how far sanctions shall be applied, what the nature of the sanctions is to be and what states shall specifically participate in their application. As we know, however, this system exists only on paper.

While the idea of collective security has, technically speaking, been formulated more effectively in the United Nations Charter, its scope has been greatly restricted. Owing to the veto rule there can be no question of sanctions against a major power (i.e., one of the five permanent members of the Security Council) or a small power that a major power may wish to protect. In the mutual relations between the major powers, particularly those between East and West (that is, in the areas central to international politics), the preservation of peace, according to the system of the Charter, is left to the self-regulating play of the balance of power.

The fact that the idea of collective security does not operate under present conditions because of the current major political schism is a historical fact that cannot exempt us from making a judgment of principle as to the force of this idea. We must determine whether its present lack of success is to be attributed to fundamental and insoluble inherent defects or whether it can be explained as being the result of accidental historical circumstances.

The basic tenet of the philosophy of collective security is that peace shall be built on the basis of law. In international relations, too, the rule of law is to be substituted for that of might. The first principle of this system must therefore be the banning of war and other forms of violence. Why go any further? The answer is obvious: It cannot be taken for granted that the states' respect for the law and the undertakings into which they have entered will in themselves be sufficient to dissuade them, when important national interests are at stake, from having recourse to violence—just as we dare not take it for granted that respect for the law will suffice to dissuade the citizens of a state from committing crimes. Thus, it is argued, a state that is guilty of a breach of peace must be punished in the same way as a criminal is punished in a state. The execution of the sanctions is entrusted to all the states that are members of a world organization and that undertake, in a charter, to uphold law and peace in this way, if anyone should attempt to violate the fundamental peace undertaking. To sum up, therefore: *The undertaking to preserve peace shall be enforced by means of an undertaking to apply sanctions.*

This is, unfortunately, the point at which the analysis and the comparison with the preservation of peace in a national society stops. But we must go further and ask ourselves: If we dare not assume that states will voluntarily—i.e., out of respect for the law— fulfill their peace undertaking, how can we rely on them to fulfill their sanction undertakings out of sheer respect for the undertakings entered into?

I do not think that a satisfactory reply can be given to this question. The idea of sanctions does not do away with, but only displaces, the difficulties. The idea is that the undertaking to preserve peace shall be enforced by another undertaking which—alas!—in itself fares no better than the first. This second undertaking is therefore in need of enforcement by means of a third undertaking, and so on *ad infinitum.*

As far as I can see, the only imaginable reply to this criticism would be that the self-interest of the states would generate sufficiently powerful motives for inducing them to fulfill their sanction obligations. However, a little thought and practical experience will soon show that this is not the case.

As already explained, collective security is characterized by its abstract and anonymous aim. A state must be prepared to apply sanctions, including, if necessary, military sanctions, against *any* peacebreaker. The need for solidarity is absolute and leaves no room for "ifs or buts." Traditional relations of friendship or enmity are wholly irrelevant. The same applies to any other consideration of interests in relation to the conflict situation that calls for sanctions. The only valid motive is the abstract desire to preserve peace. Thus Denmark may in a certain circumstance apply sanctions against Sweden in a conflict situation between Sweden and the Soviet Union, the United Kingdom shall take up arms against the United States for the sake of Cuba, and so forth. In short, states are not only to be forbidden to fight for the reason for which they have up to now resorted to war— namely, for what they regard as their vital national interests—but they are now expected, in order to defend the abstract idea of peace, to undertake to go to war against their vital interests and traditional ties. I have no further arguments for those who believe that states can be persuaded to act at variance with everything that has hitherto been the driving force of foreign policy.

It may, perhaps, be argued that the system may still be based on self-interest, if we take the long-term view. The states must learn to understand that peace can only be secured through unconditional solidarity between them. If every state, even the strongest, can be certain that *all* the other states, without discussion or conditions, will turn against it with their united power, then none will dare to start a war. In view of this, each state, conscious of its enlightened self-interest, will be prepared to sacrifice all its short-term interests and ignore its relations of friendship or enmity.

Experience in this case, as in numberless other human situations where this line of reasoning may be adopted, shows that this conception has no roots in reality. It is not difficult to understand why. Seen from the standpoint of the interests of state A, action based on solidarity will seem desirable only on condition that this principle is also followed by other states. As state A, however, has no guarantee that this will be the case, it dare not act in this way. The same applies to every other state, and so none will fulfill the requirement of collective security—unless it happens in a given situation to fit in with the interests of the state concerned.

Hans Kelsen, the leading law philosopher, dismisses these objections regarding the practical applicability of collective security, but, as I see it, his arguments are merely a sophistical play with words. He argues that if the system is effectively applied the participating states will not be exposed to any overwhelming risks. The objections that have been put forward concerning the possibility of applying the system do not therefore apply to the idea of collective security, but it is the attitude of the members of the system that deprives it of its effectiveness. What Kelsen is saying is that *if* states effectively fulfill their obligations under a collective security system, the latter will achieve its aim.

It cannot, of course, be denied that the idea in itself is a good one, but in practice the decisive question is whether, given the views and motivations that actually determine the behavior of states, there is any prospect that these will comply with the requirements of the system. In my opinion, the answer to this question is in the negative, and nothing that Kelsen has said offers any proof to the contrary. If we must accept the fact that the system cannot be applied so long as states think and behave as they do at present, it is small consolation to know that the idea is a good one and could be applied if states acted on other and more rational principles than they actually do.

The fundamental flaw in the philosophy of collective security, as I have pointed out before, is the superficial and misleading way in which relations between states are likened to relations between individuals in a civil society. A nation or nations, under the spell of the word "sanction," may believe that, so long as some action is taken that can be described as a sanction, they have thereby created a legal situation comparable with the peaceful order existing in a national society. What they overlook, however, are the profound differences as to *who* is to enforce the law and the *situation* in which this "enforcer" finds himself.

In a state, the law is enforced by authorities specially set up for the purpose. These authorities are made up of persons who, as individuals, are themselves members of the society in question. But (normally) the exercise of their official duties does not clash with their private interests or in any way endanger their welfare. The police and the judge who deal with a case of theft can carry out their duties without passion or fear, for they are not personally involved in the case and have nothing to fear from the thief.

In international relations, however, the law would be enforced by the parties involved themselves, without it being possible for the enforcing powers to dissociate their official function from ties they might have and engagements entered into with the delinquent state. Similarly, the carrying out of sanctions may involve a state in considerable risk. No, this situation cannot be compared with the peaceful order in a state but rather with the *modus vivendi* that can exist within a team of gangsters or between different teams of gangsters. It is a fact that in the American underworld there is a not insignificant trend toward the establishment of a "peaceful and lawful order" based on territorial divisions and other agreements, in conjunction with a "judicial authority" empowered to apply sanctions. But peace in that world is always precarious and threatened by the fear that someone may choose to break the existing solidarity and liquidate the chief or another rival in order to seize power. It seems to me that this underworld reflects, mirror-like, a true picture of the Great of this world.

Collective security in a community of powerful sovereign states means collective insecurity. This, as already indicated, simply follows from the nature of that community and is not the result of accidental historical circumstances. But, it may be added, the historical

circumstances reflected in recent developments have further contributed to making this idea unworkable. If the hundred or so states on
this planet were all roughly equal in power and relatively weakly
armed, the outlook would be somewhat more favorable. There
would be less risk in participating in sanctions, and there would be
more chance of being able to apply them successfully. But this does
not happen to be the case. There has, instead, been an increasing
trend toward the concentration of power resources in the hands of a
small number of states. In the mutual relations between these states,
the idea of sanctions has become meaningless, not least because
heavy rearmament would be virtually certain to make the application of military sanctions synonymous with the outbreak of an all-
destroying world war.

This analysis is borne out by historical experience. In the Covenant of the League of Nations, the idea of collective security was
defined on the basis that each of the member states was a possible
aggressor. Only once—in the case of Italy, when that country attacked Ethiopia in 1935—was any attempt made to apply economic
sanctions. This attempt did not, however, succeed in stopping the
Italians, for the very reason that power politics and other interests
clashed with the obligations assumed under the Covenant, and the
result was that the measures taken were intentionally so lenient as to
be without effect (Chap. VII.2).

In the United Nations Charter, there is little left of the idea of
collective security. Taking the realistic view that the application of
sanctions to a major power would only lead to a world war, no attempt has been made to apply this idea as regards the danger to
peace constituted by the great powers themselves. As regards the
mutual relations between the other states (in so far as there are no
competing interests among the major powers in this respect) the
Charter has established a sanctions system under the supreme authority of the Security Council. Apart from the fact that this system
does not work in practice, it is doubtful whether it can be said to
fulfill the idea of collective security. Indeed, the system provided for
in the Charter is based on the reality of power politics and not on
abstract legal ideas. Its main pillar is the political unity of the Great
Powers. So long as this unity does not exist, a state can, under this
system, start a war whenever it wishes without any risk of punishment. Conversely, if the major powers are united they can adopt

such measures as they deem effective for the preservation of international peace and security, without having to take into account which of the parties has violated the Charter as an aggressor. On the whole, the peace system laid down in the Charter is best described as an institutionalized continuation of the Great Powers' hegemony in the Concert of Europe, so that their leading role has been further strengthened by the rule that all other powers are legally obliged to assist the major powers in the application of sanctions following the instructions issued by the Security Council.

Briefly speaking, the failure of the idea of collective security can be attributed to a lack of insight in the nature of international law and to the difference between it and national law. Taking national society as an example, an attempt has been made to replace might by law, without, however, realizing that the law between states (that is, international law) belongs to a category different from that of national law and lacks the latter's capacity to canalize interests and aspirations. It is appropriate to conclude, therefore, that the problem of the preservation of peace should be settled by states instituting among themselves a legal system of the same nature and strength as the national systems. This is the program on which the movement for the establishment of a world state is based.

4. The world state (or peace through state law)

The modern movement for the establishment of a world state goes back to the years immediately preceding the Second World War, but it was the atom bomb that gave real life to it. In his brilliant book *The Anatomy of Peace* (1946), which became an international bestseller, Emery Reeves strongly emphasized the fundamental idea that there will always be wars so long as mankind is organized in groups enjoying unrestricted sovereignty and that a lasting peace could therefore only be secured if states agreed to limit their sovereignty for the sake of a powerful over-all governmental authority, in other words, a world state. This book, together with the frustrated hopes of effective co-operation between the major powers in the United Nations and the frightful threat of the atom bomb, acted as a stimulus to the creation of a great number of associations all over the world (outside the Communist bloc) whose object it was to work for the establishment of a world state. Gradually, a co-operation was organized. In the United States, where the movement made a strong impact from the beginning, a number of these associations merged to form the United World Federalists. This and other national associations joined forces in 1947 as the World Movement for World Federal Government, later known as World Association of World Federalists. This world-wide organization now has affiliated branches in more than thirty countries (all of them outside the Communist bloc).

The common aim of the movement, as indicated by the name of the organization, is the establishment of a *federal* world government. This implies an important political restriction of the terms on which peace is to be purchased. A federal state has two characteristic features: (1) the over-all state structure is provided with only *limited* governmental authority so that the constituent states are not fully absorbed into the union, but retain in a number of sectors (which may vary in scope) their governmental powers *vis-à-vis* their own citizens. Hence what is known as "sovereignty" is shared between the paramount federal state and the constituent states; (2) the constituent states participate in the federation on an equal footing, so that the over-all state is the result of the pooling by all these states equally of a part of their governmental power in a common "fund," i.e. the federation. Through these two features, a federal state differs from (1) a *unified state* in which the former states have completely lost their independent power and now exist only as a kind of administrative area; and (2) a *suzerain state* created by the unification of two or more states on an unequal basis, where the actual power is exercised by one of the participating states on behalf of all. The paramount state is known as the suzerain state and the others as vassal states.

Viewed in terms of a world state, this means that the federalists reject the idea of a world empire, whether one where the ruling state fully incorporates all other states as its own provinces or one where they are allowed as vassal states to retain a certain limited power of government. It might also be said that the federalists' aim is to bring about a freely accepted federal structure on the basis of equality as opposed to a union based on conquest and inequality.

Most of us will surely sympathize with the political judgments reflected in the stated aim of world federalism. At the same time, it must be recognized that, at any rate, before the advent of the atom bomb, it seemed more probable that a world state would be created by conquest rather than by voluntary union. Through the ages, attempts have been made to achieve world domination through war, and even today there are states that, if the risk were not too great, would be only too pleased to secure total power, not only internally but also externally. The *Pax Romana* of the Roman Empire represented the achievement of world peace in the "world" as it was at that time, and a *Pax Sovietica* could do likewise in our time if the communist ideology were to triumph.

It is also clearly assumed in the federalists' aim that the federation created by voluntary union will be organized on a democratic basis, which, in particular, means that the federation's legislative assembly will be elected by the people of the world and take decisions like a parliament. As it is difficult to imagine that the totalitarian states would agree in this way to let their peoples develop a taste for free elections, this is another obstacle to the realization of this aim.

Among the federalists there has been some disagreement as to ways and means. In fact one of the points at issue has been the question of relations with the totalitarian states. At the outset there were many who, in their anxiety to get things going, considered that a start should be made as soon as two states were prepared to unite and that for the moment it was preferable to aim only at a federation of democratic states. Most, however, realized that this would only succeed in dividing the world instead of uniting it. Hence today, universalism is a generally accepted point on the federalist program. In other words, it is intended that a federalist system should embrace all states, including the totalitarian powers, and not come into being until it has been accepted by an overwhelming majority. Clark and Sohn, who have worked out the most detailed plan for the establishment of a world government in *World Peace through World Law* (2nd ed., 1960) have formulated the following conditions for the implementation of such a plan, i.e. (1) at least five-sixths of all states must be included, (2) the states in question must represent at least five-sixths of the world's population, and (3) they must include the twelve states that at that particular time have the largest populations.

A movement of this kind is, of course, all too liable to attract dreamers whose knowledge and intelligence are not on a par with their good will. Especially at the beginning, it displayed open dis-trust toward governments and diplomats. The world state was to be set up directly by the people over the heads of all official authorities by means of a people's world convention, i.e. a world assembly that would enact a basic legislation. Indeed, such an assembly was con-vened in Geneva in 1951 on the basis of one delegate per million inhabitants, but, as only two delegates attended, the world state was not created on that occasion! Others, who did not go so far in their mistrust of the routine spirit of foreign ministries, considered that an effort should be made to win parliamentarians over to their cause, so that plans for the setting up of a world government might be adopted through the legislative channels. This view led, in 1951, to the crea-tion of the World Association of Parliamentarians for World Govern-ment. This organization is still in existence, but there cannot be many who regard it as an instrument for the realization of their ma-jor aim. The extensive support this association has received in many parliaments is the best proof of the fact that they regard it as practi-cally insignificant!

In relation to the United Nations, too, the movement has revised its strategy. At first, its attitude was one of indifference which, from time to time, turned into direct hostility, but now the generally ac-cepted policy doctrine is that the United Nations is to be regarded as the first step toward world government. The movement's immediate short-term aim is accordingly described as the strengthening and de-velopment of the existing world organization. It is hoped in this way to attain, step by step, the long-term target, i.e. the world state.

Thus it will be seen that the movement's program has become sec-ularized. The initial impetus has disappeared and the realization of a world state has been relegated to the more or less indeterminate fu-ture. Practically speaking, the movement is now a movement for the reform of the United Nations. The practical evaluation of this pro-gram accordingly centers on the actual prospects of such a reform and what hope there is of a world government being established by this method.

In order to be able to answer this question it is necessary first to define what is meant by the term "world state." There are several factors involved:

(1) Total disarmament and the creation of a world police force. As we have seen, the idea of collective security cannot be realized

because it is impossible to enforce the law with regard to states that are armed to the teeth, while the international organization is unarmed or has only minor forces at its disposal. It is on this point that the decisive difference with national legal order emerges. Individuals are unarmed, and all exercise of violence (apart from self-defense) is monopolized by society. Since no one can stand up to the organized power of the state (police, army), violence normally need only be employed to a modest extent. The fundamental importance of the coercive machinery lies in its existence and the latent threat it constitutes. If an equally effective legal order is to be instituted in the international field, the first requirement is for a similar monopoly of the means of violence and of their use, which again implies total disarmament by all states (except for lightly armed police forces necessary for the preservation of law and order) and the establishment of a central authority of military nature, sufficiently large and well armed to be able to overcome any resistance. It is only when such a regrouping of power resources has taken place that the prohibition of a state's taking the law into its own hands can be expected to be effective.

(2) A system of courts of justice to settle all legal disputes between states. This is the counterpart to the above-mentioned prohibition. It provides the legal means of redress for anyone who considers himself an injured party. It goes without saying that it will be for the law enforcement authority of the world state to see to it that the judgments are executed.

(3) A supreme legislative authority empowered to take political decisions in order to reduce tension within the world state, in the same way as the legislative authority in a national state, through its intervention and regulations, constantly adjusts the distribution of wealth and other values among various groups in society. Among the federalists there are differences of opinion on how far reaching this authority should be. The majority are "minimalists," i.e. they consider that the political power of the world state should not go beyond the point required to ensure the preservation of peace. It must therefore include, among other things, the power to levy taxes to cover its budget. Apart from this, however, it is not very clear what other powers would be required.

A detailed account of these principles will be found in Clark and Sohn's *World Peace through World Law*. It is satisfying to note that

Clark and Sohn have unreservedly emphasized the primary importance of disarmament: *until total disarmament is achieved all other measures to implement this program will be like beating the empty air.* Once this is clearly understood, together with the tremendous difficulties involved in total disarmament, only a few will still have the courage to share the authors' optimism in believing that the world state will be established by 1975! To mention only one of these difficulties: How can we be certain that the states with nuclear weapons will deliver them all up to the world government? As is known, there is no scientific method of proving the existence or locating the hiding place of such weapons.

If the argument concerning the prior necessity but practical improbability of total disarmament is accepted, then the plans to strengthen and develop the United Nations are devoid of any interest, for legal structures that do not correspond to actual social power relationships exist only on paper. Let us take, for instance, the proposed reform that consists in strengthening the authority of the General Assembly by instituting voting rules whereby each state will be assigned a fair weighted voting strength, without the major powers having any veto rights. In the first place, there is no reason to believe that the Great Powers, while continuing their rearmament, will be prepared to submit to such an authority. Secondly, let us imagine that in one way or another such a system is actually adopted. Even then there is still no reason to believe that it would survive. Or does anyone think that, for instance, the Soviet Union would act on a resolution adopted by the General Assembly asking it to withdraw from the occupied or captive states and to hold free elections under United Nations supervision? It would be acting in an unreasonable and contradictory fashion if it did. So long as states maintain their armed forces and thus base their national existence on a balance of power, it will be absurd for a state, out of respect for a resolution adopted mainly through the votes of rival states, to give up important power positions. To sum up, therefore: we are asked to create an order where might is replaced by right. How can one believe that the states will be prepared to accept such an order, so long as they retain their decentralized individual control over decisive power resources, especially in the military field? For in this way they ensure that the last word shall lie with force.

If the reader will agree with me when I say that total disarmament is an essential prerequisite for further progress, any additional arguments designed to bring out the banality and emptiness of the federalist program are superfluous. It follows that the long-term aim, namely the establishment of a world state, is relegated to some unimaginable future and that the short-term aim, i.e. the strengthening and development of the United Nations, is a fallacy. I consider this program to be banal in that it expresses the truism that peace between states cannot be preserved until they give up their sovereign rights to the means to wage war and recognize a central authority which will enjoy a monopoly of such means. I regard the program as empty because it does not suggest any feasible way of achieving this objective.

It may nevertheless be useful to analyze this line of reasoning a little more closely in order to bring out the deeper-lying reasons for its failure. Indeed, an insight into this problem can help us to gain a better understanding as to which method is most likely to lead toward a world government.

The fundamental fallacy, which, in different degrees, characterizes the reasoning of the federalists, is that they believe that a legal order is something that can be created through a resolution if the people can first be persuaded that this is right and necessary. This conception is reflected in the typical ways in which the problem is frequently raised and discussed. They speak of whether it is advisable to "institute" a given legal order, or "replace might by right," or "grant to" or "provide" the United Nations with given powers—for instance, the power to disarm all states, leaving them only with a police force. Again, the federalists speak about the "setting up" of a court, which will be "empowered" to settle all disputes between states. They do not ask *under what conditions* a given legal order is possible or *whether these conditions exist*.

At this point, anyone familiar with the history of legal thought will nod with recognition. Here we are back to the abstract rationalism of the Enlightenment! There was no doubt at that time that the sovereign—the absolute ruler, the king by divine right—like God, could create through words: Let there be Light—and there was Light! The same unhistorical and unsociological outlook was professed by the great English philosopher and legal reformer Jeremy Bentham. He never speculated as to how a legal reform could be adapted to the people's cultural tradition, customs, and prejudices. On one occasion he said that he could just as easily legislate for Hindustan as for his own parish. If this belief in the power of reason and will seems to us touchingly naïve today and strikes us as purely utopian—in other words, something unaffected by reality and leading a free existence in the world of fantasy—it is thanks to the insight into the dependence of law on the historical evolution and the cultural traditions of a people that the historical school has taught us.

It is not difficult to understand how the "magic-will" conception of the genesis of law can arise out of a superficial interpretation of the legal "facts of life." We are daily witnesses to the fact that law is created by a body of people gathering in a legislative assembly (parliament, etc.) and taking votes. Is this not proof of the power of words and will? Why should not the same magic work on the international level?

The fact is that law has never been created by words. The power of the national legislator lies in the fact that he is able to release attitudes of allegiance, respect, and obedience deeply rooted in a people which has lived together for a long time as a nation. Why do most of us obey the law? Not only and not mainly because we are afraid of punishment, but because we recognize—I could almost say, "believe in"—the validity of the constitution and accept its institutions as the instrument through which the national unity and will of the people manifest themselves. The basic feature of a people is the will to national unity. Those who want, or rather those who feel, this unity and community also accept the constitution and the authorities instituted through it. We are still very much in the dark when it comes to explaining how the feeling of community and solidarity required to fashion a nation arises in the course of time. However, the fact remains that these psychological factors, despite their somewhat mysterious character, constitute the basis of the political power of the state and are the reason why the law—unlike, say, the rule of terror imposed by an occupying power—is experienced by the citizen as a valid order meant not only to be feared but also to be respected. If this basis is in good working order, i.e., if the nation has no separatist tendencies (national, religious, or social dissenting groups) and stands united in its acceptance of the existing political system, the legislator has a rather free hand. By this I mean that he can enact laws that, though large sections of the population consider them to be unreasonable and unjust in relation to their interests, are nevertheless obeyed and respected because the forces that bind the people together into a community are stronger than the resistance prompted by self-interest.

However intangible or incomprehensible this basis of political power may be, it is still a very solid reality, which like any other reality cannot be fashioned by words or an act of will. If the legislator's "word" appears to create the law, it is only because he is working within the framework of an institutional system that, as already explained, is supported by the nation's political trust.

A further point arises. It has been said above that peace in a national society depends on the official authorities having a monopoly of the use of force backed by a special machinery set up for this purpose (police, army). One often tends to imagine that the coercive force a state is thus able to exert is a primary factor and a basis for the legal order; he who has the might can determine what the law shall be. This is a fallacy. Power is a function of law and political trust, not the other way around. The rulers' control over the machinery of coercion stems from the fact that by virtue of the constitution they occupy the key positions, which entitles them to such control. Power resources are not automatic; they must be used by men, and if men do not politically recognize the right of the authorities to rule, the would-be rulers are powerless. No dictator can rule through the sole use of physical force. At any rate, there must always be an inner circle that controls the means of force and that chooses freely to obey the dictator out of sheer political conviction.

These facts afford a further reason why the idea of establishing a world state sometime in a not too distant future must remain utopian. The sense of community and the integration of people's minds, which are the essential prerequisite for political integration, are wholly lacking in international relations. We live in a world where people's loyalty and trust are, in actual fact, bound to the national state, which is therefore the center of political and military power. Such is reality, and it cannot be altered through the mere desire to sever this bond by "establishing" a world state. One speaks of "transferring" sovereignty to a world authority. But sovereignty—if by that we mean political rule—is not something that can be transferred at will. This can only happen when conditions are ripe, in other words, when the peoples concerned are psychologically prepared for it by their historical development.

I have said above that a world state will be unimaginable until all states have carried out total disarmament and have disbanded their national armies in order to create a central military machinery to be placed at the disposal of the world authority. It seems that the federalists are beginning to understand this. However, some further considerations regarding the psychological foundations of a state show that the difficulties lie still deeper. Let us boldly imagine for a moment that the necessary centralization and monopolization of armed forces has been achieved. Even then, it is doubtful whether a world government would really work. An army is led by a staff of generals and other officers, and arms are used by soldiers. Both the officers and the ranks are human beings; the power of a world government would completely depend on the feelings of loyalty, trust, and obedience the world constitution and its institutions would inspire in these men. Is it necessary to mention instances of armies that rebelled when these requirements were not fulfilled? So long as officers and the ranks in the international army feel that they are Americans, Russians, or Indians rather than world citizens, such an army cannot be relied upon, and I believe that this is the way people would continue to feel if the world state were established today.

There would be other alarming prospects. For instance, it would certainly be tempting for a strong national faction in an international army or its general staff to seize control of decisive weapons and thereby achieve absolute world domination and establish a world empire. The world federation so neatly thought out by the federalists, in which all states would participate on an equal footing, would probably soon turn into a totalitarian authority where one state would exercise an absolute rule—in other words, a world empire or suzerain state, with all the other states as vassal states. Then peace would have come to the world as *Pax Americana* or *Pax Sovietica*.

The federalists often try to justify their optimism by saying that it is necessary to adopt their plan in order that mankind shall avoid the holocaust of a nuclear war. Apart from the fact that we have a chance of surviving even without a world authority, it is merely wishful thinking. Necessity has never made the impossible possible. If I were asked to speculate on this question, I would say that within the next hundred years the world is more likely to go under in an atomic war than to be unified into a world state.

It is not surprising that so many respectable citizens, including many politicians, are members of federalist associations or that the present Danish Minister of Foreign Affairs, Per Hækkerup, is the Danish Representative on the Executive Committee of the World Association of Parliamentarians for World Government. It is difficult to refuse to support an association that is so incontestably right in proclaiming that there would be peace on earth if its program were applied and faithfully observed. What is so convenient about such associations is that they impose absolutely no obligations—not even the obligation to think. Anyone not satisfied with the federalist platform can always create a rival association for the fulfillment of the Sermont on the Mount, which, with the same incontestable right, could promise peace on earth if its program were applied.

5. Conclusion: Functionalism

The considerations set forth in this chapter have been realistic but not optimistic. The intention has been to show that the idea of peace through law—in other words, the idea of collective security or a world state—is utopian and an illusion liable to mislead thought and action. The system under which we live and will continue to live in the foreseeable future is that of the political balance of power, and all our efforts must be concentrated on the question as to what can be done to preserve peace within this system. In particular, we must dismiss from our minds the nebulous idea that the United Nations is only a step along the way to something bigger, a seed that will grow into a world state, and that this organization should therefore be developed and be given real authority and power. We must resign ourselves to the fact that the United Nations is and will remain a special and quite useful diplomatic instrument for carrying out the balance of power policy in the field of high-level politics. The most we can hope for is a relaxation of tension in the relations between the Great Powers such as will make it possible for the United Nations to operate in accordance with the Charter, i.e. as an organization of the hegemony of the Great Powers based on the idea of the concert of nations.

I shall now attempt to put forward some considerations regarding the long-term and short-term problems arising in connection with the preservation of peace.

From the long-term point of view, the question is how to progress toward a world authority. I have already explained that the legal organization of a people into a state depends on two important factors without which the law is only an empty shell, namely (1) the existence of well-developed machinery enjoying a monopoly over the use of force, and (2) the existence of a sense of community that has crystallized into a general feeling of allegiance and obedience toward a political system and its institutions. For the sake of convenience, I shall refer to these two factors as "the machinery of power" and "ideology," respectively.

These two factors are equally important to the state's existence and are mutually dependent. Indeed, they are like the proverbial chicken and egg: it is impossible to say which came first. An effective machinery of power cannot be established or work if it is not rooted in an ideology. Conversely, any system that can be effectively maintained has a tendency to develop a corresponding ideology: eventually, all *de facto* governments become *de jure* governments. Similarly, a political ideology cannot remain suspended in mid-air but must be supported by an effective order, which, in the course of time, it helps to develop and strengthen.

I have already described elsewhere in greater detail this notable circular interplay between validity and effectiveness, right and might (*Towards a Realistic Jurisprudence*, Copenhagen, 1946). If this analysis is correct in its main lines, it means that a state develops through a lengthy historical process that involves a continuous interaction, step by step, between common external institutions and a common internal ideology, mutually strengthening one another. The sense of community, which is a necessary condition for the more developed common institutions, is created through the practice of less-developed common institutions.

The basic idea in functionalism is, precisely speaking, that the feeling of community, which is an essential prerequisite for the world state of the future, can only develop if we, however modestly, put this feeling into practice by creating common, universal institutions to further our common interests. Here I am thinking of such institutions as the Universal Postal Union and the many other specialized agencies in which practically all the nations in the world co-operate and share a sense of community. This also applies to the comprehensive work of the United Nations in the economic, social, and cultural fields and the attempt at supranational institutions represented by the European Communities.

It is important, however, to realize that the kind of solidarity that is not only perceived by the intellect but also experienced and felt, the kind of solidarity that is needed for world integration, does not lie round the corner. The road will be a long one, and many a bad year will pass before we reach our destination.

In the short run, however, we must get used to living with the balance of power and rearmament. Nuclear weapons, too, have come to stay. It may perhaps be possible to halt the arms race and achieve a limited degree of disarmament. This would be economically desirable but not in itself of decisive importance for the preservation of peace (Chap. IX). But disarmament will scarcely be possible until the present mutual distrust and fear are considerably reduced, and it is on this point in particular that we should concentrate our efforts.

There is no denying the fact that there is nothing world-shaking about drawing up a program on this basis. There is no room here for any rousing or revolutionary ideas. The task before us is a modest one, which must be pursued from day to day in both minor and major issues, in order that we may gradually succeed in eliminating international tension and promoting mutual understanding and respect. A continuous effort must also be made to improve the means and techniques employed for overcoming international crises.

A more far-reaching suggestion would be to try to consolidate shifting limits of the zones of influence of the major powers through a division of the world into an Eastern zone of interest, a Western zone, and a neutral zone. Such a scheme would be in keeping with the argument already discussed in this chapter that there is no fundamental clash of interests between East and West but that all the conflicts between them are due to the fact that each is afraid that the other will attempt to extend his power and, one day, will become strong enough to impose his rule. This argument is borne out by the fact that it is precisely in the shifting contact areas (Berlin, Korea, Congo, Cuba, and Vietnam) that the greatest dangers are to be found. If the world has to live through a series of such crises something will have to give sooner or later. Hence the desirability of dividing up the world. If it is not possible to unite into one world, the next best thing is to divide into three.

The reason this policy is not possible at the present time is the deep ideological cleavage between the two sides. Each regards the other as the enemy of humanity, with whom it is not possible to come to terms. Seen from the Western side it would be considered rank betrayal to recognize that the Iron Curtain has come down forever between the West and the captive nations.

I agree with this view and conclude that our first task should be to bridge the gulf between East and West. I cannot believe that the dogma of dialectical materialism derived from Hegel's metaphysical philosophy, which is so absolutely contrary to the principles of modern empirical science, will in the long run stand up to critical analysis. In America, the old, hard-boiled Manchester school of liberalism and individualism is clearly giving way to a growing understanding of the social role of the state and the necessity of control over the private capitalistic interest dominant in industry and commerce.

As regards an ideological *rapprochement* between East and West, the European democracies and the Nordic countries in particular may be able to play a special role by setting an example. To the dogmatic Communists we can point to ourselves as living testimony to the falseness of the Marxist claim that democracy is a fiction and that the "proletariat" will never be able to cast off its bonds under this system. We must show them that progress can go hand in hand with freedom. To the conservative Americans who only recognize the "American way of life" we must show our society as an example of a welfare state reconciled with the ideals of freedom, which are such an important part of our common culture.

I believe that the inherent power of thought is such that there is reason to hope for a breakdown of dogmas, even in a closed society where freedom lives in straitened circumstances. But it is clear that *openness* and *freedom* will speed up this development. By openness I mean the possibility for every person or every communication to cross the frontiers of any country unhindered; and by freedom I mean everyone's right to express his views, preach his faith, or proclaim his ideals. When it becomes possible for such exchanges to take place, much will have been achieved. To secure concessions in this respect is perhaps more important than many of the bases and alliances by means of which nations endeavor to preserve the balance of power.

But is this not utopian also? I do not think so. Naturally I do not expect openness and freedom to be achieved at one stroke. But there have already been signs of a thaw, tending to confirm the belief in a gradual development in this direction. There are many ways in which the West could contribute to exchanges of persons and ideas across frontiers. Indeed, this might well serve as a program for peace, not only in the sense often employed in discussions on this subject, namely that mutual knowledge and understanding between the two parties are in themselves one factor making for peace, but more in the sense that an ideological and cultural *rapprochement* is a necessary condition for achieving political stabilization of the balance of power through a division of the world.

If the hope of such a *rapprochement* between the Americans and the Russians is fulfilled, new prospects will be opened up for the United Nations and for the preservation of peace. The way will be open for the Security Council to return to the central position assigned it in the Charter and perhaps even for the application of the security system provided in Chapter VII of the Charter. These prospects will be discussed at greater length elsewhere in this book (Chap. XII.1).

References

1. CAUSES OF WAR
   Aron, Raymond, *Paix et Guerre entre les nations* (1962).
   Benedict, Ruth, *Patterns of Culture* (1934). Also published as a Mentor Book (1946).
   Niebuhr, Reinhold, *The Structure of Nations and Empires* (1959).
   Walz, Kenneth N., *Man, the State, and War* (1959).
   Wright, Quincy, *A Study of War I - II* (1942).
   The Journal of Conflict Resolution. A quarterly for Research Related to War and Peace (since 1957). Vol I (1957) in particular contains many interesting contributions to a definition of the concept of conflict and the problems and methods of conflict research.
   Psychology and International Affairs: Can We Contribute? Proceedings of the XIVth International Congress of Applied Psychology (1962).
2. BALANCE OF POWER
   Kaplan, Morton A. and Nicholas de B. Katzenbach, *The Political Foundations of International Law* (1961).
   Padelford, Norman J. and George A. Lincoln, *International Politics* (1954).
   See also the works of Aron, Niebuhr, and Wright mentioned under 1.
3. COLLECTIVE SECURITY
   Claude, Inis L., Jr., "The Management of Power in the Changing United

Nations," *International Organization* (1961), pp. 219-35 (see also Ruth B. Russel, *loc. cit.*, pp. 630-36).

Collective Security, a Record of the Seventh and Eighth International Studies Conferences of the League of Nations. Ed. by Maurice Bourquin (1936).

Hula, Erich, "Fundamentals of Collective Security," *Social Research* (1957), pp. 1-36.

Johnson, Howard C. and Gerhart Niemeyer, "Collective Security: The Validity of an Ideal," *International Organization* (1954), pp. 19-35.

Kelsen, Hans, *Collective Security under International Law; International Law Studies; 1954* (1956).

Martin, Andrew, *Collective Security* (1952).

4. WORLD STATE

Clark, Grenville and Louis B. Sohn, *World Peace through World Law* (2nd ed., 1960).

Larson, Arthur, *The International Rule of Law* (1961).

Lent, Ernest S., "The Development of United World Federalist Thought Policy," *International Organization* (1955), pp. 486-501.

Schiffer, Walter, *The Legal Community of Mankind* (1954).

Stone, Julius, *Quest for Survival* (1961).

IX ✿

THE PROBLEMS
OF DISARMAMENT

T HE idea of disarmament as a way to peace occupies a prominent place in the mind of the public the world over. This aspect of
the problem of attaining peace is more spectacular than the more
subtle aspects relating to law and political organization discussed in
the preceding chapter. The military installations and weapons of all
kinds, including the most fearful of them all, the absolute weapons
such as the nuclear bomb and the biological and chemical weapons,
are manifest realities which directly conjure up in the mind's eye a
picture of indescribable horror. Many think that rearmament, particularly when it takes the form of an arms race, is a major cause of
war. It is, of course, a fact that the possession of weapons is an
essential prerequisite for waging war. It is then easy to conclude that

war can be eliminated only if we eliminate arms and that disarmament should therefore be the most important factor in a peace policy. This view is strengthened by the fact that taxes are there to remind the citizen how fantastically expensive these death-dealing devices are.

Hence it is not surprising that disarmament has been a permanent item on the agendas of the international peace organizations from the early days of the League of Nations to the present time and has also formed the subject of countless discussions at conferences held outside the framework of the League of Nations or the United Nations. These efforts have always been observed with lively interest by the public. The greater the political tension, the louder have been the demands for disarmament negotiations and the more meager the results (or rather the prospects of results, for, apart from a couple of minor naval agreements in the 1920's, all the efforts made so far to limit armaments through agreement have failed).

This chapter deals with problems of disarmament in relation to the question of war or peace. It begins with a short account of the historical background to the disarmament question. This will be followed by a number of theoretical considerations on the role of armaments as a factor making for war or for peace, in other words the question of the desirability of disarmament and its usefulness as a means of preserving peace. Lastly, I shall discuss the practical feasibility of disarmament, i.e. the political or technical difficulties, which have so far hindered the conclusion of disarmament agreements.

1. The depressing background

THE LEAGUE OF NATIONS PERIOD

The present efforts to achieve disarmament can be traced back to the first Hague Conference in 1899. The decisive reason for Tsar Nicholas II's initiative in calling this peace congress was the desire to ease the burden on the Russian state budget by concluding a disarmament agreement. In a Russian circular of 1898, submitted to many governments, the political dangers and economic burdens of rearmament are described in words that could be used today. But although the question of the limitation of armaments was included as the first point on the program of the conference, it was agreed when the meeting began to leave it out and replace it by other points, and so the conference concerned itself mainly with the question of the peaceful settlement of disputes between states and with making war more humane. Neither at this nor at the ensuing second Hague Conference in 1907 was any result achieved in the disarmament question.

Under the influence of Wilson's ideas and the belief that armaments were a direct cause of war, a sanguine disarmament program was provided for in Article 8 of the League of Nations Covenant. The members of the League recognized "that the maintenance of peace requires the reduction of national armaments to the lowest point consistent with national safety and the enforcement by common action of international obligations." On the basis of this principle the Council, taking account of the geographical situation and circumstances of each state, was to formulate disarmament plans to be adopted by the governments concerned. As a basis for the Council's work, the members undertook to exchange full and frank information as to the scale of their armaments and armaments industry. As a result the secretariat of the League of Nations published an Armaments Yearbook containing information received from members. As there was no kind of control, there are no details available concerning the fullness and frankness of this information.

This program was as impressive as it was unrealistic. True, an attempt was made to pave the way for its application by trying to secure at the peace negotiations a compulsory reduction in German, Austrian, Hungarian, and Bulgarian armaments. Nevertheless some of the victorious allies, most particularly France, felt that it would be indefensible to leave themselves exposed to the military power of a revenge-seeking Germany so long as an effective international security system was not in existence. These powers regarded rearmament more as a symptom than as the cause of international tensions and conflicts. Disarmament was accordingly viewed as a secondary phenomenon that would automatically be realized when international tension had been eliminated and security had been achieved. If this attitude could be summed up in a slogan it might be described as "disarmament through security" (the indirect doctrine). There were, however, other countries, including the Nordic states, that supported unconditional disarmament, which they regarded as a way of eliminating tension and achieving security ("security through disarmament," the direct doctrine).

After a few unsuccessful preliminary attempts to deal with the disarmament problem directly and in isolation, the French viewpoint prevailed. The leading view was that peace was to rest on three pillars, none of which was by itself strong enough to resist the pressure of the threat of war, but jointly they would provide a secure foundation for the building of peace. These three pillars were disarmament, the peaceful settlement of disputes, and collective security through the taking of sanctions against any aggressor.

In the 1920's several attempts were made in accordance with this program to build up a security system in order to clear the way for disarmament. In 1923 unsuccessful negotiations took place for the conclusion of a mutual assistance treaty; but in 1924 apparent agreement was reached on the Geneva Protocol, which combined disarmament with arbitration and mutual assistance. This, however, faltered on account of English opposition after Ramsay MacDonald's Labour government was replaced by a Conservative government. The year 1925 saw the conclusion of the Locarno Pact, a set of treaties guaranteed by England and Italy, which was to consolidate the frontiers and the peace between Germany and her western neighbors. But this modest success was not a sufficient basis for disarmament.

In 1927 it was decided, without waiting for any other combinations, to tackle the problem directly by convening a general disarmament conference, and a committee was set up in order to prepare it. In 1932, after five years of painstaking work, the conference took place in Geneva. But, by that time, the general world situation had deteriorated to such an extent and the League of Nations had suffered such a loss of prestige that success was obviously out of the question. After Hitler had seized power in Germany in January 1933, that country withdrew from both the conference and the League of Nations in October 1933. The negotiations then came to a standstill, and in June 1934 the meetings were formally adjourned and never resumed. The aggressions committed in the ensuing years by the Japanese, Italians, and Germans put a stop to any further attempts at disarmament. Hitler gradually and openly stepped up German rearmament, and when the time came that he should have and still could have been stopped, Chamberlain, at Godesberg and Munich, gave him a free hand, because England, despite Churchill's warnings, was powerless. Here we have a historical example of an insufficient rearmament, inadequate to meet the requirements of the balance of power, being conducive to war.

The only result achieved during those years in the limitation of armaments was not obtained by the League of Nations. In 1921 the United States, which was not a member of the League, invited the major naval powers to a disarmament conference in Washington for the purpose of putting a stop to the naval arms race. The conference culminated in the Washington Treaty of February 1922, whereby the number of the largest types of warships (battleships and aircraft-carriers) was restricted in the proportion of 5:5:5:1¾:1¾ for the United States, Great Britain, Japan, France, and Italy, respectively. At the same time a ceiling was fixed as regards the tonnage and armament of such ships.

IN THE UNITED NATIONS, BEFORE KOREA

Just as the United Nations Charter has given up the unrealistic idea of the League of Nations Covenant concerning an automatic collective security, and, in its place, has created a machinery for the enforcement of peace through the concert of major powers, so the Charter has also taken up another and more realistic attitude to the armaments problem. It does not proclaim any disarmament program but contents itself (Art. 26) with entrusting the Security Council with the responsibility of formulating plans for the establishment of a system for the regulation of armaments. It is said that these plans shall be formulated in order to promote the maintenance of peace "with the least diversion for armaments of the world's human and economic resources." At the same time, the General Assembly is empowered (Art. 11) to make recommendations as regards the general principles governing disarmament and the regulation of armaments. In other words, the authors of the Charter belong to the school that regards armaments problems as secondary questions, on the ground that armaments are a symptom rather than the cause of tension and conflict. Security is the way to disarmament, not the other way around. The aim is not disarmament but the control of armaments, i.e. the prevention of an arms race.

The Charter was drawn up before the atomic bomb existed. The two bombs that were dropped on Japan at the beginning of August 1945 created a new situation and a new set of problems. This was felt so strongly that, to begin with, the atomic bomb completely stole the limelight from conventional disarmament, with the result that in the first years of the United Nations' existence (until Korea) the disarmament negotiations were conducted in two different organs, namely the Atomic Energy Commission, set up by a resolution of the General Assembly dated January 24, 1946, and the Commission for Conventional Weapons, set up by the Security Council on February 13, 1947.

The Atomic Energy Commission, which was established during the first General Assembly (but which was to report to the Security Council) consisted of 12 members: the 11 members of the Security Council plus Canada. Its task was to make proposals designed to ensure that the new source of energy would be used for peaceful ends only. It was natural that the United States, which enjoyed a monopoly of atomic energy at that time, should play the leading role. At the Commission's first meeting, in June 1946, the American delegate, Bernard Baruch, submitted a plan, later named after him, that was mainly based on the Acheson-Lilienthal report.

It was the United States itself who took the initiative in setting up the Atomic Energy Commission. When America decided to seek to internationalize atomic energy instead of holding on to its monopoly it was because it was realized that this monopoly would in any case be of only short duration and that once it was broken, if no settlement were reached, it would be followed by a costly and risky atomic armaments race.

The Baruch plan was of an unusually bold, far-sighted, and constructive nature. Had it been conceived along traditional lines, the control of atomic energy would have come under an *international* arrangement whereby the states would have entered into various obligations in regard to the use of atomic energy for peaceful purposes only and submitted to various measures of inspection and control intended to prevent contraventions. The Baruch plan, however, was based on the idea that such an arrangement would never be effective and opted instead for an arrangement whereby the decisive control over the sources of atomic energy—uranium and thorium mines and the raw materials themselves—would no longer be subject to national authority but would be vested in an international, or rather *supranational,* organ. To my knowledge, this was the first political proposal for the creation of a supranational organ endowed with such powers that it could almost be described as a world government.

In more detail the plan provided that the international organ, known as the International Development Authority, would have:

(1) the right of ownership, or at any rate operational control, over all mines and all atomic raw materials extracted therefrom;

(2) direct control over all industrial plants manufacturing fuel suitable for direct use in an atomic energy plant;

(3) direct control over all atomic energy plants;

(4) the power to apportion atomic fuels to states;

(5) the exclusive right to conduct atomic research and to allow states to carry out such research;

(6) the right to carry out inspections and control and, without veto, to apply effective measures against any state in order to ensure that atomic energy would be used exclusively for peaceful ends.

As soon as an arrangement along these lines was adopted, the United States declared itself prepared to cease production of atomic bombs, to destroy its existing bombs, and to make available all its knowledge concerning the production of atomic energy to the international authority.

Despite the far-reaching scope of this plan, it had, as any plan for the elimination of atomic weapons necessarily must have, one defect that must have rendered it unacceptable to the Russians: it assumed that the Russians would trustingly rely on the United States, which had had time to create a large stock of bombs and material for bombs, to dispose of all this stock down to the last bomb and the last ounce of atomic material. This was too great a demand to make on the mutual trust between the Leviathans of this world. Furthermore, the Russians must have feared that the powerful supranational organ would be so composed that it could be used to promote the development of the West's atomic industry at the expense of the Soviet Union.

It is not surprising therefore that the Soviet Union rejected the Baruch plan and that the ensuing lengthy negotiations—which lasted until the beginning of 1950, when the Soviets walked out of the Commission in protest against the fact that China was still repre-sented by the Formosa government—did not lead to any result. It would not be of any great interest to describe in detail the Soviet counterproposal, which was mainly based on the idea that the United States should immediately deliver up their bombs and agree not to manufacture any more. This was, of course, unacceptable to the Americans. The arguments put forward on either side were intended for public consumption and attuned to their propaganda value. They did not therefore go to the root of the matter, namely the lack of mutual trust and the impossibility of creating a neutral supranational organ.

The Commission for Conventional Armaments, set up in February 1947 and composed of the states represented in the Security Council, was no luckier. The negotiations in this Commission reflected the time-honored opposition between the doctrines of "direct" and "indirect" disarmament. The West held that relaxation of tension and security must precede disarmament and therefore demanded that the following measures be taken first:

(1) the creation of armed forces, placed at the disposal of the Security Council for the implementation of the agreements provided for in Article 43 of the Charter;

(2) effective implementation of international control over atomic energy; and

(3) conclusion of peace treaties with Japan and Germany.

The East, however, was in favor of the direct method and proposed that, without awaiting the realization of the other aims, an agreement should be concluded on disarmament and the reduction of military budgets. The point of this proposal was that it was combined with a prohibition to manufacture and employ atomic weapons. After a resolution that expressed the views of the Western powers was adopted by the Commission in August 1948—the vote being unanimous except for two countries who voted against it (the Soviet Union and the Ukraine)—the Soviet Union submitted its own disarmament proposal in the General Assembly. The gist of it was that, together with the banning of atomic weapons, the permanent members of the Security Council were all to reduce their armed forces by one-third within a year.

This proposal was effective propaganda. It was a skillful move in the game between the Great Powers, but it was not meant seriously. First of all, in view of the Soviet Union's decisive superiority in conventional armaments (kept in check only by the atom bomb) a proportional reduction would have decisively tipped the scales in the Russians' favor, particularly in Europe, where the countries of the West (this was before NATO) stood quite helpless, faced with the numerous Eastern divisions just across the iron curtain. Secondly, this plan suffered from the obvious defect that a fractional reduction is something indeterminate that cannot be controlled so long as no reliable information is available concerning the existing level of armaments. Whereas the Western powers, in view of their democratic constitutions, are unable to conceal relevant information, the opposite is true of dictatorships. In a counterproposal, the Western powers made use of this fact by asking for *disclosure* and *verification* of the existing level of armaments. The Soviet Union rejected this proposal, and the result was a stalemate. The end came when, in January 1950, the Soviet Union proceeded to boycott the Commission's proceedings.

THE OPTIMISTIC YEARS, 1953-1957

So long as the Korean conflict continued, there was no prospect of any real progress toward a disarmament agreement. Yet there was no pause in the negotiations. The United States withdrew its opposition to dealing with the disarmament problems as a whole. The two existing commissions were accordingly dissolved by a resolution adopted by the General Assembly on January 11, 1952, and were replaced by a general Disarmament Commission (made up of the same members as the Atomic Energy Commission), which was entrusted with the task of preparing a proposal for comprehensive disarmament and the banning of atomic weapons together with disclosure and verification, and subsequent inspection and control. The negotiations did not lead anywhere. The Soviet Union reiterated its proposal for a one-third reduction of military strength together with the banning of atomic weapons. The other side came back with a counterproposal providing for an absolute numerical ceiling of equal size for the armies of the United States, the Soviet Union, and China (between 1 and 1½ million men each) and for England and France (between 700,000 and 800,000 men), a proposal that must have been as unacceptable to the Soviet Union as that country's proposal was to the Western powers.

It was only after Stalin's death (March 1953) and the armistice in Korea (July 1953) that the negotiations gained a fresh lease on life. On November 28, 1953, the General Assembly unanimously (the Soviet bloc abstained) adopted an important resolution in which it not only reiterated and defined more closely the lines along which the Commission was to work but also suggested that the Commission should consider the setting up of a subcommittee "consisting of representatives of the powers principally involved, which should seek in private an acceptable solution and report to the Commission." This was in fact an open admission that public discussion had served only as propaganda and that the leading powers were now expected to sit around a table behind locked doors and negotiate in earnest.

This advice was followed and proved very effective. From 1953 to 1957 a whole series of negotiations took place, partly in secret in the subcommittee, partly in the Disarmament Commission, and partly in the General Assembly, which brought the parties very close together and aroused the hope that agreement might be reached.

The negotiations were marked by the fact that the parties involved were prepared in a realistic spirit to seek a solution. In March 1955 the United States embarked on a revision of its proposals for a disarmament policy in the light of the view that had now gained general acceptance and met with understanding in leading American circles, namely that *there is no scientific method that would make it possible to detect concealed stocks of atomic weapons or materials used for the manufacture of such weapons.* Given this fact, any demand for the complete banning of atomic weapons is nothing more or less than pure propaganda. Both parties know that neither of them dare rely on the other party to destroy its last bomb and deliver its last stocks of the appropriate raw materials.

Although the Russians continued to put forward radical disarmament proposals, they recognized the truth of this principle. As a result, the main weight of the negotiations now shifted to measures of restricted scope, which, unlike the radical schemes, were within the bounds of possibility and the realization of which would help to foster mutual trust and thereby perhaps pave the way for more far-reaching plans. Among the restricted subjects that were discussed were the banning of nuclear tests (which foreshadows the question of the restriction of the membership of the "atomic club"), control measures for preventing surprise attacks, and security measures for preventing accidental war. In the course of the spring and summer of 1957 the two parties drew increasingly close to each other—also in regard to the difficult question of international inspection and control, toward which the Russians had always displayed reluctance as the veil of secrecy is an important part of the Russian system. Suddenly, however, the negotiations took a turn for the worse. Why this happened is not altogether clear, but the reason seems to be that Dulles, the American Secretary of State, personally intervened in the negotiations in such a way that the Russians interpreted it as meaning that the Americans were not serious but merely intended to confuse the negotiations by dragging in other far-reaching and difficult problems (e.g., Germany). The Russians let it be known that they no longer wished to participate in negotiations in this Commission, which brought to an end the most hopeful period in the history of disarmament negotiations.

LAST PHASE: AFTER 1959

After the dissolution of the Disarmament Commission in the autumn of 1957, there was no longer any special United Nations organ competent to take charge of these negotiations. In November 1957, the Soviet Union submitted in the General Assembly a proposal for the setting up of a new disarmament commission in which all the member states would be represented. The creation of a commission comprising 81 members could hardly be regarded as reflecting a desire to make real progress. This proposal was rejected, and on November 19 the General Assembly decided instead to set up a new, enlarged commission of 25 members. The Soviet Union, continuing to display its hostility, refused to take part in the commission's meetings. Hence the commission was stillborn.

At the 13th General Assembly in 1958, the proposal for the setting up of an all-embracing disarmament commission came up once more, and this time it was adopted by a resolution of November 4, because it was clear that otherwise the Soviet Union would not participate in the work of any commission. This huge commission was not a suitable forum for effective discussion, and the general negotiations were not resumed until 1960. In the meantime, the four leading powers had agreed to resume their discussions in one of the organs set up by them outside the framework of the United Nations machinery, namely the Ten-Nation Committee, made up of these four countries plus Bulgaria, Canada, Czechoslovakia, Italy, Poland, and Rumania. In order to preserve some connection with the United Nations, the four powers informed the Secretary-General of the setting up of the committee, with the request that the Disarmament Commission should be convened in order to approve this step. This was done, and the committee was accordingly approved by a resolution of September 10, 1959.

During the period (between the break-up of the negotiations in 1957 and the resumption of the discussions by the Ten-Nation Committee in the spring of 1960) when no special disarmament organ had been in operation, negotiations had, however, continued between experts on the question of the cessation of nuclear tests, and general discussions on the subject had taken place in the General Assembly. The former did not achieve any result, and the latter smacked of insincerity. This was particularly true of the proposal submitted by Khrushchev personally to the General Assembly on September 18, 1959, concerning general and complete disarmament. According to this proposal, all the military forces throughout the world, whether on land, sea, or in the air, were to be permanently disbanded within a period of four years. Only minor forces would be retained for internal police purposes. At the same time, all types of weapons and ammunition, including nuclear weapons and rockets, were to be destroyed and their further manufacture forbidden. Furthermore, all military bases, ministries of war, general staffs, and military training establishments were to be abolished. The carrying out of this scheme was to be supervised by an international control organ. It is scarcely possible to imagine a grosser misuse of the Assembly or a more flagrant exploitation of naïveté for propaganda purposes. When, during the debate, it was pointed out that complete disarmament implied the prior creation of an international police force to maintain international peace and order, the Russians answered that they could not see what purpose such a police force would serve when all countries had completely disarmed and were not authorized to possess any troops or weapons.

The Ten-Nation Committee began its negotiations in Paris on March 15, 1960, and broke up without any result on June 27 of that year. A contributory factor was undoubtedly the fact that the meeting took place at an unfortunate time, when the tension between the Soviet Union and the United States was at its most acute. On May 1, 1960, an American U-2 aircraft was shot down when flying a reconnaissance mission over the Soviet Union and the pilot captured. Khrushchev made use of this opportunity to upset a planned Summit meeting in Paris.

After the Ten-Nation Committee had ended its work in an ominous fashion, the representative of the Eastern bloc having demonstratively refused to continue to take part in the negotiations, the disarmament problem figured prominently on the agenda of the 15th General Assembly, which opened on September 20, 1960. Both sides submitted proposals for plans concerning general and full disarmament, which lent a very unrealistic tone to the debate. One bright note, however, was that the American and the Soviet delegations, toward the end of the session, announced that their governments had agreed to resume, during the coming summer, direct negotiations concerning also the question of the setting up of a new negotiating organ.

These direct negotiations resulted in a common declaration submitted at the 16th General Assembly, in September 1961, concerning those disarmament principles on which an agreement had been reached and in an agreement to set up a new Eighteen-Nation Disarmament Committee. By a resolution of September 20, 1961, the General Assembly approved this proposal whereby the Committee, though not set up by the United Nations, retained a connection with the Organization. The General Assembly expressed the wish that the Committee negotiate a plan for general and complete disarmament on the basis of the common declaration and report to the United Nations Disarmament Commission.

The special feature of this Committee was that, of its 18 members, eight did not belong to any alliance. The Committee began its discussions in Geneva in March 1962 and, after a pause, resumed them in November of that year. One of the members, France, as a protest against plans to check France's development as an atomic power, refused to take part in the meetings.

A modest success was reached when direct negotiations between the three atomic powers of that time, the Soviet Union, the United States, and the United Kingdom, resulted in a treaty signed in Moscow on August 5, 1963, banning nuclear weapons tests in the atmosphere, in outer space, and under water—but not underground. The treaty is open to all states for signature, and many states have signed and ratified it—unfortunately not, however, those two states whose adherence would have been of consequence: France and Communist China.

2. Rearmament and the danger of war

This section deals with the functional relationship existing between armament and the danger of war as a basis for assessing the actual value of disarmament as a peace promoting device and of the endeavors of the United Nations to that end. The question of the practical feasibility of a given disarmament policy will be dealt with in the next section.

I shall begin by discussing two extreme views, both of which I regard as manifestly erroneous.

It may seem self-evident to say that as war cannot be waged without weapons the surest way to peace is through absolute disarmament. This is true, but on one condition, namely that simultaneously with national disarmament, a supranational rearmament is carried out within the framework of an effective legal order—in other words, that a world government is set up, provided with the necessary overwhelming power and based on a universal common ideology. This requirement was discussed in the preceding chapter, where it was shown that the realization of this idea is unfortunately far beyond the bounds of possibility in a foreseeable future.

So long as this requirement is not fulfilled, in other words, so long as the world remains as it is today, it is nonsense to say that complete disarmament will guarantee peace. On the contrary, it will act as a stimulus to war, particularly in the case of certain states.

What is meant by "complete disarmament"? The usual reply is that it means disarmament down to the level required for maintaining peace and order within the state. This level, however, cannot be identified with that of the police forces existing under normal conditions, because military forces, though intervening only under special conditions, are also concerned with the maintenance of order. The minimum security level may be assumed to vary considerably from country to country. While Denmark, for example, and other firmly established democratic states would be satisfied with very little, say, roughly their present police forces—as their governments are based on law and freedom—we would certainly find that states under dictatorial rule based on coercion and oppression would require a "people's police" equipped with tanks and aircraft, tantamount to a highly efficient army. Disarmament along those lines would mean providing the dictatorships with a free pass to unrestricted aggression against the democracies. So much for the fox that preaches to the hens!

But let us now, for the sake of argument, imagine that all states enjoy equal inner political stability and that all disarm down to the same police level, in other words down to the bare minimum. What is there, in such a case, to prevent a modern industrial state, in the absence of strong supranational control, from resuming the production of weapons with which it could easily achieve world domination, since all the other countries would be helpless? The reasoning behind the idea of complete disarmament is naïve, as it concentrates on the elimination of existing weapons, whereas the decisive fact must be to ensure that their production cannot be resumed.

I admit that the line of reasoning adopted here has a strong air of unreality about it, but that is not my fault. The reason is that we have left aside for the moment the question of practicability. As this chapter will show, total disarmament is utopian and, for that reason, this discussion on the desirability of total disarmament is concerned with imaginary circumstances unrelated to facts. To put it briefly, the idea that war between states can be abolished, simply because they lack the weapons with which to fight each other, is unreasonable, not least in relation to modern industrial societies.

It cannot be objected that disarmament should be accompanied by a prohibition of rearmament coupled with international inspection and collective sanctions. In the preceding chapter it was shown that prohibitions and sanctions based on international law cannot guarantee peace. No inspection system can prevent a state planning aggression from gaining a decisive lead in rearming.

If the idea of "peace through total helplessness" is an illusion, this is no less true of its exact opposite, namely peace through *total terror*. On the assumption that the current atomic rearmament has a restraining effect on the nuclear powers' inclination to start a war even with conventional weapons, it might be tempting to draw the conclusion that the best thing would be for all states to possess these frightful weapons. Total terror would then exercise a maximum restraining effect on any warlike ambitions. On the other hand, the risk of total disaster, which can *perhaps* be kept under control so long as only a few countries possess such weapons, would then increase considerably. Hence this idea is hardly worth discussing.

It is generally recognized that any considerable difference in the level of armaments as between potential enemies is a peace-threatening factor. The recognition of this fact is part and parcel of the general theory of the balance of power. If the arms lead of one party is so large as to make that party believe that it can wage a successful war, this may incite it to take advantage of the situation in order to achieve certain political aims. As regards atomic weapons, the position is a special one. If the aggressor is unable, with his first blow, completely to destroy his opponent, so that the latter has no possibility of retaliating (in other words, if the aggressor may expect to receive a dose of his own medicine), the expression "prospect of winning a war" is meaningless. Hence the decisive factor is not the number of bombs or their size but the technical and strategic conditions relating to the possibility of retaliation. A dangerous "over-balance" would be created if one of the parties considers itself able to destroy its opponent without any risk of retaliation.

The importance of a balance of armaments is obvious and undisputed, but the policy to which such balance can give rise is in practice more likely to take the form of a rearmament than of a disarmament program. Where there is an imbalance of armaments, it is clearly desirable, in accordance with the basic principles of power politics, for the party that is lagging behind to catch up by rearming, whereas the party that has forged ahead has only economic reasons for disarming. The true problem of armaments, therefore, is concerned not with the *balance* of armaments but with the impact of the *level* of armaments on war and peace, given a state of equilibrium. The question is whether war is more likely if the parties concerned are equally armed at a high level than if they are equally armed at a low level.

It seems to me probable that the answer to this question must be in the negative. Indeed, I am even inclined to believe that a high (and equal) level of armaments contributes to some extent to the preservation of peace, though the value of such a contribution is reduced by the fact that a war under these conditions, even if less probable, would be all the more frightful if it actually occurred. I really cannot see how a high level of armaments as such can constitute a reason for starting a war. It might perhaps be thought that in a society that devotes considerable sums to military ends, the military authorities may come to play a dominant role in public life, which may be conducive to an aggressive policy as the natural tendency of a military apparatus is to prove itself in war. I do not think that this reasoning is correct. At any rate, neither in America nor in Russia have there been signs of any tendency to restrict the full and absolute responsibility of the civil authorities in matters of foreign policy. I believe, moreover, that military authorities are professionally inclined to cold calculation, so that military influence on national policy is just as likely to promote the preservation of peace as to be conducive to war, for example in a situation where an excited public opinion demands action which the military authorities may consider hazardous. It is well known that Hitler's generals, on many occasions, in connection with the march into the Rhineland in 1935 and during the Second World War, were more careful and cautious than Hitler himself and his National Socialist Party, who considered that they could disregard the academic calculations of their military staff.

On the other hand, a high level of armaments means that the stakes that are being played for are correspondingly higher. If the opposing armies consist only of infantry armed with conventional weapons, and the fleets only of light surface vessels, the stakes (i.e. the losses that the party that declares war is willing to risk) are relatively small. Under present circumstances, however, the stakes, even without taking into account nuclear weapons, are very high. A country that goes to war exposes itself to considerable destruction through air raids carried out on its towns, the sinking of ships in its ports, etc. This fact may serve as a sober warning to think again before taking the plunge.

It may be asked what is the explanation of the widespread view, expressed also in Article 8 of the Covenant of the League of Nations, that a high level of armaments is in itself a factor making for war. I wonder whether the reason does not lie in a confusion between causes and symptoms, which so often occurs also in the fight against disease. It is obvious that a high level of armaments exists precisely in historical periods when the political atmosphere is full of tension; just as, when a thunderstorm is gathering, people are full of nervous tension and fear, wondering when the lightning will strike it. It would be a fallacy to couple these two phenomena, regarding rearmament as the cause of political friction, whereas in actual fact it is the friction that has led to the rearmament.

Particularly widespread is the view that an arms race must inevitably culminate in war. If there is any truth in this it must be interpreted in the light of what has just been said—it is not continued rearmament but the underlying tensions that cause the "lightning."

The peace-preserving function of rearmament raises special problems in the case of nuclear rearmament. It is generally recognized in Western strategic thinking (and there is no reason to suppose that this does not also apply to the East) that a nuclear war is ruled out in so far as each of the parties concerned is in possession of means of retaliation that cannot be put out of action in an attack. In these circumstances, deliberate nuclear war seems inconceivable, for no rational reason can be put forward for starting a war that would inevitably cause enormous losses and perhaps even the total destruction of the party starting it. "I cannot conceive," former Secretary of State Christian Herter said in the United States Senate on the occassion of the hearings on his nomination, "of any President involving us in an all-out nuclear war unless the facts showed clearly we are in danger of all-out devastation ourselves." (Quoted from Brennan, *Arms Control and Disarmament*, p. 26). The problem, therefore, is not—as a shortsighted public opinion, aided and abetted by a cynical "peace propaganda" carried on as part of the cold war, wants to believe—the banning of nuclear warfare. First, no nuclear power is in a position to start a nuclear war without suffering the same treatment, so that the banning of this type of warfare is like forbidding someone to commit suicide. Secondly, such a ban, assuming that a state were determined to embark on anything so frightful as nuclear aggression, would lack any real force. Or can one imagine that a state sufficiently callous to mount such an attack, knowing that in the space of a few hours it would cause many millions of deaths and untold suffering, would refrain from taking this fatal step because it realizes that there is some kind of ban on it by virtue of a United Nations resolution? The paradox of a ban stems from the fact that the force of the ban is of a moral nature but its intention is to prevent a crime of such enormity that it is inconceivable that anyone contemplating it would be moved by moral considerations.

The real challenges raised by the existence of nuclear weapons are as follows:

(1) It is supposed that State A will retaliate in kind if, and only if, it is *itself the victim of a nuclear aggression*. The same applies to State B. This makes it imperative for States A and B to conclude agreements specifying what is meant by the terms "nuclear aggression" and "itself." Such a definition of the circumstances in which retaliation may be expected is intended to ensure that a nuclear war will not start because of a *misunderstanding* as to what the opposing party will regard as a first blow calling for a counterblow. Unfortunately, what makes the solution of this problem difficult is that each of the parties has a strategic interest in leading the opposing party to believe that retaliation will be more extensive than is actually the case. The question is whether their joint interest in preventing a nuclear war through a misunderstanding will be strong enough to prevail over the special interests acting in the opposite direction. At the moment it obviously is not, but the more it proves possible to solve current problems and the more a common external danger (China) brings the nuclear powers closer together, the better will be the chances of solving this important problem.

(2) Even if neither of the parties intends to start a nuclear war, there is a danger that it may nevertheless be triggered *by accident*. It should be the task of each of the parties concerned to take all possible individual and joint measures to prevent an accidental nuclear war.

For instance, a state may blunder into atomic war as a result of a technical or human error because it believes itself to be the victim of a nuclear attack. It is possible that certain natural phenomena may be wrongly interpreted by the warning system as the beginning of an attack, the error being either purely technical or the result of a fault by the men operating the system. It is also conceivable that the misunderstanding may be based on reality in the sense that something unusual *has* happened—something interpreted as an attack but wrongly so because what happened was due to a technical or human deficiency. For example, it is imaginable that a rocket may be sent up by mistake or that an aircraft carrying an atomic bomb may, as a result of the pilot's illness (physical or mental) or death, lose its way over the other side's territory and cause an explosion there; or that a mentally deranged person presses the button that sets the whole nuclear machinery in motion. It is likewise possible that a third country that wishes to start a nuclear war deliberately acts in such a way as to create misunderstandings of the kind described above. Such misunderstandings may also be caused by military or diplomatic information sources. For example, A may consider itself in possession of definite information to the effect that an attack by B is imminent.

(3) The argument that deliberate nuclear war is unthinkable rests on the assumption that the behavior of the parties concerned will be dictated by rational considerations. Everything must therefore be done to ensure that cold reason shall not yield to *irrationality* and violent emotion. Here the danger is that one of the parties, through threats and boastful speeches, may have committed itself to such an extent that it is unable, for prestige reasons, to retreat if its blustering behavior has not had the intended effect on the opposing party. In such cases, a situation can easily arise where each of the parties, believing that the other party is bluffing, gradually takes more and more risks and is so caught up in its risky game that disaster becomes inevitable (*escalation*, or the moving staircase principle). The voice of reason may also go unheeded because of exacerbated national sentiment.

The practical problems mentioned under (1) and (3) involved in the prevention of a nuclear war would all become very much more complicated and difficult if a great number of states possessed atom bombs. This sets us another task, namely,

(4) to prevent any increase in the membership of the "atomic club." The banning of nuclear tests is a step in that direction, but, of course, far from sufficient in itself. In particular, it is in the interest of both the West and the Soviet Union that China should be prevented from developing an effective atomic arms potential. The same also applies to France, for it is in the interest of the whole world that there should be no more than two nuclear powers. It should still be possible to achieve this result if the

United States and the Soviet Union in unity would accept and live up to their joint responsibility for the fate of the world and spare no pains to uphold their authority.

The practical points mentioned under (1) to (4) as part of a program intended to avert the danger of a nuclear war are examples of the kind of thinking and peace policy that is known as "arms control." It is, I believe, the most important task of the present day, as regards meeting the challenge of the nuclear bomb, that the best scientific, technical, and political brains should be employed in dealing with the far-reaching problems raised by arms control and in working out all the details of such a program. It is then for the nuclear powers individually and in co-operation to ensure the application of this program in the best possible way and to keep it under constant review in the light of new technical or political conditions. "Co-operation" must be emphasized, for many of the points in this program can only be implemented in this way. It is high time that the two major nuclear powers understand that, as a result of the atom bomb, their fate and interests are linked together and that this should prove stronger than the ideological opposition and the rivalry in power politics dividing them.

I have already discussed the fact that, given a rational arms control, nuclear armament tends to make nuclear war inconceivable. Another question is the effect that such armament may be assumed to have on the possibility of conventional war.

It has been argued that the possibility that an attack with conventional weapons would be met with strategic nuclear bombing would also make a war with conventional weapons impossible between two nuclear powers. American strategy for the defense of western Europe was, for a long time, based on the doctrine that any attack of any kind would be met with "massive" retaliation. Such a strategy could be justified so long as the United States enjoyed such superiority over the Soviet Union that no Russian nuclear retaliation of any importance was to be feared. When this requirement is no longer fulfilled, as is the case at the present time, the argument that the threat of nuclear war is capable also of preventing conventional war does not hold water. If we accept, as we have done above, the principle that a nuclear war is automatically ruled out because none of the parties concerned will start such a war but will only use nuclear weapons when it has itself been the victim of *nuclear* aggression, the logical conclusion is that the existence of nuclear weapons cannot have the same effect in relation to an attack with conventional weapons. This principle, indeed, gives a state that has attacked another with conventional weapons reason to believe that it will not be subjected to nuclear bombing in return.

The apparent paradox in the view that the atom bomb makes it impossible to start an atomic war but not a conventional war, follows quite simply from the fact that an atomic war (assuming that both parties are capable of retaliation) would be so frightful that it would not constitute a suitable "sanction" against a conventional war of aggression. What purpose could be served by applying a "sanction" that would do just as much harm to the victim as to the guilty party and would probably be synonymous with the total destruction of both parties and lead to tremendous losses and untold suffering in the rest of the world? That is why the United States was able without risking atomic retaliation to stand firm on its demand for the withdrawal of offensive weapons from Cuba. The Soviet Union, which understood that America could and would back up its demands with the use of force under conditions favorable to the latter, thought it as well to accept these demands of its own free will. There is a corollary to this, which should not be overlooked by the West: namely, that the Soviet Union can, in the same way and without risk, back up with force its claims to disputed positions in Europe. Or does anyone really believe that if the Russians were, for instance, to occupy Berlin, the United States would start a nuclear war that would probably cost 25-50 million American lives, destroy New York and other large cities, and leave a legacy of illness, need, and suffering to generations of Americans? I cannot believe that the Americans would react in this way. Hence, in order to prevent a conventional war in Europe in which the balance of power favors the Russians, an earnest attempt must be made to secure the settlement of outstanding conflicts by negotiation.

Even if the atom bomb does not in any way rule out the possibility of a limited conventional war in Europe, it is nevertheless probable that owing to the escalation danger it acts as a damper on any inclination either of the parties may have to use force.

3. Feasibility of disarmament

The preceding analysis of rearmament did not provide any support for the assumption that disarmament as such contributes to the cause of peace. We have tried to show that a high level of armaments probably reduces the risk of war but that, on the other hand, it increases the horrors of war, if war comes. In a theoretical calculation, the real magnitude of the danger of war is determined as the product of the probability of the risk and the size of the losses that the war is likely to cause. Naturally, none of these factors are susceptible of accurate or even approximate calculation. Hence in my opinion, we cannot say whether a high level of armaments increases or reduces the actual danger of war. An extreme case is that of maximum rearmament: atomic weapons, coupled with means of retaliation, reduce the risk of nuclear war toward nil but increase to infinity the size of the damage caused by such a war.

But even if disarmament cannot be justified as a means of preventing war, it may be justified on other grounds. Rearmament today is costing the world fantastic sums, estimated at around 120 thousand million dollars per annum, or 8 to 9 per cent of the total world production of goods and services. A substantial measure of disarmament would make for a considerable increase in the national product available in the various countries to satisfy nonmilitary needs. Here, however, we must bear in mind that disarmament by agreement would call for a very comprehensive international control system embracing not only military institutions, installations, and equipment but also the sizable part of industry that can be converted without great difficulty from peace-time production to war production. Even if the cost of such control were high, there can scarcely be any doubt that it would be less than present military expenditure and require less manpower. Thus on economic grounds there is no doubt that disarmament would be beneficial. For this reason, whatever one may think of the role of disarmament in the preservation of peace, it is necessary to discuss how far disarmament is feasible.

The basic principle of a practical disarmament policy is that the *existing atomic weapons cannot be got rid of.* They are here to stay and we must learn to live with them. This applies, at any rate, so long as no scientific method exists whereby concealed weapons or stocks of materials used for their manufacture can be detected. The truth of this principle is recognized both by the Americans and by the Russians (as explained above in the section on negotiations in the Disarmament Commission and its subcommittee, 1953-57), as well as by all the experts with whose opinions on this question I am familiar. Here I would like to quote what has been said by someone particularly qualified in this field. As far back as 1955, Eugene Rabinowitch, publisher of the *Bulletin of Atomic Scientists,* wrote an article entitled "Living with A-bombs" (Jan. 1955, p. 6) in which he said, among other things:

The technical feasibility of atomic disarmament depends now on a reliable *inventory* of existing stocks of fissionable materials. Considering the extremely small bulk of these materials, and the absence of penetrating radiations emanating from them, . . . the only possibility of inventorying them is for the agents of the U.N. control body to be led to the stockpiles by national officials who know where they are located. Neither the West nor the USSR can be expected to base their own atomic disarmament on the faith that the other side has not concealed a substantial part of its stockpile. . . . If this conclusion is true, then we may have to add, to the appalling knowledge of the material and biological damage of an atomic war, the recognition that time for an effectively controlled atomic disarmament has irretrievably passed, and that attempts to find a compromise solution . . . are therefore bound to remain futile. . . . Mankind will have to live, from now on, with unlimited and unchecked stockpiles of atomic and thermonuclear explosives piling up, first in America and the Soviet Union, then in Great Britain, and later in other countries as well.

It is astonishing how little understanding of this elementary fact has penetrated the public mind. Indeed, it makes the antinuclear campaign and the agitation for the elimination of nuclear weapons and the banning of the manufacture and use thereof seem at best empty talk and at worst a cynical move in the cold-war propaganda contest.

If the banning of nuclear weapons is ruled out, what practical arms reductions can be considered with these weapons?

A disarmament program whereby the parties concerned undertake to reduce their stocks of bombs of different types in accordance with definite rules is probably neither of any special interest nor feasible in practice. Any such program of reductions must, like total banning, be based on reliable information on the size of existing stocks, but this is something that cannot be secured. As the figures supplied by each of the parties cannot be controlled, none of them dares accept the other party's information as a reliable basis for its own disarmament.

It is also very doubtful whether there is any prospect of being able by means of an agreement to halt the continuation of the quantitative and qualitative arms race. Since the actual number of bombs, once a certain order of magnitude has been reached, is not of decisive importance (If 100 bombs are sufficient for the total destruction of one's opponent, there is nothing to be gained by increasing the number to 1,000.), particular interest attaches to the halting of the qualitative arms race, i.e. of the extensive and costly efforts to devise, by means of scientific and technological research, new offensive or defensive weapons, instruments, methods, etc. In so far as the qualitative rearmament requires the continuation of test explosions, the sending up of satellites, or similar measures which lend themselves to control, it may perhaps be possible, through prohibiting such measures, to restrain the qualitative arms race. Apart from this, the application of restrictions under an agreement seem hardly feasible. It seems more likely that both parties, after a general relaxation of political tension and growing mutual trust, will decide each for itself to cut their arms programs.

However, the various programs for arms control outlined in this chapter, aiming at the prevention of nuclear war due to a misunderstanding, accident, escalation, or increased membership in the atomic club, may be regarded as feasible on the basis both of unilateral measures and of mutual arrangements between the nuclear powers.

As regards conventional weapons, complete disarmament is equally inconceivable. The idea that the powers concerned should be prepared to give up these weapons if they possess atomic weapons is unrealistic, because the use of atomic weapons is self-defeating but, as we have seen, their possession does not rule out the use of conventional weapons.

As experience shows, it is extraordinarily difficult to arrive at international agreements on disarmament or even on halting rearmament. Since 1920, virtually uninterrupted negotiations have taken place on this point, but all that has come out of these thousands of hours of discussions and mountains of paper is the relatively insignificant naval agreement concluded in Washington in 1922. The difficulties involved, which are both technical and political, can be summed up as follows:

(1) technical difficulties in working out concepts and units in terms of which the arms potential of a state can be expressed and measured,

(2) political difficulties in agreeing on standards for an authorized maximum level of armaments, and

(3) technical and political difficulties in the supervision and enforcement of arms agreements.

All agreements on arms reduction aim, on the basis of certain standards, at fixing a ceiling for the arms potential of the signatory states. Whether these standards directly fix the level authorized or indirectly refer to the *status quo* (for instance by freezing the existing arms level or by providing for a specific percentage reduction of this level), it is a prerequisite in all cases that a state's level of armaments should be describable in terms suitable for quantitative measurement. This raises many difficulties. It does so first of all as regards the objects, persons, and installations that are to be included in the calculation. What is military equipment? A bomb is military equipment and so, of course, is a tank. But what about aircraft and motor vehicles that can speedily be converted to military uses? Even more important than the question of conversion is that of remanufacturing. Many military articles of equipment cannot, at the first stage of production, be distinguished from similar objects used for peaceful purposes. A state can therefore increase its arms potential by building up stocks of semifinished products that could be further processed for military purposes. To what extent should such articles be included among military equipment? Similar problems arise in the case of military personnel. There are numerous examples of the existence, side by side with official troops, of large formations of a "paramilitary character," such as police forces, gendarmeries, protection corps, citizen corps, etc. all the way down to camouflaged gymnastics and athletics associations. Even if these questions are cleared up, major problems of measurement arise. One soldier cannot simply be compared to another. To take an extreme case, there is a great difference between a fully trained professional soldier and a soldier who has been called up for military service for a single six-month period. How can capacity in one field, for example that of submarines, be compared with capacity in another, say aircraft?

The political difficulties are just as great. For a politician, it is of decisive importance that the balance of power should not be disturbed to his country's detriment. He will act on the assumption that any proposal put forward by the other party or for that matter any proposal the other party is prepared to accept, must, *ipso facto,* be regarded as working in the other party's favor and consequently as detrimental to himself. The reason it is so difficult to come to an agreement in this field lies in a special feature that is not found in other kinds of bargaining. Most contracts effect a mutual exchange of performances beneficial to both parties. Both the salesman and the buyer are richer after the sale than they were before, and their bargaining is concerned with the apportionment of the gain. However, a disarmament agreement, viewed from the standpoint of the balance of power, differs from this in that a gain for one party is synonymous with a loss for the other.

From the point of view of power politics, therefore, any willingness displayed by the opposing party must be interpreted as a danger signal making for circumspection. This mutual mistrust could perhaps be overcome if it were objectively possible to assess the impact of a disarmament proposal on the arms potential of the parties involved. As already stated, however, such assessment is impossible. Furthermore, each of the parties lacks reliable information concerning the state of armaments in the opposing country. It will, therefore, deem it necessary to allow itself a certain safety margin in its calculations and be inclined to reject any arrangement from which it does not clearly derive some advantage. As, however, there is no question of any arrangement being advantageous to both parties, no agreement is possible.

Hence there is no prospect of any disarmament agreement, unless the parties negotiate on a basis that is not solely that of power politics. Disarmament or a halt in rearmament would be beneficial to each of them from the economic and social point of view. Hence, a precondition for success when dealing with the disarmament problem is that the parties concerned should be prepared to give economic considerations precedence over hesitations rooted in power politics. The chance of this condition being fulfilled grows with the size of the arms burden and with the general atmosphere of political *détente* in which the negotiations take place.

The last-named factor explains the disturbing inverse proportionality existing between the public demand for disarmament negotiations and the prospect for the success of such negotiations. The greater the public anxiety created by political tensions and conflicts, the stronger will be the public's demands for disarmament and the less the politicians will be willing to enter into disarmament agreements. But none of the parties dare, for fear of being regarded as an enemy of peace, back out of these negotiations, and so the discussions drag on in an atmosphere of insincerity.

Any agreement that restricts a state's freedom to rearm touches one of the most sensitive nerves in the national consciousness. It is not so much that the inspection measures required under a control system may be felt as an infringement of sovereignty—whatever this may mean in the present context. The sore point is that under such an agreement a state deprives itself of the right to improve its position in the military balance of power, if it finds that the political situation has altered or that the initial estimates on which it based itself have proved to be erroneous. Of course, agreements can always be denounced or broken, but a state taking either of these two courses would find world public opinion unfavorable. This adds further to the difficulty of concluding disarmament agreements.

The difficulties involved in the control system are both of a technical and political nature. Germany's secret rearmament under Hitler, the extent of which was for a long time successfully concealed from the Allies, showed that an effective control system requires very extensive machinery empowered to inspect military installations, factories, etc. In particular, it is necessary to carry out a comprehensive control of that part of industry that can, without any major difficulties, be converted to war production. Such extensive inspection would be particularly disadvantageous for a country whose political system enables it, to a considerable extent, to conceal the state of its armaments and its industrial capacity. But the opposite country, if it is to feel confident that the agreement will be observed, must, precisely because of this secretiveness, demand an effective control system. This dilemma has been very clearly reflected in the disarmament negotiations that have taken place in the United Nations. The Soviet Union has continually opposed or adopted a reserved attitude to the far-reaching demands for inspection on the part of the West, which it has described in stereotyped fashion as camouflaged espionage. It would be incorrect to interpret this as a sign of the Soviet Union's secret intention not to observe any agreements entered into. Without accepting the argument that inspection would only be a cover for espionage, one must recognize the underlying fact that inspection—although carried out in a completely lawful manner—would nevertheless help to remove the smoke screen and weaken the effect of secrecy.

This pessimistic analysis of the prospects of success for disarmament agreements seems to accord well with historical experience. I think it fair to say that no other topic has come in for so many international negotiations without practical results. The Washington Agreement of 1922 concerning heavy warships is the exception that confirms the rule. It is clear that battleships and aircraft carriers occupy a special place from the technical point of view, both as regards the stipulation of maximum levels (expressed in tons of weight, firepower, engine power, etc.) and as regards control measures. From the political standpoint, the naval agreement was part of a wider arrangement whereby the parties, in an atmosphere of political détente, settled a whole series of questions regarding China and their interests in the Pacific.

What role can the United Nations be expected to play in pursuit of arms control and disarmament? The above analysis indicates—and this is confirmed by experience—that the General Assembly is the worst possible forum for negotiations to this end. Belief in disarmament as the way to peace is too widespread in world public opinion for anyone to dare let slip the opportunity of posing as a champion of peace by launching disarmament projects. After Khrushchev personally presented in the General Assembly his program for general and complete disarmament, the other side did not dare lag behind, and the discussions have since been conducted on the basis of this program, which, as both sides know full well, is illusory. Is there no little child in the Assembly who will stand up and tell frankly that the Emperor is not wearing any clothes? The answer is no: The General Assembly is no place for children but only for clever politicians.

In my opinion, if negotiations on disarmament or arms control are to be expected to produce some results, the first requirement is that they should take place behind locked doors. The second requirement is that they should be conducted directly between the immediately interested parties, possibly with the assistance of nonaligned mediators. The importance of these requirements is recognized by the United Nations itself. The section of this chapter called "The Depressing Background" mentions the resolution of November 28, 1953, whereby the General Assembly recommended the Disarmament Commission to set up a sub-committee which would meet *in private* and the resolution of December 20, 1961, whereby they approved the establishment of the Eighteen-Nation Disarmament Committee, whose special feature was that it included the representatives of eight *nonaligned* countries.

Actually, the United Nations has, to a large extent, ceased to be a forum for these negotiations. The Disarmament Commission on which all the members of the Organization are represented is no more suitable for real negotiations than is the General Assembly. Neither the existing Eighteen-Nation Committee nor the preceding Ten-Nation Committee are actual United Nations organs but are loosely connected with the Organization, which sponsored their establishment and requested them to report to the Disarmament Commission.

In my view, it is desirable that these negotiations be conducted more discreetly away from the public eye. Disarmament negotiations that do not produce any results are worse than no negotiations at all. The high expectations aroused ("general and full disarmament") and the resulting constant disappointment, frequently coupled with violent mutual recriminations, reproaches, and insinuations, can only add to international disquiet and tension and make it more difficult to conduct discussions in an objective spirit.

While the value of disarmament as a contribution to the preservation of peace is questionable, the problems dealt with under section 2, "Rearmament and the Danger of War," concerning arms control are undoubtedly of the greatest consequence. The very survival of our culture may depend on a satisfactory solution of these problems. They are definitely not suitable for public discussion in the United Nations but only for direct and discreet negotiations between the nuclear powers. What the United Nations must and should do is to make the nuclear powers realize, at this late hour, their responsibilities and to ensure that they examine this problem jointly, first on the level of the experts and subsequently on the political level.

References

1. THE DEPRESSING BACKGROUND

Bechhoefer, Bernhard G., *Postwar Negotiations for Arms Control* (1961).

Documents on Disarmament, 1945-1959, Vol. I-II. Department of State Publication 7008 (1960).

Martin, Andrew, *Collective Security* (1952).

As regards the unity achieved during the years 1955-57 and the collapse of the negotiations, see Philip E. Jacob, "The Disarmament Consensus," *International Organization* (1960), pp. 233-60.

2. REARMAMENT AND THE DANGER OF WAR

Aron, Raymond, *Paix et Guerre* (1962), pp. 622-53.

Beaton, Leonard and John Maddox, *The Spread of Nuclear Weapons* (1962).

Brennan, Donald B., ed., *Arms Control and Disarmament* (1961).

Claude, Inis L., Jr., *Swords into Plowshares* (2nd ed., 1959), pp. 296-323.

3. FEASIBILITY OF DISARMAMENT

Economic and Social Consequences of Disarmament, Report of the Secretary-General transmitting the study of his Consultative Group. Doc. E/3593/Rev. I (1962).

X 🏵

CO-OPERATION
FOR PROGRESS

I n Chapter III I said that the United Nations' ultimate aim could be expressed with the slogan "peace and progress." In the last three chapters the work of the United Nations on behalf of peace was described and analyzed, and its value assessed. The present and following chapters deal with the United Nations' activities on behalf of progress. This chapter is concerned with co-operation in achieving progress toward general well-being, and the subsequent ones deal, in particular, with improving the welfare of dependent peoples, especially their progress toward political independence, in which respect the work of the Organization has also a political aspect.

The two ultimate aims of peace and progress are interdependent. At any rate, there can be no doubt that peace contributes to progress and well-being. Conversely, progress and prosperity are probably peace-promoting factors, since need and poverty may arouse bitterness and hate which can lead to revolutions and wars. But it would be a mistake to think that social and economic progress is necessarily synonymous with progress toward peace. For instance, there is no reason to assume that teaching Negro children to read or to believe in human rights always furthers the cause of peace. The ability to read and the realization of their human dignity and equality opens up new horizons for them—with the possibility, however, that the new outlook will lead to protests against the existing order and demands for better political and social conditions. As we know, it is not the most destitute who start revolutions. The process of decolonization that has taken place in the last few decades has clearly shown that progress does not always mean peace.

Hence, if a choice had to be made between peace and progress as an ultimate aim, preference should be given to progress. The United Nations Charter, however, has it the other way around. Article 55 says that the Organization's work in promoting international social and economic co-operation shall be carried on "with a view to the creation of conditions of stability and well-being which are necessary for peaceful and friendly relations among nations." Thus co-operation for progress is justified in terms of its usefulness to the highest aim, namely the cause of peace. The constitutions of some of the specialized agencies have also been drawn up along these lines, their specific aim being described as serving as a means of promoting peace and security. Article I of the UNESCO Constitution says that "the purpose of the Organization is to contribute to peace and security by promoting collaboration among the nations through education, science and culture. . . ." In the Preamble to the ILO Constitution, that organization's work for the improvement of the worker's lot is justified on the grounds that social justice is a necessary basis for a universal and lasting peace.

From this definition of aims, however, it should not be concluded that the scope of co-operation should be restricted depending on whether it can or cannot be proved that progress toward well-being in a given field really serves the cause of peace. The above quotations from the United Nations Charter and the constitutions of the specialized agencies may be regarded as declarations of belief that motivate but do not restrict such co-operation.

That the Charter regards co-operation for economic and social progress as a subsidiary object justified on the sole grounds of its contribution to the cause of peace, is understandable in view of the considerations that led the various states to create the United Nations. The major powers placed the emphasis on the Organization's political character as an instrument whereby they could exercise their concerted hegemony for the preservation of international peace and security. The Soviet Union even went so far as to advocate that the United Nations should be concerned only with political security and that welfare questions should be left to existing or new institutions outside the United Nations—an attitude that stems from the Marxist point of view that international co-operation for the promotion of general well-being is nothing but a delusion which can only delay the inevitable collapse of the capitalist states and the triumph of the Communist world revolution in accordance with the inexorable laws of historical evolution. At the confidential conference between the great powers in Dumbarton Oaks, held from August to October, 1944, the Soviet Union, after putting up considerable opposition, accepted the setting up of the Economic and Social Council because it was agreed that the ultimate aim of the Council's work would be of a political nature, namely to preserve international peace and security. Furthermore, the Council's functions were defined in brief and abstract terms. At the San Francisco Conference (April to June, 1945) other views were put forward. Many of the smaller states regarded nonpolitical co-operation as very important and valuable in itself. They urged successfully that the functions and powers of the Economic and Social Council be defined in a more positive and concrete manner. Although Article 55 of the Charter took over from the Dumbarton Oaks Conference the latter's reference to the ultimate aim of the Council's activities, there cannot now be any doubt that the welfare questions entrusted to the Council are firmly established in their own right irrespective of their value to the realization of the political aim.

In two respects, there is a characteristic difference between the rules laid down in Chapters VI, VII, and VIII of the Charter concerning the United Nations' political functions, on the one hand, and the rules embodied in Chapters IX and X concerning economic and social co-operation, on the other. As regards the former, as already explained (Chap. VII.4), the rules in question are based on the principle that responsibility for the preservation of peace is centralized in and exclusively rests with the United Nations, or, more specifically, with the Security Council. As regards the enforcement of peace, the Organization claims a monopoly, in that regional organizations may not resort to such enforcement measures without the consent of the Security Council and can therefore never—under the system provided for in the Charter—be more than an instrument in the hands of the Council, without any responsibility of their own. Secondly (Chap. III.2 and V.2), the Security Council is empowered to act on behalf of all the member states and to give them binding instructions as to their participation in the application of enforcement measures for the preservation of peace. Thus the Security Council is internationally empowered to issue orders. In its activities concerned with achieving progress toward well-being, however, the United Nations does not claim any monopoly and has no authority to issue orders. Although the nonpolitical aims laid down in Article 55 are defined in such broad terms as to cover any subject that may in practice lend itself to international co-operation, it is not intended that the United Nations should render superfluous all other co-operation institutions. On the contrary, it is assumed that many other international institutions will remain in existence and that new ones may be set up for special purposes. Thus in this sector, the Charter adopts the principles of *specialization and decentralization.* In order, however, to bring some order and system into this extensive activity, it expresses the wish that the various specialized agencies should be brought into relationship with the United Nations through freely concluded agreements. The result of this decentralization is that the United Nations acts partly on an equal footing with the specialized agencies for the solution of special problems which are not attended to by any of these, and partly as a supreme organ for co-ordinating the work of these agencies. In the whole field, however, the United Nations, whether dealing with the supplementary or the co-ordinating tasks is *without any authority to issue orders.* That is why the Charter speaks of international economic and social co-operation, which in fact implies that every single step taken by a state in this field is taken freely and that the Organization as such can never take any action beyond information, discussion, recommendation and operational actions on its own account.

It is because of these two factors, namely decentralization and the absence of authority to issue orders, that the rules in Chapters IX and X concerning co-operation for progress are not set out with as much detail and precision as the rules in Chapers VI, VII, and VIII concerning the settlement of disputes and the preservation of peace. This applies to both the definition of the Organization's functions and to the stipulation of the obligations assumed by the members. One has the impression that the wording frequently was the result of a compromise: an effort has been made to meet the wish expressed by certain states that far-reaching aims should be set for economic and social co-operation and, at the same time, to respect the definite reluctance on the part of other states to accept any obligations at all in this respect. The result is a wordy and well-sounding text, but much of the wording is obscure, imprecise, or hollow. No attempt was made to resolve the major difference between the opposing tendencies, reflected in the contradiction between the aim laid down in Article 55, namely that the Organization shall promote, among other things, higher standards of living and full employment in the various member states (i.e. conditions that are normally considered internal state matters), and the restrictive principle laid down in Article 2(7) to the effect that nothing shall authorize the United Nations to intervene in matters that are essentially within the domesic jurisdiction of a state.

Even a brief outline of the extensive work being done by the United Nations and the specialized agencies in order to promote well-being in many different fields would be beyond the scope of this work, whose purpose is to give a broad picture of the nature and activities of this organization and to discuss some of the more general problems arising therefrom. The present Chapter is therefore essentially concerned with describing the general framework for the Organization's activities as laid down in Chapters IX and X of the Charter. First, I shall discuss in more detail the aims of economic and social co-operation; second, I shall deal with a number of organizational problems; third, I shall describe the various forms of co-operation, that is, the different ways in which the aims laid down may be achieved; and last, I shall give a brief outline of the work actually being done for the solution of a series of problems.

1. The aims of co-operation

In Article 55 of the Charter the aims of international nonpolitical co-operation are described as follows. The United Nations is to promote:

    a. higher standards of living, full employment, and conditions of economic and social progress and development;

    b. solutions of international economic, social, health, and related problems; and international cultural and educational co-operation; and

    c. universal respect for, and observance of, human rights and fundamental freedoms for all without distinction as to race, sex, language, or religion.

This wording is more detailed and far-reaching than the corresponding provision in the Dumbarton Oaks proposals, which merely said that the Organization should:

facilitate solutions of economic, social, and other humanitarian problems and promote respect for human rights and fundamental freedoms.

The broader wording in the Charter is the result of the protracted tug-of-war that took place at the San Francisco Conference between, on the one hand, many of the lesser powers, led, in particular, by Australia and Canada, whose wish it was that the modern democratic ideas and aims of the welfare state should also be accepted on the international level, and on the other hand, other states, first and foremost the United States of America, which were opposed to the idea of giving the Organization the power to intervene in matters that have traditionally been regarded as being within the domestic jurisdiction of the state. For the American delegation, the thought of the fate of the Covenant of the League of Nations must have been a kind of nightmare, urging it to keep a constant eye on the Senate's possible reactions. When the Americans yielded to overwhelming pressure and accepted the more comprehensive and binding wording, it was because it was agreed at the same time that the reservation in respect of domestic affairs—which in the Dumbarton Oaks proposals had concerned only the rules governing the settlement of disputes—be made into a general principle binding upon all the organs concerned in the performance of their duties (see Art. 2.7 of the Charter). Furthermore, the American representative in the technical committee dealing with this question persuaded this committee unanimously to adopt the following statement for inclusion in the *rapporteur's* report:

The members of Committee 3 of Commission II are in full agreement that nothing contained in Chapter IX [Chapters IX and X of the Charter] can be construed as giving authority to the Organization to intervene in the domestic affairs of member states.

Armed with this declaration and the reservation embodied in Article 2(7) the Americans accepted the wording of Article 55. As there is no rule in Chapters IX and X empowering any organ to issue binding orders, the emphasis on the meaning of the above reservation within the context of those Chapters seems to imply that "intervention" takes place even where only discussions or recommendations are involved. If this is assumed, the aims set out in Article 55 become illusory, as this article does in fact mainly refer to matters that are usually regarded as coming within the domestic jurisdiction of a state. The negotiations at the San Francisco Conference provide no clue as to how this inner contradiction may be resolved. In practice, only on rare occasions have objections been raised against the Security Council's competence, except in connection with questions relating to the respect and protection of human rights (see Chap. III.3).

Broadly speaking, the aims set forth in Article 55 mean that the United Nations accepts the progressive and constructive ideas that in America are known under the name "New Deal" and in Europe as welfare policy. The Organization and its individual members (see section 3 of this chapter) have thereby undertaken to continue on the international level the work these states are carrying out on a national level to achieve economic and social well-being. It may perhaps be surprising that the United States accepted such aims—aims that reflect a philosophy of society that is far from being accepted by all sections of American society. But the declaration in Article 55 loses its sting when we remember that the Organization has no authority to issue orders and that the obligations of the members are formulated in such a vague manner that their freedom of action is in no way impeded.

Viewed in detail, the formulation of the aims laid down in Article

55 is unclear from the point of view of logical structure. In particular, one cannot understand in what way the three sections of this article are systematically interrelated. When subparagraph (b) talks about the solution of *international* problems this seems to imply that the matters mentioned under (a) and (c) are not international but purely national. This assumption is, of course, fallacious. All the matters mentioned in Article 55 are of a directly national character and governed in each state by national legislation. They assume an international character when they give rise to international discussions and co-operation. Moreover, most of the special aims laid down seem superfluous in so far as the general wording employed under subparagraph (a): "conditions of economic and social progress and development" may cover these aims if the terms "economic" and "social" are understood in the normal way as including also health, humanitarian, and cultural (including educational) matters.

There is, however, no point in trying to work out a precise interpretation of Article 55 in its various details. This article's *legal* significance lies solely in the fact that, in practice, it gives ECOSOC unlimited powers to deal with any matter which might appropriately give rise to international co-operation. Apart from this, it is merely a declaration of ideals and intentions.

2. Organizational problems

With regard to the composition, operation, and organization of ECOSOC, reference should be made to Chapter V.3. Here it is sufficient to point out that the machinery through which economic and social co-operation is carried out is extremely complex and reflects a high degree of decentralization, in that various tasks are apportioned among a great number of different organs and institutions. This machinery is made up of:

(1) the General Assembly;
(2) the Assembly's Second, Third, and, to some extent, Fifth Committee;
(3) the Economic and Social Council;
(4) the four standing committees of the Economic and Social Council and a varying number of *ad hoc* committees and working parties;

(5) seven functional commissions and one subcommission;

(6) four regional commissions;

(7) fourteen specialized agencies; and

(8) eight special bodies, i.e. bodies that are not set up by ECOSOC and are not subsidiary to it, but that are, to some extent, connected with it, e.g. the Permanent Central Opium Council, the United Nations International Children's Emergency Fund (UNICEF), and the Technical Assistance Council (TAC).

Particular importance attaches to the 14 specialized agencies. These are not United Nations organs but autonomous institutions with their own constitutions embodied in an independent treaty stipulating the tasks to be carried out by each agency. The reason for dealing with them here within the context of the United Nations is that, by means of agreements, a certain relationship has been established between them and the United Nations, the idea being that they all form a comprehensive whole, "the United Nations family," as it is often called, whose various members co-operate harmoniously in the pursuit of their common goal, i.e. the promotion of well-being.

There has been a great deal of discussion on whether it would not have been better to wind up all the specialized agencies and centralize all economic and social co-operation under a single authority in the United Nations. In favor of this idea, it can be argued that extensive decentralization carries with it a danger of lack of harmony in the work, reflected in overlapping or in gaps, and a lack of co-ordination in the solution of problems that are many-sided in their nature and therefore require the co-operation of specialists from different fields. From the administrative point of view, a lack of unity could lead to a waste of energy and money. On the other hand, the multiplicity and vastness of the problems is such that a central authority could hardly be more than a figurehead. The questions dealt with, for instance, by the Universal Postal Union, the International Bank for Reconstruction and Development, and UNESCO are so variegated that one cannot imagine their being dealt with by one and the same staff. Any centralization, therefore, could only consist in the establishment of some kind of formal superstructure under which each of the specialized institutions would still continue to function as independent departments. There are also political reasons that militate in favor of decentralization. When the United Nations was set up, some of the specialized agencies, or at least their predecessors, were already in existence, and the considerable interests invested in these bodies made it easier to continue to operate on the existing basis than to create a new one. When tasks are apportioned among different institutions, it is easier to mobilize the generous impulses of states that are interested in a special field. To sum up, therefore, we can say that the idea of centralization is very impressive in theory, but the realities of life definitely militate in favor of working in a more piecemeal fashion. But it then becomes a major task to fit the various pieces together into a coherent whole.

Before turning to the problems of co-ordination, an account should be given of the distribution of functions and responsibilities as between the different organs within the Organization.

Although ECOSOC is, under Article 7 of the Charter, included among the main organs of the United Nations, it is far from occupying a position at all comparable with that enjoyed by the Security Council in political matters. While the Charter has placed the primary responsibility for the maintenance of international peace and security upon the Security Council and given the General Assembly certain additional and subsidiary powers in this field, ECOSOC is completely under the authority of the General Assembly. Article 60 says that responsibility for the discharge of the functions of the Organization in economic and social matters shall be vested in the General Assembly and, under its authority, in the Economic and Social Council, which shall have for this purpose the powers set forth in Chapter X. Examining the relevant provisions in detail, it can be seen that in quite a number of cases these powers reflect the dependent status of the Council in that the exercise of these powers is subject to the express consent of the General Assembly (Art. 62.3, 62.4, 63, 66.2 and 96.2).

Article 60, taken in conjunction with Articles 10 and 13, must surely mean that in all respects, including also the powers that are unreservedly granted to the Council in Chapter X, the General Assembly has authority over the Council, including authority to issue binding instructions and to alter decisions already taken. On the other hand, the Council is not merely an auxiliary organ set up by the General Assembly. Its functions derive directly from the Charter, and, in so far as the General Assembly's consent is not expressly required, it must be able to carry out these functions on its own initiative.

Although, in practice, the General Assembly's superiority has not manifested itself in the extreme form of orders or modifications but has always been expressed in the shape of recommendations and advice, it has not been without practical significance. In several cases, the General Assembly has returned to the Council resolutions adopted by that organ with a request that the question be reconsidered in the light of certain desiderata. Similarly, the Assembly has, on a number of occasions, addressed itself directly to the Council's subsidiary organs, such as its functional commissions.

This tendency on the part of the General Assembly to bring its decisive influence to bear in economic and social questions, which seems to have become more pronounced in recent years, reflects a political difference between the composition of the Assembly and that of the Council. While in the General Assembly the less-developed countries can muster a strong majority of votes, in the Council they are definitely in a minority of 4 or 5 out of the 18 members of the Council. The leading industrial and capital-exporting states have traditionally been permanently represented in the Council, with the result that its attitude to the radical demands for economic assistance has throughout been one of marked conservatism and cautiousness. Realism and rationalism are more at home in the Council than they are in the Assembly and its committees, which are an ideal arena for rhetorical and propagandistic outpourings.

The General Assembly's control over economic and social matters, however, can never be either thorough or effective; there is too much work, and the Assembly and its committees with their tangled membership of over a hundred are too cumbersome an instrument for this purpose. It has been said that the Assembly's attempt at control gives the impression that this many-headed giant is enthusiastically humanitarian, but has an unfortunate tendency toward organizational cumbersomeness and over-politization and is unbusinesslike and overambitious—which is even truer today than when it was set up.

How cumbrous the machinery of the United Nations is in this field can be seen when one thinks of the many repetitive stages involved in the procedure through which a proposal must go. Let us imagine, for instance, that a question is raised in one of the functional commissions. Frequently such a proposal will be referred for preliminary discussion to a small committee or a working party. The latter's report is then discussed in the commission and may possibly result in a proposal, which is submitted to ECOSOC, where a fresh discussion takes place, possibly resulting in the adoption of a resolution, which is then referred to the General Assembly. First of all, it will go to their Second Committee (on economic questions) or the Third Committee (on social, humanitarian, and cultural questions), and then the final debate takes place in the General Assembly. To a large extent, it is the same people who are called upon to deal with the questions at various stages, which is not, of course, calculated to make this repetitive procedure any more exciting.

In Chapter V.3 it is said that the enormous increase in membership that has taken place in recent years has led to a strong demand for increased participation of the Afro-Asian group in ECOSOC. In December 1963 the General Assembly passed a resolution that the membership of the Council should be increased from 18 to 27 members, but it is doubtful whether this amendment to the Charter will ever enter into force. An attempt has been made to meet the demand part of the way by increasing the number of members in the functional commissions from 15 to 21, with the exclusion, however, of the Statistical Commission and the Population Commission, which now have 18 members as compared with 12 formerly. At the same time, the standing Technical Assistance Committee has been enlarged to include 30 members—an unusual feature in that the committees are otherwise made up of representatives of countries that are members of the Council.

As regards co-ordination problems, I shall define the aim of such co-ordination, the legal principles on which this co-ordination is based, the ways and means available for achieving the desired results, and, lastly, the machinery that has been created for this purpose.

The co-ordination problems are partly of a technical and partly of an administrative nature. From the technical point of view it is sought to harmonize both the distribution and the solution of the various tasks. The first means that the functions of the different agencies are mutually limited in such a way as to avoid both gaps and overlappings. The last means that the working programs and specific projects prepared by the various agencies are mutually adapted so that they fit together well instead of pulling in different directions. Frequently this requires agreement as to the order in which a series of questions shall be tackled and willing co-operation between different bodies in solving a problem of extensive scope. If, for example, it is a matter of helping a newly created state to overcome certain teething troubles, contributions will be required from many quarters. It may be desired to carry out, with the assistance of the UN Special Fund, investigations concerning the use of certain resources. FAO's assistance may be required for the promotion of agriculture, WHO may be asked to help build up a health administration, UNESCO's help may be needed in the educational field, and so forth. Clearly, to achieve a satisfactory result, it is necessary that the various agencies concerned deal with the matter on the basis of a common plan, along similar lines.

From the administrative point of view, the purpose of co-ordination is to solve the technical problems by means of machinery operating as effectively and cheaply as possible. It may, for example, be advantageous to establish, to a greater or lesser extent, common services in respect of headquarters, staff, library, statistical research, the preparation of programs, etc., or, at any rate, to co-operate in the recruitment or exchange of staff or the solution of many administrative tasks of a technical nature.

From the legal standpoint, a distinction should be drawn between internal and external co-ordination. The former, i.e. co-ordination in respect of the mutual relations between the different commissions set up by ECOSOC, presents no problem. As subsidiary organs created by the Council, these commissions are subject to its authority. The Council does not, however, enjoy corresponding authority over the autonomous specialized agencies. The legal basis of external co-ordination consists exclusively of the agreements that have been concluded with these institutions. In theory, it might have been thought that by virtue of these arrangements the United Nations would be given real power to direct with authority economic and social co-operation in all fields and perhaps firmly to integrate the many separate agencies into a large organizational whole. However, this has not happened. The agreements entered into uniformly recognize the autonomy of the specialized agencies and do not, on any point, grant a dominating position to the United Nations. In the main, these arrangements do not stray outside the usual framework of free co-operation between two equal partners. They concern, for instance, representation at meetings, mutual consultation (e.g. on agendas for meetings), the exchange of information and documents, various forms of mutual assistance and co-operation in the administrative field. Moreover, the specialized agencies undertake to report at regular intervals on their work and recognize the right of ECOSOC to submit recommendations for reference to the competent organ. The discussions on these recommendations then form the subject of a special report. Such recommendations may concern technical programs and activities as well as administrative questions, especially those of a budgetary nature.

In certain cases, co-ordination is even looser and little more than make-believe. It is understandable that institutions such as the International Bank and the International Monetary Fund, which carry out their activities in a businesslike fashion and whose members have a voting strength proportional to the capital they contribute, should wish to restrict the right of the well-meaning but economically irresponsible United Nations bodies to have a voice in their decisions. It has accordingly been decided, in agreement with these institutions, that no formal recommendations shall be made before mutual consultation has taken place and that, in particular, no recommendations at all shall be made to BANK concerning specific loans and financing terms. Furthermore, information obligations and the right to be represented are restricted.

The means that can be employed to implement co-ordination wholly depend on the agreements entered into. When the United Nations Charter was drawn up it was not possible to know what measures the specialized agencies would be willing to agree upon. However, a series of provisions in the Charter (Art. 17.3, 58, 59, 63, 64, and 70) show that it was expected that such agreements would involve at least the following minimum measures:

(1) mutual representation, Art. 70;
(2) consultation, Art. 63(2);
(3) submission of regular reports on the work of the specialized agencies, Art. 64;
(4) recommendations to the specialized agencies concerning the framing of their policy and the carrying out of their activities

aiming at both technical and administrative co-ordination, Art. 58 and 63(2);

(5) submission of special reports on the steps taken by a specialized agency to give effect to ECOSOC recommendations, Art. 64; and

(6) budgetary arrangements enabling the United Nations to exercise a certain influence, with particular reference to the administrative budgets of the specialized agencies, Art. 17.

The agreements in question have, as will be seen from the above considerations—that is, apart from BANK and FUND—fulfilled these minimum conditions.

In addition, ECOSOC may, without any agreement being required for this purpose, promote co-ordination designed to fill in gaps in the distribution of tasks, by taking the initiative in arranging for negotiations between the appropriate states with a view to the setting up of new specialized agencies.

Responsibility for the implementation of co-ordination rests primarily with the General Assembly in so far as it is this body that approves the agreements with the specialized agencies and issues the main directives and recommendations to the Council, the specialized agencies, and the member countries on the policy of co-ordination. But it goes without saying that the Assembly is not qualified to deal with concrete questions.

It is ECOSOC that deals with the day-to-day routine questions of general and administrative co-ordination. But this organ, too, is not directly in a position to take up these questions, partly because it only meets from time to time and partly because it lacks the expert knowledge required in the many different fields of activity of the specialized agencies and commissions. The Council is therefore assisted by the Secretary-General and a committee specially set up for this purpose, namely the Administrative Committee for Co-ordination (ACC), consisting of the Secretary-General, who is the chairman, and the corresponding senior official from each of the specialized agencies. This Committee, which, therefore, is not an ordinary Council Committee but a body of staff officials with an all-round expert knowledge, is entrusted with the task of working out priority and other co-ordination proposals. In addition, the Secretary-General prepares surveys of programs covering a certain number of years. A general discussion then takes place in the Council in order to arrive at a joint assessment of all the programs relating to the economic and social activities carried on within the United Nations "family."

Certain tasks call for particularly close co-operation between many institutions and special machinery for the organization of this co-operation. An instance of this occurred in 1949 when the United Nations, inspired by President Truman's "Point Four Program" adopted the Expanded Program of Technical Assistance (to under-developed countries). Two special organs were set up for the organization of an extensive co-operation, namely the Technical Assistance Committee (TAC) and the Technical Assistance Board (TAB). TAC is a standing committee under the authority of ECOSOC and at present consists of the 18 members of the Council plus 6 others elected by the Council. This committee is responsible for planning and directing the Expanded Assistance Program. In this task it is assisted by TAB, which is an organ of experts made up of a director in addition to the leading official of each of the organizations participating in the Expanded Program, i.e. 9 specialized agencies in addition to the United Nations. Those taking part in TAB's meetings also include, as observers, representatives of BANK, FUND, and the Special United Nations Fund, which, without formally participating in the Expanded Program, closely co-operate with TAB. In 1962 there was also set up a co-ordinating body known as the Special Committee, which, in co-operation with ACC and TAC is to submit proposals as regards assistance activities carried out within the context of the program known as the United Nations Development Decade.

It must, no doubt, be admitted that under the existing and in itself justified decentralization of economic and social activities, it is in practice an insoluble problem to weld all these more or less independent efforts into a coherent whole. The most important source of difficulties is, I believe, not so much the lack of a higher authority responsible for planning and directing, as the complicated nature of this task. The solution of the co-ordination problem itself requires the co-ordination of many factors, namely those relating to political and economic responsibility and those relating to expert knowledge. Even if the result is not ideal or, for that matter, does not even fulfill the hopes of genuine integration entertained during the drawing up of the Charter, it must nevertheless, in my opinion, having regard to the prevailing circumstances, be regarded as satisfactory—which, of course, does not mean that there is no need for continued efforts to achieve greater effectiveness and simplification.

3. Ways and means

According to Article 55 (see Art. 1.3) it is, as explained in more detail in section 1 of this chapter, the task of the United Nations to work for progress toward greater economic and social well-being in all fields, for example, higher standards of living, full employment, better health and education, etc. As these aims are, in each member country, subject to the national legislation and political measures of the state in question (for the promotion of employment, social welfare, education, etc.) and as the United Nations has no power in these fields either to take any direct measures (supranational power) or to issue binding orders to the states as regards the taking of certain steps (international power to issue orders), the question arises: What are the ways and means whereby the United Nations can work for the improvement of situations and conditions over which it has no power?

The reply is self-evident. Influence can be exercised in other ways than by the legal power to issue orders, for instance by information, discussion, and consultation; by criticism; or by economic means, in so far as it is possible, wholly or in part, to pay for the implementation of projects which one is not empowered to command. These methods, which, from the point of view of effectiveness, are often comparable to the legal technique, are the methods that the United Nations has to fall back on. The Organization must endeavor to achieve its aims by informing, teaching, stimulating, and admonishing—in so far as it is not in a position directly to pay, out of its own funds and in agreement with the state concerned, for the carrying out of welfare projects. The powers enjoyed by the Organization in this respect are nonpolitical, and the amount of influence it exercises depends on expert knowledge, public opinion, and the funds available.

I shall deal first with the obligations directly laid upon the members under the Charter. Then, under the headings "Information,"

"Discussion," "Recommendations," and "Stimulation," I shall go on to discuss various forms of activity aimed at influencing the actions of states on either the national or international level. Lastly, under "Action," I shall deal with the welfare activities undertaken and directly paid for by the United Nations (and the associated specialized agencies).

Members' obligations. In Article 56 of the Charter it is stipulated that "all members pledge themselves to take joint and separate action in co-operation with the Organization for the achievement of the purposes set forth in Article 55." The wording is unclear and the result of a compromise. At the San Francisco Conference, a wording was originally proposed whereby each individual state pledged itself separately, i.e. under its national legislation, to promote the purposes set forth in Article 55—for example, full employment. The United States representative in the relevant Commission would not accept so far-reaching an obligation. Hence the present wording of Article 56. The obligations of members thus include both action taken "jointly" with other states, i.e. international arrangements, as well as "separate" action, i.e. purely national measures. In both cases, however, this obligation is limited to measures taken "in co-operation with the Organization."

A member's obligation therefore implies a certain obligation to co-operate with the United Nations to carry out such international or national measures as are proposed by the Organization. This is not, of course, to say that members are bound to execute the Organization's recommendations, for this would mean that in reality these would not be recommendations but binding orders; and there has, quite definitely, never been any question of this. What then are actually the members' obligations? Legally speaking, they boil down to nothing, since the indefinite obligation to promote certain aims does not imply an obligation to take any specific action, for the aims in question must be weighed against other considerations. The obligation laid down in Article 56 is of the same loose and moral nature as the provision of the Danish Constitution (Art. 75.1), which calls upon the government and parliament to ensure that every able-bodied citizen shall have the possibility of working under conditions that will enable him to lead a secure existence. The fact that full employment is a desirable aim does not, of course, mean that it should be promoted at the expense of everything else. The provision, legally speaking, does not carry any definite obligation but is in the nature of a moral-political declaration.

Information. Facts often speak for themselves. To set them forth soberly, to analyze them, and to bring out their dependence on factors we are in a position to influence—this is often the strongest incentive for taking a certain political action. In recognition of this fact, Article 62 of the Charter mentions, first and foremost among the functions and powers of ECOSOC, that the Council may "make or initiate studies and reports" with respect to any matter falling within its competence. The Council has made extensive use of this, the most basic weapon in its armory. Over the years, hundreds of studies have been carried out in every possible social sector. If nothing else can be agreed upon, it is often an easy way out to agree merely that a question should be the subject of closer studies.

In most cases the Council has left it to the Secretary-General to initiate a study or a report, but there have also been cases where the question has been referred to a special working party of experts or to one of the commissions or a specialized agency. The Secretariat is the most appropriate body for dealing with questions that require only the factual gathering and analysis of information. If the solution of the problem calls for a political decision, it may be appropriate to call in a political organ, which can accept responsibility for this particular aspect of the question.

The result of the study normally takes the form of a report which is usually submitted to ECOSOC, which may then take various steps. For instance, it may decide simply to publish the report, to draw the attention of the interested parties to it, or to use it as a basis for further discussion and consultation either in the Council itself or in one of its subsidiary or associated organs.

Special importance attaches to the extensive and continuous work devoted to the gathering, processing, and publication of statistical data. All the agreements with the specialized agencies contain provisions on a certain division of labor whereby the national statistical offices supply information partly to the United Nations and partly to the specialized agencies. After these have been analyzed and otherwise processed they are published in periodicals or special publications, summarizing on a world-wide scale the data received from the various states (for example, the United Nations *Statistical Yearbook, Demographic Yearbook, World Economic Report, Report on the World Social Situation*).

Considerable difficulties of both a political and technical nature have arisen, and to some extent are still arising, in connection with this work. The Soviet Union and the other countries of the Eastern bloc have, to a large extent, been unwilling or unable to supply the desired information, thereby causing extensive gaps and uncertainties. From the technical point of view, the collating or comparison of statistics requires a standard classification. The United Nations has done valuable work to promote the desired standardization of statistics, for example in working out the *Standard International Trade Classification, Standard Industrial Classification of all Economic Activities,* and other similar surveys, which have gradually been accepted by nearly all states as a basis for their own statistics in the relevant sectors.

Discussion. In all the many different organs and institutions concerned with economic and social matters, problems give rise to a discussion involving opposing arguments and opinions. Each individual member state has, particularly in the General Assembly and its committees, the possibility of airing its views and upholding its special interests. Even if the flood of speeches may often seem interminable and aimed toward purposes other than purely objective ones, it must nevertheless be admitted that debates as such, apart from any decisions they may lead to, can be valuable in themselves. To a great extent, a debate will be useful from the information point of view, in so far as the participants submit facts and views that were not generally known before. At best, an exchange of ideas can help to clarify and thereby to solve the problems. At worst, the debate can degenerate into propaganda aimed at discrediting certain other states and at showing oneself in a sympathetic light. In many cases, the main value of the discussions lies in the moral judgments and criticisms to which they give rise, for example by throwing light upon and condemning violations of human rights occurring in a given country. Experience has shown that no state, not even the mightiest, is completely indifferent to such condemnation, particularly where a virtually unanimous world public opinion is concerned.

This does not, of course, mean that the criticized party will always alter its behavior in the light of the criticisms, but, nevertheless, they cannot be said to be altogether without practical effect.

Recommendations. Under Article 62(1) the Council may make recommendations to the General Assembly, to members of the United Nations, and to the specialized agencies concerned. The commissions and other subsidiary organs are not named in this article because they are, as such, fully under the instructions of the Council.

In so far as a recommendation is addressed to the General Assembly or to a specialized agency, it must, by the very nature of things, aim at further international action—for example, a study, a conference, and so forth. If the recommendation is addressed to the member states, the same may hold true, but in that case the recommendation may also aim at action at the national level, that is, the creation of certain economic and social conditions in the state concerned, which, after all, is the ultimate aim of all efforts in this field.

In practice, the Council has made extensive use of these powers also *vis-à-vis* states, as just explained. Hundreds of resolutions have been adopted, of which a great number concerned violations of human rights. The recommendations were addressed to the members in general; to specific groups of members, for example, the states which have applied for technical assistance; or to specific states mentioned by name. The view that the last-named were outside the Council's province has been rejected. The discussion on this point is bound up with the difficult question of the interpretation of the proviso in Article 2(7) of the Charter in regard to domestic jurisdiction. In the light of what has been said in Chapter III above, what matters is not to whom the recommendation is addressed—any recommendation, indeed, even the discussion in itself, is in my opinion an "intervention" within the meaning of Article 2(7)—but the actual nature of the subject: a matter is essentially within the domestic jurisdiction of a state if it does not affect the rights of other states or, essentially, their interests. United Nations practice, also so far as ECOSOC is concerned, may be interpreted in this light.

A restriction of the Council's competence to make recommendations follows from the general restriction of its field of activities to economic and social matters. On one or two occasions it was suggested in certain quarters that the Council should submit proposals for the settlement of a dispute on economic questions between two member states, but the Council rightly declared itself incompetent to express any opinion since the dispute was also of a legal nature.

Stimulation. According to Article 62(3) and (4), the Council may prepare draft conventions and call international conferences, in both cases, of course, only with respect to matters falling within its competence. This activity goes further than simple recommendations. The Council does not then content itself merely with recommending the conclusion of a convention or the holding of a conference but actively intervenes by taking preparatory action designed to encourage the states concerned to take further steps in the desired direction.

It goes without saying that states are free to decide whether they wish to accede (sign and ratify) a given draft convention or take part in a conference called by the Council. In order to improve the chances of success, the Council always contacts members in advance by means of questionnaires and in other ways in order to sound them out with respect to any proposed action.

A draft convention is normally submitted to the General Assembly, which decides what further action shall be taken. The Council can also avail itself of its powers to call a conference of states, to which it can submit the draft.

The "international conferences" that can be called by the Council may be state or nonstate conferences. Rules of procedure to be followed in such cases have been laid down by the General Assembly.

The Council has to a considerable extent made use of its competence to elaborate draft conventions. More than a score of such drafts have been submitted to the General Assembly, and about half as many to international conferences. At the moment, the Third Committee of the General Assembly is discussing two draft conventions on human rights, one draft convention on free consent to marriage, and one on freedom of information. Of the specialized agencies, the International Labor Organization (ILO) has made extensive use of this technique. It has elaborated well over 100 conventions concerning working conditions, an overwhelming majority of which have subsequently come into effect.

When a state has acceded to and ratified a convention and when this convention has become effective, the state in question is bound to carry out its provisions. Unfortunately, such obligation is not always synonymous with actual observation of the agreement. To encourage observation, a provision has in many cases been adopted to the effect that the state shall report every year on the action it has taken in fulfillment of its obligations. ILO has gone a step further. Under its Constitution, both workers' trade unions and employers' organizations are entitled to set in motion a procedure of complaint alleging that a state has not fulfilled the relevant obligations.

Action. The methods described so far have this in common—that they are designed, directly or indirectly, to stimulate states to take certain measures to promote well-being. To a certain extent, however, an international agency takes direct action in respect of such measures. It goes without saying that these measures are never applied in the territory of a state without the consent of that state's authorities.

The best-known example of this is the extensive activity carried out under the auspices of the United Nations Programs for Technical Co-operation, which cover both the regular and the expanded program of technical assistance to the less-developed countries.

Direct action is involved also in various assistance measures taken in emergencies, such as by UNRRA (United Nations Relief and Rehabilitation Administration), which was set up immediately after the Second World War to assist the liberated countries, UNKRA (United Nations Korean Reconstruction Agency), and UNRWA (United Nations Relief and Works Agency for Palestine Refugees).

Of a more permanent nature are the programs on behalf of children and refugees carried out respectively by UNICEF (United Nations Children's Fund) and UNHCR (United Nations High Commissioner for Refugees).

A further example of living up to the slogan "not only words but also action" is the activity carried out by the International Bank (IDA and IFC; see "Financial help" in section E of this chapter) and the International Monetary Fund.

4. *Brief survey of the different sectors of economic and social co-operation*

A. ECONOMIC QUESTIONS

International Trade. It is a disturbing fact that until very recently the economic life, production, and trade of states had scarcely been subject to international regulation. Each state independently determines its own trade policy. In the struggle for raw materials, markets, and employment, each state pursues its own aims, and the clashes of interests arising in this connection can, even when the countries concerned are militarily at peace, lead to commercial warfare.

True, since 1860 a great number of trade agreements have been concluded. But practically all of these have been bilateral agreements, a means of bargaining for concessions and preferences, but without any provision for international co-ordination. After most countries had given up orthodox free trade, such arrangements have pimarily been concerned with setting limits to customs tariffs and other measures of trade protection.

Nevertheless, in the years before the First World War, this unorganized process of adaptation achieved not altogether insignificant results. A network of trade arrangements was woven around the world, offering possibilities for a maximum exchange of goods. The standing "most-favored-nation clause," whereby a contracting state is assured of treatment as favorable as that enjoyed by the country which is or will become in the future the most favored nation, brought a certain unity into the variety of these trade arrangements.

After the First World War, this development toward free trade came to a complete halt. Influenced, among other things, by military considerations, various states adopted a policy of self-sufficiency, which was bound to lead to similar reactions on the part of other states that really favored free trade. Everywhere controls were imposed on imports, and trade arrangements no longer merely set the level of customs tariffs but stipulated also export quotas and prices. The culmination of this process was reached when even England, through the Ottawa treaty of 1932, gave up the idea of free trade for the system of Empire preference. The most-favored-nation clause was undermined and was replaced partly by the idea of "preference," whereby states inside a given group grant one another mutual trade advantages. The Geneva Convention of 1927, signed by a great number of states, concerning the abolition of import and export restrictions, stands as a monument to liberal ideas, but subsequent developments prevented it from ever having any practical effect. The great economic depression, which began with the Wall Street crash in 1929, obliged the states to stick to restrictionism. (In Denmark, legislation for the protection of Danish currency was introduced in the early 1930's.) Two later attempts by the League of Nations, in 1930 and 1933, were equally unsuccessful. And so, until the time of the Second World War, the system of restrictions, preferences, and bilateral agreements continued to spread, to the great detriment of international trade.

After the end of the Second World War, a major drive was launched for peace in world trade and the establishment of a plan for the harmonious development of the world economy. To this end, the Havana Charter was adopted in 1948. In this instrument, signed by 53 countries, a whole series of principles were laid down in order to promote full employment, the full exploitation of the world's economic resources, the development of the underdeveloped areas, the restoration of war-damaged property, and, in particular, the liberalization of trade policy, aimed at ensuring free and equal access by all to all markets and raw materials. An International Trade Organization (ITO) was to be set up for this purpose. No doubt because it aimed too high and its ideas were too abstract, its Charter failed to obtain the necessary number of ratifications to enter into force, and ITO never became a reality. The more limited General Agreement on Tariffs and Trade (GATT), which has been more particularly concerned with the breaking down of trade barriers, was more fortunate. The GATT agreement was concluded in 1947. After a great number of states had acceded to it, there was set up in 1955 an institution known as the Organization for Trade Co-operation (OTC) for the purpose of administering the GATT agreement and to examine and foster international co-operation in trade. This organization's constitution, which has not yet come into force (1965), offers the possibility that the organization may, in agreement with the United Nations, become a "specialized agency."

In recent years, the efforts toward a world-wide liberalization of trade have, to some extent, clashed with the efforts made on a regional basis to unite states in free trade areas or customs unions based on mutual adjustment of economies. In Europe, these efforts have resulted in the creation of the European Economic Community (EEC, the Common Market, "the Six") and the European Free Trade Association (EFTA, "the Seven").

In international trade, raw materials occupy a special place. For each state, it is a matter of life and death to have access on the free market, on equal terms with other countries, to the raw materials it lacks. For many of the less-developed countries, whose economies are very largely dependent on the export of raw materials, stable raw material prices are of crucial importance for the sound and regular development of their economy.

ECOSOC has concerned itself with these problems. In 1947, it took the initiative in setting up a special body known as the Interim Co-ordinating Committee for International Commodity Arrangements (ICCICA), which comprises representatives from the United Nations, FAO, and GATT. Its task is to promote and co-ordinate efforts to arrive at arrangements on raw materials problems. After the setting up of this committee, the United Nations called a number of conferences to discuss various important raw materials. This resulted in arrangements on tin, sugar, wheat, and olive oil. In addition, cocoa, copper, lead, rubber, wool, and tea have been the subject of studies, negotiations, and certain regulations.

In 1954 ECOSOC set up a new functional commission known as the Commission on International Commodity Trade (CICT), which was entrusted with the task of preventing undesirable fluctuations in the price of raw materials and, more generally, of studying and supervising international trade in raw materials, with particular reference to its effects on the economy of the less-developed countries.

The Council has also made various efforts to improve the legal and commercial conditions of international trade. On its initiative, a conference took place in New York in 1958 which led to the conclusion of a Convention on the Recognition and Enforcement of Foreign Arbitral Awards. Agreements on and methods of limiting competition have, for a long time, formed the subject of studies and consultations.

International financial relations. A policy of self-sufficiency and the resulting restrictions in international trade also lead to currency restrictions, i.e. notes cease to be convertible into gold and the purchase of foreign currency is restricted. This in turn does away with the "natural" rates of exchange based on gold convertibility, and each state fixes the exchange rates for its own currency. Under a restrictive trade policy, it may be tempting to resort to devaluation as a means of promoting exports, but, like other regulations of this kind, its weakness is that it induces other states to take similar countermeasures, and the result is a stalemate.

When, after the end of the Second World War, all energies were bent to the task of liberalizing international trade, it was found necessary, at the same time, to try to create free and stable international monetary conditions. The International Monetary Fund (FUND) was set up for this purpose at a conference held at Bretton Woods, New Hampshire, in 1944. FUND is recognized as one of the United Nations specialized agencies. Its task is to foster international co-operation in the monetary field in order to create stable and balanced payments conditions for the benefit of international trade. To this end, by means of quotas apportioned among the participants, a gold and currency fund was established on which the members, in accordance with specific rules, may draw, by purchasing the currency they need, to cover any deficit in their balance of payments. They are expected to repurchase their own currency within a given period of time. Furthermore, a gold parity is fixed for the currency of each member, and limits are set to the freedom to alter such currency rates by more than 10 per cent.

The International Bank and allied financial institutions are described below in connection with the question of assistance to the less-developed countries

Traffic (transport of goods, persons and communications). It is quite obvious that the traffic problems of states can only be solved by means of international co-operation. What use would it be to a country to have the finest transport system if this were not co-ordinated with the transport systems of other countries in such a way that transport could easily continue beyond the individual states' borders? Indeed, it was in this field that the first international administrative union was created, namely the international telegraph union set up in Paris in 1865. Today a large part of the traffic comes under international regulation and control under the responsibility of four specialized agencies:

The International Telecommunications Union (ITU), which covers telegraph, telephone, radio, and television, is based on the International Telecommunications Convention signed in Madrid in 1932 and since frequently revised. The Union itself does not perform any kind of service in the field of telecommunications, its sole aim being to foster international co-operation for the improvement of telecommunications. A particularly important field of activities has been the apportionment of radio wave lengths and measures for the prevention of harmful interference.

The Universal Postal Union (UPU), which organizes international postal traffic, is based on the principle of free transit, which does not, however, exclude the payment of certain charges. The whole Union constitutes a common postal area having the same postage charges irrespective of distance. No mutual settling of accounts take place, each state keeping its own postage revenue in full.

The International Civil Aviation Organization (ICAO), set up by a convention signed in 1944, is based on the principle that every state enjoys full and exclusive sovereignty in the air space over its territory. Thus, under general international law, it does not recognize any right of passage in the air corresponding to that applying to foreign ships at sea. Under the convention, however, the participants recognized one another's right to fly over and land in their territory. This only applies to civil aircraft and only in peacetime and not to regular air traffic. In supplementary agreements, which have not been signed by all the members of ICAO, further rights are granted, including that of making regular flights. ICAO is permanently concerned with the improvement of techniques and safety in air traffic. In this connection, ICAO has set up a North Atlantic weather reporting service based on nine floating and stationary stations in Greenland, the Faroe Islands, and Iceland. This information is available to the 18 countries whose airlines cross the Atlantic.

The Inter-Governmental Maritime Consultative Organization (IMCO) is concerned with promoting navigation and safety at sea and encouraging the removal of flag discrimination and other restrictions. The Organization's activities are based on various treaties, the most important of which is a convention on the safety of human life at sea, together with various regulations concerning the prevention of collisions at sea and a convention to prevent the pollution of the sea by oil.

Development of natural resources. In order to raise living standards, most particularly in those parts of the world where people live on the verge of hunger, it is most important that the earth's natural resources, agricultural land, the resources of the sea, and sources of energy all be exploited as rationally as possible for the production of foodstuffs and other substances necessary to life. International activity in this field has been apportioned as follows: FAO concerns itself with agriculture, IAEA with the development of atomic energy, and ECOSOC with the remaining resources and sources of energy.

The Food and Agriculture Organization of the United Nations (FAO) was set up for the purpose of satisfying the most fundamental of all needs, the need for food. The living standards we enjoy in our countries make it difficult for us to imagine the full extent of this basic problem. We are so overwhelmed with statistics that we cannot take in the significance of these figures. Can we really imagine what it means for nearly half of the earth's population, i.e. about one and a half thousand million people, to suffer from constant hunger or undernourishment? Nor is this the kind of hunger with which we are familiar, the stimulating sensation that comes before a good meal, but a state of chronic weakness leading to apathy, pain, sickness, and death.

The problem is greatly aggravated by the fact that in recent times the population of this planet has been increasing at an unprecedented rate. And so we have a race between growth of population and the increase of food production, a race that in many parts of the world is being won by the former. This unfortunate situation is the concomitant of an achievement that otherwise is one of the benefits of civilization of which the poorer countries have also had their share, namely the reduction of the mortality rate, particularly among children, thanks to medical treatment and hygiene. Whereas in former days the death rate more or less kept pace with the birthrate, the population of countries that have great difficulty in feeding their inhabitants is increasing by 2 to 3.5 per cent per annum (India, 2%; China, 2.5%; Colombia, Venezuela, Malaya, Ceylon and others, 3 to

3.5%). Compared with this, the population of Denmark is increasing by less than 1 per cent per annum, and that of the world as a whole by 1.7 per cent. The total annual increase is 50 million people a year, or about 140,000 each day. Of these, by far the greater part are born in the underdeveloped countries. It is these countries, therefore, that must be provided with extra supplies of food through the further development of food production, and this is where the FAO comes in.

Naturally, there is another and very much more effective way of tackling the problem: that is to teach the peoples concerned birth-control as a means of reducing their increase in population. Unfortunately, it is to be expected that for a long time this method will come up against a series of obstacles, such as complete inability even to understand the significance of the question, religious objections, the traditional idea that it is a blessing to have a lot of children, and the lack of means to purchase contraceptives. In the long run, therefore, it is a question of overcoming these obstacles by means of information and economic progress. Proposals to this end made in the United Nations have come up against a wall of prejudice, stupidity, and irresponsibility. Faced with the problem that, next to the threat of the nuclear bomb, is the major challenge of our times, the Roman Catholic Church has ruthlessly cast aside all considerations of human suffering and happiness in order to uphold religious dogmas and to ensure the triumph of religious fanaticism over rational humanism. In my opinion, this is nothing less than a crime against humanity.

The FAO's field of activity covers not only agriculture but also forestry, fisheries, and nutrition problems in general. A major campaign has been launched for the five-year period 1960-65, with the slogan "Freedom from Hunger," that involves information and education as well as research and national action. Among the methods available for increase in production, particular importance attaches to the following: bringing new land under cultivation (only about one-fourth of the earth's arable land is under cultivation); improvement of soil under cultivation (for example, through the use of fertilizers, irrigation, elimination of erosion and sand, etc.); improvement of crops; control of plant and cattle diseases; improvement of methods of cultivation in conjunction with the introduction of better equipment; the improvement of distribution and marketing in order to reduce the tremendous losses that occur during storage and transport due to fungus, insects, rodents, worms, etc. But all these and other methods require, first and foremost, an improvement in the human material through information aimed at overcoming stupidity and prejudice, and improving the health of the populations concerned in order to break the vicious circle of sickness and poverty.

Atomic energy opens up fresh prospects of increasing production in all sectors. This new source of energy seems to have been discovered at the right historical moment, just when the exhaustion of the other existing sources of fuels, in particular coal and oil, seemed to be in sight. Atomic energy can be used primarily for the production of electricity, which is the form of energy that is the easiest to transport and that can be used in both small and large industrial plants. In medicine and agriculture, too, the enormous forces locked up in these tiny particles can be used for promoting research, experiments, therapy, and techniques. But the use of atomic energy is no simple matter, depending as it does on a high degree of scientific knowledge, constant research and the building of large plants. The investment required is such that international co-operation is the best solution, particularly as many more or less undeveloped countries would hardly be in a position to carry out such investments on their own.

It is for this purpose that the International Atomic Energy Agency (IAEA) was set up. Its task is to further and increase the contribution of atomic energy to peace, health, and well-being throughout the world. The United Nations and the IAEA have concluded an agreement on co-operation, but, as this did not take place in accordance with the provisions of Articles 57 and 63 of the Charter, IAEA cannot be formally described as a "specialized agency"—though in reality it is on an equal footing with these bodies, apart from the fact that it reports directly to the General Assembly and the Security Council, not to ECOSOC. This organization, which was set up in 1956, has sent investigating commissions to a series of less-developed countries to make preliminary inquiries. It has provided consultants and experts and granted study fellowships. It has fostered scientific research and organized conferences. The results of this research have been disseminated by holding special courses and organizing other educational activities.

To supplement this work carried out by FAO and IAEA, ECOSOC has concerned itself with a number of other questions in this field. Partly through its Standing Committee for Industrial Development and partly by holding special conferences and setting up study groups, the Council has given its attention to the question of the utilization of natural sources of energy and resources such as water power and oil, land reform, the protection of natural resources in the sea, and other similar problems.

Regional co-operation. The above-mentioned activities carried out by the United Nations and some of its specialized agencies relate to economic problems on a world-wide scale. The four regional economic commissions—namely, for Europe (ECE), Asia and the Far East (ECAFE), Latin America (ECLA), and Africa (ECA)—deal with similar problems on a regional basis. These are all subsidiary organs working under ECOSOC, but in practice they have achieved a large measure of independence, as may be seen in particular from the fact that they are competent to submit recommendations direct to the governments of the member countries concerned. The more limited geographical scope of these commissions means that the problems with which they deal are often more wieldy and that they are more likely to have concrete and constructive tasks to perform. As a United Nations organ, the European Commission has no connection with the different European communities organized by the Western European states. Hence it assumes special importance as the only European organization where the states of the Eastern bloc also are represented.

B. SOCIAL AND HUMANITARIAN QUESTIONS

Protection of workers. In recognition of the fact that social injustice and the need and misery associated with it are a danger to world peace, Chapter 13 of the Versailles Treaty provided for the setting up of an independent and permanent institution, the International Labor Organization (ILO), entrusted with the task of improving working conditions. After a revision of its constitution in 1945-46, the organization in 1946 became a specialized agency related to the United Nations.

From the organizational point of view, the ILO occupies an interesting and special position in that not only the participating governments but also workers and employers are directly represented in the executive organs of the organization. To the leading organ, the General Conference, each of the member countries sends four representatives, two of whom are appointed by the governments and one each by the most representative workers' and employers' organizations (where these exist). The Governing Body, which is the ILO's executive organ, has the same triangular composition (20-10-10). In addition, both workers' and employers' organizations are entitled to report to the ILO whenever any member has "failed to secure in any respect the effective observance within its jurisdiction of any convention to which it is a party."

The ILO concerns itself with improving the well-being of workers, in particular by elaborating draft conventions laying down certain minimum standards, for example in respect of working hours; prevention of unemployment; protection of children, young people, and women; minimum wages; trade union rights; night work; weekly day of rest; holidays with pay; old age and accident insurance; etc. Such drafts can be adopted by the General Conference with a two-thirds majority. The conventions are binding only upon those member states that accede to (ratify) the drafts, but the governments are bound to submit them to the national organ competent to legislate in the field in question and are likewise bound to report on the implementation of the conventions to which they have acceded. The purpose of these conventions is to encourage those states in which conditions are the worst to improve these conditions and bring them up to the level of the stipulated minimum standards. Thus no purpose is served by fixing too high a level, for then the chances are that the draft convention will not be ratified precisely by those countries for which the convention is primarily intended. Since its inception in 1919, this organization has done effective work. Well over 100 draft conventions have been adopted, the great majority of which have been ratified by many of the member countries. A similar number of recommendations have also been adopted.

Health. Until the 19th century every country sought to deal with the worst contagious diseases, in particular the plague, cholera, and yellow fever, by means of strict quarantine rules which were designed to act as a local barrier. Gradually, it was realized that this common enemy must be fought jointly and that the fight must be taken to the enemy from the outset. The opening of the Suez Canal in 1869 and the closer contact that ensued with sources of contagion in Asia gave rise to various international conventions whereby an international sanitary police was established to supervise the sanitary administration in the East and co-operation was instituted between the various states in implementation of their protective measures.

Co-operation in this field is at present the responsibility of the World Health Organization (WHO), set up in New York in 1946, which superseded the previous Office International d'Hygiène Publique in Paris and the Health Organization of the League of Nations. Its headquarters are in Geneva. Its statutes lay down certain general aims and principles, but apart from this they are of an organizational nature and do not take the place of the existing health conventions. That the main aim of this organization now goes further than combatting certain dangerous contagious diseases is shown by the fact that health is defined as "a state of complete physical, mental, and social well-being and not merely the absence of disease or infirmity," and is at the same time considered a fundamental human right to be enjoyed by all and of fundamental importance for the attainment of peace and security.

The diseases that originally gave rise to international co-operation in this field have now been practically wiped out. WHO has particularly conerned itself with the control of malaria, tuberculosis, and venereal disease and is now aiming at the total eradication of a whole series of contagious diseases. It is also working for the promotion of higher nutritional and sanitary standards.

The advent of atomic energy has provided new tasks for international co-operation in the field of health. On the credit side, there is the fact that radioisotopes can be used in medical research, diagnosis, and treatment. On the debit side, however, we have the radioactive fall-out caused by nuclear test explosions, which can be a serious danger to public health and possibly even cause genetic damage affecting future generations. Both aspects of the question give rise to tasks calling for organized research and co-operation.

One special aspect of the efforts made to improve public health is the fight against the abuse of narcotics, which in certain countries has been responsible for more misfortunes than the worst diseases. Natural narcotics are extracted mainly from three plants, namely the opium poppy, the coca leaf, and the cannabis plant. Opium is used for producing morphine and other opiates, while the coca leaf yields cocaine. Cannabis is also known as marijuana, hashish, etc. The last-named substance is creating particularly difficult problems owing to the fact that it is geographically the most widespread and the most difficult to control, since, apart from the fact that it grows wild, it is also used for industrial purposes. In addition, a great number of synthetic drugs have been introduced in recent years.

International activities in this field are carried on by a series of bodies specially set up for this purpose. The leading authority is the Commission on Narcotic Drugs, which is one of the commissions of ECOSOC. A majority of its members are major producers of narcotics. Administration and control are in the hands of two of ECOSOC's special bodies, namely the Permanent Central Opium Board and the Drug Supervisory Body, in liaison with the Committee on Addiction-Producing Drugs of WHO. The activities of these bodies are based on eight international conventions.

This system is now about to be developed and simplified. In 1961, on the initiative of ECOSOC, a conference took place in New York at which a new convention was adopted, the Uniform Convention on Narcotic Drugs. This made it possible to (1) codify the rules laid down in the eight conventions concerned; (2) to extend control, which had hitherto been mainly concerned with drugs trafficking, to include also the production of the raw materials; and (3) to simplify the organizational machinery by merging the two above-mentioned special bodies. The Uniform Convention has not yet been ratified by a sufficient number of countries to come into effect (early 1965).

Assistance to children. In 1946 the General Assembly decided that as part of the postwar reconstruction program, there should be set up an international fund to assist children, particularly in those countries that had suffered most from the effects of the war. This fund is known as the United Nations International Children's Emergency Fund (UNICEF). After a few years the task of healing the scars left by the war had been largely accomplished. In 1950, and again in 1953, it was decided that UNICEF should continue its activities as a permanent institution for giving assistance to children on a broader basis, with particular reference to the underdeveloped countries. The organization changed its name to the United Nations Children's Fund, but the initials UNICEF were so well known that they were retained unaltered.

The United Nations Children's Fund is now a special body operating under ECOSOC. It does, however, enjoy a considerable measure of independence and obtains its fund not from the United Nations budget but through voluntary contributions, of which about 85 per cent comes from about 100 governments and the rest is derived from private gifts, the sale of Christmas cards, etc.

As there are over one billion children in the world, of which more than half are needy, there is plenty for UNICEF to do. Its working program is primarily concerned with the fight against sickness, the improvement of sanitary conditions and nutrition—including the direct distribution of milk and other essential foodstuffs—assistance in the event of natural disasters, and general welfare measures to assist children and families. Since 1961, the program has been expanded to include educational and vocational training assistance.

Measures to assist refugees. The violent political upheavals and the two world wars that have taken place in recent times created an extremely serious and difficult refugee problem. In the 1920's, Fridtjof Nansen and the League of Nations gave assistance to the Armenians escaping from Turkish persecution and to the Russians who left their homeland after the revolution. After 1933, thousands of Germans and Austrians, many of them Jews, fled from Hitler's persecution. The Second World War added a new category of refugees, the displaced persons. The Nazis moved millions of people from their homes in the various occupied countries and transported them to concentration camps or to factories in Germany. Many people also fled from the Baltic countries before the Russian advance. Later, the dictatorships behind the Iron Curtain added to the stream of the homeless. The Hungarian uprising in 1956 resulted in over 200,000 people fleeing the country. Between half a million and a million Chinese have fled from the Communist regime to Hongkong, and the stream shows no sign of drying up. The hostilities that took place at the time of the foundation of the state of Israel in 1948 led nearly a million Arabs to flee from Palestine to the neighboring Arab states. Lastly, the eight-year-long fighting and terrorism in Algeria resulted in the creation of 300,000 more refugees. In addition, there are many smaller groups from all parts of the world that have been the scene of armed conflicts or political upheavals.

These people are in an unfortunate position. Being refugees from their home country, they have no national status and consequently require international legal assistance. The main task is that of sending home refugees who want to return and resettling elsewhere those who do not. Moreover, until some definite decision is taken, all these refugees must be housed and decently looked after.

When the Allied armies entered Germany, they liberated and sent back to their countries about 7 million people (by the end of 1946). But there were still over a million refugees left, living in camps, most of whom did not wish to be repatriated. In order to help these and other refugees, the International Refugee Organization (IRO) was set up in London in 1946 as an autonomous specialized agency. When, at the end of 1951, it ceased its activities, it had returned to their home countries 93,000 refugees and resettled more than a million.

Since then, this work has been continued directly by the United Nations, which has, for this purpose, set up a special body under the authority of the General Assembly, namely the office of the United Nations High Commissioner for Refugees (UNHCR), whose activities at the present time are concerned with the welfare of about one and a quarter million refugees. The Office's administrative expenses are covered by the United Nations budget, but the actual assistance measures are paid for out of private contributions. In order to increase public interest in the problem, a World Refugee Year was held in 1959-60. The UNHCR operates along the same lines as the former IRO. In other words, it is concerned with repatriation, resettlement, maintenance, and legal assistance. On its initiative, a convention on the legal status of refugees was adopted in 1951.

Assistance to Arab refugees from Palestine is specially administered by the United Nations Relief and Works Agency for Palestine Refugees (UNRWA), which is a subsidiary organ working under the General Assembly. The cost of assistance is covered by voluntary contibutions. This refugee problem is particularly difficult because the humanitarian aspect is complicated by the political enmity between the Jews and Arabs. As a result, it has proved very difficult either to send these refugees home or to resettle them elsewhere. At the time of writing (1965), the registered Arab refugees number one and a quarter million divided between Jordan, Gaza, Lebanon, and Syria. Of these, 879,000 are entitled to all forms of assistance. Approximately half of them are children. About 40 per cent of the refugees are living in camps (there are 54 such camps), and UNRWA is therefore faced not only with the task of feeding these people (basic rations provide 1,500-1,600 calories per day per person) but must also provide health services, schools, further education, and other essential facilities. Each camp is equipped with the most important facilities required for administering UNRWA assistance, i.e. schools, kitchens, canteens, and clinics.

On many occasions, the United Nations has granted emergency assistance, particularly after a war. During the years immediately following the Second World War, the initial assistance toward European recovery was granted through the United Nations Relief and Rehabilitation Administration (UNRRA). Similarly, after the end of the Korean conflict, assistance toward Korea's recovery was organized through a special body, United Nations Korean Reconstruction Agency (UNKRA), whose activities came to an end in 1960.

Supplementary Activities of ECOSOC. To supplement the tasks described above, which are all carried out by special organs set up for this purpose, the Economic and Social Council and its commissions deal with a whole series of social and humanitarian questions. As human rights and assistance to the less-developed countries will be dealt with later in this chapter, only the following tasks need be mentioned here:

(1) social welfare programmes and associated administrative problems, including the care of families, young people, and children; the care of the aged; help to the disabled; the training of social workers; and the like;

(2) social development, including reports on social trends and programmes on a world-wide scale in conjunction with studies on the question of international comparison of living standards;

(3) social defense, including the fight against crime, in particular juvenile delinquency, and the treatment of offenders; the fight against prostitution; the white slave trade; and

(4) population problems, including the growth in population and living standards, migrations, and the classification of population into productive and nonproductive groups.

C. CULTURAL QUESTIONS

The main organ in this field is the United Nations Educational, Scientific, and Cultural Organization (UNESCO), which is one of the specialized agencies. The organization is based on the idea "since wars begin in the minds of men it is in the minds of men that the defenses of peace must be constructed," and its purpose is to

contribute to peace and security by promoting collaboration among the nations through education, science and culture in order to further universal respect for justice, for the rule of law and for the human rights and fundamental freedoms which are affirmed for the peoples of the world, without distinction of race, sex, language or religion, by the Charter of the United Nations.

This organization's work in the field of education has been primarily influenced by the fact that about half the adults in the world can neither read nor write and that about 250 million children do not go to school. The fight against illiteracy is justified not merely because the ability to read and write is in itself a cultural accomplishment, but also because this ability is a necessary prerequisite for any further education in the fight against sickness, poverty, and social injustice. A major project in progress at the present time aims at creating schools and providing teachers for children in 20 Latin American countries. It is estimated that there is a shortage of 400,000 teachers in that part of the world.

In the scientific field UNESCO seeks in particular to foster research, which calls for organized co-operation between nations. Among the current projects in the sphere of the natural sciences is one concerned with areas suffering from drought, the practical purpose of which is to improve living conditions in 16 countries located in the dry belt that runs from North Africa through the Middle East to South Asia. A characteristic UNESCO project within the field of social sciences is the promotion of research in conflict and conflict resolution.

In the cultural field, UNESCO considers that its primary task is to spread knowledge and understanding of the cultural achievements of other peoples in the realms of art, science, religion, and philosophy, with a view to furthering international understanding. For instance, a ten-year plan is now in progress for fostering mutual understanding and appreciation of the cultural achievements and values of East and West.

Certain branches of science which are particularly dependent on international co-operation are dealt with by other specialized agencies. This applies, for instance, to meteorology, the theoretical and practical aspects of which come under the World Meteorological Organization (WMO). Theoretical nuclear physics are the responsibility of IAEA, which was mentioned above in the section dealing with economic problems.

A cultural problem of special importance is international co-operation for the codification and development of international law. Under Article 13 of the Charter, the General Assembly is required to initiate studies and make recommendations to this end. In 1947, the Assembly accordingly set up an International Law Commission made up of (at present 21) persons of recognized competence in international law and representing the main forms of civilization and the principal legal systems of the world. Its task is to examine problems of international law and prepare draft conventions. The commission may take up a question on its own initiative, but most of its tasks have been entrusted to it by the General Assembly. The commission has only minor achievements to its credit and, by and large, must be reckoned a disappointment. It has concerned itself with more than a dozen topics, but only in three of them has a convention been agreed upon: four conventions on the law of the sea adopted at an inter-state conference in Geneva in 1958, a convention on the reduction of statelessness (New York, 1961), and a convention on diplomatic relations (Vienna, 1961).

In other fields, too, the commission has prepared draft conventions, but without finding sufficient interest or support on the political side to warrant their adoption. This is particularly the case with the series of problems relating to the definition of the concept of aggression, the elaboration of an international code of offenses against the peace and security of mankind, and the setting up of an international criminal court to punish those guilty of aggression or other violations of peace. After lengthy discussions during the period

1950-57 in the commission, the General Assembly, and its Sixth Committee, the question may now be regarded as dropped. It is beginning to be realized, I believe, that it is fallacious to apply the principles of criminal law in this field and that it is illusory to believe that international peace and security can be preserved in this way. On this point, the International Law Commission has not proved equal to its task. Instead of being carried away by the "idealism" that regarded the Nuremberg trial and judgment as the beginning of a new legal era in the fight against war, these jurists should have had enough realistic knowledge of the nature and technique of law to recognize this project for the chimera it was and to spare themselves and the United Nations all these useless efforts. (It should be added that three of the Commission's members expressed themselves against an international criminal jurisdiction.)

Apart from the International Law Commission, the General Assembly has made other contributions to the development of international law. On December 9, 1948, it unanimously adopted a Convention on the Prevention and Punishment of the Crime of Genocide. It is difficult to imagine a clearer example of a solemn-sounding but empty and useless declaration. Under that convention, which was ratified by a great many states, the signatory states undertake to punish persons who have committed genocide, i.e. who have performed certain acts, in particular killing, with intent to destroy, in whole or in part, a national, ethnical, racial, or religious group as such. The example those concerned had in mind at that time was, of course, Hitler's attempt to destroy the Jews. Such acts, however, are scarcely conceivable as the work of one man, but would have to be planned and carried out by the apparatus of the state. What the convention is asking therefore is that a government which has been so criminal and corrupt as to commit genocide shall then be so upright as to ensure its own punishment in its own national courts (the convention makes no provision for any international proceedings). The worst of it is that, apart from a small circle of empty-headed "idealists," the authors of this convention and the governments that ratified it must have realized perfectly well that it was pure nonsense. But no one had the courage to say so and spoil the impression given to the whole world that the United Nations had really done something to prevent a repetition of the world's most horrible crime.

D. HUMAN RIGHTS

The United Nations Charter expressly describes the Organization's task as being to promote "universal respect for and observance of human rights and fundamental freedoms for all, without distinction as to race, sex, language, or religion" (Art. 55.c. Cf. Art. 1 and 13). No such aim was embodied in the Covenant of the League of Nations. In the intervening period the world experienced the kind of barbarism that results when a state loses the respect for human beings that is at the heart of the Christian and humanistic tradition and its government cynically preaches racial myths and hatred and asserts its right, as a "master race," to dominate, humiliate, or even annihilate other peoples or races. The Charter's provisions concerning respect for human rights are based on the belief that a mentality such as that of the Nazis is a threat to peaceful relations between peoples, and that it must therefore be one of the tasks of the organization to ensure that humanistic ideals based on respect for man, which can be accepted by all, irrespective of race, religion, or political ideology, shall be affirmed and honored everywhere.

This aim sets the Organization an extraordinarily difficult task. It does so, first of all, because this problem, in so far as it is fundamentally of a moral nature, really lies outside the scope of state or international institutions. There is hardly any subject that has produced such a spate of words or left such a depressing impression of insincerity and lack of substance behind these words. The second reason is the profound differences between the cultural traditions and economic and political ideologies of the different peoples and states, which make it difficult, without resorting to untruths, ambiguities, or camouflage, to draw up definitions acceptable to all.

The work in this field has been carried out almost exclusively within the United Nations. ECOSOC has set up a special Commission on Human Rights together with a Subcommission on the Prevention of Discrimination and Protection of Minorities. In addition, a Commission on the Status of Women has been set up, most of whose activities come within the province of human rights. Proposals prepared by the commissions are transmitted to ECOSOC, which, after discussing them, refers them to the General Assembly. There the question is first discussed in the Third Committee and then at a plenary sitting of the Assembly.

In the Charter, the idea of human rights is regarded as a standard or an ideal calling for moral respect and practical realization, but nowhere does it say what these human rights are. Hence the Organization's first and most important task was to define these rights as a kind of humanistic basic law and to secure a pledge from the member countries that they would undertake to observe this law (see section (1), below). This basis was then developed in two specific ways: first, certain particular rights embodied in the basic law were subjected to closer scrutiny and classification (see section (2)); second, special treatment was given to the rights of certain groups of persons (3). In addition to these efforts to codify human rights, the United Nations has also endeavored in other ways to foster moral respect for, and the practical observance of, these rights (4).

(1) *The definition of human rights.* The work on the basic formulation of human rights was carried out in two stages. First of all, a document was drawn up that proclaimed the moral ideals and aspirations inherent in the idea of human rights, without, however, setting the states any legal obligations. This stage was completed when, on December 10, 1948, the General Assembly adopted the Universal Declaration of Human Rights. The Organization was then faced with the much more difficult and delicate problem of working out the draft of one or more conventions on human rights whereby states acceding to, or ratifying, these conventions would accept certain specific legal obligations. The Organization has not yet managed to complete this task.

Apart from the two introductory and general articles, the Universal Declaration falls into two sections. Articles 3-21 deal with civil and political rights of the kind normally dealt with in the constitutions of the democratic states, the purpose of which is to restrict the competence of state organs, in particular the legislative organs, to interfere with certain rights, such as the right to freedom of expression, freedom of religion, and freedom of peaceful association, protection against arbitrary arrest, etc. These rights can be invoked by a citizen in his country's courts. Articles 22-27 are concerned with the social and economic rights commonly dealt with in the constitutions of the Communist states, whose special feature is that they are merely lofty declarations and political proclamations setting certain legislative aims, without, however, providing any grounds for claims or objections that may be invoked in a domestic court. These rights include, for example, the right to social security, to work under reasonable conditions, to a satisfactory standard of living adequate for the health and well-being of the worker and his family, etc.

The Universal Declaration does not carry any legal obligations but is only a proclamation of ideals constituting a common standard, which, as stated in the preamble, should constantly be kept in mind by every individual and every organ of society. Its value, which is intended to be of a moral nature, is greatly reduced by the fact that the states, while proclaiming these ideals, were anxious to emphasize that they undertook absolutely no legal obligation to apply them. The Declaration was adopted by 48 votes (in favor) to 8 abstentions (including those of the Eastern bloc); 2 countries were absent. This relative unanimity was achieved partly because the Declaration was not binding and partly because in some cases on which there was disagreement that could not be resolved, these differences were smoothed over by means of verbal formulas, which in reality meant nothing but which gave the impression that a principle was being proclaimed.

The Universal Declaration has been referred to as mankind's Magna Carta and described on numerous occasions, in glowing terms, as an enterprise of the greatest consequence. The United Nations itself has been busily publicizing the Declaration, recommending, among other things, that all states and interested organizations proclaim the tenth of December of every year a Human Rights Day on which the Declaration would be celebrated. For my own part, I doubt whether politico-legal institutions are suitable instruments for the dissemination of moral ideals. What we expect of these organizations is legal and political action and not moral pronouncements.

When, after the adoption of the Declaration, the next step was taken, namely that of turning these ideals into binding obligations, the enthusiasm began to wane and yield to caution. It took the Commission over five years to draw up two draft conventions, one on civil and political rights and one on economic, social, and cultural rights. Since 1955 both drafts were under discussion in the General Assembly. They were slowly fought out, paragraph by paragraph, and in 1963 the main articles of both conventions were finally adopted. However, the rules concerning the implementation of both conventions have not yet been adopted and will no doubt also give rise to considerable discussion before the covenants are signed and ratified.

The question of implementation is of special interest in regard to the Convention on Civil and Political Rights, for only this convention can give rise to definite claims that might be advanced before a court. The implementation rules will be of decisive importance as regards the actual practical value of the convention once it has been adopted. It is typical of the cautious attitude states adopt when there is a question of binding obligations, that an Australian proposal advocating the setting up of an International Court of Human Rights found little support. The Soviet Union has consistently been against implementation provisions of any kind. Thus all this draft convention does is to recognize the right of complaint in respect of the participating states alone, in such a way that the complaint can only lead to investigation, conciliation, and the submission of a report. To this end it is proposed to set up a special human rights committee to which a complaint can be submitted when the parties concerned have not succeeded in reaching a settlement by direct negotiation.

Even if these two draft conventions, with implementation rules, can be pushed through the General Assembly—which may happen, thanks to the dominating voting strength of the smaller and the less-developed states—the chances of ratification by a substantial number of larger states are not great. The Soviet Union has, as already mentioned, always been opposed to any implementation rules, in other words to any possibility of putting the conventions into effect. In the American Senate there has been growing reluctance in recent years to accept international control in human rights matters. Many other states are likely to follow this example.

If, as I am inclined to believe, the conventions, or at least the one on civil and political rights, come to nothing, this is bound to have consequences as regards the value attached to the Universal Declaration. It will no longer be possible to respect the Declaration, when it has been demonstrated that states are all too willing to preach moral sermons, particularly where the behavior of others is concerned, but refrain from entering into any effectively binding obligations to translate these ideals into reality.

(2) *Particular rights.* Both draft conventions on human rights contain an introductory provision proclaiming the right of all peoples and nations to self-determination, which can be more closely

defined as the right freely to determine their own political, economic, social, and cultural status. This provision has given rise to considerable controversy, partly because it cannot be said to grant any rights to the individual and partly because it represents an indeterminate political principle rather than a right that can be given legal shape (Chap. III.7). Furthermore, the right to self-determination is bound up with the delicate question of "sovereignty" over natural wealth and resources. In spite of this opposition, this provision was pushed through by the states that pounce on every chance to protest against the remnants of colonial rule. The question of the "permanent sovereignty of nations and peoples over natural wealth and resources" was investigated and discussed by a special commission set up in 1958. On the basis of this commission's report, the General Assembly adopted on December 14, 1962, a resolution, which is described in greater detail at the end of this chapter.

Article 14 of the Universal Declaration contains a provision on the right to asylum (which is largely devoid of any value). The Commission on Human Rights has worked out a draft declaration on the general principles that should be followed by states in questions concerned with the grant of asylum. The Council has referred the draft to the General Assembly, which was scheduled to deal with it at its 19th session in 1964. Unfortunately, this session was unable to accomplish its work, owing to disagreement on dues and payments.

Freedom of association (Art. 21 of the draft convention) has given rise to two special conventions for the protection of trade union rights adopted by the ILO, namely the Convention on the Freedom of Association and the Right to Organize (1948) and the Convention on the Right to Organize and on Collective Bargaining (1949).

Slavery, institutions and practices similar to slavery, and forced labor have given rise to special studies, partly in co-operation with ILO. For a long time, various treaties have been concluded in an effort to stop the slave trade and the transport of slaves. ECOSOC has taken up this question for further consideration. At a conference organized by the Council in Geneva in 1956, a Supplementary Convention on Slavery, the Slave Trade, and Institutions and Practices Similar to Slavery was adopted, which deals also with debt-bondage, serfdom, bride-price, and the exploitation of child labor.

On the basis of the many reports on inhuman conditions existing in forced labor camps in the various totalitarian states, the United

Nations in 1951 set up jointly with ILO a committee to investigate these conditions. This committee found that forced labor was practiced on a wide scale, partly as a means of dealing with political opposition and partly on economic grounds. The United Nations adopted several resolutions condemning this practice, and ILO in 1957 adopted a convention on the abolition of forced labour.

Likewise, since 1946, freedom of information and the like has formed the subject of numerous negotiations. At a conference in 1948 three draft conventions were drawn up concerning (1) the gathering and international transmission of news; (2) the institution of a right of correction; and (3) freedom of information. The first two were adopted by the General Assembly, but the third is still on the Assembly's agenda and continues to give rise to lively controversy.

Personal freedom from arbitrary arrest, detention, or deportation has formed the subject of special studies in a committee set up for this purpose by the Human Rights Commission. This committee has expressed its opinion in the form of a declaration of principle, which is still under discussion. Another question that has been referred to a special committee is that on the right of prisoners to remain in contact with their lawyers.

(3) *Group rights.* The Commission on the Status of Women has concerned itself with the promotion of the legal and practical equality of women with men in regard to political, educational, economic, family, and nationality rights. Of particular importance is the Convention on the Political Rights of Women, which was adopted by the General Assembly in 1952 and was subsequently acceded to and ratified by many countries. It can be said to have contributed to the fact that in practically all countries women now have the same political rights as men. The Commission has co-operated with ILO in drawing up two conventions concerning the position of women on the labor market that were later adopted at an ILO conference, namely one relating to equal pay for men and women doing equal work (1951) and the other concerning discrimination in employment (1958). For a number of years, the Commission dealt with the question of equal citizenship rights for women. As a result of this work, the General Assembly in 1957 adopted a Convention on the Nationality of Married Women, which subsequently secured the necessary

support to become effective. Its central substantive provision is that neither the celebration nor the dissolution of a marriage between one of a state's nationals and an alien, nor the change of the husband's nationality during marriage, shall automatically affect the nationality of the wife.

After the preparatory work carried out by the Human Rights Commission together with the Social Commission, the General Assembly unanimously adopted in 1959 a Declaration on the Rights of the Child. This, like the Universal Declaration, is a declaration of principle which is not legally binding. In this declaration the rights of children are formulated under ten points. These include, for instance, the right of children to grow up in an atmosphere of love and security and, as far as possible, under the care of their parents; the right to protection against all forms of corruption, cruelty, and exploitation; and so on. Here it may also be mentioned that the General Assembly adopted in 1962 a convention drawn up by the Commission on the Status of Women on Consent to Marriage, Minimum Age for Marriage, and Registration of Marriages, which is designed to prevent child marriages and eliminate other primitive customs practiced in some of the less-developed countries.

According to general humanitarian principles, national minorities should be given special protection, partly in order to prevent the state where this minority lives from persecuting or otherwise discriminating against such a minority and partly for the more positive purpose of granting such groups special rights regarding the use, (including for official purposes) of their own language, the right freely to practice their religion, the right to establish (with the assistance of the state) their own private schools, and special provisions for the use of the minority language in state schools. However, the granting of such rights presupposes that the minority in question loyally supports the state of which its members are nationals. If that is not the case, that is if this minority, instead of endeavoring loyally to cooperate with the state in which it lives, allows itself to be used by its national state of origin as an element of unrest and a destructive fifth column intended to prepare the way for aggression, then, of course, the protection of a minority is no longer a peaceful humanitarian measure but an instrument of national hatred and aggression.

History provides interesting illustrations of the conflict between these two aspects of the protection of minorities. After the First World War the humanitarian aspect was dominant. Through the peace treaties and a series of special treaties, as well as declarations made before the League of Nations, something like a European minority law was created for the protection of national minorities in a great number of European states, not including, however, the victorious powers. This protection was enforced by means of a right of petition, that is, the right both of the members of a minority and of their state of origin to draw the attention of the League of Nations to any violation of their rights. The experience gained in this field between the two world wars was not, however, encouraging. The protection of minorities was a constant source of unrest and interference in matters traditionally regarded as coming within the "domestic jurisdiction" of states, and the use made of the German minority in Eastern Europe as tools in a policy of aggression convinced many that the protection of minorities did not serve the cause of peace. They take the view that if this question cannot be settled radically by means of population movements, minorities should not be granted any special privileges but should be content with the protection afforded by the general prohibition of discrimination based on, among other things, national origin (see Universal Declaration of Human Rights of Dec. 10, 1948, Art. 2, and Art. 14 of the European Convention on Human Rights). Accordingly, after the last war, no effort was made to re-establish a European law on minorities, and only the peace treaty with Italy contains a single modest provision concerning the protection of the German-speaking minority in Italian Southern Tyrol. Thus this question has been transferred from the concrete sphere of political treaties to the more general and rarefied atmosphere of human rights.

In 1946, the Commission on Human Rights set up a special Subcommission on the Prevention of Discrimination and the Protection of Minorities. It was not, apparently, intended to draw up any general conventions on the protection of minorities. Subsequently, the subcommission, partly in co-operation with ILO and UNESCO, examined various special discrimination problems in different fields, such as, education, employment, freedom of worship, political rights, and the right freely to leave and to return to one's country. These studies, which also concern, but are not specially directed against, national discrimination, have so far resulted in two conventions, one on discrimination in education adopted in 1960 by UNESCO, and the other on discrimination in employment adopted in 1958 by ILO.

(4) *Other efforts.* The activities described in the first three sections are all concerned with general principles or more special rules intended to define the norms involved in the idea of human rights. The United Nations has also sought in other ways to foster and to uphold respect for human rights.

There is no provision in the Charter for any right of petition, i.e. there is no procedure whereby anyone who feels that his human rights have been violated can complain to the Organization with the result that some kind of machinery will be set in motion to examine his complaint. This does not, of course, prevent a constant influx of complaints from individuals, groups, and organizations all over the world. These complaints are entered, without any indication as to the identity of the complainant, on a confidential list, together with a short summary of the subject of the complaint. The list is submitted to the members of the Commission on Human Rights, meeting in camera, and each member state is informed of the complaints concerning it, again without revelation of the complainant's identity. It is then up to the governments concerned, if they so wish, to take action and report on it to the United Nations.

Alleged violations of human rights in a given country have often given rise to debates in the General Assembly, which, in a number of cases, have resulted in the adoption of resolutions condemning the country concerned. This procedure has aroused protests on the grounds that it clashes with the proviso concerning domestic jurisdiction in Article 2(7). Without taking up any formal position on the question of competence, the General Assembly, adopting the view that the question of the respect of human rights is treated in the Charter as a question of international concern, has not allowed these protests to prevent it either from discussing the question or from adopting resolutions directed against specific states. It is, in particular, conditions in the Union of South Africa that have given rise to repeated complaints concerning the treatment of persons of Indian origin and concerning South Africa's racial policy (apartheid). The Bulgarian, Hungarian, and Rumanian governments have been condemned for violations of religious freedom in connection with the persecution of priests in those countries, including the imprisonment of Cardinal Mindszenty (1949). The Soviet Union, too, has repeatedly been accused of flagrant violations of human rights, such as the existence of forced labor camps (1949-56), failure to release prisoners of war (1950-57), and refusal to give Soviet women married to foreign nationals permission to leave the country to join their husbands (1948-49). In several cases, a resolution has been adopted directly condemning the Soviet Union.

A valuable source of information concerning legal conditions throughout the world is the *Yearbook on Human Rights* published by the United Nations. This contains information on constitutional provisions, laws, regulations, judicial decisions, etc. relating to human rights in the various countries of the world, including also those that are not members of the United Nations. It also reports important international measures taken in this field.

In 1956 ECOSOC introduced a system whereby all member states are required to submit at three-year intervals a report on the progress made and the difficulties encountered by them in the field of human rights. Three series of reports have been submitted, covering the years 1954-56, 1957-59, and 1960-62. The governments that contributed to the last of these numbered 49—a number considerably lower than in the preceding two first series. The Commission on Human Rights has set up a special committee for the purpose of examining and commenting on the reports. In the light of these comments, the Council then makes observations and recommendations on the reports. This system may be regarded as still on trial.

Lastly, it should be mentioned that ECOSOC advises and assists states in various ways at their request, for instance in connection with legislation and administrative procedures in these matters.

E. HELP TO THE LESS-DEVELOPED COUNTRIES

Just as in a national society a distinction may be made between different social groups or classes according to their economic position, so on the international level it is possible to distinguish between rich and poor states. But, while the economic differences and the discrepancies to which these give rise in modes and standards of living in societies such as that of present-day Denmark are so small that the words "poor" or "rich" have practically ceased to apply, the difference between the most- and the least-favored countries are such as to justify the use of these two adjectives. Thus the United States of America, whose population accounts for 1 per cent of the world's total population, enjoys an income amounting to about 6 per cent of the world's total income, while the corresponding figure for the poor countries is only one quarter of one per cent. In other words, the average standard of living in the rich countries is about 25 times that of the poor countries. The seriousness of these figures can only be fully grasped when it is further considered that the poor countries do not constitute a small backward fraction of humanity or a kind of international slum district spoiling an otherwise pretty picture; they comprise the great majority (up to three-quarters) of the population of the world. This discrepancy in the distribution of goods goes far beyond the inequalities existing between different social groups in, say, Denmark, where the highest incomes (after tax has been deducted!) are at most four to five times as high as the lowest.

Unfortunately, if no deliberate and systematic efforts are made to deal with this state of affairs and if matters are allowed to take their own course, the gulf between rich and poor will grow ever wider. Once capital investment, technology, and science have reached the stage now achieved by the Western nations, further progress becomes almost automatic, since there is always a possibility of saving in order to increase investments and of research aimed at increasing knowledge. Another important factor is international trade, which encourages specialization, division of labor, and consequently a better use of the means of production. In the underdeveloped countries, conditions are very different. Capital investment and technological development are stagnant. Living standards are so low that there is very little left to save, and industry, if any, is not competitive. These countries are therefore obliged to practice a policy of national protectionism, which deprives them of the advantages of a division of labor and leads to unemployment. Their only source of wealth is the export of raw materials, and their economy is therefore one-sidedly and unfavorably tied to the level and stability of raw material prices.

Why should the rich countries be concerned by this misery? It is not easy to give a simple and definite reply to this question. As is so often the case with major constructive ideas, the underlying motives are a shifting blend of altruism, a sense of human obligation, and enlightened self-interest. In the long run, it is difficult for people to deny others the advantages of the ideals that they have fought to secure on their own behalf. The more the Western states consist of societies that have fought their way under the banners of freedom, equality, and fraternity, the more difficult it will be for them to turn a deaf ear to the growing wave of protest rising from the poor countries as they gradually become aware of their poverty and the possibility of improving their lot. The desire for freedom has been so strong that the colonial system has now practically ceased to exist and this has happened in a much shorter time than anyone could have believed 15 years ago. Now there is a demand for greater equality which cannot be dismissed. It is simply not possible to set up an organization representing the people of the whole world for the purpose of promoting peace and progress and founded on the belief in the equal value and rights of all men and nations, and, at the same time, to tolerate the continued existence of conditions that are so manifestly contrary to those ideals.

Now human beings are not angels, and I am quite prepared to admit that if humanitarian idealism were not backed up by or clearly clashed with selfish motives, the organization of help would be much slower. What happens in fact is that in the long run enlightened self-interest acts as a support for and blends with idealism. It is now more or less realized that there will be no peace in the world either externally or in man's conscience so long as such terrible inequality exists. True enough, the underdeveloped countries do not constitute a military threat, and would not, even if they were all to unite. But the wish for a "place in the sun" can, as we have seen, very easily lead to struggle and war. Even if such wars, for instance the conflict in the Congo, compared with what a war between the major powers would mean today, seem more like games with tin soldiers, they can still be full of political dynamite, for the simple reason that the whole world today forms one political system. Isolation is no longer possible. Any disturbance in any political sector is of some consequence to the central balance of power. For this reason, the Great Powers are afraid of even the most minor wars. Moreover, the underdeveloped countries can in other ways, particularly in view of their important raw material resources, create unrest and other sundry disturbances of considerable inconvenience. Other more tangible and direct interests may be involved. When help is given on a bilateral basis, i.e. directly from the donor to the receiving state, such help, even if no specific political strings are attached, may create a state of dependence, in that the receiver may realize that this help may cease if he steps on the donor's toes.

From the outset, the United Nations has been very conscious of its responsibility in this field, but it is only in recent years that the point has been reached where it can be said that assistance to the underdeveloped countries is the question that most arouses the interest of the Organization's members and their willingness to make sacrifices, and makes the greatest call on its and the specialized institutions' time and energy. On the proposal of President Kennedy, the General Assembly resolved on December 19, 1961, to proclaim the 1960's "United Nations Development Decade," with the aim of raising the standard of living of the underdeveloped countries by 5 per cent per annum. A comprehensive program was drawn up for this purpose, and it is very gratifying to note that it envisages long-term planning in the various countries concerned, in conjunction with regional co-operation stimulated by the United Nations regional economic commissions for Asia and the Far East, Africa, and Latin America. This calls for an increase in the members' voluntary contributions. The idea was that in 1963 these should make available a total of $150 million (for the Expanded Program and the Special Fund together, see below) and that this sum shall thereafter increase each year, according to the amount of voluntary pledges made by each government. Actually, for the 1965 calendar year the sum pledged is $145.5 million, of which up to $60 million will come from the United States. That country has undertaken each year to contribute not more than two-thirds of the sum provided by all the other countries taken together—in other words, not more than 40 per cent of the total amount. Denmark has undertaken to contribute over $5 million in 1965, which makes it the seventh largest contributor, ahead of such countries as the Soviet Union, France, and Italy. If all those concerned contributed in the same proportion the proposed target would be left far behind.

The underdeveloped countries need (a) technical knowledge and know-how and (b) capital. The assistance given them in this connection through United Nations programs and agencies accordingly falls into two main sections:

Technical help in the United Nations is administered by means of two different programs, known as the Regular and the Expanded Programs of technical assistance. The Regular Program is a continuation of the work that, from the very beginning, has been done by the United Nations (on its own), the expenditure for which is charged to the Organization's budget. The Expanded Program of Technical Assistance (EPTA) consists of measures taken jointly with nine of the specialized institutions, the cost of which is covered by voluntary contributions from the member states. The Expanded Program is by far the larger of the two, having a budget of around $40 million, as compared with the $2 million budget of the Regular Program. To stress the fact that many of the states *receiving* help also *grant* assistance in their turn, it was decided in 1960 that these two programs, while retaining their individual names, would be known jointly as the *United Nations Programs for Technical Co-operation.*

The nine specialized agencies that participate in the assistance program comprise all these institutions except the Inter-Governmental Maritime Consultative Organization and the four financial institutions (BANK, FUND, IDA, and IFC). In fact, however, the last-named co-operates regularly with the administration of the assistance programs.

The Expanded Program, which was adopted by the General Assembly in 1949, was inspired by President Truman's famous "Point Four Program," in which he called for a "bold new program for making the benefits of our scientific advances and industrial progress available for the improvement and growth of underdeveloped areas." From the very beginning, American initiative and funds have borne and continue to bear the brunt of this assistance.

As the Expanded Program is the joint effort of ten different organizations, it requires a special administrative machinery. The effective authority lies with the Technical Assistance Board (TAB), which is made up of a permanent chairman and senior administrative officials of the participating organizations. The Board reports to the Technical Assistance Committee (TAC), which is made up of the 18 members of ECOSOC plus another 6 members appointed by ECOSOC. This Committee has a supervisory function and is required to report to ECOSOC, which in its turn reports to the General Assembly.

Technical assistance is needed because of the frequent desperate lack of trained personnel and experts in all fields. In addition to technical experts, properly speaking, there is a need for administrators, doctors, jurists, teachers, trade experts, agricultural experts, veterinary surgeons, fishery experts, etc., not to mention the scientists on whom all the other experts are dependent. The central idea of the program is not that the experts sent out shall solve the problems that the local population is unable to solve on its own, but that they shall teach and train the population in such a way as to enable it gradually to overcome its difficulties by its own efforts.

The General Assembly has laid down a series of leading principles for carrying out this work. The particularly important principles are that this help can only be given to or through a government, that it must be free of any political strings and may not in any way be used as a means of interfering in the receiving state's domestic affairs. It must be given irrespective of the political structure of the country concerned or the race or religion of its people. Such help can be given not only to independent states but also to territories with a colonial or other dependent status.

By far the greater part of the work (about three-quarters) consists of sending out consultant experts, either singly or in small groups. Altogether, by the end of 1960, over 10,000 such experts had been sent out for varying periods. It goes without saying that it is very difficult to find the right people for this type of work, for they are required not only to possess the necessary professional qualifications but also the human qualities necessary to make contact with and earn the confidence of the populations concerned. In order to facilitate the experts' working conditions, permanent TAB representatives are available on the spot in a number of countries, who, over the years, have gained an understanding of and a sympathy with local conditions and authorities—an understanding of great value to the newly arrived expert.

Where a more general and higher training is required, the method employed consists in the grant of fellowships enabling suitable persons to study in the highly developed countries, either at ordinary educational establishments or by attending courses or seminars especially established for that purpose.

To a lesser extent, permanent demonstration establishments, for example a dairy or a clinic, are set up to show the local population what results can be obtained through the use of rational methods.

The assistance thus given covers every conceivable social sector.

The term "technical" should not be understood here in its narrower sense. First of all, a start has been made on the development of agricultural production and on the improvement of health conditions, followed by industrialization, the utilization of resources, education, and training embracing all the subjects that have been previously described under the headings "economic," "social," "humanitarian," and "cultural" as constituting the United Nations' field of activity for the achievement of progress and well-being.

One special task, for which there is otherwise no counterpart in the United Nations' work for progress, is the technical assistance given to public administrations. Many of the newly created states have not undergone the necessary preliminary training in self-government and are not therefore in a position to solve by themselves the problems involved in the setting up and operation of state machinery. For many years the United Nations has given such assistance in the usual forms, especially by sending out consultant experts and awarding fellowships enabling those concerned to attend seminars and receive other forms of education and training. As the process of de-colonization gradually proceeded in areas where the population was not yet ripe for self-government, it became clear that the usual forms of assistance were not adequate. Frequently, the new states were so destitute that they were quite unable to recruit the necessary public administration personnel. In order to remedy this state of affairs, the General Assembly decided in 1958 to institute a new program, known as Provision of Operational, Executive, and Administrative Personnel (OPEX), aimed at recruiting experts, who are then sent to work in the public administration of the states concerned. They are paid ordinary salaries, which are then supplemented by the United Nations. The idea is that the experts will remain in the public service of these countries until they have been able to train a member of the local population to take their place. This type of assistance has aroused great interest. The means at present available, however, are not nearly sufficient to meet all the requests.

Closely associated with the Expanded Program of Technical Assistance is the United Nations Special Fund, set up in 1958. This is not a financing institute, properly speaking, intended to make capital investments in the underdeveloped countries; rather, it forms a link between technical and financial aid in that it provides technical assistance for research, studies, and education aimed at determining the sectors where capital investment is possible and desirable. The fund is therefore primarily interested in major projects providing for a survey of a country's natural resources and a study of the possibilities of making effective use of them. As an example I would mention the following survey carried out in Ghana. The river Volta, which crosses that country, periodically floods the surrounding land, which cannot therefore be used. The Fund has, through FAO, set in motion an extensive survey of this area in order to find out whether it would be possible, by means of dams, irrigation, and the like, to transform this waste land into fertile agricultural land. Only when this problem has been solved can the question of capital investment arise at all. In this way the Special Fund bridges the gap between purely consultative assistance and investment. It has become customary to refer to the Fund's undertakings as "preinvestment projects."

The Fund is, like EPTA, financed by means of voluntary contributions.

Financial help is designed to promote capital investment in the less-developed countries. Even if the technical assistance for the development of the population's capabilities, knowledge, and practical know-how may be expected in the long run to give better results than capital investment and is in any case a prerequisite without which investment cannot succeed or bear fruit, the fact remains that investment, for instance in the form of the building of an electric power station or of roads, provides more immediately tangible advantages for the local population. That is why the underdeveloped countries are constantly pressing for the conclusion of arrangements aimed at promoting investment, but apparently not always with the realization that certain conditions must be fulfilled if such investment is to foster their development and not merely to waste.

The capital invested may be either public or private. The former comes from national or, as is particularly appropriate in this connection, international institutions or funds. The latter comes from the private capital market. In both cases, the capital can be supplied in the form of a loan (or a gift or a part loan–part gift) or of a direct investment in a specific undertaking in which the investor thus participates to some extent.

The international supply of capital takes place through three financial institutions, all of them specialized agencies of the United Nations.

The first of these is the International Bank for Reconstruction and Development (BANK), set up in 1944. As its name indicates, BANK was created for a dual purpose, namely in order to speed up postwar reconstruction and to promote the economic development of the member countries. In the early postwar years, the primary aim was reconstruction in Europe, but since 1948 loans have increasingly gone to the underdeveloped countries. Loans are granted only to states or, subject to state guarantee, to private undertakings and then only for productive purposes such as will promote the economic development of the receiving country. About one-third of the total loans granted have been used for building electric power plants, another third for developing the transport network (railways, roads, and air routes), and the remainder for developing agriculture and industry.

The interest charged is 1 per cent more than the current rate BANK has to pay on the loan market. BANK is non-profit-making, and any favorable balances are paid into the reserve. By June 30, 1964, the Bank had granted to about 60 countries and territories loans totaling about $8 billion.

BANK has a registered capital of $10 billion, divided up into 100,000 shares of $100,000. About one-third of the capital is subscribed by the United States. BANK's working capital is increased through the sale of its own bonds on the world capital market.

BANK's main organ is a Board on which all the members are represented. Each member has 250 votes, plus 1 vote for each share it has subscribed.

As may be seen from the above, the conditions under which BANK grants loans are very strict. First, the interest charged and the period of repayment are such that, even if they are advantageous considering the recipient's credit position, these loans can be a burden to its balance of payments. Secondly, the loans are granted only to states or under state guarantee. In order to satisfy further demands for credit, two more financial institutions have been set up, both of which are recognized as specialized agencies of the United Nations. They are autonomous organizations but are branches of BANK in the sense that they are administered by it.

The International Development Association (IDA) was set up in 1960 with a registered capital fixed at one billion dollars. Its aim, like that of BANK, is to promote economic development in the member countries, but it can do so on easier terms with regard both to the projects that can be financed and the actual loan terms. Thus loans can also be granted in respect of social projects (water and sanitary installations, housing, etc.) that have only an indirect effect on economic growth. According to circumstances, longer repayment periods or more favorable rates of interest may be granted. Loans are chiefly granted to states but can also be granted to private undertakings without a state guarantee. By June 30, 1964, the loans made by IDA totalled about $800 million.

The International Finance Corporation (IFC) was established in 1956. Its registered capital is much more modest and amounts to barely $100 million, that is, a tenth of IDA's capital which, in turn, is only a tenth of BANK's capital. The reason for this is that IFC is solely concerned with financing private undertakings by means of direct investments. Up to now, it has confined itself to large firms, mainly of an industrial character. The capital invested has varied between $100,000 and $2,000,000 and has never amounted to more than half of the firm's total capital. Altogether, by June 30, 1964, IFC investments totaled $103 million divided up among 75 undertakings.

Apart from its registered capital, the IFC also works with funds supplied by private investors.

The less-developed countries are far from satisfied with the financial possibilities offered by BANK and the two financing institutes. They have brought special pressure to bear in order to secure the setting up of a capital development fund within the framework of the United Nations itself, because, for one thing, thanks to their voting strength in the United Nations organs, they would be able to exercise over such a fund an influence they cannot exercise over BANK, IDA, and IFC, since the voting strength in these organizations is proportional to capital contributions. This question has been under discussion since 1953, and, understandably enough, the idea has met with resistance on the part of the states that would be expected to contribute the capital, that is, first and foremost, the United States. These negotiations led in 1958 to an American proposal for the setting up of a United Nations Special Fund. As explained above under "Technical help," this fund is not a financing institute, properly speaking, but an extension of the Expanded Program of Technical Assistance. The demands for an investment fund have therefore continued. Under pressure from the underdeveloped countries, the General Assembly in 1960 adopted a resolution whereby it was decided "in principle" to establish a United Nations Capital Development Fund and to set up a committee to prepare it. The qualifications that the resolution would be valid only "in principle" was made on the initiative of the Danish delegation and others, having regard to the fact that the capital-exporting countries, the United States in particular, were opposed to the establishment of the Fund. The preparatory committee has since —without the co-operation of the United States and the other capital-exporting countries—adopted a draft statute for the Fund, so worded that the decisive influence lies with a general conference of all the participating countries, in other words with the underdeveloped countries themselves. This draft has been referred by ECOSOC to the General Assembly, which has not yet definitively dealt with it.

It is possible that the large majority of underdeveloped countries will succeed in forcing the matter through the General Assembly. Then the Fund can be set up, and it will have everything—except money. If so, the resolution will have provided one more example of the fact that the less-developed countries have not yet understood the limited scope of their formal voting strength in the organs of the United Nations.

In addition to the internationally organized supply of capital, the countries poor in capital are also interested in attracting private capital looking for investment possibilities. In this connection, however, conditions have not been satisfactory, as the inflow of private capital in the 1950's and early 1960's has been smaller (in terms of real value) than in the 1920's. The reason for this may presumably be sought partly in the pressure of nationalism and anticolonialism, which have accompanied colonial liberation. Nearly all the underdeveloped countries dislike the idea of foreign capital control, particularly of their natural resources, an attitude reflected in the more or less unfavorable treatment given to foreign capital interests, which may go as far as nationalization against more or less nominal compensation. Such a reaction may be understandable from the emotional point of view, but it cannot be denied that it does not stimulate investment.

The United Nations has repeatedly concerned itself with this problem, partly from the point of view of what has been referred to as "the nation's permanent sovereignty over its natural wealth and resources" and partly in conjunction with the question of the need of the underdeveloped countries for private capital.

In 1952, Uruguay submitted a resolution recommending that the states recognize "the right of each country to nationalize and freely exploit its natural wealth as an essential factor of economic independence." This proposal, which must be viewed against the background of the Anglo-Iranian conflict over Iran's nationalization of its oil resources, gave rise to a lengthy debate. The United States fully recognized the right to nationalize but wanted it to be added that when a state made use of this right it should respect the principles of international law and existing international agreements. An American amendment to this effect was, however, rejected, and the General Assembly adopted a resolution that was in the nature of a compromise in that it recommended states, when exercising their sovereignty over their natural resources "to have due regard, consistently with their sovereignty, to the need for maintaining the flow of capital in conditions of security, mutual confidence, and economic co-operation among nations." As I see it, this resolution, while not taking up any definite position on the question of compensation, reminds those countries that need capital that it is in their own interest to be reasonable. In 1958 this question was taken up once more, and the General Assembly decided to set up a commission to consider the problem of permanent sovereignty over natural wealth, due regard being shown to the rights and duties of states under international law and to the importance of encouraging international co-operation in the economic development of the underdeveloped countries. The commission's deliberations resulted in the General Assembly's adopting on December 14, 1962, by an overwhelming majority (87-2-12), a resolution in which rational considerations took precedence over emotions. There it is clearly said that invested capital must be treated in accordance with international law and, more particularly, that in the case of nationalization or expropriation the owner shall be paid appropriate compensation in accordance both with the law of the nationalizing or expropriating country and with international law.

Both the General Assembly and ECOSOC have concerned themselves with the problem of stimulating private investment. In 1954 the General Assembly adopted a resolution that recommended both the capital importing and exporting countries to observe various rules in this connection. At the same time, it instructed the Secretary-General to report periodically on developments on the international capital market and on the measures adopted by the states in this connection. Since then, the Secretary-General has submitted such a report every year. These reports show that a considerable number of states in need of capital have, by means of tax concessions, the avoidance of dual-taxation, recognition of the right to re-export capital home, and similar facilities, sought to improve investment conditions and that there has also been a certain upward trend in the volume of investments.

References

Asher, Robert E., "Economic Co-operation under UN Auspices," *International Organization* (1958), pp. 288-302.

Asher, Robert E. et al., *The United Nations and the Promotion of the General Welfare* (1957).

Cheever, Daniel S. and H. Field Haviland, Jr., *Organizing for Peace* (1954), pp. 159-280 and 507-670.

Myrdal, Gunnar, *Beyond the Welfare State* (1960).

Peaslee, Amos J., *International Governmental Organizations: Constitutional Documents*, Vols. I-II (2nd ed., 1961).

XI ❧

THE TERMINATION OF
THE COLONIAL SYSTEM

I n the preceding chapter, I described the help given by the United Nations to the less-developed countries in order to improve the living conditions of their population from the economic, social, and cultural points of view. This assistance, which is organized on the basis of the rules laid down in the Charter's Chapters IX and X on economic and social co-operation, has two characteristic features. First of all, it is voluntary. The Charter does not in any way oblige the members to participate in this assistance and does not give the Organization's organs any authority to take any binding measures to this effect. Agitation for such assistance must therefore, both within and outside the United Nations, take the form of an appeal to good will and understanding, idealism and sacrifice, and farsighted self-interest. On this basis, help to the underdeveloped countries has indeed contributed to world-wide solidarity and good will among peoples. Second, it is important that this voluntary help shall have no political strings attached to it. In order to qualify for such help, the decisive factor is a territory's status as underdeveloped from the economic and social standpoints regardless of the population's political status. Assistance is given both to independent states and to areas with a colonial or other dependent political status. The help given is free from any political ties or conditions.

Chapters XI, XII, and XIII contain rules concerning a special welfare task of the United Nations, namely the promotion of the welfare of the dependent colonial peoples. The work of the United Nations in this field can be regarded as a special function to further the object of the Organization in the social and economic fields: progress toward well-being. In regard to the two features just mentioned, however, this welfare activity differs radically from the economic and social co-operation described in the preceding chapter, including especially the help given to the underdeveloped countries.

In the first place, the rules for the promotion of the welfare of the colonial peoples are not based on the voluntary principle. Here, the Charter directly places upon the ruling colonial powers certain very vaguely formulated obligations to foster development toward greater well-being in the colonies and also gives the Organization certain powers to supervise the fulfillment of these obligations. There is no question, however, of any authority to order to apply sanctions against a colonial power that has not observed these rules. Here, too, the United Nations' influence is restricted to public debate and criticism.

Second, the promotion of welfare in this context also has political aims. The idea is not only to achieve *good* colonial government, that is, an administration that takes a paternal and human interest in the needs of the native population, but also eventually to *end* colonial government. The aim, in fact, is self-government. Good colonial government is not accepted as a substitute for self-government. The decisive factor, as far the territories covered by Chapters XI-XIII are concerned, is therefore solely the political status of the territory: the territories covered are those "whose peoples have not yet attained a full measure of self-government" (Art. 73).

These differences show why the discussions held both within and outside the United Nations on colonial government and its termination have been so different from the debates on assistance to underdeveloped countries. The vagueness of the Charter's provisions concerning the obligations of the colonial powers and the control powers of the Organization, together with the strong emotional tensions that are bound up with the granting of freedom to the colonial peoples, have created ideal conditions for unrational and uncompromising discussion full of legal quibbling and only calculated to aggravate the present antagonism. As a result of the cold war, the Eastern bloc has also been there to fan the flames and support any anticolonial propaganda campaigns in order to weaken the prestige of the West and to create a split between the European colonial powers and the United States.

Led by the steadily growing group of Afro-Asian states, most of which have only recently gained their independence, and supported by the Eastern bloc and often also by the Latin American states, the General Assembly has succeeded in imposing an interpretation of the Charter's provisions on supervision going far beyond what was intended at San Francisco. Borne by, and at the same time urging on, the nationalistic, anticolonialist wave, it has activated the process of liberation and, without considering whether the economic and social conditions were suitable, demanded the immediate liquidation of the last remnants of the system—a completely irresponsible demand in view of the chaotic conditions, internal conflicts, corruption, and dictatorship that regularly follow in the wake of premature decolonization (for example, in the Congo).

The basic idea in the Charter's rules on the non-self-governing peoples, namely that the administering countries must be responsible to the Organization and world public opinion for their colonial government, may, at first sight, seem attractive and consistent with the principles of parliamentary democracy. But this presupposes positive and responsible criticism. This is to a certain extent guaranteed in parliamentary democracy in that the opposition must be prepared to make good their word when they take over the reins of government. There is no similar guarantee in the United Nations system. Naturally, there has been and still is much in the remaining colonial rule that can give rise to justified criticism. But from a perusal of the reports of the proceedings in the Trusteeship Council and, in particular, in the General Assembly and its Fourth Committee, one cannot avoid the impression that to a great extent the criticism has been negative and irresponsible and used as a political weapon. While the League of Nations Permanent Mandate Commission was made up of persons elected in their personal capacity as experts, all the United Nations organs that deal with colonial questions consist of representatives from states that have a political interest in the question—a fact that has not been conducive to positive criticism. The loudest criticism often comes from the newly independent states eager to set themselves up as supporters of progress—in other states. At all events, this criticism is irresponsible in so far as there can never be any question of the critics of the United Nations as an Organization taking over the administration and living up to their own demands. It is no wonder that such debates and criticism have been humiliating, in particular for the most honest and reasonable colonial powers, and have aggravated rather than resolved the conflicts. Given this background, it is understandable that the United Nations General Assembly should have been referred to in the British House of Lords, on a certain occasion, as an Assembly of 58 back-seat drivers.

Although the work of the United Nations on behalf of the non-self-governing countries is based on principles other than those underlying help to the underdeveloped countries, in actual practice the two functions are closely bound up together. The non-self-governing territories may all be said to belong to the underdeveloped areas, and there can scarcely be any doubt that a certain economic and social development is a necessary precondition for a satisfactory transition to self-government. With this in mind, the anticolonial group argue strongly in favor of increased technical and financial assistance to the remaining colonial areas. On the other hand, it is maintained—but this is more open to doubt—that political independence is the best stimulus to economic progress, which furnishes another powerful argument in favor of the termination of every remaining colonial administration. Whatever may be thought of this mutual effect between economics and politics, it is a fact that the remaining colonial territories need assistance and development in both the economic and political sense and that these two aspects should therefore be coordinated and synchronized.

The Charter's rules on the "territories whose peoples have not yet attained a full measure of self-government" are based on a division of colonial territories into two groups, which are given different treatment, namely those that come under the trusteeship system and those that do not. This lacks any rational foundations and is solely due to accidental historical circumstances. After the First World War, the victorious allied powers created the mandate system, which was designed to meet at one and the same time, on the one hand, the idealistic demands of President Wilson and British liberal public opinion that victory should not be exploited for imperialistic ends and territorial annexations, and, on the other hand, the demands of the British conservatives and the French, who wanted to control the former German colonies and Arab areas in the Middle East that had formerly been under Turkish rule. The mandate system was intended to fulfill the promises made during the war to the Arabs concerning national independence in the Middle East, while at the same time allowing the victors to continue to exercise control over these areas. The mandate system could be used to reconcile these contradictions because the powers of control over these areas, which were entrusted to some of the victorious powers, were interpreted not as giving them the right to rule in their own interests but as a trusteeship, a sacred task entrusted to them in the interest of the peoples concerned and on behalf of the League of Nations. Article 22 of the League of Nations Covenant states the idea in this way:

> To those colonies and territories which as a consequence of the late war have ceased to be under the sovereignty of the States which formerly governed them and which are inhabited by peoples not yet able to stand by themselves under the strenuous conditions of the modern world, there should be applied the principle that the well-being and development of such peoples form a sacred trust of civilization and that securities for the performance of this trust should be embodied in this Covenant.
>
> The best method of giving practical effect to this principle is that the tutelage of such peoples should be entrusted to advanced nations who by reason of their resources, their experience or their geographical position can best undertake this responsibility, and who are willing to accept it, and that this tutelage should be exercised by them as Mandatories on behalf of the League.

The hollowness of this conception is obvious. If it is really intended to establish and acknowledge the principle that the well-being and development of those peoples that are not yet politically mature form a sacred trust of civilization, what justification can there be for applying this principle only in the former colonies of the defeated powers and not in those of the victorious powers? Naturally, no such justification could be given. The decisive factor was pure power interests. In other words, the idealistic conception of the mandate system was but a pious fraud. There were to be no annexations, but the mandate was to give the leading powers the necessary excuse for exercising control.

Thus the result was a division of the colonial territories on the basis of power politics: the areas that had previously been under German or Turkish rule were now as mandated territories subject to a certain measure of international control, but all other areas remained a purely internal matter for the colonial power concerned.

This arbitrary division has, with certain modifications and adaptations, been taken over in the United Nations Charter. What has happened in the meantime was that the former Turkish possessions in the Middle East, which had constituted Class A mandates (Lebanon, Syria, Palestine, Transjordan, and Iraq), either had already gained or were about to gain their full national independence. All that remained were 11 Class B and C mandated territories consisting of the former German colonies, some in Africa and some in the Pacific. Even though according to the Charter any colony can come under the trusteeship system if the ruling power accepts this arrangement voluntarily by concluding a trusteeship agreement with the United Nations, there is no doubt that the trusteeship system was conceived as a continuation of the old League of Nations mandate system. This is, in fact, how it has worked out in practice. All 11 mandated territories became trust territories—except South-West Africa, because the Union of South Africa has consistently refused to recognize that it has any obligations toward the United Nations in respect of this territory. Apart from the former mandated territories, no colonial territory has been brought under trusteeship, with the exception of the former Italian colony, Somaliland, which in 1960 gained its independence as Somalia. The trusteeship has been taken over by the former mandatory powers, except in the case of the Pacific islands that used to be Japanese mandated territories and have now become trust territories of the United States.

Although this arbitrary division has been retained in the Charter its relevance has been weakened in that the solemn declaration concerning the duties of the governing states toward the peoples under their control—corresponding to the above-mentioned proclamation in Article 22 of the Covenant of the League—has now been extended to cover *all* non-self-governing territories, that is, also those that do not come under the trusteeship system. In addition, the anticolonial states have in practice pressed for and, to a great extent, succeeded in imposing an interpretation of the Charter that attenuates the difference. Obligations and control measures, which in the Charter refer only to the trust territories, have been made applicable also to the ordinary colonial areas.

Hence a description of the United Nations' activities for the promotion of the welfare of the non-self-governing peoples and their development toward independence must fall into two main sections, namely one concerned with the institutionalized trusteeship system and the other relating to the remaining non-self-governing territories. As the trusteeship system, however, is now practically speaking only of historical interest, all the trust territories, except a few islands in the Pacific with a total population of under one and a half million, having achieved full independence, a brief survey of the trusteeship machinery will be sufficient.

1. The trusteeship system

As will be seen from the accompanying table, the League of Nations mandates were classified into three groups referred to as A, B, and C. Class A mandates consisted of the former Turkish possessions in the Arab Middle East. Article 22 of the League of Nations Covenant stated that the existence of these communities as independent nations could be provisionally recognized, subject to the rendering of advice and assistance until they were able to stand alone. This was to cover the promises made to the Arab peoples during the war. Iraq became independent in 1932, but the other territories not until the Second World War or after.

The Class B and C mandates consisted of the colonial territories that had previously been German possessions. The League of Nations had made no provision for their future independence. The intention had been solely to ensure *good* colonial government, i.e. one that sought to promote the welfare of the native peoples and in particular to protect them from abuses and exploitation. To this end, the Covenant provided that the mandatory power should report every

MANDATED AND TRUST TERRITORIES

Area	Administering State	Date of independence
Class A Mandate		
Lebanon	France	1944
Syria	France	1945
Palestine	United Kingdom	1948
Transjordan	United Kingdom	1946
Iraq	United Kingdom	1932
Class B Mandate, subsequently trust territories		
Togoland, British[1]	United Kingdom	1957
Cameroons, British[2]	United Kingdom	1961
Tanganyika	United Kingdom	1961
Togoland, French[3]	France	1960
Cameroons, French[4]	France	1960
Ruanda-Urundi[5]	Belgium	1962
Class C Mandate, subsequently trust territories		
South-West Africa[6]	Union of South Africa	
Pacific Islands	Japan, U.S.A.	
New Guinea	Australia	
Nauru	Australia	
West Samoa	New Zealand	1962
Former Italian Colony, later trust territory		
Somaliland[7]	Italy	1960

[1] As a result of a plebiscite, British Togoland united with the Gold Coast to become the independent state of Ghana.

[2] Following local voting, the northern part of this territory joined, as an independent province, the Federation of Nigeria, whereas the southern part joined the Cameroon Republic.

[3] Independent under the name of Togo Republic.

[4] Independent under the name of Cameroon Republic.

[5] Independent as two states: the Republic of Rwanda and the Kingdom of Burundi.

[6] South-West Africa, owing to the opposition of the Union of South Africa, has not come under the trusteeship system but is governed solely by the Union, which refuses to admit to any obligations toward the United Nations.

[7] Independent under the name of Somalia.

year on the situation in the areas entrusted to their care and that a permanent commission should be set up to examine these reports and advise the League about them. This commission, known as the Permanent Mandate Commission, was made up of nine persons elected by the League in their capacity as experts, without any official connection with the governments concerned, so that a majority of them belonged to the nonadministering states. Eventually, this commission came to play a role of some importance, having succeeded in winning respect and high regard for its objectivity and good judgment. Here it should be remembered that the League of Nations mandate system did not lay down any political obligations but had purely humanitarian aims and was administered by an organization the overwhelming majority of whose members represented the same culture and ideology as the colonial powers.

The United Nations trusteeship system is basically a continuation and extension of the mandate system. The extension concerns both the duties of the administering states and the institutional control over the fulfillment of these obligations.

As regards the former, the essential factor is that the Charter imposes on the administering state the obligation not only to promote the economic and social welfare of the indigenous peoples but also to foster their "progressive development towards self-government or independence" (Art. 76). Even if the term "self-government" as employed in the Charter is something less than "independence" and the latter is not, therefore, regarded as an unconditional goal for the administering power, a completely new ideological principle has been stated, namely that the purpose of the trusteeship system is not only good and humane colonial government but also the termination of such government.

In the latter respect, that is with regard to supervision, the supervisory authorities, namely the General Assembly and, under its authority, the special Trusteeship Council (Chap. V.4), were provided with the means of voicing more effective criticism, as they were empowered not only to examine reports but also to receive petitions (requests, complaints) from the peoples concerned and to organize periodic visits to trust territories.

Even though, in principle, the Charter proclaimed that the aim of the trusteeship system was self-liquidation, hardly anyone in 1945 could have imagined that, practically speaking, this aim would be substantially realized within 20 years (see Chap. V.4). The 11 territories that came under this system had a total population of around 20 million. All that is left now are three territories with a total population of under one and a half million. These are: islands in the Pacific Ocean with a population of about 70,000, under American trusteeship; the little island Nauru (about 4,000 inhabitants, of which only about 2,500 are Nauruans); and New Guinea (about 1,360,000 inhabitants)—both the latter being under Australian administration. In these areas the transition to political independence involves special difficulties. In New Guinea, the greater part of the population still lives at the very lowest level of civilization. As for the Pacific Islands, these are scattered over a sea area as large as the continent of Australia. In these areas there is no real colonial problem justifying the continued existence of a special Trusteeship Council, which, moreover, can no longer have the membership stipulated in the Charter's rules (Chap. V.4). The only interests that might conceivably give rise to a debate are the United States' strategic interests in the Pacific Islands. But as this mandated area has been designated a strategic area, control is in the hands of the Security Council (see Art. 82 and 83).

South-West Africa is the only former mandated territory that has not been brought under trusteeship. With regard to this area an uncompromising struggle has been going on since 1946 between the United Nations and the mandatory power, the Union of South Africa. Initially, the latter wanted to absorb this territory. But when the General Assembly turned down this idea and proposed instead the conclusion of a trusteeship agreement, the Union gave up the idea and declared itself prepared to continue to administer the territory in accordance with its mandate. In 1947, it accordingly submitted a report for 1946, but as, in its view, the United Nations made unjustified use of this report it ceased henceforth to submit any reports and completely refused to recognize the United Nations' right to inspect and control its administration in South-West Africa.

Thereafter, the legal position became obscure. Was the Union, despite the disappearance of the League of Nations, still bound to carry out its obligations under the mandate agreement? If so, who could carry out the control which according to that agreement was the responsibility of the League of Nations? Was South Africa automatically covered by the trusteeship system, or was it in any case legally bound to conclude an agreement to this end? In order to clear up this and other similar questions, the General Assembly decided in 1949 to ask the International Court of Justice for an advisory opinion on the international legal position in regard to this territory. In 1950, the Court expressed its advisory opinion: (1) this territory did not come under the United Nations' trusteeship system and the Union of

South Africa was not obliged to enter into an agreement to this end, and (2) South Africa's obligations under the mandate agreement were to continue, but control, which under the mandate agreement was to be exercised by the League of Nations, must now be transferred to the United Nations. In particular, the Union must submit annual reports to the Organization and transmit to it petitions from the people of the territory.

Although the General Assembly approved the International Court's definition of the legal position, the Union of South Africa has refused to accept it. In 1953, the General Assembly set up a special committee for South-West Africa (superseded by another in 1961) to examine the situation in that territory and negotiate with the Union with a view to persuading it to recognize the United Nations' control rights. In the absence of any reports by the Union, an effort has been made to obtain information in other ways, in particular through petitions and reports from persons who have left the territory. It was even planned that the Committee would on its own initiative send a visiting mission to South-West Africa. Of course nothing came of this, for the South African government refused to grant the members of the Committee a visa and stated that it would prevent any illegal attempt to cross the border. As the mandate agreement did not provide for any right of inspection and as the territory is not subject to the rules of the trusteeship system, South Africa was perfectly within its rights in opposing this plan, which in any case had only been intended as a kind of demonstration. However, the chairman and vice-chairman of the committee received and accepted an invitation from the government of the Union of South Africa to pay a visit to the territory. This visit took place in May 1960 and lasted about 10 days. The report on the visit said that the administration of South-West Africa was pervaded by the policy of apartheid, which was in utter contradiction with the mandate, the United Nations Charter, and the Universal Declaration of Human Rights; that nothing was being done there to develop the territory for self-government or independence; and that it was the overwhelming desire of the African population that the United Nations assume direct administration of the territory.

Over the years there have been many negotiations aimed at achieving United Nations supervision and control over that territory. For its part, South Africa still refuses to recognize that the United

Nations has any right of inspection but has declared itself prepared to conclude an agreement with France, the United Kingdom, and the United States as the three remaining members of the main allied and associated powers of the First World War—a proposal that, of course, has no chance of being accepted.

As the negotiations did not seem to be leading anywhere it was wondered whether it might be possible to secure a final settlement of the dispute by legal means. The advisory opinion given by the International Court of Justice in 1950 (later supplemented with two more opinions on technical points) is, as such, only intended for the guidance of the General Assembly, and the South African government is not bound by it. There is one difficulty, however, that arises with the legal method: namely, that under the Statute of the International Court the United Nations cannot itself be one of the parties to a dispute before the Court. Only states can be parties to such disputes. It was thought, however, that the mandate agreement gave every former member of the League of Nations the possibility of coming before the International Court as a plaintiff in connection with disputes concerning the interpretation and application of the mandate and that, as a corollary, the Union of South Africa was bound to submit to such proceedings. The General Assembly drew the members' attention to this possibility and encouraged them to make use of it.

The result was that in 1960 two African states, Ethiopia and Liberia, both former members of the League of Nations, instituted proceedings against the Union of South Africa and requested that a judgment be given to the effect that on a great number of points, in particular through the application of the policy of apartheid in the territory, South Africa had failed to carry out its obligations under the mandate and the Covenant of the League of Nations. The Union denied that these two countries had any competence to institute such proceedings and asked that the case be dismissed. It was therefore necessary first of all to decide this preliminary question of competence. The decision, rendered in 1962 by 8 votes to 7, affirmed the Court's competence to hear the dispute on the merits. The vote clearly shows that opinion was divided. I myself consider that this judgment was wrong. The matter is now taking its own course, and it is probable that South Africa will be found guilty of having violated its mandate obligations. But there is less likelihood that such a judgment will be accepted by that country or will induce it to alter its policy.

Even though I have as little sympathy as anyone else in Denmark for the Union of South Africa, and in particular for its policy toward South-West Africa, I cannot close my eyes to the fact that the way the United Nations has dealt with this case has not been calculated to bring about any real improvement in the conditions under which the population of that territory lives. My impression is that the primary aim of the General Assembly's policy has not been to effect such improvements but to carry out a political demonstration against South Africa. This may have been a way of relieving certain feelings, but only at the cost of the actual interests that were meant to be safeguarded.

2. Supervision over colonial government

The trust territories with their 20 million inhabitants constituted only a small fraction of the territories subject to colonial government. It is estimated that just before decolonization began, during and after the Second World War, the colonial territories had a population of over 500 million people, that is, nearly one-quarter of the world's population. Today this figure is under 50 million. With the end of British rule in India, the countries of Pakistan, Ceylon, and Burma also became independent. All the British and French mandate territories in the Middle East have become self-governing states. After a hard struggle, France has had to withdraw from French Indochina (Cambodia, Laos, Vietnam) and grant Tunisia, Morocco, and Algeria their independence. In the same way, the former Dutch possessions in the Far East became the Republic of Indonesia. The United States has given up the Philippines. Virtually the whole of Africa, where twenty years ago there were only a few independent states, has been or is about to be freed from colonial rule.

When the United Nations was set up in 1945, India's accession to independence brought the population of the colonial territories down to about 215 million. Today, as I have said, the corresponding figure is under 50 million. Apart from certain isolated large territories, such as the Portuguese possessions Angola and Mozambique, the rest of the non-self-governing territories consist of small scattered areas with a total population of under 1 million. In 14 of the remaining British territories the population numbers under 100,000. If, during the coming years, the world is not to be enriched with the creation of some 50 or so new, independent, but miniature-sized states, we must solve the problem of how we can not only terminate the colonial status of these territories but also fit them in some appropriate way into already existing states.

During the preparatory work on the United Nations Charter, there was considerable uncertainty and diversity of opinion concerning the attitude the Organization should take to the colonial problem. In the Atlantic Charter, Roosevelt and Churchill had confirmed the right of all peoples to choose their own government. While Churchill did not want this declaration to be understood as applying also to the colonial peoples and was completely unwilling to allow the Organization any right to interfere with conditions in the British Empire, there was a growing liberal public opinion in America that considered that all colonial government should be subject to full supervision until the colonial system was completely ended. This was the line adopted by President Roosevelt and his Secretary of State, Cordell Hull, and an internal preliminary draft prepared by the State Department in 1943 was based on the principle that the trusteeship system woud apply to all non-self-governing territories. However, this idea met with resistance not only from the British but also from the Army and Navy Departments in Washington. That is why the draft prepared during the confidential negotiations at Dumbarton Oaks in the summer of 1944 left the question open. It was not until the Yalta Conference in February 1945, that it was agreed that the trusteeship system beyond the former mandate areas would apply only to such other territories as were placed voluntarily under the system by the states responsible for their administration.

At the San Francisco Conference, Chapters XII and XIII of the Charter were drafted accordingly. In order to meet the wish of growing liberal public opinion concerning the recognition of the right of peoples to self-determination and the related principle that the administration of colonial territories shall be regarded as a means of promoting the population's welfare and independence, a Chapter XI was added, which contained a "Declaration regarding non-self-governing territories."

The obligations that Chapter XI (Art. 73) imposes on *every* state

that administers a non-self-governing territory are not very different
from those laid down in Chapter XII for the administration of the
trust territories. The obligation to promote the political independence of a people is perhaps a little less explicit in that Article 73
mentions only the obligation to promote "self-government" whereas
Article 76 (dealing with the trust territories) refers to "self-
government or independence." In practice, however, no importance
has been attached to this shade of difference. In both cases, the
United Nations considers that its task will not be completed until the
colonial peoples have achieved full independence. The fundamental
difference between Chapter XI and Chapter XII lies in the rules on
the control machinery and the obligation to transmit reports and information, which, is the most important basis for this machinery.
While under Article 88 the administering states are required to make
annual reports to the General Assembly on the basis of a questionnaire drawn up by the Trusteeship Council concerning the political,
economic, social, and educational advancement of the area, all that
is said in Article 73(e) is that the administering state shall regularly
(that is, not necessarily annually) transmit to the Secretary-General
(that is, not the General Assembly) for information purposes (as
compared with Art. 87, which says that the reports shall be considered by the General Assembly and the Trusteeship Council) statistical and other information of a technical nature relating to economic,
social, and educational conditions in the territories. It will be noticed
that there is no question of any report, that nothing is said about an
obligation to answer any questionnaire and that the obligation to
supply information does not cover political conditions, which, as it
happens, are frequently the most delicate and controversial. Moreover, the obligation to supply information under Article 73(e) is
limited by considerations relating to the security and constitution of
the administering state. Furthermore, Chapter XI does not mention
any form of control organs or functions. Nothing is said about the
possibility that the General Assembly or any other special organ set
up for this purpose might supervise the colonial government, and no
reference is made to the possibility of organizing or receiving visiting
missions.

These profound differences reflect the opposition displayed at the
time of the Charter's establishment by the leading colonial powers
against the idea of extending the trusteeship system to areas other

than the former mandated territories. They were prepared to accept a declaration of principles couched in general terms on the aims and obligations of colonial governments, but they were not prepared to submit to organized supervision and control.

Nevertheless, the General Assembly, under pressure from the anti-colonialist powers and with the support of the Eastern bloc has, in practice, contrary to the principles underlying the Charter, interpreted and extended Chapter XI in such a way as to subject every colonial government to supervision and control similar to that provided for under the trusteeship system. Thus the General Assembly has set up a Committee on Information from Non-self-governing Territories, which, like the Trusteeship Council, is made up of representatives of the administering states and an equal number of representatives from the nonadministering states and whose task it is to gather information and report to the General Assembly. Furthermore, it has insisted on a questionnaire being answered and exerted strong pressure in order to obtain information also on the political development in the territories in question. Again, petitions have also been received from the populations, and in one case the United Nations even went so far as to try to organize a visiting mission (South-West Africa). The colonial powers, especially the United Kingdom, have repeatedly protested against this extension of their obligations but without going so far as to refuse to co-operate (except for Portugal and the Union of South Africa) in supplying such information and discussing it in the various organs concerned.

From the formal point of view, justification for this development has been found in Article 10 of the Charter, which empowers the General Assembly to discuss any questions or matters within the scope of the Charter, and in Article 22, which authorizes it to set up such subsidiary organs as it deems necessary for the performance of its functions. This is a politically motivated interpretation, similar to the interpretation whereby the Western powers have made it possible for the General Assembly, to a large extent, to carry out functions that, according to the Charter, were to be carried out by the Security Council (Chap. I.5 and VI.2).

If the more reasonable of the colonial powers have, however reluctantly, accepted the placing of ordinary colonies on an equal footing with the trust territories, this is due to the fact that the separation of these two types of territories, as explained in the introduction to this chapter, lacks any rational basis. No reasonable ground can be given for applying special rules to colonial territories that were once under German rule. Once it has been recognized that the United Nations shall have powers of supervision and control over these territories, it is difficult, if one does not wish to split hairs, to argue that the same should not hold true for other colonial territories.

As far as the application of Chapter XI is concerned, a major and difficult problem is to determine which territories shall be covered by this Chapter's provisions. Article 73 says that these obligations shall apply to territories whose peoples have not yet attained a full measure of self-government. Although this sounds very impressive, it is, however, more a phrase than a definition.

The difficulty here does not lie so much in the fact that there may be some doubt as to what is meant by a full measure of self-government. It is natural to interpret this expression as being synonymous with independence and this, in fact, is how it has been understood in practice.

The real difficulty stems from certain unmentioned premises. Especially, there is the premise that the territory has a population that in a given sense constitutes a separate "people" and therefore naturally aspires to an independent national existence as a state. If this premise is not accepted, the phrase may be applied to any area that constitutes a part of the territory of a state. For instance, in Denmark the island Funen might well be claimed to be an area "whose people have not yet attained a full measure of self-government." If it has not occurred to anyone to invoke Chapter XI in respect of Funen, it is because it has not occurred to anyone to regard the population of that region as a people in its own right with a natural aspiration to self-government.

Hence the field of application of this Chapter depends on the scope of a people's right to self-determination. This is discussed and analyzed in Chapter III, where it is shown that it is impossible to give a precise meaning to this principle—partly because it cannot be determined under which conditions a minority group constitutes a "people" and has therefore the right to claim self-determination, and partly because it is not possible to determine how this principle shall be restricted by opposite considerations, say geographical conditions of economic, traffic, or strategic consequence.

As a result, no general definition or criteria can be found for determining the territories to which Chapter XI applies. In each particular case it is a matter of weighing the question whether the population of the territory can be said to constitute a people that can justifiably lay claim to self-determination and independence. This does not, however, rule out the possibility of singling out certain typical features applicable in typical situations.

It is, in fact, because of the weight ascribed to such typical features that the practical difficulties involved in determining the field of application of Chapter XI have not been so great as theoretical analysis led one to expect. It was tacitly assumed on all sides that the provisions of this Chapter should be applicable only to territories of the *colonial type*. These are characterized by the fact that (1) the territory in question is separate from the mother country and frequently situated overseas at a great distance and (2) the indigenous population in the territory is ethnically and culturally different from that of the mother country and has a less-developed civilization. This last requirement is clearly reflected in the wording of Article 73, which speaks of the development of free political institutions according to the varying stages of advancement of the population. In most cases, it can clearly be seen whether a given area and its population belong to this type or not. Clearly outside its scope falls, e.g., the oppression of formerly independent nations under imperialist rule, such as the Soviet rule over the Baltic states and other oppressed areas. The problem of the liberation of these countries is something the United Nations has not dared to tackle, even though the principle of a people's right to self-determination is just as obviously applicable to these oppressed peoples.

The preceding analysis explains why, despite many efforts, it has never proved possible to find an acceptable definition of the phrase "non-self-governing territories" and why it has nevertheless been possible to administer Article 73 without serious difficulties. The General Assembly has, from the very outset, repeatedly demanded or directly endeavored to devise such a definition, but without success. Most countries have not been dissatisfied with this state of affairs, because they could approve the list of administered territories—a list drawn up in reply to a circular letter of the Secretary-General in 1946. At that time, eight member states declared that they were prepared under Article 73(e) to supply information on a total of 74 territories that they regarded as coming under the provisions of

Chapter XI. A practical problem first arose when, in the following years, some of these eight countries ceased to supply information on certain of the 74 territories. But the problem here was not the difficult, fundamental question of whether the principle of the right to self-determination was applicable to a given territory as being of the colonial type, but the more technical and practical question of whether the development toward independence could be said to be completed because the population had actually achieved a full measure of self-government and joined the ranks of other independent states or had, in some other way, become master of its destiny.

These unilateral acts gave rise to thorough discussions and studies aimed at reaching an agreement on certain principles or criteria to settle the question as to which territories are covered by Chapter XI and the conditions under which the obligation to supply information ceases because the development toward self-government may be regarded as completed. After many years of work on the part of a special committee, the General Assembly adopted in 1953 a Resolution enumerating 34 factors as being characteristic of either independence, various degrees of self-government, or free union with another state. This resolution, however, did not secure general approval, and in 1959 a new working committee was set up to study the problem. This committee's work led to the adoption of Resolution 1541 (XV) of the General Assembly on December 15, 1960, concerning the *Principles which should guide members in determining whether or not an obligation exists to transmit the information called for under Article 73e of the Charter*. This resolution formulates 12 such principles. Particular importance attaches to the principles (1) that Chapter XI shall be applicable only to areas generally regarded as colonies, (2) that the obligation to supply information must be taken to apply only to territories that are geographically separated from the administering state and distinct ethnically and/or culturally from the country administering it, and (3) that a full measure of self-government can be reached by: (a) emergence as a sovereign independent state, (b) free association with an independent state, or (c) integration with an independent state. This is subject in the last two of these alternatives to a number of conditions, in particular that the association or the integration shall be decided by the people in a free plebiscite.

The debate on these principles, which secured general support (the Resolution was adopted by 69-2-21), was particularly directed at Spain and Portugal, which, since their entry into the United Nations in 1955, had refused to recognize any obligation to furnish information. While Spain, however, during the debate in 1960, relented and declared itself prepared to fulfill its obligation in future in accordance with the Charter, Portugal continued to deny the existence of any such obligation on the grounds that the former Portuguese colonies (of which Angola and Mozambique are the most important) had been granted the status of provinces of the mother country. The General Assembly refused to accept this declaration. Resolution 1542 (XV) of December 15, 1960, stated that in the light of the principles approved in Resolution 1541 (of the same date) nine of the territories administered by Portugal, including Angola and Mozambique, were non-self-governing within the meaning of Chapter XI of the Charter, and Portugal was asked to fulfill its obligation to furnish information.

From November 28, to December 14, 1960, on Khrushchev's proposal, the General Assembly held an extensive debate on the colonial problem, during which no less than 120 statements were made.

Khrushchev had submitted a draft resolution in which, among other things, it was requested that all non-self-governing colonial territories should immediately be given full independence irrespective of whether they were trust territories or not. To this was attached, as a "rider," the demand that all possessions or leased areas on another state's territory (i.e., bases) should be eliminated. The United Kingdom delegate said that he was shocked by the manner in which the Soviet Union had tried to exploit for its own ends the profound desire of millions of people for independence. He pointed out that since 1939 about 500 million people formerly under British rule had achieved freedom and independence, whereas, during the same period, six countries with a population of 22 million had been partly or wholly absorbed by force into the Soviet empire. Moreover, many of the Asian and African states protested against the colonial problem being exploited for cold war purposes. Khrushchev was unsuccessful in his manoeuver, for the Asian and African states rejected his proposal and put forward instead their own draft in the nature of a Declaration on the Granting of Independence to Colonial Countries and Peoples, which on December 14, 1960, was adopted as Resolution 1514 (XV) by 89-0-9. The Resolution stated that the colonial system in all its forms and manifestations should be brought to a speedy and unconditional end. Immediate steps were to be taken in all the non-self-governing territories to transfer power to the peoples of these territories, and inadequacy of political, economic, social, or educational preparedness should never serve as a pretext for delaying independence. A Russian attempt to strengthen the demand for unconditional and immediate independence, by asking for all the territories concerned to be given their freedom by the end of 1961, was rejected.

The demand that an inadequate level of economic and social development in the territories should never serve as a pretext for deferring their accession to independence was repeated in another resolution adopted the following day, namely Resolution 1535 (XV) of December 15, 1960, in which the General Assembly expressed its views on a Report on Progress Achieved in Non-self-governing Territories under the United Nations Charter, prepared by the Secretary-General. The terms used are unclear and ambiguous. If by "pretext" is meant an untenable excuse for not carrying out an obligation, the wording reflects a truism, namely that these circumstances may not be invoked when they do not provide adequate grounds for postponing the grant of independence. But this meaning can scarcely have been intended. It may be assumed that the intention was to affirm that the invoking of inadequate preparedness should never be taken at its face value but should always be regarded as an untenable excuse. Thus understood, this demand is irresponsible. In the course of the major debate on colonial questions, the United Kingdom delegate drew attention to the fact that 14 of the remaining British colonial territories had a population of under 100,000. Their future raises serious problems, and the mere withdrawal of the colonial power would be far from sufficient to solve them.

In the 20 years or so that have elapsed since the establishment of the United Nations, a tremendous process of development has taken place, which has completely altered the political map of the world and the cast of actors on the world political scene. The colonial system, which, since the days of the great discoveries, i.e. nearly four hundred years ago, has been a deeply rooted feature of high politics, has in this short space of 20 years been submerged under an irresistible wave of anticolonialism. No one today will deny that the days of colonial rule are definitely over. The only question is how the system can be ended in the most reasonable and safest way.

It might be tempting to interpret this coincidence in time in terms of cause and effect, and to explain colonial liberation as being due to the driving force of the United Nations. Such an interpretation, however, would not be correct. The colonial liberation movement rests on forces and impulses that have been neither created nor conjured up by the United Nations. A better explanation is that both the world Organization and the colonial liberation movement are the common products of the Second World War. Even if the United Nations had not been created, the colonial system would still inevitably have been doomed to disappear.

Under these circumstances, the most that could have been expected of the United Nations was that the Organization would act as a cautious midwife. This has not, however, been the case, because the General Assembly, under the pressure of strong emotions and cynical speculation, has been more concerned with getting in the mother's way than with looking after the child.

References

Asher, Robert E. et al., *The United Nations and Promotion of the General Welfare* (1957), pp. 815-1020.

Fletcher-Cook, John, "Some Reflections on the International Trusteeship System, with Particular Reference to its Impact on the Governments and Peoples of the Trust Territories," *International Organization* (1959), pp. 422-30.

Haas, Ernest, B., "The Reconciliation of Conflicting Colonial Policy Aims: Acceptance of the League of Nations Mandate System," *International Organization* (1952), pp. 521-36.

————— "The Attempt to Terminate Colonialism: Acceptance of the United Nations Trusteeship System," *International Organization* (1953), pp. 1-21.

Jacobsen, Harold Karan, "The United Nations and Colonialism: A Tentative Appraisal," *International Organization* (1962), pp. 37-56.

Murray, James N., *The United Nations Trusteeship System* (1957).

Robinson, Kenneth, "World Opinion and Colonial Status," *International Organization* (1954), pp. 468-83.

XII ❦

RESULTS

AND PROSPECTS—

ILLUSIONS AND REALITIES

Aᴼᴼᴼ FTER our step-by-step survey of the development and activities of the United Nations, the time has come to try to take stock and to draw up a balance sheet. What has the United Nations achieved and what can we reasonably expect of it in the future? These two questions hang together; a forecast for the future must rest on a diagnosis of the past, and an assessment of future possibilities on an analysis of past experience. It is obvious that, to a large extent, the United Nations has not fulfilled the expectations aroused by its creation. But the question is why? Are these unsatisfactory results due to relatively accidental circumstances, which might conceivably change for the better? Or are they due to organizational shortcomings, which could be remedied? Or does the explanation lie rather in some deeply rooted feature in the nature of international society that from the very outset rules out any possibility of an organization of this type living up to mankind's hopes and expectations, at least in the foreseeable future? If we plant a shoot in the expectation that it will develop into a mighty tree, and all we obtain is a sorry-looking bush, we may wonder whether this disappointing result should be attributed to the climate, or other unfavorable conditions that might be remedied, or if the reason is simply that what was planted was not actually a tree and was not therefore predisposed under favorable conditions to grow into a tree. The same question may be asked in the case of the United Nations. What was planted in 1945? Was it a seed that only required a little sun, fertilizer, and care in order to develop into a world government where war and poverty, as in Shangri-La, are things of the past? Or was it something sterile, a hollow shell, an elegant setting for periodic interstate conferences, that allows the world to continue the chaotic and lawless game of the balance of power? Or does the truth lie between these two extremes?

It is important to try to answer this question, in so far as this can be done, because a realistic understanding of the Organization's difficulties and limits is the necessary basis for a policy in respect of the United Nations aiming at something other and better than mirages. Many affirm that the United Nations is and should be the cornerstone of national foreign policy and that their aim is to strengthen the Organization. It is difficult, particularly for a small country, to disagree with this; but the question is what is really meant by the vague expression "to strengthen the United Nations"? A more precise definition depends on one's ideas on the nature and development possibilities of the Organization in relation to the international community.

A balance sheet of the Organization's work must necessarily cover the different aspects of its extensive field of activities: the preservation of peace, arms control, welfare work, and the termination of the colonial system.

1. Preservation of peace and settlement of disputes

As I have repeatedly stated in this book, the United Nations Charter is based on the idea of the concert. By and large, the Charter's peace-

keeping system can be described as an institutionalized continuation
of the Great Powers' hegemony in the Concert of Europe, whereby
the leading role of the Great Powers has been consolidated by means
of rules legally obliging the other powers to assist them in the application of sanctions and, to this end, to follow the directives issued by
the Security Council. When the Charter was drawn up it was hoped
that this system could be implemented through the leading powers
agreeing to organize the peace by concluding peace treaties with the
defeated enemy countries and thereafter administering the peace
jointly as a continuation of their wartime co-operation.

As is known, this hope remained unfulfilled. Peace treaties were
concluded with Finland and Italy and with Bulgaria, Rumania, and
Hungary, but no treaty has yet been concluded with Germany, and
in the case of Japan, West and East have concluded separate treaties
with that country. Instead of the concert, we got the cold war. As a
result, the Charter's plan in Chapter VII concerning the organization
of armed forces to be made available to the Security Council for the
purpose of maintaining peace has never been carried out in practice
and the Council's authority has been undermined by an inner split.

For this reason, the world has never witnessed the example of a
peace-breaker being met by an organized peace force with a power
as overwhelming as that exercized by the police *vis-à-vis* an individual in a national state. The improvised Korean police action is about
as near we have managed to get to the Charter's idea of a peace-
enforcing police action, but here the "police" was so far from enjoying the necessary superiority over the offender that in the early days
the action almost ended in a fiasco, and ultimately it degenerated
into a war that lasted several years. The action in Korea was an
isolated phenomenon made possible by the Soviet Union's boycott of
the Security Council. The United Nations Emergency Forces in the
Gaza strip and the operations in the Congo do not have the character
of sanctions against a peace-breaker but are a form of assistance
given at the request of the lawful government of the state for the
purpose of maintaining peace and order under circumstances that
could otherwise represent a threat to peace. While the watch along
the frontier between Israel and Egypt may be described as a modest
but undisputed success and perhaps the United Nations' most significant contribution to the preservation of peace, there has been
considerable controversy concerning the political value and the

legality from the point of view of the Charter of the lengthy operations in the Congo. We are frequently told that it is directly contrary to the United Nations' mission for peace to become involved in military operations of a regular warlike nature entailing the use of tanks and bombers. The answer is that, in itself, the use of armed forces in the Organization's name and under its leadership for the purpose of maintaining peace is in no way inconsistent with the Charter; on the contrary, it is a realization of the ideas on which the Charter is based. In itself the use of armed force is as little at variance with the idea of the preservation of peace as is the idea of a policeman having to use his gun to keep peace and order. What is objectionable is what actually happened in the Congo and in Korea, namely that what was originally conceived as a police action, i.e. an action carried out with overwhelming force by organs representing the community and backed by its authority and supremacy, was in fact carried out with so little power and authority that the operations degenerated into regular warfare between equally matched parties. Not only does the United Nations risk being made responsible for military abuses, which are inevitable when the Secretary-General has to rely on a force made up of many different national contingents without common traditions, training, or discipline. The more the Organization is dragged into internal conflicts and is obliged to adopt a definite position toward them, the more it is likely to arouse the suspicion that its peace-keeping action is not being carried out in a completely objective and impartial manner but under the pressure of one or other of the Great Powers in order to further this or that interest.

At the time of writing (early 1965) the situation in the Congo is not yet fully clear. Even if the final outcome of the ONUC is favorable, in the sense that it succeeds in ensuring the stability of the Central Congolese Administration in Leopoldville and in restoring peace and order in all the provinces without any interference from other countries, this experiment has been so expensive in terms of both money and prestige that it is not likely to be repeated for a long time. Those who helped and believed that the UNEF under the command of the Secretary-General would be the beginning of a larger United Nations Army are presumably doomed to disappointment.

Even though in certain cases the United Nations has succeeded, without the use of armed force, either in putting an end to a breach of peace or in averting a threatened breach of peace—here I am thinking, for example, of the Organization's intervention during the Suez crisis in 1956 or the dispute about West New Guinea in 1962 —it must be clearly recognized that the United Nations has not succeeded in performing its peace-keeping function, which the Charter intended to be its main task. This task has now been taken over by NATO and other regional arrangements. "Why?" one may ask. The answer is important in regard to what we may expect in the future.

The answer is simply that the reason for the inactivity of the Security Council is the split between East and West, the cold war, which has made it impossible for the major powers to act in concert in order to enforce the preservation of peace and the settlement of disputes between other states. One of the fundamental ideas set out in this book is that the political idea underlying the United Nations Charter, namely that of the Concert of the Great Powers, is a sound and strong idea that provides a realistic basis for the work of an organization concerned with keeping the peace—provided that the harmony between the leading powers, which the system presupposes, can be ensured. Up to now, this requirement has not been fulfilled, but there is no reason to suppose that this will necessarily continue to be the case and that this system will never be made to work. After all, by and large, the Concert of Europe worked satisfactorily for about a century.

Perhaps there is still reason to hope that the destructive split between the two groups may be brought to an end. The main reasons for the Russians' decision to break off their wartime co-operation with the Western powers were, first, the Marxist doctrine of the historical necessity of world revolution, which makes any co-operation with the capitalist states open treason to the cause of Communism; and, second, the Americans' unilateral possession of the atomic bomb, which meant that the Soviet Union could not meet the leading Western power on an equal footing and with confidence—for confidence in politics is only possible between parties of equal strength. On both points, there has been a development toward equality and a *rapprochement*. The Marxist beliefs, which, like other dogmas, are so obviously contrary to rational thought and to experience, cannot in the long run, not even under a dictatorship, remain intact in the face of the undermining influence of critical thought. Even if, as is usually the case under authoritarian systems, one con-

tinues to pay lip-service to these beliefs, the spirit in which the doctrine is interpreted changes. A development in this direction clearly
emerges from a comparison between an old Communist country such
as the Soviet Union, where the "Gospel" has already become an established "Church," with a young Communist country such as
China, where the faith still possesses the blind enthusiasm typical of
the early days of Communism. Simultaneously with the gradual lift-
ing of the ideological barriers, a social and cultural development is
taking place, which is bringing the leading elite in the Soviet Union
into closer contact with Western culture, which, after all, formed the
soil from which Communism orginally sprang. But most important of
all is the fact that the Soviet Union, having itself built up an atomic
force, has achieved that equality with the United States which is a
prerequisite for negotiation and compromise. The fearful possibilities of nuclear weapons, and the need to ensure that control of these
weapons shall remain in the hands of the few, binds the world's two
leading powers together in a community of interest that makes it
necessary for them, before it is too late, to try to achieve mutual
understanding, a settlement of their differences, and the establishment of joint and exclusive nuclear control.

If this hope of an American-Russian *rapprochement* is realized, it
seems likely that in the United Nations the Security Council will
resume its position as the Organization's central organ for dealing
with political problems and genuinely assume the main responsibility for the maintenance of international peace and security. Any possibility of reverting to the Charter's original idea in this respect will
be strengthened thanks to the transformation undergone by the General Assembly during the last few years. Decolonization has led to
the emergence of a great number of sovereign states, some of which
(a dozen or so) are miniature states with less than one million inhabitants, many of them economically and politically underdeveloped
and unable to conduct their own affairs without help, but all eager to
appear on the stage of the world organization and to intervene in the
settlement of difficulties—in *other* states. The membership of the
General Assembly has thus grown out of all proportion and will indeed continue to do so until the colonial system has been completely
ended. Perhaps a membership of around 125 to 150 does not seem so
unreasonable, compared with the membership of many national parliaments. But here it must be remembered that, unlike parliaments,

the General Assembly is not organized into parties whose members are subject to party discipline. The General Assembly is made up of as many individual delegates as there are members and each of them is equally entitled to be heard. Lobbying, which to some extent should make up for the lack of parliamentary organization and guarantee a certain measure of leadership, has become almost unmanageable in so large an assembly, and it is becoming increasingly difficult for either of the major powers to muster the two-thirds majority that in most cases is required for the adoption of a resolution.

It seems to me grotesque for the world's burning problems to be discussed in an Assembly where up to 10 per cent of the sovereign states represented are smaller than a single municipality in Denmark and about half are smaller than Denmark. Side by side with representatives of these states there will sit, when the question of the representation of Communist China has been settled, delegates from two states (India and China) that together represent about a billion people, that is about one-third of the earth's population. Whatever one may think of the introduction of a weighted vote in the General Assembly (Chap. VI.1), a voting reform in itself will not turn the General Assembly into an effective organ for political debate.

The incapacity of the General Assembly is further increased by the fact that it normally meets only once a year for a session of a couple of months.

Thus there are strong grounds for the major powers wishing to shift the political emphasis back to the organ where they are certain to muster a majority of the votes if they act in unison. If this happens, new prospects will arise. One can imagine a situation in which Communist China, having taken up its seat in the Security Council, will become the dissenting power that through its veto will threaten to paralyze the Security Council. We had better wait until then before we speculate on how this difficulty can be overcome. It is not likely, however, that the General Assembly's subsidiary competence will once more be resorted to.

If the major powers succeed in establishing the concert that is the foundation upon which the United Nations is erected, it may well prove possible to apply the security system provided for under Chapter VII of the Charter. It is then conceivable that the major powers, and possibly a number of other states, will conclude the agreements referred to in Article 43 of the Charter as regards making armed forces available to the Security Council so that at any given time an effective force will be available for speedy and effective en- forcement of the peace. Such a development would involve an enormous strengthening, not only of the Council's peace-keeping powers but also of its functions in connection with the settlement of disputes. Legally speaking, the Council will still not be empowered to make binding arbitration decisions. But there is no doubt that if the Council functions as an organ of a harmonious concert of the major powers and is backed by effective armed forces, its recommen- dations and exhortations in pursuance of Chapter VI of the Charter will have much greater political weight than they have under present conditions, and will act more or less as a binding law.

I would not go so far as to say that a development along the lines I have just mentioned is probable. I merely say that it is conceivable, meaning that even if it meets with difficulties or possibly insur- mountable obstacles, any failure will not be due to something inher- ent in the nature of the international community and international politics. It will perhaps be argued that the mutual fear and jealousy inseparable from any power struggle in the field of high politics makes it impossible to bring about the unity between the giant powers that is a prerequisite for such a development. This argument carries some weight. If I believe, nevertheless, in the possibility of unity, it is because I expect that this mutual fear can be overcome by another and greater fear, namely the common fear of total destruc- tion in a nuclear war.

On the other hand, I think it illusory to believe that the United Nations could develop into a world government by granting to the General Assembly extensive powers and authority to make binding decisions through the institution of a weighted voting system. This, in fact, is what the world federalists aspire to. I cannot understand how anyone with any political experience can imagine the world be- ing governed through resolutions adopted by an assembly such as that of the United Nations. In Chapter VIII above, I said that the establishment of a world government—as, indeed, of any other government—implied two things, namely (1) the existence of a highly developed machinery enjoying a monopoly over the use of force and consequently the total disarmament of the states, and (2) the existence of a feeling of solidarity that has crystallized into a general attitude of allegiance and obedience toward the institutions and organs of the community. I added that it was inconceivable that these two requirements could be fulfilled so long as the human feelings of solidarity and loyalty were bound up with national states. These social and psychological facts are not, as might be thought, nebulous phenomena that easily arise and just as easily disappear, but hard realities that develop and change slowly. Any legal order must rest on this basis. Experience shows that the broadening of the feeling of solidarity and loyalty, which is a necessary precondition for any voluntary political integration, is extremely difficult to achieve and requires a long period of development under favorable conditions. For example, what has become of Scandinavian unity despite all the talk of Scandinavian fellowship and solidarity? We must take it, therefore, that not only is a world state not "just around the corner"—it is not in sight in even the most remote future our imaginations can conjure up.

What then are the United Nations' present possibilities in the political field? Its task is to realize the plan for an oligarchic government of the Great Powers through the Security Council, laid down in the Charter. This plan does not solve all the difficulties but, within its limits, it is both strong and realistic. Under that plan, the United Nations is essentially a new dimension for the policy of balance of power and for the formal establishment and institutionalization of the leadership of the Great Powers. This idea is rooted in the realities of political life. On the other hand, it is an illusion to believe that the United Nations is like a larva, which one fine day will burst out of its cocoon as a magnificent butterfly, in the form of a world government (a democratic world government, at that, based on liberty and equality) and rule a world where the rule of law has superseded power politics, because we all, both great and small, obey the resolutions of the General Assembly. This belief, which makes short work of all the difficulties, is nothing but a dream.

We can all agree that the United Nations should be "strengthened." But what exactly do we mean by this? Realistically speaking, it must mean trying to ensure that the Security Council shall be able to carry out its functions in accordance with the Charter. There is not perhaps very much that the smaller states can do to that end, for the realization of the Charter's plan depends on harmonious cooperation between the Great Powers. What we can do, however, both within and outside the United Nations, is stimulate public opinion to demand the end of the cold war, the settlement of outstanding disputes, constructive agreements on arms control, and positive co-operation in the Security Council. This demand must first and fore-most be directed at the United States and the Soviet Union as the two powers that are chiefly responsible for the world's fate. As far as the rest of us are concerned, all we can do is hope that those who bear this responsibility will live up to it.

The terrible thing is that time presses. Once China succeeds in building up a nuclear force with retaliatory power, the chances of avoiding a nuclear war will be greatly reduced.

This, then, is what "strengthening the United Nations" means. Yet I am afraid that many of those who use this expression mean some-thing quite different by it. In their lofty enthusiasm for law and de-mocracy, coupled with their lack of understanding of the nature of these things and the conditions governing their existence, they be-lieve that the future lies with a democratic General Assembly, pro-vided with legislative authority, and with the Court of Justice, pro-vided with obligatory jurisdiction in all disputes between states. Such is the radiant vision beheld by the ideologists.

2. Disarmament and arms control

Here I would in the main refer the reader to what has already been said in Chapter IX. Although negotiations have been in progress al-most uninterruptedly, since the United Nations was created until the present time, the result so far has been virtually nil. In this field there is no reason to expect that the Organization will be able in the future to make any significant contributions. The General Assembly is the worst imaginable forum for such negotiations. The way to achieve results is for confidential negotiations to take place directly between the immediately interested parties, possibly with the assistance of neutral mediators. This, in fact, has been recognized by the United Nations itself. Although the General Assembly (and its First Com-mittee) continue to put forward and discuss proposals concerning plans for general and full disarmament, the real negotiations are go-ing on in Geneva, partly in the form of confidential discussions be-tween the United States, the Soviet Union, and the United Kingdom and partly in the Eighteen-Nation Committee on disarmament,

which is not a United Nations organ but has a somewhat loose connection with it, in that the United Nations approved its establishment and expressed the wish that it would report on its work to the UN Disarmament Commission.

The United Nations' work in the sphere of disarmament and armament control must be judged negative rather than positive. Since September 18, 1959, when Khrushchev personally submitted in the General Assembly a proposal for general and full disarmament to be completed within a period of four years, the discussions in the Assembly have been dominated by propaganda considerations. The Americans did not want to lag behind the Russians and therefore submitted their own projects, and so, misleading the public at large, the General Assembly has continued to debate ideas and plans that, it knows perfectly well, have no connection with reality.

3. Welfare work

The most solid if not the most sensational achievements of the organization must be sought in the broad international co-operation organized by the United Nations and the members of the United Nations "family" in all sectors of social life. The machinery may be cumbersome and clanking and may often break down altogether, but the international extension of national administration is at the present time an inescapable necessity. Perhaps it is precisely the humble everyday nature of much of this work that allows it escape public attention.

Yet some of the tasks taken up by the United Nations stand out sharply and attract attention. First and foremost, there is the assistance to the underdeveloped countries. In this sector, on American initiative and with overwhelming American support, the United Nations has launched an important program. This has proved capable of appealing to the imagination and idealism of the public, which does not, of course, mean that the willingness to make sacrifices does not also spring from enlightened self-interest in the long term. While the United Nations must, because of the fanaticism and rashness with which the process of decolonization has been carried out, bear part of the responsibility for the difficulties faced by the helpless states that have come into the world prematurely, the Organization has ample opportunity of making up for it through its assistance work. As I have said before, apart from the results achieved, the actual work that is being done in this cause all over the world is of value as an education for international understanding and solidarity.

Another field that has received public attention is the work being done to further respect for human rights. The United Nations has itself publicized its work in this sphere, launching the Universal Declaration of Human Rights as a milestone in the history of mankind. I find it difficult to share in the general enthusiasm. There has been an unending stream of fine words on the subject but little willingness to get down to realities and accept controls. The actual influence of the Universal Declaration—which, as the reader will recall, is not legally binding—is, in my opinion, questionable. I am not impressed by the fact that, as it is often affirmed, the Declaration has left a mark on the constitutions and legislations of many of the newly created states. The work on the drawing up of the two legally binding conventions on human rights has gone on over a good many years and will not, all things considered, lead to any practical results, because the conventions, once adopted, are not backed by any legal machinery whereby an individual can obtain redress from the state—which, after all, is the heart of the problem. The Convention on Genocide (see Chapter X.6), loudly praised by many, is a case of the specific United Nations disease reminiscent of the disease called tympanites (a distention of the abdomen, caused by air accumulation) and manifesting itself in inflated language which bursts when a pin is stuck in it.

The work of the Law Commission, too, has, by and large, proved a disappointment. This is partly due to the fact that the Commission, which should have known better, has allowed itself to be drawn into taking up subjects that are hopeless from the start, for instance the idea of criminalizing acts of aggression as an offense against the peace and security of mankind. Moreover, the explanation no doubt lies in the fact that our times do not lend themselves to the task of codifying international law. Inherited international law is of European origin and is mistrusted by the new states as the expression of colonial interests and a conception of law based on these interests. However much or little truth there may be in this, it is undoubtedly true that the inherited European legal tradition cannot be maintained unchanged in a world where so many new peoples belonging to so many different cultural traditions agitate on the international scene demanding that their interests be taken into account and that they be heard on questions of international law. On the other hand, no new common conception of law has yet arisen. Thus we find ourselves in a period of transition in which any attempt to codify a law uniting all nations meets with special difficulties.

4. Colonial liberation

Here it is easier to agree on the facts than on how they should be interpreted. Even though the forces that during the past 20 years have led to the collapse of the colonial system were not conjured up by the United Nations, there can scarcely be any doubt that the Organization has precipitated this process. In the General Assembly, anticolonialism has found a ready platform for its propaganda, which has not neglected any opportunity of fanning the flames and stirring up passions. The more the former colonial territories (now independent and sovereign states) crowded into the General Assembly—50 of the new members were formerly colonies—the more one-sided and insistent the Assembly became in its demand for the unconditional and immediate ending of all colonial rule. The Eastern bloc states have, of course, supported this demand as a move in the cold war and the competition to gain friends and win sympathy among the young states. Apart from the colonial powers, the Western powers have been split by conflicting tendencies. Although, in principle, they were in sympathy with the ideas of self-determination and freedom, they were also soberly aware of the fact that the successful implementation of these ideas required careful preparation and gradual application. However, the propaganda proved so powerful and the fear of being stamped "imperialist" so great that these powers have increasingly tended to vote with the majority or, at least, abstain.

In this connection, there are no future prospects to be discussed. The colonial system will soon only be a thing of the past, and care for the welfare and liberation of the non-self-governing peoples will soon disappear forever from the program of the United Nations. In retrospect, many will no doubt consider that the United Nations earned imperishable glory for having presided over and precipitated the liquidation of the bankruptcy of the colonial system. Others, including myself, consider that the Organization failed to fulfill its true task, which was to ensure that this process would be carried through at lowest possible cost and with the fewest possible losses. Indeed it is a well-known fact that a headlong realization of an asset is not the way to achieve the highest return.

The process of colonial liberation has, however, created a problem for the future which cannot but have serious consequences for the internal organization and distribution of power within the United Nations. Independence and the nationalism that goes with it—in many cases tribalism would be the better term—have led to the paradoxical result that whereas, from the technological and economic points of view, the world is increasingly drawing toward unity, it is at the same time breaking up into an increasingly large number of political units. The paradox lies not so much in the actual number of equal and sovereign units but in the overwhelming number of miniature states created on tribalistic grounds, and completely incapable of an independent existence in the technical, economic, and political sense of the term. One may wonder whether we shall have reached the extreme of this situation with Nauru. This "people," which is demanding independent existence as a sovereign state, consists of about 2,500 persons, in other words roughly the population of a large housing block.

This development has created a serious problem. It makes it a task for the United Nations to further an integration of the many small units into larger units in the form of either a full merger or some sort of federation. This is above all necessary in order to render these states viable from the technical and economic point of view. The problem, however, also has an internal and organizational aspect. As already explained above in section 1, this development has turned the General Assembly into a parody of a world forum, dominated by a profusion of small states that are not representative in terms of population, political power, or civilization, states that have a natural right to ask for assistance but not to dominate the World Organization. To this, it may be objected that no great harm is done, as the General Assembly has no power of decision but derives its authority solely from its public debates and the public opinion that is created and expressed as a result of such debates. But even expressions of opinion will lose their representative significance under such one-sided conditions. In a period of transition like the present, a resolution adopted by the General Assembly will continue to carry a certain amount of authority. Many countries and statesmen are, in principle, in favor of supporting and strengthening the United Nations, and any decision taken on behalf of the United Nations has, within certain limits, been able to draw on this fund of good will. But this good will will quickly evaporate if the anticolonial majority pushes through the Assembly resolutions that cannot be expected to secure compliance, such as, for instance, the resolution of November 6, 1962, on sanctions against the Union of South Africa (see Chap. VII.2).

I believe, therefore, that the General Assembly has seen its heyday and is heading for a crisis of confidence. Moreover, the political use made of the Secretary-General's functions has come in for severe criticism from many sides, and it is scarcely possible that the far-reaching powers granted during the Congo episode will be resorted to again in the future.

The prospect for political initiatives and leadership on the part of the United Nations are not, therefore, very bright—unless the major powers can agree to restore to the Security Council the functions assigned to it under the Charter.

APPENDIX I ❀

CURRENT ABBREVIATIONS
OF THE NAMES
OF INSTITUTIONS

ACC	Administrative Committee for Co-ordination
ANZUS Pact	Pact of September 1, 1951, between Australia, New Zealand, and the United States
BANK	International Bank for Reconstruction and Development
CICT	Commission on International Commodity Trade
ECA	Economic Commission for Africa
ECAFE	Economic Commission for Asia and the Far East
ECE	Economic Commission for Europe
ECLA	Economic Commission for Latin America
ECOSOC	Economic and Social Council
EEC	European Economic Community
EFTA	European Free Trade Association
EPTA	Expanded Program of Technical Assistance
FAO	Food and Agriculture Organization of the United Nations
FUND	International Monetary Fund
GATT	General Agreement on Tariffs and Trade

IAEA	International Atomic Energy Agency
ICAO	International Civil Aviation Organization
ICCICA	Interim Co-ordinating Committee for International Commodity Arrangements
IDA	International Development Association
IFC	International Finance Corporation
ILO	International Labor Organization
IMCO	Inter-Governmental Maritime Consultative Organization
IRO	International Refugee Organization
ITO	International Trade Organization
ITU	International Telecommunication Union
NATO	North Atlantic Treaty Organization
ONUC	United Nations Operations in the Congo
OPEX	Provision of Operational, Executive and Administrative Personnel
OTC	Organization for Trade Co-operation
SACEUR	Supreme Allied Command in Europe
SACLANT	Supreme Allied Command in the Atlantic
SEATO	Southeast Asia Treaty Organization
SHAPE	Supreme Headquarters of the Allied Powers in Europe
TAB	Technical Assistance Board
TAC	Technical Assistance Committee
UNCIO	United Nations Conference on International Organization
UNEF	United Nations Emergency Force
UNESCO	United Nations Educational, Scientific, and Cultural Organization
UNHCR	United Nations High Commissioner for Refugees
UNICEF	United Nations Children's Fund
UNKRA	United Nations Korean Reconstruction Agency
UNRRA	United Nations Relief and Rehabilitation Administration
UNRWA	United Nations Relief and Works Agency for Palestine Refugees
UPU	Universal Postal Union
WHO	World Health Organization
WMO	World Meteorological Organization

APPENDIX II ❀

THE CHARTER OF
THE UNITED NATIONS

WE THE PEOPLES OF THE UNITED NATIONS DETERMINED

to save succeeding generations from the scourge of war, which twice in our lifetime has brought untold sorrow to mankind, and

to reaffirm faith in fundamental human rights, in the dignity and worth of the
human person, in the equal rights of men and women and of nations large
and small, and

to establish conditions under which justice and respect for the obligations arising from treaties and other sources of international law can be maintained,
and

to promote social progress and better standards of life in larger freedom,

AND FOR THESE ENDS

to practice tolerance and live together in peace with one another as good neigh-
bours, and

to unite our strength to maintain international peace and security, and to ensure by the acceptance of principles and the institution of methods, that armed force shall not be used, save in the common interest, and

to employ international machinery for the promotion of the economic and social advancement of all peoples,

HAVE RESOLVED TO COMBINE OUR EFFORTS TO ACCOMPLISH THESE AIMS.

Accordingly, our respective Governments, through representatives assembled in the city of San Francisco, who have exhibited their full powers found to be in good and due form, have agreed to the present Charter of the United Nations and do hereby establish an international organization to be known as the United Nations.

Chapter I. Purposes and principles

Article 1

The Purposes of the United Nations are:

1. To maintain international peace and security, and to that end: to take effective collective measures for the prevention and removal of threats to the peace, and for the suppression of acts of aggression or other breaches of the peace, and to bring about by peaceful means, and in conformity with the principles of justice and international law, adjustment or settlement of international disputes or situations which might lead to a breach of the peace;

2. To develop friendly relations among nations based on respect for the principle of equal rights and self-determination of peoples, and to take other appropriate measures to strengthen universal peace;

3. To achieve international co-operation in solving international problems of an economic, social, cultural, or humanitarian character, and in promoting and encouraging respect for human rights and for fundamental freedoms for all without distinction as to race, sex, language, or religion; and

4. To be a centre for harmonizing the actions of nations in the attainment of these common ends.

Article 2

The Organization and its Members, in pursuit of the Purposes stated in Article 1, shall act in accordance with the following Principles.

1. The Organization is based on the principle of the sovereign equality of all its Members.

2. All Members, in order to ensure to all of them the rights and benefits resulting from membership, shall fulfil in good faith the obligations assumed by them in accordance with the present Charter.

3. All Members shall settle their international disputes by peaceful means in such a manner that international peace and security, and justice, are not endangered.

4. All Members shall refrain in their international relations from the threat or use of force against the territorial integrity or political independence of any state, or in any other manner inconsistent with the Purposes of the United Nations.

5. All Members shall give the United Nations every assistance in any action it takes in accordance with the present Charter, and shall refrain from giving assistance to any state against which the United Nations is taking preventive or enforcement action.

6. The Organization shall ensure that states which are not Members of the United Nations act in accordance with these Principles so far as may be necessary for the maintenance of international peace and security.

7. Nothing contained in the present Charter shall authorize the United Nations to intervene in matters which are essentially within the domestic jurisdiction of any state or shall require the Members to submit such matters to settlement under the present Charter; but this principle shall not prejudice the application of enforcement measures under Chapter VII.

Chapter II. Membership

Article 3

The original Members of the United Nations shall be the states which, having participated in the United Nations Conference on International Organization at San Francisco, or having previously signed the Declaration by United Nations of 1 January 1942, sign the present Charter and ratify it in accordance with Article 110.

Article 4

1. Membership in the United Nations is open to all other peace-loving states which accept the obligations contained in the present Charter and, in the judgment of the Organization, are able and willing to carry out these obligations.

2. The admission of any such state to membership in the United Nations will be effected by a decision of the General Assembly upon the recommendation of the Security Council.

Article 5

A Member of the United Nations against which preventive or enforcement action has been taken by the Security Council may be suspended from the exercise of the rights and privileges of membership by the General Assembly upon the recommendation of the Security Council. The exercise of these rights and privileges may be restored by the Security Council.

Article 6

A Member of the United Nations which has persistently violated the Principles contained in the present Charter may be expelled from the Organization by the General Assembly upon the recommendation of the Security Council.

Chapter III. Organs

Article 7

1. There are established as the principal organs of the United Nations: a General Assembly, a Security Council, an Economic and Social Council, a Trusteeship Council, an International Court of Justice, and a Secretariat.

2. Such subsidiary organs as may be found necessary may be established in accordance with the present Charter.

Article 8

The United Nations shall place no restrictions on the eligibility of men and women to participate in any capacity and under conditions of equality in its principal and subsidiary organs.

Chapter IV. The General Assembly

COMPOSITION

Article 9

1. The General Assembly shall consist of all the Members of the United Nations.

2. Each Member shall have not more than five representatives in the General Assembly.

FUNCTIONS AND POWERS

Article 10

The General Assembly may discuss any questions or any matters within the scope of the present Charter or relating to the powers and functions of any organs provided for in the present Charter, and, except as provided in Article 12, may make recommendations to the Members of the United Nations or to the Security Council or to both on any such questions or matters.

Article 11

1. The General Assembly may consider the general principles of co-operation in the maintenance of international peace and security, including the principles governing disarmament and the regulation of armaments, and may make recommendations with regard to such principles to the Members or to the Security Council or to both.

2. The General Assembly may discuss any questions relating to the maintenance of international peace and security brought before it by any Member of the United Nations, or by the Security Council, or by a State which is not a Member of the United Nations in accordance with Article 35, paragraph 2, and, except as provided in Article 12, may make recommendations with regard to any such question to the state or states concerned or to the Security Council or to both. Any such question on which action is necessary shall be referred to the Security Council by the General Assembly either before or after discussion.

3. The General Assembly may call the attention of the Security Council to situations which are likely to endanger international peace and security.

4. The powers of the General Assembly set forth in this Article shall not limit the general scope of Article 10.

Article 12

1. While the Security Council is exercising in respect of any dispute or situation the functions assigned to it in the present Charter, the General Assembly shall not make any recommendations with regard to that dispute or situation unless the Security Council so requests.

2. The Secretary-General, with the consent of the Security Council, shall notify the General Assembly at each session of any matters relative to the maintenance of international peace and security which are being dealt with by the

Security Council and shall similarly notify the General Assembly, or the Members of the United Nations if the General Assembly is not in session, immediately the Security Council ceases to deal with such matters.

Article 13

1. The General Assembly shall initiate studies and make recommendations for the purpose of:
   a. promoting international co-operation in the political field and encouraging the progressive development of international law and its codification;
   b. promoting international co-operation in the economic, social, cultural, educational, and health fields, and assisting in the realization of human rights and fundamental freedoms for all without distinction as to race, sex, language, or religion.

2. The further responsibilities, functions and powers of the General Assembly with respect to matters mentioned in paragraph 1(b) above are set forth in Chapters IX and X.

Article 14

Subject to the provisions of Article 12, the General Assembly may recommend measures for the peaceful adjustment of any situation, regardless of origin, which it deems likely to impair the general welfare or friendly relations among nations, including situations resulting from a violation of the provisions of the present Charter setting forth the Purposes and Principles of the United Nations.

Article 15

1. The General Assembly shall receive and consider annual and special reports from the Security Council; these reports shall include an account of the measures that the Security Council has decided upon or taken to maintain international peace and security.

2. The General Assembly shall receive and consider reports from the other organs of the United Nations.

Article 16

The General Assembly shall perform such functions with respect to the international trusteeship system as are assigned to it under Chapters XII and XIII, including the approval of the trusteeship agreements for areas not designated as strategic.

Article 17

1. The General Assembly shall consider and approve the budget of the Organization.

2. The expenses of the Organization shall be borne by the Members as apportioned by the General Assembly.

3. The General Assembly shall consider and approve any financial and budgetary arrangements with specialized agencies referred to in Article 57 and shall examine the administrative budgets of such specialized agencies with a view to making recommendations to the agencies concerned.

Article 18

1. Each member of the General Assembly shall have one vote.

2. Decisions of the General Assembly on important questions shall be made by a two-thirds majority of the members present and voting. These questions shall include: recommendations with respect to the maintenance of international peace and security, the election of the non-permanent members of the Security Council, the election of the members of the Economic and Social Council, the election of members of the Trusteeship Council in accordance with paragraph 1(c) of Article 86, the admission of new Members to the United Nations, the suspension of the rights and privileges of membership, the expulsion of Members, questions relating to the operation of the trusteeship system, and budgetary questions.

3. Decisions on other questions, including the determination of additional categories of questions to be decided by a two-thirds majority, shall be made by a majority of the members present and voting.

Article 19

A Member of the United Nations which is in arrears in the payment of its financial contributions to the Organization shall have no vote in the General Assembly if the amount of its arrears equals or exceeds the amount of the contributions due from it for the preceding two full years. The General Assembly may, nevertheless, permit such a Member to vote if it is satisfied that the failure to pay is due to conditions beyond the control of the Member.

PROCEDURE

Article 20

The General Assembly shall meet in regular annual sessions and in such special sessions as occasion may require. Special sessions shall be convoked by the Secretary-General at the request of the Security Council or of a majority of the Members of the United Nations.

Article 21

The General Assembly shall adopt its own rules of procedure. It shall elect its President for each session.

Article 22

The General Assembly may establish such subsidiary organs as it deems necessary for the performance of its functions.

Chapter V. The Security Council

COMPOSITION

Article 23

1. The Security Council shall consist of eleven Members of the United Nations. The Republic of China, France, the Union of Soviet Socialist Republics, the United Kingdom of Great Britain and Northern Ireland, and the

United States of America shall be permanent members of the Security Council. The General Assembly shall elect six other Members of the United Nations to be non-permanent members of the Security Council, due regard being specially paid, in the first instance to the contribution of Members of the United Nations to the maintenance of international peace and security and to the other purposes of the Organization, and also to equitable geographical distribution.

2. The non-permanent members of the Security Council shall be elected for a term of two years. In the first election of the non-permanent members, however, three shall be chosen for a term of one year. A retiring member shall not be eligible for immediate re-election.

3. Each member of the Security Council shall have one representative.

FUNCTIONS AND POWERS

Article 24

1. In order to ensure prompt and effective action by the United Nations, its Members confer on the Security Council primary responsibility for the maintenance of international peace and security, and agree that in carrying out its duties under this responsibility the Security Council acts on their behalf.

2. In discharging these duties the Security Council shall act in accordance with the Purposes and Principles of the United Nations. The specific powers granted to the Security Council for the discharge of these duties are laid down in Chapters VI, VII, VIII, and XII.

3. The Security Council shall submit annual and, when necessary, special reports to the General Assembly for its consideration.

Article 25

The Members of the United Nations agree to accept and carry out the decisions of the Security Council in accordance with the present Charter.

Article 26

In order to promote the establishment and maintenance of international peace and security with the least diversion for armaments of the world's human and economic resources, the Security Council shall be responsible for formulating, with the assistance of the Military Staff Committee referred to in Article 47, plans to be submitted to the Members of the United Nations for the establishment of a system for the regulation of armaments.

VOTING

Article 27

1. Each member of the Security Council shall have one vote.

2. Decisions of the Security Council on procedural matters shall be made by an affirmative vote of seven members.

3. Decisions of the Security Council on all other matters shall be made by an affirmative vote of seven members including the concurring votes of the permanent members; provided that, in decisions under Chapter VI, and under paragraph 3 of Article 52, a party to a dispute shall abstain from voting.

PROCEDURE

Article 28

1. The Security Council shall be so organized as to be able to function continuously. Each member of the Security Council shall for this purpose be represented at all times at the seat of the Organization.

2. The Security Council shall hold periodic meetings at which each of its members may, if it so desires, be represented by a member of the government or by some other specially designated representative.

3. The Security Council may hold meetings at such places other than the seat of the Organization as in its judgment will best facilitate its work.

Article 29

The Security Council may establish such subsidiary organs as it deems necessary for the performance of its functions.

Article 30

The Security Council shall adopt its own rules of procedure, including the method of selecting its President.

Article 31

Any Member of the United Nations which is not a member of the Security Council may participate, without vote, in the discussion of any question brought before the Security Council whenever the latter considers that the interests of that Member are specially affected.

Article 32

Any Member of the United Nations which is not a member of the Security Council or any state which is not a Member of the United Nations, if it is a party to a dispute under consideration by the Security Council, shall be invited to participate, without vote, in the discussion relating to the dispute. The Security Council shall lay down such conditions as it deems just for the participation of a state which is not a Member of the United Nations.

Chapter VI. Pacific settlement of disputes

Article 33

1. The parties to any dispute, the continuance of which is likely to endanger the maintenance of international peace and security, shall, first of all, seek a solution by negotiation, enquiry, mediation, conciliation, arbitration, judicial settlement, resort to regional agencies or arrangements, or other peaceful means of their own choice.

2. The Security Council shall, when it deems necessary, call upon the parties to settle their dispute by such means.

Article 34

The Security Council may investigate any dispute, or any situation which might lead to international friction or give rise to a dispute, in order to determine whether the continuance of the dispute or situation is likely to endanger the maintenance of international peace and security.

Article 35

1. Any Member of the United Nations may bring any dispute, or any situation of the nature referred to in Article 34, to the attention of the Security Council or of the General Assembly.

2. A state which is not a Member of the United Nations may bring to the attention of the Security Council or of the General Assembly any dispute to which it is a party if it accepts in advance, for the purposes of the dispute, the obligations of pacific settlement provided in the present Charter.

3. The proceedings of the General Assembly in respect of matters brought to its attention under this Article will be subject to the provisions of Articles 11 and 12.

Article 36

1. The Security Council may, at any stage of a dispute of the nature referred to in Article 33 or of a situation of like nature, recommend appropriate procedures or methods of adjustment.

2. The Security Council should take into consideration any procedures for the settlement of the dispute which have already been adopted by the parties.

3. In making recommendations under this Article the Security Council should also take into consideration that legal disputes should as a general rule be referred by the parties to the International Court of Justice in accordance with the provisions of the Statute of the Court.

Article 37

1. Should the parties to a dispute of the nature referred to in Article 33 fail to settle it by the means indicated in that Article, they shall refer it to the Security Council.

2. If the Security Council deems that the continuance of the dispute is in fact likely to endanger the maintenance of international peace and security, it shall decide whether to take action under Article 36 or to recommend such terms of settlement as it may consider appropriate.

Article 38

Without prejudice to the provisions of Articles 33 to 37, the Security Council may, if all the parties to any dispute so request, make recommendations to the parties with a view to a pacific settlement of the dispute.

Chapter VII. Action with respect to threats to the peace, breaches of the peace, and acts of aggression

Article 39

The Security Council shall determine the existence of any threat to the peace, breach of the peace, or act of aggression and shall make recommendations, or decide what measures shall be taken in accordance with Articles 41 and 42, to maintain or restore international peace and security.

Article 40

In order to prevent an aggravation of the situation, the Security Council may, before making the recommendations or deciding upon the measures provided for in Article 39, call upon the parties concerned to comply with such provisional measures as it deems necessary or desirable. Such provisional measures shall be without prejudice to the rights, claims, or position of the parties concerned. The Security Council shall duly take account of failure to comply with such provisional measures.

Article 41

The Security Council may decide what measures not involving the use of armed force are to be employed to give effect to its decisions, and it may call upon the Members of the United Nations to apply such measures. These may include complete or partial interruption of economic relations and of rail, sea, air, postal, telegraphic, radio, and other means of communication, and the severance of diplomatic relations.

Article 42

Should the Security Council consider that measures provided for in Article 41 would be inadequate or have proved to be inadequate, it may take such action by air, sea, or land forces as may be necessary to maintain or restore international peace and security. Such action may include demonstrations, blockade, and other operations by air, sea, or land forces of Members of the United Nations.

Article 43

1. All Members of the United Nations, in order to contribute to the maintenance of international peace and security, undertake to make available to the Security Council, on its call and in accordance with a special agreement or agreements, armed forces, assistance, and facilities, including rights of passage, necessary for the purpose of maintaining international peace and security.

2. Such agreement or agreements shall govern the numbers and types of forces, their degree of readiness and general location, and the nature of the facilities and assistance to be provided.

3. The agreement or agreements shall be negotiated as soon as possible on the initiative of the Security Council. They shall be concluded between the Security Council and Members or between the Security Council and groups of Members and shall be subject to ratification by the signatory states in accordance with their respective constitutional processes.

Article 44

When the Security Council has decided to use force it shall, before calling upon a Member not represented on it to provide armed forces in fulfilment of the obligations assumed under Article 43, invite that Member, if the Member so desires, to participate in the decisions of the Security Council concerning the employment of contingents of that Member's armed forces.

Article 45

In order to enable the United Nations to take urgent military measures, Members shall hold immediately available national air-force contingents for combined international enforcement action. The strength and degree of readiness of these contingents and plans for their combined action shall be determined, within the limits laid down in the special agreement or agreements referred to in Article 43, by the Security Council and with the assistance of the Military Staff Committee.

Article 46

Plans for the application of armed force shall be made by the Security Council with the assistance of the Military Staff Committee.

Article 47

1. There shall be established a Military Staff Committee to advise and assist the Security Council on all questions relating to the Security Council's military requirements for the maintenance of international peace and security, the employment and command of forces placed at its disposal, the regulation of armaments, and possible disarmament.

2. The Military Staff Committee shall consist of the Chiefs of Staff of the permanent members of the Security Council or their representatives. Any Member of the United Nations not permanently represented on the Committee shall be invited by the Committee to be associated with it when the efficient discharge of the Committee's responsibilities requires the participation of that Member in its work.

3. The Military Staff Committee shall be responsible under the Security Council for the strategic direction of any armed forces placed at the disposal of the Security Council. Questions relating to the command of such forces shall be worked out subsequently.

4. The Military Staff Committee, with the authorization of the Security Council and after consultation with appropriate regional agencies, may establish regional subcommittees.

Article 48

1. The action required to carry out the decisions of the Security Council for the maintenance of international peace and security shall be taken by all the Members of the United Nations or by some of them, as the Security Council may determine.

2. Such decisions shall be carried out by the Members of the United Nations directly and through their action in the appropriate international agencies of which they are members.

Article 49

The Members of the United Nations shall join in affording mutual assistance in carrying out the measures decided upon by the Security Council.

Article 50

If preventive or enforcement measures against any state are taken by the Security Council, any other state, whether a Member of the United Nations or not, which finds itself confronted with special economic problems arising from the carrying out of those measures shall have the right to consult the Security Council with regard to a solution of those problems.

Article 51

Nothing in the present Charter shall impair the inherent right of individual or collective self-defence if an armed attack occurs against a Member of the United Nations, until the Security Council has taken measures necessary to maintain international peace and security. Measures taken by Members in the exercise of this right of self-defence shall be immediately reported to the Security Council and shall not in any way affect the authority and responsibility of the Security Council under the present Charter to take at any time such action as it deems necessary in order to maintain or restore international peace and security.

Chapter VIII. *Regional arrangements*

Article 52

1. Nothing in the present Charter precludes the existence of regional arrangements or agencies for dealing with such matters relating to the maintenance of international peace and security as are appropriate for regional action, provided that such arrangements or agencies and their activities are consistent with the Purposes and Principles of the United Nations.

2. The Members of the United Nations entering into such arrangements or constituting such agencies shall make every effort to achieve pacific settlement of local disputes through such regional arrangements or by such regional agencies before referring them to the Security Council.

3. The Security Council shall encourage the development of pacific settlement of local disputes through such regional arrangements or by such regional agencies either on the initiative of the states concerned or by reference from the Security Council.

4. This Article in no way impairs the application of Articles 34 and 35.

Article 53

1. The Security Council shall, where appropriate, utilize such regional arrangements or agencies for enforcement action under its authority. But no enforcement action shall be taken under regional arrangements or by regional agencies without the authorization of the Security Council, with the exception of measures against any enemy state, as defined in paragraph 2 of this Article, provided for pursuant to Article 107 or in regional arrangements directed against renewal of aggressive policy on the part of any such state, until such time as the Organization may, on request of the Governments concerned, be charged with the responsibility for preventing further aggression by such a state.

2. The term enemy state as used in paragraph 1 of this Article applies to any state which during the Second World War has been an enemy of any signatory of the present Charter.

Article 54

The Security Council shall at all times be kept fully informed of activities undertaken or in contemplation under regional arrangements or by regional agencies for the maintenance of international peace and security.

Chapter IX. *International economic and social co-operation*

Article 55

With a view to the creation of conditions of stability and well-being which are necessary for peaceful and friendly relations among nations based on

respect for the principle of equal rights and self-determination of peoples, the United Nations shall promote:
   a. higher standards of living, full employment, and conditions of economic and social progress and development:
   b. solutions of international economic, social, health, and related problems; and international cultural and educational co-operation; and
   c. universal respect for, and observance of, human rights and fundamental freedoms for all without distinction as to race, sex, language, or religion.

Article 56

All Members pledge themselves to take joint and separate action in co-operation with the Organization for the achievement of the purposes set forth in Article 55.

Article 57

1. The various specialized agencies, established by inter-governmental agreement and having wide international responsibilities, as defined in their basic instruments, in economic, social, cultural, educational, health, and related fields, shall be brought into relationship with the United Nations in accordance with the provisions of Article 63.

2. Such agencies thus brought into relationship with the United Nations are hereinafter referred to as specialized agencies.

Article 58

The Organization shall make recommendations for the co-ordination of the policies and activities of the specialized agencies.

Article 59

The Organization shall, where appropriate, initiate negotiations among the states concerned for the creation of any new specialized agencies required for the accomplishment of the purposes set forth in Article 55.

Article 60

Responsibility for the discharge of the functions of the Organization set forth in this Chapter shall be vested in the General Assembly and, under the authority of the General Assembly, in the Economic and Social Council, which shall have for this purpose the powers set forth in Chapter X.

Chapter X. The Economic and Social Council

COMPOSITION

Article 61

1. The Economic and Social Council shall consist of eighteen Members of the United Nations elected by the General Assembly.

2. Subject to the provisions of paragraph 3, six members of the Economic and Social Council shall be elected each year for a term of three years. A retiring member shall be eligible for immediate re-election.

3. At the first election, eighteen members of the Economic and Social Council shall be chosen. The term of office of six members so chosen shall expire at

the end of one year, and of six other members at the end of two years, in accordance with arrangements made by the General Assembly.

4. Each member of the Economic and Social Council shall have one representative.

FUNCTIONS AND POWERS

Article 62

1. The Economic and Social Council may make or initiate studies and reports with respect to international economic, social, cultural, educational, health, and related matters and may make recommendations with respect to any such matters to the General Assembly, to the Members of the United Nations, and to the specialized agencies concerned.

2. It may make recommendations for the purpose of promoting respect for, and observance of, human rights and fundamental freedoms for all.

3. It may prepare draft conventions for submission to the General Assembly, with respect to matters falling within its competence.

4. It may call, in accordance with the rules prescribed by the United Nations, international conferences on matters falling within its competence.

Article 63

1. The Economic and Social Council may enter into agreements with any of the agencies referred to in Article 57, defining the terms on which the agency concerned shall be brought into relationship with the United Nations. Such agreements shall be subject to approval by the General Assembly.

2. It may co-ordinate the activities of the specialized agencies through consultation with and recommendations to such agencies and through recommendations to the General Assembly and to the Members of the United Nations.

Article 64

1. The Economic and Social Council may take appropriate steps to obtain regular reports from the specialized agencies. It may make arrangements with the Members of the United Nations and with the specialized agencies to obtain reports on the steps taken to give effect to its own recommendations and to recommendations on matters falling within its competence made by the General Assembly.

2. It may communicate its observations on these reports to the General Assembly.

Article 65

The Economic and Social Council may furnish information to the Security Council and shall assist the Security Council upon its request.

Article 66

1. The Economic and Social Council shall perform such functions as fall within its competence in connexion with the carrying out of the recommendations of the General Assembly.

2. It may, with the approval of the General Assembly, perform services at the request of Members of the United Nations and at the request of specialized agencies.

3. It shall perform such other functions as are specified elsewhere in the present Charter or as may be assigned to it by the General Assembly.

VOTING

Article 67

1. Each member of the Economic and Social Council shall have one vote.
2. Decisions of the Economic and Social Council shall be made by a majority of the members present and voting.

PROCEDURE

Article 68

The Economic and Social Council shall set up commissions in economic and social fields and for the promotion of human rights, and such other commissions as may be required for the performance of its functions.

Article 69

The Economic and Social Council shall invite any Member of the United Nations to participate, without vote, in its deliberations on any matter of particular concern to that Member.

Article 70

The Economic and Social Council may make arrangements for representatives of the specialized agencies to participate, without vote, in its deliberations and in those of the commissions established by it, and for its representatives to participate in the deliberations of the specialized agencies.

Article 71

The Economic and Social Council may make suitable arrangements for consultation with non-governmental organizations which are concerned with matters within its competence. Such arrangements may be made with international organizations and, where appropriate, with national organizations after consultation with the Member of the United Nations concerned.

Article 72

1. The Economic and Social Council shall adopt its own rules of procedure, including the method of selecting its President.
2. The Economic and Social Council shall meet as required in accordance with its rules, which shall include provision for the convening of meetings on the request of a majority of its members.

Chapter XI. Declaration regarding non-self-governing territories

Article 73

Members of the United Nations which have or assume responsibilities for the administration of territories whose peoples have not yet attained a full measure of self-government recognize the principle that the interests of the inhabitants of these territories are paramount, and accept as a sacred trust the obligation to promote to the utmost, within the system of international peace and security established by the present Charter, the well-being of the inhabitants of these territories, and, to this end:

a. to ensure, with due respect for the culture of the peoples concerned, their political, economic, social, and educational advancement, their just treatment, and their protection against abuses;

b. to develop self-government, to take due account of the political aspirations of the peoples, and to assist them in the progressive development of their free political institutions, according to the particular circumstances of each territory and its peoples and their varying stages of advancement;

c. to further international peace and security;

d. to promote constructive measures of development, to encourage research, and to co-operate with one another and, when and where appropriate, with specialized international bodies with a view to the practical achievement of the social, economic, and scientific purposes set forth in this Article; and

e. to transmit regularly to the Secretary-General for information purposes, subject to such limitation as security and constitutional considerations may require, statistical and other information of a technical nature relating to economic, social, and educational conditions in the territories for which they are respectively responsible other than those territories to which Chapters XII and XIII apply.

Article 74

Members of the United Nations also agree that their policy in respect of the territories to which this Chapter applies, no less than in respect of their metropolitan areas, must be based on the general principle of good-neighbourliness, due account being taken of the interests and well-being of the rest of the world, in social, economic, and commercial matters.

Chapter XII. International trusteeship system

Article 75

The United Nations shall establish under its authority an international trusteeship system for the administration and supervision of such territories as may be placed thereunder by subsequent individual agreements. These territories are hereinafter referred to as trust territories.

Article 76

The basic objectives of the trusteeship system, in accordance with the Purposes of the United Nations laid down in Article 1 of the present Charter, shall be:

a. to further international peace and security;

b. to promote the political, economic, social, and educational advancement of the inhabitants of the trust territories, and their progressive development towards self-government or independence as may be appropriate to the particular circumstances of each territory and its peoples and the freely expressed wishes of the peoples concerned, and as may be provided by the terms of each trusteeship agreement;

c. to encourage respect for human rights and for fundamental freedoms for all without distinction as to race, sex, language, or religion, and to encourage recognition of the interdependence of the peoples of the world; and

d. to ensure equal treatment in social, economic, and commercial matters for all Members of the United Nations and their nationals, and also equal treatment for the latter in the administration of justice, without prejudice to the attainment of the foregoing objectives and subject to the provisions of Article 80.

Article 77

1. The trusteeship system shall apply to such territories in the following categories as may be placed thereunder by means of trusteeship agreements:
   a. territories now held under mandate;
   b. territories which may be detached from enemy states as a result of the Second World War; and
   c. territories voluntarily placed under the system by states responsible for their administration.

2. It will be a matter for subsequent agreement as to which territories in the foregoing categories will be brought under the trusteeship system and upon what terms.

Article 78

The trusteeship system shall not apply to territories which have become Members of the United Nations, relationship among which shall be based on respect for the principle of sovereign equality.

Article 79

The terms of trusteeship for each territory to be placed under the trusteeship system, including any alteration or amendment, shall be agreed upon by the states directly concerned, including the mandatory power in the case of territories held under mandate by a Member of the United Nations, and shall be approved as provided for in Articles 83 and 85.

Article 80

1. Except as may be agreed upon in individual trusteeship agreements, made under Articles 77, 79, and 81, placing each territory under the trusteeship system, and until such agreements have been concluded, nothing in this Chapter shall be construed in or of itself to alter in any manner the rights whatsoever of any states or any peoples or the terms of existing international instruments to which Members of the United Nations may respectively be parties.

2. Paragraph 1 of this Article shall not be interpreted as giving grounds for delay or postponement of the negotiation and conclusion of agreements for placing mandated and other territories under the trusteeship system as provided for in Article 77.

Article 81

The trusteeship agreement shall in each case include the terms under which the trust territory will be administered and designate the authority which will exercise the administration of the trust territory. Such authority, hereinafter called the administering authority, may be one or more states or the Organization itself.

Article 82

There may be designated, in any trusteeship agreement, a strategic area or areas which may include part or all of the trust territory to which the agreement applies, without prejudice to any special agreement or agreements made under Article 43.

Article 83

1. All functions of the United Nations relating to strategic areas, including the approval of the terms of the trusteeship agreements and of their alteration or amendment, shall be exercised by the Security Council.

2. The basic objectives set forth in Article 76 shall be applicable to the people of each strategic area.

3. The Security Council shall, subject to the provisions of the trusteeship agreements and without prejudice to security considerations, avail itself of the assistance of the Trusteeship Council to perform those functions of the United Nations under the trusteeship system relating to political, economic, social, and educational matters in the strategic areas.

Article 84

It shall be the duty of the administering authority to ensure that the trust territory shall play its part in the maintenance of international peace and security. To this end the administering authority may make use of volunteer forces, facilities, and assistance from the trust territory in carrying out the obligations towards the Security Council undertaken in this regard by the administering authority, as well as for local defence and the maintenance of law and order within the trust territory.

Article 85

1. The functions of the United Nations with regard to trusteeship agreements for all areas not designated as strategic, including the approval of the terms of the trusteeship agreements and of their alteration or amendment, shall be exercised by the General Assembly.

2. The Trusteeship Council, operating under the authority of the General Assembly, shall assist the General Assembly in carrying out these functions.

Chapter XIII. *The Trusteeship Council*

COMPOSITION

Article 86

1. The Trusteeship Council shall consist of the following Members of the United Nations:

a. those Members administering trust territories;

b. such of those Members mentioned by name in Article 23 as are not administering trust territories; and

c. as many other Members elected for three-year terms by the General Assembly as may be necessary to ensure that the total number of members of the Trusteeship Council is equally divided between those Members of the United Nations which administer trust territories and those which do not.

2. Each member of the Trusteeship Council shall designate one specially qualified person to represent it therein.

FUNCTIONS AND POWERS

Article 87

The General Assembly and, under its authority, the Trusteeship Council, in carrying out their functions, may:
a. consider reports submitted by the administering authority;
b. accept petitions and examine them in consultation with the administering authority;
c. provide for periodic visits to the respective trust territories at times agreed upon with the administering authority; and
d. take these and other actions in conformity with the terms of the trusteeship agreements.

Article 88

The Trusteeship Council shall formulate a questionnaire on the political, economic, social, and educational advancement of the inhabitants of each trust territory, and the administering authority for each trust territory within the competence of the General Assembly shall make an annual report to the General Assembly upon the basis of such questionnaire.

VOTING

Article 89

1. Each member of the Trusteeship Council shall have one vote.
2. Decisions of the Trusteeship Council shall be made by a majority of the members present and voting.

PROCEDURE

Article 90

1. The Trusteeship Council shall adopt its own rules of procedure, including the method of selecting its President.
2. The Trusteeship Council shall meet as required in accordance with its rules, which shall include provision for the convening of meetings on the request of a majority of its members.

Article 91

The Trusteeship Council shall, when appropriate, avail itself of the assistance of the Economic and Social Council and of the specialized agencies in regard to matters with which they are respectively concerned.

Chapter XIV. *The International Court of Justice*

Article 92

The International Court of Justice shall be the principal judicial organ of the United Nations. It shall function in accordance with the annexed Statute, which is based upon the Statute of the Permanent Court of International Justice and forms an integral part of the present Charter.

Article 93

1. All Members of the United Nations are *ipso facto* parties to the Statute of the International Court of Justice.

2. A state which is not a Member of the United Nations may become a party to the Statute of the International Court of Justice on condition to be determined in each case by the General Assembly upon the recommendation of the Security Council.

Article 94

1. Each Member of the United Nations undertakes to comply with the decision of the International Court of Justice in any case to which it is a party.

2. If any party to a case fails to perform the obligations incumbent upon it under a judgment rendered by the Court, the other party may have recourse to the Security Council, which may, if it deems necessary, make recommendations or decide upon measures to be taken to give effect to the judgment.

Article 95

Nothing in the present Charter shall prevent Members of the United Nations from entrusting the solution of their differences to other tribunals by virtue of agreements already in existence or which may be concluded in the future.

Article 96

1. The General Assembly or the Security Council may request the International Court of Justice to give an advisory opinion on any legal question.

2. Other organs of the United Nations and specialized agencies, which may at any time be so authorized by the General Assembly, may also request advisory opinions of the Court on legal questions arising within the scope of their activities.

Chapter XV. The Secretariat

Article 97

The Secretariat shall comprise a Secretary-General and such staff as the Organization may require. The Secretary-General shall be appointed by the General Assembly upon the recommendation of the Security Council. He shall be the chief administrative officer of the Organization.

Article 98

The Secretary-General shall act in that capacity in all meetings of the General Assembly, of the Security Council, of the Economic and Social Council, and of the Trusteeship Council, and shall perform such other functions as are entrusted to him by these organs. The Secretary-General shall make an annual report to the General Assembly on the work of the Organization.

Article 99

The Secretary-General may bring to the attention of the Security Council any matter which in his opinion may threaten the maintenance of international peace and security.

Article 100

1. In the performance of their duties the Secretary-General and the staff shall not seek or receive instructions from any government or from any other

authority external to the Organization. They shall refrain from any action which might reflect on their position as international officials responsible only to the Organization.

2. Each Member of the United Nations undertakes to respect the exclusively international character of the responsibilities of the Secretary-General and the staff and not to seek to influence them in the discharge of their responsibilities.

Article 101

1. The staff shall be appointed by the Secretary-General under regulations established by the General Assembly.

2. Appropriate staffs shall be permanently assigned to the Economic and Social Council, the Trusteeship Council, and, as required, to other organs of the United Nations. These staffs shall form a part of the Secretariat.

3. The paramount consideration in the employment of the staff and in the determination of the conditions of service shall be the necessity of securing the highest standards of efficiency, competence, and integrity. Due regard shall be paid to the importance of recruiting the staff on as wide a geographical basis as possible.

Chapter XVI. Miscellaneous provisions

Article 102

1. Every treaty and every international agreement entered into by any Member of the United Nations after the present Charter comes into force shall as soon as possible be registered with the Secretariat and published by it.

2. No party to any such treaty or international agreement which has not been registered in accordance with the provisions of paragraph 1 of this Article may invoke that treaty or agreement before any organ of the United Nations.

Article 103

In the event of a conflict between the obligations of the Members of the United Nations under the present Charter and their obligations under any other international agreement, their obligations under the present Charter shall prevail.

Article 104

The Organization shall enjoy in the territory of each of its Members such legal capacity as may be necessary for the exercise of its functions and the fulfilment of its purposes.

Article 105

1. The Organization shall enjoy in the territory of each of its Members such privileges and immunities as are necessary for the fulfilment of its purposes.

2. Representatives of the Members of the United Nations and officials of the Organization shall similarly enjoy such privileges and immunities as are necessary for the independent exercise of their functions in connexion with the Organization.

3. The General Assembly may make recommendations with a view to determining the details of the application of paragraphs 1 and 2 of this Article or may propose conventions to the Members of the United Nations for this purpose.

Chapter XVII. Transitional security arrangements

Article 106

Pending the coming into force of such special agreements referred to in Article 43 as in the opinion of the Security Council enable it to begin the exercise of its responsibilities under Article 42, the parties to the Four-Nation Declaration, signed at Moscow, October 30, 1943, and France, shall, in accordance with the provisions of paragraph 5 of that Declaration, consult with one another and as occasion requires with other Members of the United Nations with a view to such joint action on behalf of the Organization as may be necessary for the purpose of maintaining international peace and security.

Article 107

Nothing in the present Charter shall invalidate or preclude action, in relation to any state which during the Second World War has been an enemy of any signatory to the present Charter, taken or authorized as a result of that war by the Governments having responsibility for such action.

Chapter XVIII. Amendments

Article 108

Amendments to the present Charter shall come into force for all Members of the United Nations when they have been adopted by a vote of two-thirds of the members of the General Assembly and ratified in accordance with their respective constitutional processes by two-thirds of the Members of the United Nations, including all the permanent members of the Security Council.

Article 109

1. A General Conference of the Members of the United Nations for the purpose of reviewing the present Charter may be held at a date and place to be fixed by a two-thirds vote of the members of the General Assembly and by a vote of any seven members of the Security Council. Each Member of the United Nations shall have one vote in the conference.

2. Any alteration of the present Charter recommended by a two-thirds vote of the conference shall take effect when ratified in accordance with their respective constitutional processes by two-thirds of the Members of the United Nations including all the permanent members of the Security Council.

3. If such a conference has not been held before the tenth annual session of the General Assembly following the coming into force of the present Charter, the proposal to call such a conference shall be placed on the agenda of that session of the General Assembly, and the conference shall be held if so decided by a majority vote of the members of the General Assembly and by a vote of any seven members of the Security Council.

Chapter XIX. Ratification and signature

Article 110

1. The present Charter shall be ratified by the signatory states in accordance with their respective constitutional processes.

2. The ratification shall be deposited with the Government of the United States of America, which shall notify all the signatory states of each deposit as

well as the Secretary-General of the Organization when he has been appointed.

3. The present Charter shall come into force upon the deposit of ratifications by the Republic of China, France, the Union of Soviet Socialist Republics, the United Kingdom of Great Britain and Northern Ireland, and the United States of America, and by a majority of the other signatory states. A protocol of the ratifications deposited shall thereupon be drawn up by the Government of the United States of America which shall communicate copies thereof to all the signatory states.

4. The states signatory to the present Charter which ratify it after it has come into force will become original members of the United Nations on the date of the deposit of their respective ratifications.

Article 111

The present Charter, of which the Chinese, French, Russian, English, and Spanish texts are equally authentic, shall remain deposited in the archives of the Government of the United States of America. Duly certified copies thereof shall be transmitted by that Government to the Governments of the other signatory states.

IN FAITH WHEREOF the representatives of the Governments of the United Nations have signed the present Charter.

DONE at the city of San Francisco the twenty-sixth day of June, one thousand nine hundred and forty-five.

INDEX

Note: Common abbreviations of organizations' names are given in Appendix I. Entries in the Index use the complete name.

The major organs of the UN are indexed under their names, not as subheadings of the United Nations entry.